Race in the 21ˢᵗ Century

Ethnographic Approaches

JOHN HARTIGAN, JR.

The University of Texas at Austin

SECOND EDITION

New York   Oxford

OXFORD UNIVERSITY PRESS

Oxford University Press is a department of the University of Oxford.
It furthers the University's objective of excellence in research,
scholarship, and education by publishing worldwide.

Oxford   New York
Auckland   Cape Town   Dar es Salaam   Hong Kong   Karachi
Kuala Lumpur   Madrid   Melbourne   Mexico City   Nairobi
New Delhi   Shanghai   Taipei   Toronto

With offices in
Argentina   Austria   Brazil   Chile   Czech Republic   France   Greece
Guatemala   Hungary   Italy   Japan   Poland   Portugal   Singapore
South Korea   Switzerland   Thailand   Turkey   Ukraine   Vietnam

For titles covered by Section 112 of the US Higher Education
Opportunity Act, please visit www.oup.com/us/he for the
latest information about pricing and alternate formats.

Published in the United States of America by
Oxford University Press

198 Madison Avenue, New York, NY 10016
http://www.oup.com

Oxford is a registered trade mark of Oxford University Press.

Library of Congress Cataloging-in-Publication Data
Hartigan, John, 1964-
    Race in the 21st century : ethnographic approaches / John Hartigan. -- Second edition.
        pages cm
    Includes bibliographical references and index.
    ISBN 978-0-19-937437-3
    1. Race--Social aspects--United States. 2. Ethnology--United States.
3. Ethnopsychology--United States. 4. Human population genetics--United States.
5. Blacks--Race identity--United States. 6. Whites--Race identity--United States.
7. Race awareness--United States. 8. Race discrimination--United States.
9. United States--Race relations. I. Title.
    GN560.U6H37 2015
    305.800973--dc23
                                                                    2014004925
Printing number: 9 8 7 6 5 4 3 2 1

Printed in the United States of America
on acid-free paper

For my students,
in gratitude
for all you helped me learn

CONTENTS

～

A Cultural Perspective on Race

The purpose of this book is to introduce students to the study of race via qualitative approaches. Anthropologists and sociologists have produced an enormous number of insightful analyses of racial dynamics via fieldwork in the United
States. In surveying and summarizing this research, my aim is to offer students the
opportunity both to think through and to pose basic, important questions about
race in relation to their present circumstances and contexts. The view taken here
is that, though we know a great deal about how race matters based on the record
of ethnographic research, there is still more to learn about how racial meanings are
transforming and being reproduced. The "field," as it is variously construed, is the
preeminent location for learning more about these developments.

A prominent feature of informed public discussions about race in this country
over the past several decades has been our inability to settle on a definitive assessment of the "state of race relations." Partly, this is due to the contrary orientations
and dispositions people bring to these discussions. The view looks much different
to whites, generally, than it does for people of color; then add to the mix competing optimistic and pessimistic assessments concerning whether we, as a nation, are
making progress on ending racial discrimination and prejudice. Then, too, many
of the findings we have from social scientists can be seen, to some extent, as contradictory. Depending on the subject matter—residential segregation versus elec-
toral politics, for instance—the conclusions they reach about the significance of
race can appear quite opposite. To top it off, the enormous amount of survey data
generated on race in this country can be confusing. While majorities of whites and
blacks, for instance, can be shown to view key events in starkly opposed terms,
what about the minorities of both races who see things commonly or in contrast
to majority racial views? Then there is a range of literally conflicting findings,
those that suggest whites, in particular, alternately do and do not believe racism
remains a problem in this country. If we cannot establish shared assessments of

how race matters across the nation at large, what hope do we have of advancing informed discussions and conversations of these difficult topics?

Race in the 21st Century takes a somewhat different approach to this considerable, initial problem. The focus in these pages is on ethnographic research, which generally turns attention away from the "big picture" in order to examine particular settings and situations. The premise of ethnography, generally, is that local, place-based dynamics are of considerable significance in shaping peoples' sensibilities about and understandings of the world. This approach to racial matters can generate great insight because it shifts the focus away from general statements about race and develops an attention, instead, to the particular contexts where people actively engage and respond to racial meanings and identities. But ethnography involves more than an attention to place. At its core, ethnographic research highlights the active cultural work people pursue in their daily lives as they interpret the words and actions of others and as they strive to make sense of events unfolding around them in everyday settings. Ethnography, as a means of producing social knowledge, prioritizes an attention to peoples' engagement with the structures of meaning all around them. This perspective holds great promise as a means of addressing the nettlesome questions of why and how race continues to matter so profoundly in our daily lives.

Race in the 21st Century features a project-based approach to the study of race. The bulk of this book is devoted to summarizing and explaining the current state of social science knowledge on race in the United States, with a priority given to ethnographic findings. Based on this overview, the second feature of this text is its inquiry-driven orientation. Appendix A, *Taking It to the Field*, offers a developed series of suggestions and templates for how to reexamine or extend the types of research findings and questions covered in this book. In Appendix B you'll find a series of discussion topics and research prompts that encourage students to examine these issues and debates for themselves. Such inquiries need not be elaborate undertakings; many can be pursued in the routine course of daily life by maintaining a heightened, critical awareness of the breadth and depth of racial meanings in our society. Race is all around us, and, in a sense, we are experts about its operations, though we often are unsure of its functions and are frequently loathe to address its significance directly.

The same is true of culture as well, which this book also examines in detail, linking it to an array of racial processes. The approach featured in this book assumes, first, that we have more to learn about how race matters than we know currently and, secondly, that readers, as well-positioned "natives" of this culture, are the perfect people to generate more knowledge on this topic by pursuing inquiries that examine race in everyday life in the United States. For all that we know about race at this moment, the dynamism of America's demographics, politics, and public cultures assures that the significance of race will keep changing. The inquiry-driven orientation of this book aims exactly to address these changing circumstances, in part by drawing attention to the cultural dynamics that underlie these transformations.

THE ROLE OF CULTURE

When we think of *culture*, we often assume it refers to "traditional" peoples and exotic locales. But really it is quite mundane and all around us. Culture primarily involves meaning and social conventions—the structures of significance that shape our thoughts and actions. Culture is the means by which we articulate our identities and establish important matters of social belonging and difference. We pursue these activities by drawing on a plethora of signs and signifiers embedded in the language we speak, the ways we pose and use our bodies, the apparel we wear, the foods we eat, and the various ways we seek entertainment and engagement with the world around us. The central activity of culture is interpretation: we read and appraise the actions and words of people all around us, just as we imagine or project ourselves being understood by others. Culture is fundamental to human existence—it is something we do quite well without a second thought—but its basic operations are not generally well understood. This book takes culture as its central focus, based on the conviction that it explains a good deal of the ways we "do" or perform race in routine, ordinary circumstances.

In a two-step process, *Race in the 21st Century* presents key concepts for the study of race in conjunction with an explication of related cultural processes that inform how race matters. For instance, in explaining *color-blind racism*, it helps to be able to point to the fundamental operation of culture in making some things visible while obscuring others. The ability to "see" race or to ignore it altogether rests on both a person's social position and his or her cultural conditioning with regard to beliefs about the significance of skin color and the meanings we assign to physical features. It matters also to understand that social conventions inform what we feel we can and cannot observe or say about race. And it is important to recognize that speaking a "color-blind discourse" involves certain kinds of social boundary work that may or may not differ across racial lines. In each of these, comprehending racial matters is facilitated by grasping fundamental cultural dynamics that shape our socialization into a world where race so powerfully shapes discrepant life chances and circumstances.

Race in the 21st Century proceeds in systematic fashion to delineate the basic operations of culture and then to demonstrate how these inform the ways we make sense of race. Chapters 1 and 2 lay out the basic elements of racial analysis today, introducing key concepts such as *racial formation* and *racialization* (in addition to *color-blind racism*) while also examining the manifold ways racial inequality manifests in this country. In parallel fashion, these chapters also introduce key concepts in cultural analysis and then present a series of ethnographic vignettes featuring racial situations where cultural dynamics are quite vivid and tangible. Race involves more than skin color and encompasses more than forms of social advantage and disadvantage. Race is meaningful, and it is a fundamental part of how we make sense of the world around us—that is, it is cultural, too. These chapters detail the advantages a cultural perspective brings to the task of making sense of race, in part just because it moves discussion away from attitudinal registers and into domains of social interaction. This is where the strength of ethnography as a mode of research and analysis comes powerfully to the fore.

Chapter 3 extends this cultural perspective by addressing a range of controversies over whether there is a biological or genetic basis to racial identities. These are some of the most pressing, important issues related to race today, but our debates about these matters are generally convoluted. This is not surprising, given the complexity of the technical aspects of these issues. An equally daunting factor is that the basic facts of human diversity (biological and genetic) are so poorly understood. For that matter, we are also generally oblivious to the immense amount of cultural work involved in how we think about and reference "nature." Chapter 3 addresses each of these aspects in turn: examining both historical and contemporary uses of biology and genetics in conjunction with racial interests; then focusing on the fundamentals of human diversity as well as the variety of systems of racial classification that have tried to parse this diversity into absolute social categories. These discussions focus on the "traffic between culture and nature," which is a constant characteristic of humans' comprehensions of the natural world. A distinctive feature of this chapter is that, rather than reprising arguments about the "social construction" of race, it promotes a *biocultural* perspective as crucial to grasping the biological impacts of social forces such as racism, which play a key role in racial health disparities.

In the subsequent chapters, the discussion shifts entirely toward a survey of classic and current ethnographic studies of race. Three chapters, in turn, examine whiteness, blackness, and the "racial middle" between these two racial formations. This arrangement acknowledges the defining role that whiteness and blackness—as primary poles of racial signification—play in shaping our social landscape while also being attuned to the cultural complexity in the fast-growing "middle" zone between these prominent orders. A distinguishing facet of *Race in the 21st Century* is that, in contrast to most textbooks on race and ethnicity, it features a primary attention to cultural dynamics that crosscut particular racial formations and domains. Textbooks on this subject generally take a cataloguing approach by having separate chapters on every racial or ethnic group. Despite certain advantages, such an approach can inadvertently reproduce the notion that these groupings reflect essential differences, rather than demonstrating—counter to essentialist racial thinking—that we share more in common than differentiates us. In attending to the crucial differences that racial formations inscribe, the approach of this book is to focus time and again on the cultural dynamics that underlie and animate the operation of racial distinctions.

Chapter 4 presents a series of key concepts in relation to the study of whiteness, such as *white skin privilege, unmarked* identities, and the *wealth factor*. This chapter then tacks back and forth between an antiracist angle on whiteness afforded by these concepts and a series of ethnographic perspectives on whites in particular locales. These alternating frameworks allow for a developed understanding to emerge of how white racial identity both manifests and varies from one social location to another. An additional aspect of this chapter is its focus on the concept of *discourse*. Beginning with sociologist Ruth Frankenberg's qualitative analysis of three racial discourses (*essentialist racism, color- and power-evasive discourse*, and *race-cognizant discourse*), this chapter then offers a developed discussion of *merit discourse* as a common means by which Americans struggle with the significance of race. *Merit* can be construed as primarily a racial discourse, or it can be seen as deriving from key categories in American culture such as "individual" and "group." From this latter viewpoint, it becomes possible to recognize simultaneously racial and nonracial operations in discourse on "merit." The advantage gained is in comprehending the *equivocal* aspects of public cultural discourses that varyingly key on race or ostensibly ignore it altogether. The second half of this chapter surveys a range of ethnographic studies of whites that works out these more abstract matters in concrete situations.

Chapter 5 turns to questions of blackness, moving initially through some of the relational aspects of these two racial formations and then quickly shifting to an extensive exploration of the cultural dynamics shaping the lives of African Americans. This chapter begins with a critical assessment of sociologists' and anthropologists' past efforts to understand blackness, framing the problematic "*racial optic*" that white researchers have deployed in these endeavors. But this chapter also highlights an alternative tradition within the social sciences—initiated by W. E. B. Du Bois— that makes use of the same basic set of ethnographic research tools to produce a rather different view of African Americans' social and cultural predicaments. This chapter additionally features a discussion of "the hidden cost of being African American" (Shapiro 2004) and a detailed glimpse of the "black public sphere," particularly in relation to debates about Barack Obama's blackness during the 2008 presidential election. These discussions are carried further in the second half of the chapter, which also surveys a range of recent ethnographic projects. These ethnographies highlight the diversity within, and contested aspects of, blackness by focusing on the range of class circumstances of African Americans. This chapter ends with a detailed description of the *performative model of racial identity*, as developed by anthropologist John L Jackson in the course of his fieldwork in Harlem.

Chapter 6 examines the *racial middle*—that broad, fast-changing social landscape "between" whiteness and blackness. This chapter opens by reviewing recent charged debates over the *whitening thesis* and the *browning thesis*, which represent contrary views on current demographic, political, and social trends suggesting that Latinos and Asian Americans are being drawn to one or the other of these powerful racial poles. But the opening of this chapter also juxtaposes these debates with another set of public discussions over processes of *Latinization* and *Asianization* that may well be undermining the dominant "black and white" racial framework. As well, this chapter points to common experiences of racialization that these groups all share, in the enduring perception of their "foreignness" over and against whites and blacks.

The two primary concerns of this chapter are first, to examine how the cultural circumstances of these fastest-growing groups in America have the potential to reconfigure the U.S. system of racial classification; second, to consider how these same circumstances suggest the need to move beyond a strict reliance on forms advantage and disadvantage as the key explanatory principle for racial analytics. The end of Chapter 5 lays the groundwork for both these discussion by highlighting the broad social spectrum of black identities. But Chapter 6 takes this line of thinking much further by simultaneously keeping in view the overlapping but distinct social situations of Latinos and Asians in the United States. After explaining the differential aspects of the linked discourses of *ethnicity* and *race* in the U.S. public sphere, Chapter 6, too, shifts to an extensive surveying of recent ethnographies. Although the ethnographic record is not as extensive for either of these groups as it is for whites and blacks, recent ethnographic work on Latinos and Asian Americans features a great deal of sophistication and nuance. Part of this is due to the greater complexity of representational issues for these groups, who are alternately coveted by marketers (and hence valorized) and yet pushed from view in terms of representations of belonging to the nation as a whole. The ethnographic portions of this chapter also include discussions of diasporic identities and the variety of cultural practices of colorism.

Chapter 7 turns to the task of synthesizing various matters of method and analysis from the three previous chapters in order to delineate some basic components of ethnographic approaches to race. Principally, the concern here is to guide readers in how to formulate further ethnographic inquiries that either extend or revisit central findings from the works surveyed in this book. In reaching this last chapter, students should have gained a good grasp of the range of issues, problems, and questions regarding particular cultural circumstances of racialization in the United States. What then remains is to think a bit more broadly about what cultural analysis, in general, entails and to consider how best to bring it to bear in making sense of particular racial situations and settings.

As the work of race theorists is adopted and transformed by anthropologists and sociologists engaged in qualitative research, we see concepts like whiteness and blackness being reconfigured in the course of their application in fieldwork settings, particularly via an attention to performance. The *performance model* (Goffman 1959, Bauman 1977, Carlson 1996), a mainstay of ethnographic research for many years, frames social reproduction and change as occurring in particular locales through everyday interactions as people draw upon various expressive media to project a sense of self and group identity. Through a performance framework, the contingent aspects of racial identity are highlighted, because it is viewed as both a process and outcome of the interactive, interpretive work of situated social subjects. The question, then, is how research from this cultural perspective can, in turn, inform the thinking of race theorists.

The cultural perspective developed in this book reflects my sense that one of the impediments to advancing discussions about how race matters in this country is Americans' great difficulty in comprehending culture and its dynamics. Without some appreciation of the fact that our experience of the world is culturally contoured, it is hard to regard racism as more than just an individual failing or a vaguely perceived "institutional" byproduct. Without a recognition of the interlocking aspects of cultural perceptions and categorical identities, "race" appears as just another isolated topic of concern. But by starting with basic cultural dynamics, it is easy to show how race both inflects and is shaped by judgments Americans make about whether certain people appear to be "nice" or "friendly" or "hard-working"—each reflecting crucial categorical demarcations that ostensibly make no mention of race but that certainly operate at times in racial registers.

A cultural perspective allows us to place race simultaneously in the mix of everyday life, shaping perceptions that outwardly do not appear racial, but without reductively asserting that "everything" is about race. As well, in a cultural analysis the signifiers of race, class, and gender are seen as a series of interlocking codes by which patterns of inequality are maintained and reproduced in perceptions of similarity and difference. This view productively circumvents heated philosophical and political arguments about which of these three critical registers of difference has primacy in determining social circumstances today.

In broadest terms, culture, as an analytical perspective, treats collective dynamics of belonging and differentiation, the assigning of social meaning to arbitrary biological traits, the naturalization of certain orders of inequality or dominance, the forms of etiquette or decorum that discipline bodies and behaviors, the styles of narrative that organize each of these into tangible forms of meaning that people encounter in a multitude of reinforcing or challenging circumstances, and finally the forms of performance in which categorical identities and more fluid constructions of self are recognized and reproduced or revised. Each of these dynamics informs the interpretive work of cultural subjects in making sense of their world and negotiating the uneven social terrains that shape their individual and collective identities. These dynamics provide a powerful basis by which we can grasp the workings of race and its enduring significance in our daily lives.

In focusing on the underlying cultural dynamics that shape our racial sensibilities, *Race in the 21st Century* does not aim to present a comprehensive view of all racial/ethnic groups and their particular social circumstances, historically and contemporarily. As a result, many groups are not given sufficient attention in this book—particularly Native Americans and Arab Americans. For that matter, there is little discussion here of race in a global framework or of ethnographies conducted outside the United States. But *Race in the 21st Century* is not meant to serve as an encyclopedic compendium on racial groups; nor does it provide historically and sociologically detailed descriptions of distinct collectives. Rather, the focus here is on *a cultural analysis of the categories Americans predominantly rely upon in making sense of race*: white, black, Latino, and Asian.

What this book gives up in completeness of coverage it hopefully recoups with incisiveness, in terms of the analytic perspective it brings to bear on the role of culture in shaping how we think about and reproduce racial identities. In this view, the ethnographic approaches surveyed here are applicable to other groups beyond those highlighted in these pages. An attention to the circumstances of particular groups is important to understanding the history and politics of racial identity. But such a focus can actually direct us away from thinking about underlying cultural dynamics that shape how Americans generally perceive, project, and perform racial identities. My hope is that, in foregoing a well-warranted descriptive attention to the array of distinctive groups that comprise the American racial landscape, something else important will come into view—*the relational aspects of racial identity and the basic cultural operations that structure the meanings of race.* This book will be successful if students are able to recognize the underlying patterns of marking and unmarking race that inform our most basic perceptions and discussions of racial matters.

NOTE ON THE SECOND EDITION

In the short time since this book first appeared, race has only increased in its significance, and uncertainties about its enduring relevance are hardly dissipating. Fortunately, high-quality ethnographic research continues to advance, providing us yet more insightful and detailed case studies that render the complexity and nuance of racial identities and conflicts in full. This second edition of *Race in the 21st Century* features a new chapter, "Postracial America?," which squarely frames and examines contentious arguments about whether or how race still matters in the United States today. "Postracial" is an intensely disputed phrase in scholarly debates about race, but it usefully poses both the expectations that we should, someday, finally be done with race while reminding us, also, of the immense difficulties and challenges entailed in accomplishing this end. The new chapter ranges, initially, through a variety of contemporary scenes that highlight the increasing social and analytical complexity of racial matters. The core dynamics informing these scenes are studiously linked to earlier discussions in the book, such as the fundamental role nonracial categories (e.g., "individual" and "group") play in informing racial thinking. Then the chapter turns to a variety of recent ethnographies that survey changing terrains of whiteness, blackness, and the racial middle. Drawing from these ethnographies, readers are provided a variety of fascinating examples of how to think through the fast-changing landscapes of race in the United States. As well, these ethnographies offer a series of new key concepts that are useful in formulating qualitative research on race. This new chapter aims to fully engage readers in the important question of what "postracial America" might mean or look like.

ACKNOWLEDGMENTS

As always, I want to thank my colleagues in the Department of Anthropology and at the University of Texas for their steady support. Both from their collegiality and the examples of their respective research projects, I learn so much. Many thanks to Deborah Bolnick, John Hoberman, Martha Menchaca, Ted Gordon, João Vargas, Katie Stewart, Richard Flores, Sam Wilson, Ward Keeler. As well, I want to thank more far-flung colleagues, such as Clarence Gravlee, Ron Eglash, Linda Hunt, Sandra Soo-Jin Lee, and Pamela Sankar. I also am deeply indebted to our many excellent graduate students, who push my thinking in interesting and productive ways, both through seminar discussions and in dialogue with their ethnographic research. Many thanks to Mathangi Krishnamurthy, Ken MacLeish, Abdul Chang, Amanda Morrison, Santiago Guerra, Jerry Lord, Jackie Doyle, Ritu Khanduri, and Dan Gilman. I am particularly indebted to those who worked as teaching assistants in my introductory course on race: Naomi Reed, Amy Brown, Alysia Childs, Sandra Cañas, Alex Dodson, and Emily Lynch. They each improved the course and class discussions through contributions they made based on their own, fascinating dissertation research. In this regard, I am particularly grateful to Emily, Naomi, and Sandra for reading early drafts of some of these chapters; and Emily, thanks for your persistence in taking these questions seriously and the insights you offered in relation to your ethnographic projects. As well, I am very grateful for Scott Webel's excellent copyediting work. In terms of how this book made it to your hands, I want to thank the reviewers: John Bodinger de Uriarte, Susquehanna University; Dorothy Dillard, Delaware State University; Jennifer Roth Gordon, University of Arizona; Miranda Hallett, Otterbein College; Joanne Poehlman, Mount Mary College; Marvin Sterling, Indiana University-Bloomington; Bobby Vaughn, Notre Dame De Namur University. Thanks also to Cory Schneider for his editorial prowess; to Jan Beatty for working with me on this when it was just an idea; and for Sherith Pankratz who was willing to let this go further. Thank you all!

CHAPTER 1

Recognizing Race

On a bright, bitterly cold January afternoon in 2009, Barack Obama was inaugurated as president of the United States. As the first African American elected to the highest political office in the country and the first to occupy the White House, which was constructed with slave labor, Obama's ascendancy to the presidency was a historic moment. His election victory was heralded across the nation and around the world as a clear indication that the significance of race was fundamentally changing.

In the brilliance and import of the moment, it was easy to lose sight of the many ways that race matters were not altered one whit by Obama's accomplishment. Nothing dramatically changed on that day regarding the stark racial disparities in this country in terms of health, access to financial resources, and rates of incarceration. Nothing was modified concerning the increasing residential segregation in this country or the forms of discrimination people of color face in housing or loan or job markets or in accessing medical care. The stunning racial differential in life expectancy—African Americans' average lifespan is five years shorter than whites—remained entirely unchanged after Obama completed the oath of office.

How do we think about this gulf between what was transformed on that momentous day and what was left unaltered in the ways race matters in the United States? Undoubtedly, American public discourse will be irrevocably changed by the powerful figure of Obama as the voice of authority for the nation as a whole. But what impact, if any, does this transformation affect in the more mundane and routine ways that Americans continue to practice varied forms of racial exclusion and inclusion?

There is no single answer to these questions. Rather, they stand as an open-ended invitation to inquiry—to examine and wrestle with the issues of race for which the primary certainty now seems to be increasing uncertainty. The one thing we can be sure of from this moment on is that racial matters will grow more complicated and nuanced; we are unlikely ever to return to a situation in which race was a simple, clear-cut matter of "black and white." The purpose of this book is to provide some guidance on how to explore effectively the increasingly open-ended question of how race matters today. Pursuing this question successfully requires a basic understanding of the dynamics shaping racial identities and meanings across our fast-changing social landscape. *Race in the 21st Century* addresses this challenge by introducing readers both to processes of social science knowledge production on race and to an array of critical concepts and theories that frame and explain its enduring significance.

QUESTIONING RACE

The first question we have to ask is, what do you know about race? For that matter, where do your ideas about race come from? We are surrounded by images of race in movies, ads, and music. American history, all the way up to our current moment, is saturated with race. Everyday life is typically full of instances when our implicit understandings of race are affirmed in gossip, jokes, and news events. Based on where we live, these often unconscious notions generally are reinforced or go unchallenged by our neighbors and friends or family members.

This book is about how we learn and perform race. The goal is to lead readers to recognize the manifold ways that we *do* race everyday. When we look around the classroom or walk down a city street, we see race continuously. When we socialize—finding friends, choosing a place to sit and eat, or open our mouths to speak—race is usually very close at hand, manifesting in the ways we present ourselves and evaluate others. We learn these types of seeing and acting very young, and they generally stay with us, unconsciously, throughout our lives. These aspects of race are cultural—that is, they are learned and shared (though not always agreed upon) and actively reproduced. This latter, active dimension involves the ways we do or *perform* racial identities, roles, meanings, and anxieties on a regular basis. The striking point about these cultural aspects is that they exceed the ways we usually think of race, in terms of racism.

Race entails a system of classifying people into groups, either explicitly or implicitly promoting the notion that these groups are ranked in terms of superiority or inferiority. But race is meaningful in a variety of ways, many of which are changing rapidly and that we can barely control. The sharpest impact of the meaningfulness of race is that people are alternately advantaged and disadvantaged by their racial identity. Race remains a problem because it is the basis for pervasive forms of social inequality. But the range of racial meanings that we both consume and generate on a daily basis is not entirely reducible to the problem of inequality or discrimination. The cultural perspective developed here suggests that, given the extent that race permeates our culture, we need more than the concept of racism to explain why it matters so intensely. But this view is not one that you need assent to in order to get anything out of this book. *Race in the 21st Century* is an empirically focused, inquiry-driven project that both surveys the range of recent ethnographic research on race and suggests lines of investigation that you can pursue in examining racial matters. In the end, you should be able to assess and then conclude something substantive regarding the role of race in our cultural experiences today.

Race in the 21st Century deploys a cultural approach to understanding the significance of race. In discussing how notions such as whiteness, blackness, and "people of color" shape our ideas about family, strangers, and crime—as well as about intelligence, work, and comfort—this book shows that making sense of race today involves understanding how culture works. This is particularly difficult for Americans, because we are intensely attached to the idea of **individualism** and the attendant belief that each of us personally experiences the world in a unique manner.[1] We believe this so deeply that it is hard for us to recognize this belief as a particular cultural perspective on the world—that identity, in many cultures, is not similarly conceived or experienced. We experience this view as natural because our society is largely organized around confirming this sensibility. We encounter cultural messages that constantly affirm our uniqueness and individuality, mostly as consumers in a society based, ironically, on mass consumption. The crucial point about culture is that it precedes the personal, shaping our interactions and thoughts even before we become fully aware of them. **Culture** shapes the terms of an interaction even before individuals are entirely sure how they personally feel about a situation. Consider, for example, how many times you ritually greet someone— "Hi, how are you?" "I'm fine"—before you are entirely clear how you feel about the other person or yourself at that moment. This is the power of culture and why it is hard to grasp and comprehend. This book offers a detailed explanation of how culture works, particularly as it shapes our ways of thinking and talking about race.

Culture works simultaneously to make some things obvious and others difficult to recognize. Race is a perfect example of this—we immediately see it on each others' faces, yet we generally do not recognize the broader social significance of race. That is, we see it all over the place but often miss crucial social dimensions of race and how it matters. The most important fact about race—that it drastically contours social life in terms of advantage and disadvantage—is not widely acknowledged by most Americans. There are differences across racial lines in terms of how clearly or to what extent the facts of racial inequality register—people of color are typically more attuned to it than whites, for instance—but Americans generally prefer not to concede the social importance of race. Part of this denial stems from our strong belief in individualism: that group circumstances are shaped by social inequality flies in the face of the ideal that we are all equal as individuals. Since race fundamentally shapes Americans' life chances, our first step is to review what social science research reveals about the facts of racial inequality. Then we will consider the role culture plays in making aspects of race alternately visible or fairly invisible to us. In this effort, we will consider the roles that central features of American culture, such as individualism, play in shaping and reproducing our ideas about race in the twenty-first century.

---

[1] Definitions of boldface terms are in the glossary.

THE FACTS OF RACIAL INEQUALITY

Seeing Race Clearly

We know that race continues to matter a great deal in our society because research on discriminatory practices is so conclusive. But we also know, mostly from survey data, that these facts are not apparent to everyone. In particular, whites and blacks diverge greatly in their assessments that people are advantaged or disadvantaged in terms of race. In 2008, as the nation faced the historic prospect of electing an African American to the office of president, a great deal of effort was spent by pollsters trying to gauge the current state of racial thinking. Their findings largely confirmed what previous surveys found: whites and blacks view the significance of race rather differently. One poll, by CBS News/*New York Times* (June 2008), posed the question, "Are race relations in the United States generally good or bad?" A majority of whites (55%) replied, "generally good," while a majority of blacks (59%) voiced the opposite opinion, that they are "generally bad." On the crucial question, "Who has a better chance of getting ahead in today's society?," the racial divide is just as pronounced. Whereas a majority of whites considered these two races as "both equal" in their prospects and opportunities, blacks predominantly (64%) thought that whites had a better chance.

Obviously, it is crucial to ask who is right and who is wrong in these assessments. But it should be equally obvious that doing so is challenging because, as this polling data suggests, *race shapes our views and experiences of the world.* Though we imagine settling such questions by turning to the facts of the matter, things are not that easy with race because it shapes not just your view of the facts but also how they are generated and reproduced. For that matter, our ideas about race shape our very ability to produce social data about the subject. An interesting and disturbing aspect of this study—as with many surveys in the United States—is that the question of race was limited to white and black respondents. Other respondents were disregarded if they did not fit either of these categories. This is a reflection of how our ideas about race profoundly shape how we produce data about race—a process to which we will devote considerable attention throughout this book. Another overlooked aspect of this poll involves how minority views of white and black respondents—those whites who do not and those blacks who do see race relations as "good"—are downplayed in favor of an analysis that emphasizes the polar opposition of white and black views on race. These survey results indicate, at the very least, that whatever facts social scientists present on these matters will run up against a deep, prior conditioning in terms of race. If whites and blacks, in general, see things so differently, how can they be expected to see a given set of facts in a similar manner?

This question raises the issue of **interpretation**, which is the central work of culture. Rather than throwing up our hands in frustration in the face of competing and perhaps irresolvable interpretive dimensions of race, this is where an attention to culture becomes valuable. In taking a cultural approach, this book offers a view of the conventions and dynamics that guide the interpretive ways we engage with race, in order to suggest more effective means of understanding how and why it matters. Race is not unusual in this regard, in that most facts and all aspects of everyday life involve interpretation. Culture provides the means we rely on for determining what constitutes a good or bad interpretation. The challenge is to consider what empirical social science research has to show, while also taking into account the role that culture plays in shaping both our perception of those facts and the ways they are produced. This is a challenging task but, fortunately, a very interesting and worthwhile undertaking.

The Difference Race Makes

There is an enormous and consistent amount of social science research that shows conclusively that racial discrimination is a fact of American life. Importantly, this fact is evident in a variety of distinct domains—at home, in the workplace, on the highways, and, most critically, in terms of access to capital. In the first sphere, on the home front, blacks and Hispanics face considerable racial impediments when they look for a place to live. Whether seeking to buy a home or rent an apartment, blacks and Hispanics encounter discrimination on a regular basis across the country. The U.S. Department of Housing and Urban Development tests both the rental and housing markets for discriminatory practices by sending out testers of different races posing as prospective buyers or tenants. More than one in five potential black renters are told that no places are available, though subsequent white renters are offered places to rent; Hispanic renters receive this discriminatory treatment 25% of the time. Both black prospective home buyers (17%) and Hispanic buyers (19.7%) face similar discrimination, compared with white prospective buyers. Such practices reinforce patterns of residential segregation, which in turn reproduce racial segregation in the schools. Though the country made strides toward desegregation in the wake of the 1954 Supreme Court ruling *Brown v. Board of Education*, that trend has been reversed in the last two decades. Nationally, rates of school segregation—as measured by shrinking percentages of black and Latino students attending predominantly white schools—have increased substantially, returning to levels when Martin Luther King Jr. was assassinated in 1968.

Discriminatory practices, though now illegal, are long-standing in this country. They have resulted in huge disparities between whites, blacks, and Latinos in terms of overall wealth. These disparities are crucial because they, in turn, produce differential life chances by race. Wealth disparities result from practices that restricted black and Latino participation in the massive process of suburbanization that transformed this country over the last fifty years. From the 1960s through the 1990s, disproportionately denied access to credit as well as to housing markets, many blacks and Latinos remained confined in central cities while whites poured out of urban cores. While suburban housing values soared—due in large part to massive federal subsidies for highway, water, and sewage systems—aging central-city housing values declined. Jobs, too, shifted from urban to suburban zones, leaving high rates of unemployment in their wake. Even when blacks and Latinos made inroads in various economic sectors during boom periods, those gains were largely reversed in subsequent recessions. This was particularly noticeable in the wake of the recession that started in 2008: white families lost about 11% of their wealth, compared to 31% lost for black families and 44% for Latino families, in the period between 2007 and 2010 (Urban Institute 2013). Prior to the recession, white families were about four times as wealthy as nonwhite families, but that ratio increased substantially, leaving whites about six times as wealthy as nonwhites.

Another impact of these residential practices linked to race involves the role of **environmental racism**. This term refers to the intentional or unintentional placement of environmental hazards and wastes in or near minority communities. Research on this topic began in the late 1980s, when James Hamilton examined zip codes for correlations between race and concentrations of waste dumps. He found that areas targeted for hazardous-waste facilities were disproportionately minority communities. Decisions on locating landfills, incinerators, or toxic-waste treatment operations may not reflect intentional racist practices—certainly economics plays a role, with poor minority communities faring badly in these processes. As well, long-term trends of racial segregation by neighborhood factor in the background of these decisions. But it is clear that people of color bear a disproportionate burden regarding how toxic wastes are treated in this country (Downey 2007).

Another domain of American life where racial discrimination is prevalent is in the practice of **racial profiling**. This involves racially selective judgments made by police officers concerning who to stop and search on highways or neighborhood streets. Such practices make it more likely that blacks and Latinos will encounter law enforcement officials directly. The inconvenience and danger this entails—in the disproportionate use of lethal force by police against minorities as well as in disparate rates of incarceration—places blacks and Latinos at a decided disadvantage in American public spaces. Strikingly, this practice flies in the face of some basic facts about crime in the United States. In terms of drug use, for instance, according to the Centers for Disease Control and Prevention, whites are far more likely to be engaged in drug use (ranging from cocaine to crack and from marijuana to heroin) than are blacks (Centers for Disease Control 2003). Furthermore, in contrast to media and police stereotypes, white youths are far more likely to sell drugs than are their black counterparts. White males are also far more likely to drive drunk or carry a weapon in school than are black males. And yet, school disciplinary practices are disproportionately directed at black youths (Wise 2001).

Racial Judgments

But perhaps the most sobering facts concerning the relative question of who is better able to "get ahead" come from the job market. Employers often racially discriminate in hiring practices. A study designed to gauge the detrimental effects of having a criminal record for job applicants produced a stunning finding pertaining to race. Whites *with* a criminal record were more likely to receive favorable treatment (callbacks, hiring, etc.) than were blacks *without* a criminal record (Prager 2003). This reflects a huge advantage just by being white. This advantage works at an even more sinisterly subtle level than skin color. Another study, conducted by researchers at the Graduate School of Business, University of Chicago, examined the differential value of race in terms of resumes. This field experiment involved sending resumes in response to help-wanted ads in Boston and Chicago. In the initial stage, all the resumes featured the same set of credentials; they were differentiated only by the name listed on the resumes. The researchers alternated these by assigning the resumes "black names" and "white names," drawing these from the top-ten names for babies assigned by whites and blacks according to the U.S. Census. Strikingly, "white names elicit about 50% more callbacks than African American names" (Bertrand and Mullainathan 2002). In a second stage of the study, the researchers improved the credentials listed in the resumes. For whites, this resulted in 30% more callbacks, but for blacks the success rate remained unchanged.

This study raises an intriguing question: Would these prospective employers consider themselves racist? It is not possible to know for certain, but it is easy to imagine that either they are "closet racists" or they sincerely believe that they do not harbor racist thoughts at all. Regardless, fixating on their attitudes directs attention away from the role of culture in all this. Remember, culture precedes the individual, which is very clear in this study—before any black applicant is considered in individual terms he or she is identified according to the meanings assigned to blackness in the culture at large. Whatever the personal beliefs of these personnel managers, they are influenced by a frame of cultural reference that devalues blackness in the occupational sphere. The meanings they attach to race are clearly shared, which is what produces the discrepant racial outcomes documented in this study. Whatever they may believe individually, the results of their actions are the same: Black applicants are not afforded the same assumption of "belonging" in the workplace as are white applicants, which goes a long way toward explaining the disproportionately high unemployment rates facing blacks.

Now imagine this particular process of applying for jobs amplified and repeated on a broader scale, in applications for car or business loans as well as for home mortgages, all of which also evidence continued forms of racial discrimination. Consider the cumulative impact of these overlapping and mutually reinforcing decisions by a variety of loan officers. Combine these with the extensive history of residential discrimination—which continues long after such practices were made illegal—that still makes it difficult for blacks to accrue wealth in their homes the ways that whites have in this country. Add in the effects of a variety of racial profiling practices, ranging from who store detectives decide to follow and who police stop and frisk, alongside the higher rates of infant mortality for African Americans and the resegregation of American schools. This bigger picture, which indicates so clearly that race matters powerfully in determining an individual's life chances in this country, also helps frame the role of culture in all this.

In cultural terms, race involves a *worldview*—a patterned system of meanings—that profoundly shapes peoples' thoughts and actions before they are clear on their own personal attitudes about its significance. This worldview both derives from and responds to the cumulative ways that race matters in this country, which, in turn, powerfully shapes our experiences and perceptions of race. As we have seen, where you live is influenced by race, and that deeply contours your view of the world; whether you have access to credit, are exposed to industrial toxins, or can land a good job, all profoundly affect how you see the world. Decisions made in terms of race—and the way these decisions shape a social world that is differentially structured in terms of race—are interrelated ways in which American culture powerfully forms how people both perceive and experience race.

THE CHANGING ROLE OF RACISM

Americans generally believe that racism is a personal failing and an individual problem. But the significance of race importantly precedes any particular individual's beliefs and sensibilities. For the racial disparities recounted here to pertain across the nation, they must involve more than personal opinions or sentiments. Rather, they reflect a shared set of beliefs and behaviors. But how do we characterize this common sensibility? The easy answer is **racism**—the belief that racial identity is an inherent and inherited human characteristic, linked to innate capacities assumed to be permanent and common across a particular race. Racism also involves the belief that these races are hierarchically ranked or differentially valued in terms of capacities (e.g., intelligence) judged inferior and superior. The problem with this answer, though, is that openly racist sentiments—whether in the forms of public speech or in responses to attitudinal surveys—have notably dwindled in the mainstream currents of American social life. Also, officially sanctioned racist practices—denying people the rights of citizenship as well as economic and social liberty on the basis of race—were largely rendered illegal as a result of the civil rights movement. That discrimination persists indicates the enduring role of racism, but that it operates and looks different than it did in the past also impels us to consider the possible limits to what it explains about the ways race matters today.

One approach to this problem involves updating and expanding on the concept of racism. Sociologist Eduard Bonilla-Silva accomplishes this by pairing a far broader range of examples of the pervasiveness of racial discrimination than I have presented with survey results that report whites claiming to "not see any color, just people." In *Racism without Racists: Color-Blind Racism and the Persistence of Racial Inequality in the United States* (2006), Bonilla-Silva asks, "How is it possible to have this tremendous degree of racial inequality in a country where most whites claim that race is no longer relevant?" More pointedly, he asks, "How do whites explain the apparent contradiction between their professed colorblindness and the United States' color-coded inequality?" The answer Bonilla-Silva offers—based on his extensive survey research on white racial attitudes—is that a new racial ideology has emerged, one that he labels **color-blind racism**. This form of racial thinking foregoes the ostensible references to race—racist comments and blatant discriminatory acts—for a more subtle series of practices that racially differentiate while professing an adherence to the ideal of being color-blind. These practices seek to elude the charged conflicts over race linked to the open expression of racist beliefs and ideals in the public sphere. Yet they are equally effective as blatant racist acts in maintaining strict boundaries (in housing, hiring, and policing) between whites and people of color.

This is an important, developing area of social inquiry and will likely continue to generate crucial insights into the dynamics of racial thinking, particularly as it pertains to the reproduction of social inequality. Along with Bonilla-Silva, other researchers are developing additional concepts, such as *symbolic racism, silent racism, modern racism, subtle racism,* and *new racism.* Each of these is keyed around understanding the same dynamic—while whites increasingly disavow racist sentiments and expressions, evidence of racial discrimination continues to mount. But the elusive and treacherous character of racial thinking indicated here raises an important question: Is race alone sufficient to explain how and why race matters? Sociologist Michele Lamont suggests that it is not. While similarly pursuing questions about the new forms racism takes, Lamont turns to a broader dimension of our cultural conditioning in order to comprehend this development. She examines how people draw symbolic boundaries in terms of group identity generally, then asks how this activity pertains to the ways that we do race. Importantly, Lamont arrives at this perspective by expanding the frame of analysis beyond what whites, in particular, might think, to looking comparatively at how differently raced people interpret their social world.

In her book *The Dignity of Working Men: Morality and the Boundaries of Race, Class, and Immigration,* Lamont examines the varied media and modes by which workers in the United States construct **social boundaries** in moral, class, and racial terms. She observes, "for black and white workers alike, moral boundaries on the one hand, and class and racial boundaries on the other, often work together to provide them with a space in which to affirm their worth and preserve their dignity, a space for expressing their own identity and competence" (2000, 4). Lamont found "that whites and blacks alike subtly move from drawing moral boundaries to drawing racial boundaries" and that an "'us' versus 'them' dynamic animated by two different conceptions of morality is closely associated with the collective identities of the two groups" (93). Lamont's approach leads in a rather different direction than Bonilla-Silva's, though both are interested in a similar subject: how racial boundaries continue to be drawn and reproduced in an era when Americans increasingly disavow the importance of such boundaries. Instead of linking racial thinking back to originary or core racist sensibilities, Lamont sees racial boundary work, for both whites and blacks, as related to larger processes of viewing the world in moral terms. This suggests the importance of engaging racial thinking not as an abstract function of ideology but as a more convoluted and complex product of socialization. Processes of socialization are at the heart of culture.

THE CULTURAL DOMAIN

When we learn culture—typically as infants and children—we learn categories for making sense of the world around us. We learn meanings for these categories, particularly as they relate to words, sounds, and gestures as well as to clothes, food, and behaviors. Of course, we learn categories of people too—"nice" or "bad," initially, and then "friend" and "stranger" ("Don't talk to strangers!"), "neighbor" and "kin" or "family." We learn that there are *kinds* of people, too: "men" and "women," for instance, but also "girls" and "boys," who each do different kinds of things, wear different kinds of clothes, and act in certain ways. At the same time, we may well learn that these differences are not important or should not matter, an assertion that appears to belie the fact that we retain and enforce these categories in daily encounters that ratify their relevance. A similar process occurs with race, and no matter how much we may resist the process, we *learn* race as a matter of different kinds of people. Commonly, Americans learn that this form of difference is not supposed to matter—people are alternately "all the same" and each equally "different," as in being unique. But the social world around us also conveys the contrary point that this kind of difference is indeed meaningful, for the very simple reason that, if it were not, we would not need or retain these categories for people: white, black, Latino, Asian, Arab, and so forth. The interesting dimension that a cultural perspective brings to the subject of race concerns how people deal with these seemingly contradictory assertions—that "people are just people," yet there are different kinds of people; or that "race doesn't matter," yet it is clearly meaningful.

Culture centrally involves the realm of meaning, and, as you well may realize, meaning is often quite complicated. Culture points us toward a broader register of categorical thinking and classifying practices that extend well beyond any particular set of beliefs, such as racism. A cultural view on the role of racial thinking expands the frame of analysis beyond an effort to identify the origins of peoples' perceptions and attitudes, in order to get at the active interpretive and performative work we do when we encounter or engage the significance of race. The important aspect of culture is that it involves the realm of meaning generally. The fundamental characteristic of **meaning** is that it is established relationally via mutually reinforcing structures of significance; it derives from and is reproduced in social interactions with other people but also with and in particular social contexts. Race is meaningful not just because of racist ideology or practices, but also because it is a set of categories imbued with meanings that we learn early in life for making sense of the world and, notably, for describing or characterizing our sense of comfort or uneasiness. This all becomes quite dense because the ways we think about race are ensconced in a larger system of classification (American culture) that also shapes how, as Americans, we think about such categories as home and family, neighbors and strangers, friends and criminals.

Consider, again, the concept of color-blind racism. The central implication Bonilla-Silva develops in deploying this concept is that whites are being disingenuous when they claim to "not see any color, just people." Bonilla-Silva uses this concept effectively to highlight the ways whites apparently contradict this assertion, as evidenced by so many forms of ongoing discrimination. But in doing so, he misses the important way that this color-blind ideology mimics or mirrors the basic categorical sensibility or tenet in American culture—individualism. Perhaps white Americans are not simply trying to hide their true racist beliefs as much as they are challenged by the task of simultaneously maintaining that "everyone is an individual" while recognizing that race remains significant. Or, perhaps, whites—and maybe even all racially identified people in the United States—are socialized, implicitly, to recognize people of their own color, first and foremost, as *individuals*, allotting everyone else to that crucial shadow category for the individual—*groups*. The problem, then, is not simply racial ideology, to whatever extent that remains pervasive in this country, but that the way Americans see the world in terms of the crucial categories, *individuals* and *groups* (e.g., "There are two kinds of people . . ."), profoundly shapes the way we think about the meaningfulness of race.

One way of illustrating this cultural dimension is to consider that people of color, even though they are often subjects of discrimination, can also have a difficult time recognizing this racial dynamic. In part, as we will examine in more detail later, individualism makes it very difficult to perceive group circumstances. You can easily get a sense of this if you ask anyone what causes poverty or ill health, topics we cover in detail in Chapter 3. Chances are that whomever you ask will stress individual responsibility every time. Social explanations are practically a nonstarter for most Americans. But another way to recognize what is going on here is to consider how personally we each take individualism. This is perhaps most poignantly illustrated in instances when African Americans, for example, are presented with evidence of racial discrimination and yet they insist that this is not really what is happening. Contrary to the complaint by many whites, as documented by Bonilla-Silva, that blacks too often "cry racism," a variety of polls indicate that African Americans are just as likely *not* to perceive racial discrimination as they are to detect it. This finding is most strikingly evidenced in the case of fieldwork conducted by sociologist Jay MacLeod, recounted in his excellent ethnography *Ain't No Making It: Aspirations and Attainment in a Low-Income Neighborhood* (2009).

MacLeod followed the life trajectories of two groups of kids from an East Coast housing project—one white and one black—over several years as they shifted from high school to the world of work. Consistently, MacLeod found instances where the black youths were unfairly treated by employers, even though they maintained a much stricter adherence to the ideals of the American dream than did their white counterparts. But when confronting the black youth (now men) with this finding, the respondents emphatically rejected his conclusion that they were subjected to racist practices. Instead, MacLeod found, they "explicitly discount racism as a handicap in their occupational careers" (2009, 222). One of them explains to MacLeod that, as a rule, he "never looks at it thatta way." As

MacLeod concludes, these young men view themselves strictly as individuals. From that vantage point, they only blame themselves when they are passed up for promotions or routinely docked for minor infractions that go unnoticed with white workers, or when they are unable to tap the social networks that their white counterparts rely on for finding jobs in the first place. This manner of cultural conditioning in terms of individualism makes it very difficult for Americans— even those who suffer from discrimination—consistently to see race at work.

RACE IN RELATION TO CULTURE

The simple fact that race is meaningful places it in the domain of culture, although it certainly can be also located in the domains of law, economics, and politics. The cultural aspects of race are the subject of this book, and we will see in the chapters ahead how the central method of cultural analysis—ethnographic fieldwork such as that practiced by MacLeod—generates crucial insights into the ways Americans contend with the significance of race in everyday life. But it is important to note that stressing the cultural dimension of race is not an assertion that race is only reducible to cultural dynamics. There are many more forces at work shaping the significance of race in addition to cultural ones, and it is critical, in considering the role of culture, not to blunt a broader attention to race. The advantage of focusing on culture in relation to race, though, is that it allows us to recognize the nuanced ways that racial meanings are imbricated throughout our social world. To capture the interplay between the cultural realm of meanings and the wide array of other domains that shape how race matters, sociologists Michael Omi and Howard Winant formulated the concept of **racial formation**. This concept "refers to the process by which social, economic, and political forces determine the content and importance of racial categories, and by which they are in turn shaped by racial meanings" (1986, 61). The idea is that the way we talk and think about race—its categories and meanings—is affected by developments across the national landscape.

This is evident in Bonilla-Silva's analysis, which depicts whites as reformulating their public statements on race and rephrasing their expressions of concern or interest, all in response to the way changes in public discourse have made expressions of openly racist sentiments taboo. But Omi and Winant's notion of racial formation also opens a wider reading of race than the attitudinal register or ideological dimension that Bonilla-Silva targets in his analysis. Specifically, as Winant later elaborated, this approach "looks at race as a phenomenon whose meaning is contested throughout social life" (1994, 23). This broader view of the social sphere, where a wide series of conventions and expectations shape our thoughts and actions, begins to point in another direction than the form of ideological analysis concerned with racism.

We get a glimpse of the power and pervasiveness of **cultural conventions** when we recognize that the basic dynamic highlighted by the concept of color-blind racism is one in which people may feel one way but express rather contrary beliefs and ideals. That is, social contexts and interactions—particularly how people anticipate they will be perceived and regarded by others—matter a great deal in how we formulate and articulate our views. When we deal with the realm of meaning and the social conventions shaping how people articulate or disavow those meanings, we are assuredly in the domain of culture. And one of the characteristic features of this domain of meaning and convention is that things are rarely straightforward. Indeed, ambiguity is as common as clarity, in that our cultural encounters and expressions are often less than certain and typically involve feelings of ambivalence.

The concept of color-blind racism frames this dense aspect of racial thinking, wherein people may hold contradictory ideas about race. The advantage of a cultural approach is to raise the additional consideration that perhaps the "real" core of their feelings and beliefs may be ambivalent, uncertain, or changeable. This makes for a challenging subject of study, in qualitative terms, because it involves getting beneath or behind someone's stated perspectives and claims—in a sense, reading against the grain a person's statements and professed sentiments. This type of research, in fact, *requires* a qualitative approach because we are dealing extensively with the realm of meaning. The particulars of how to pursue ethnographic work in relation to questions about people's perceptions and understandings of race will be covered in detail in Chapters 4, 5, and 6.

In another regard, one of the challenges highlighted by the concept of color-blind racism is that racial meanings change; they are dynamic and mutable, responding to developments in the public sphere. In this process, new and old social forms can acquire racial meanings. The concept of **racialization**—also from the work of Omi and Winant (1986)—is useful here because it refers to "the extension of racial meanings to a previously racially unclassified relationship, social practice or group" (66). This concept highlights the developing and unfolding novel ways that racial meanings operate, changing and shifting in conjunction with broad, national developments. If race is constantly changing, why should we expect that it would continually conform to the ways it has mattered in the past? Only if we assume that a primary ideological impulse of racism animates whites today as it did three hundred years ago could we maintain such a stance.

From a cultural perspective, that would be surprising, because culture is something learned anew with each generation. Certainly, there are plenty of consistencies (*traditions*, if you will) that are the basis by which culture remains shared through the years. But the process of learning continually takes place in circumstances that have changed, reflecting the impact of history. In this way, a cultural worldview is fashioned anew in the process of socialization, even though there are overarching consistencies. The challenge in studying something like race from a cultural perspective is to maintain an awareness of the historical aspects of racial dynamics while being astute about the constantly changing influence of cultural dynamics.

CULTURAL ANALYSIS

The cultural perspective on race developed in this book focuses primarily on how the meanings of racial categories are interpreted in everyday life by people in particular social settings. So before proceeding further, we need to be clear about what cultural analysis involves. Cultural analysis moves beyond the attitudinal register targeted in polls and surveys and orients toward the widest possible reading of how we do race—that is, how we perform and interpret it in daily life. In its fundamental operation, culture is concerned with matters of **belonging** and **difference**. These concerns are often considered abstractions, but in cultural terms they are active means of processing the images and impressions we glean from other people every day, usually in quite mundane and unconscious ways. As we take fleeting notice of how people speak or stand, what they wear, and how they look, we appraise whether they belong with "us" or not. These judgments are subtle and may well be fleeting, overturned by subsequent information; also, the projected collective identity may be mutable—at one moment framed by class, in turn by gender, at another moment by race, then by generation, region, or neighborhood or other affiliations. This process is interactive, in that we are similarly being read by others, which is what makes it so dynamic. The markers of belonging and difference are not just static emblems—clothes, for instance—but things we socially perform in the varied ways we form our speech and pose our bodies. Signs of ease or discomfort, poise or languor, are physical inflections we give to the socially conditioned ways we learn to occupy and pass through space. These are the media in which we sort out matters of belonging and difference, not just with race but with all manner of social distinctions.

An easy mistake to make in thinking about culture is to assume that it is what makes people different. This is certainly an aspect of culture, and it is what typically comes to mind when people reference it. But culture, more fundamentally, is how people recognize or establish that they share something in common. That is, culture is about determining sameness; in the process, we subsequently classify people as different when they do not fit our expectations. Think of what you do when you first meet someone: You try to establish what you have in common. Typically, this starts with a shared language—if you don't have that, the process often goes no further—and then moves on to shared topics of interest or conversation (where you are from, what you do, what views you hold, what types of music or entertainment you favor). Running out of commonalities does not indicate that you do not share a culture. Americans differ and disagree in many ways, yet they retain many more commonalities overall. The basic dynamic of culture, shaping our view of the world, instills within us ways of organizing and arranging degrees of difference within or across imagined cultural boundaries. But this perception of and interest in sameness is fundamental to how culture works, much more so than the items we often equate with culture, such as different styles of dress, eating, or behaviors.

This dimension of culture is central to how Americans do race. A crucial criterion in the perception of sameness is skin color. It is not that we cannot see sameness in the face of differences in skin tone, but doing so generally requires a little more interpretive effort for Americans. That is partly because skin remains one of our most ingrained signifiers of difference, but it is also because we are socialized into the world by our color in ways that provide, alternately, advantages and disadvantages. There may or may not be essentially "white" or "black" ways of standing, talking, dancing, or singing. But these are the registers in which "differences" are frequently associated with ideas and narratives about whiteness and blackness, as we will see in Chapters 4 and 5. The point is not to fixate on cataloguing these differences in order to make some authoritative statement about categorical identities but, rather, to attend to the way people process the social world via these categories. The goal is to examine belonging and difference as ongoing determinations made in unending processes of classifying and interpreting the actions and words of others while we also present ourselves in various interactions as certain kinds of persons—serious, professional, diffident, and so on—that we would like to be.

The central cultural activity is *interpretation*. Think of all the many varied things we interpret in the course of a day: words and comments from family, friends, and strangers; gestures (facial, bodily, or verbal) from people we pass by or may know well; sounds, ranging from traffic and construction to music; colors that people wear or that saturate signs, lights, and surfaces all around us; symbols, in ads or official media (traffic signs, flags, and emblems) or in the adornments people wear marking status, belonging, or difference; the texts we send and receive each day; and the stories, jokes, or gossip we hear at home or at work. All this requires an enormous amount of interpretation that generally functions at an unconscious level, which is why we are so good at it. But we are also accomplished at it because we organize our interpretive practice around sets of beliefs or ideas that let us distinguish certain styles, genres, and structures in what people around us say or do. These are commonly characterized as **interpretive repertoires**: collections of stories, examples, narratives, and images on which we rely to make sense of any particular situation. The idea here is that people express opinions and articulate their experiences with a fairly fixed set of narrative conventions and linguistic tropes. These repertoires are linked to the places we inhabit and traverse, in that they resonate with how these setting are arranged, maintained, and reproduced. These repertoires are largely shared, which is what makes our expressions and sentiments intelligible to ourselves and to others. Because they are shared, we are able to map them out through the process of ethnographic fieldwork. Ethnography is the primary approach developed in this book, and, before going any further, we need to have some more concrete examples of how it works, especially in relation to race.

ETHNOGRAPHIC EXAMPLES

The following ethnographic vignettes involving race each feature fairly mundane instances from everyday life. These are hardly spectacular, gripping, or dramatic moments; rather, like most things cultural, they are incidents that barely draw conscious attention and would otherwise not appear notable to anyone involved. This is one of the distinctive aspects of culture: It generally seems unimportant and routine, which indicates that these patterns of perception and interpretation are pervasive and taken for granted. If you think about it, most of our day is concerned with exactly this type of exchange, encounter, or experience—moments to which we barely give any thought, and yet we navigate them with remarkable dexterity; a sign that we do so by relying on both a deep social conditioning and a confidence that those we pass or encounter in the course of a day are similarly socialized. The power of culture lies in its being both barely noticed and utterly pervasive, informing and reinforced by overlapping moments when nothing of import seems to be going on. But such moments actually involve a great deal of cultural work. We can glimpse this work through just a few ethnographic encounters and insights.

These vignettes provide specific glimpses of how culture operates in relation to race, shaping our differential perceptions of bodies, the constraints we feel against saying certain things, and the sense of ease or discomfort we experience in particular social settings. What you should begin to glimpse in the following examples are the registers in which culture is most powerful—the sense of *conventions* that guide what we say and do, the array of *meanings* we read into bodily features, and the *interpretive frameworks* on which we rely in making sense of other peoples' words and actions. These forms are most powerful when we barely recognize them; indeed, you might notice them only when you make an effort to push against social conventions—maybe by coming unwashed or poorly dressed to school one day or by speaking nonsense to friends or strangers or by bumping into people on the street instead of following the host of unspoken cues we rely on to navigate crowded public spaces. Indeed, for all our highly touted individuality, our actions are deeply shaped by social conventions that we hardly notice until we transgress them in some way. But there is a systematic, empirical method for recognizing these forms—short of violating all kinds of decorum, rules of etiquette, or social norms—and that is through ethnographic observation.

Who Smells?

Hortense Powdermaker is an example of how long anthropologists have been involved doing fieldwork on race issues in the United States. She started her fieldwork in Indianola, Mississippi, in 1932. Upon completing her first fieldwork project (1929–1930) in Lesu, a village on the east coast of New Ireland, she was casting about for a next project. In a discussion with one of her mentors, Edward Sapir, she quickly settled on doing a study of African Americans in the Deep South. At the time, her decision was quite unusual. Almost no ethnographic attention was being paid to "modern communities" (versus indigenous groups) in the United States. But Powdermaker (1966) relates that as soon as she started writing grant applications to support the study she realized that "I must have been thinking, consciously and unconsciously, for a long time about this type of research problem"

(132). As she reflected on her choice, she recalled her various experiences with race growing up in Baltimore in a German Jewish home in the 1910s and 1920s. One incident stood out in her recollections as an initial moment that made her curious about race. Powdermaker describes the setting:

> I was coming home on a streetcar late one hot August afternoon from the playground where I taught during some summer vacations while a college student. White and Negro men who had obviously been digging and working in the sun boarded the car. They were all dirty and sweaty. The car was crowded and people had to stand close to each other. A white woman standing by me complained of the smell of the Negroes; they did smell. I wondered about the white workers and moved next to them; they smelled, too. The blue cotton uniform which I wore as a playground teacher was wet with perspiration from my strenuous day. I then became aware that I smelled. The streetcar incident stood out as a discovery. (1966, 132)

That moment of discovery for Powdermaker involved recognizing how profoundly race conditioned her thinking. She did not realize suddenly, in a personal sense, that she harbored racist sentiments. Rather, she confronted the system of classifications and conventions that made her and fellow riders view people differently in terms of race. The classifications related to race worked then, as they still do, to shape not only how we think about bodies—their substances and attributes— but also the type of meanings we attribute to them. Bodily smells pervaded that streetcar, but only "Negroes" were associated with the odor, even though the smell emanated from white bodies, too. Racial classification shaped in advance how the bodies and their attributes were differently perceived. Secondly, she realized these classifications were linked to cultural conventions. The other white woman felt perfectly free to complain about the black passengers, but no one on the car would make the same complaint about the white workers. Nor would anybody be so "rude" to mention that this hardworking young, white female teacher smelled, even though, as Powdermaker recognized, she clearly did. The point is that our racial classifications are accompanied by conventions that govern what people feel they can or cannot do or say in relation to race.

In cultural terms, race operates as a series of frames linking identities and behaviors, which we rely on for sorting out bodily experiences in our daily lives. Powdermaker explored these intently in her ethnography *After Freedom: A Cultural Study in the Deep South* (1993, 1939), which examined the ways whites and blacks in Indianola, Mississippi, lived lives that were elaborately entwined while being maintained as utterly distinct. Such a complex social arrangement rested on deeply ingrained cultural mores and taboos, which in turn were policed and maintained both institutionally (in terms of economics and politics) and, at times, by violence. We will consider these cultural dynamics in some detail in Chapter 4, which focuses on questions about whiteness. But first, a couple of more contemporary examples of ethnographic approaches to race will provide a somewhat more tangible depiction of what this mode of producing social knowledge entails.

Friendly Americans

Throughout the 1980s and 1990s ethnographic fieldwork in the United States became more common, and it gradually shifted from the study of "minorities" or "subcultures" to looking at Americans broadly in cultural terms. One of the influential books in this trend was Michael Moffatt's *Coming of Age in New Jersey: College and American Culture* (1989). The title makes playful reference to one of the most influential early ethnographies, *Coming of Age in Samoa* (1928), by Margaret Mead. Moffatt wanted to understand better the worldview of his students at Rutgers University, so he took up residence in a dorm for a year, observing their socializing and interviewing them about their beliefs and practices. Moffatt's analysis of student life is wide-ranging, but for our purposes the most interesting material he considered involved how Americans think about race.

The dorm floor on which Moffatt did his study was structurally divided, with two wings of rooms linked by an elevator lobby and a set of fire doors. The floor was also socially separated. One side of the dorm was home to the single black special-interest section at the university, named after Paul Robeson (one of Rutgers' most illustrious alumni). The other side was mostly white students, who anticipated that the whole floor would form a single community—holding regular meetings, programs and parties, and so forth—as was common practice on campus. Moffatt recounts how conflicts arose almost immediately when white and black expectations clashed over how the students would mutually occupy this shared space. You might expect that, as an anthropologist, Moffatt would find that this clash stemmed from two distinct cultures coming into conflict. Instead, what he concluded was that the conflicts arose out of a series of confusions stemming from the way race differentially shapes perceptions within our common culture. Both sets of students shared American culture in common, a culture that emphasizes "friendliness" in social interactions. Where they differed sharply was in how they recognized, or more often misrecognized, *signs of friendliness.*

Following the lead of many social scientists and commentators, Moffatt characterizes "friendliness" as a central discourse in American culture. This is an important point that many Americans might not easily get, because—as a cultural construct—it is something mundane that we assume to be completely natural or real. But rather than existing as an essential, abstract quality, friendliness is something we actively construct as we perform social roles and interpret others' efforts at sociality. It is what we perform when we smile and say, "Hi, how are you?" answering, in return, "I'm fine," without giving it much thought. Friendliness, in this regard, is something we do so readily and consistently that we really only notice when it seems missing or lacking in an exchange. Friendliness is so primary a register for evaluating and performing our social interactions that it may be difficult for you to realize this is not a universal social expectation. Rather, it fits tightly within a set of conventions that Americans maintain for managing social interactions and classifying people. Along with "nice," "friendly" does an awful lot of work for Americans. The striking observation that Moffatt (1986) makes is that "all the students, black and white, gave virtually identical formal definitions of a 'friend'" (164). In this regard, he concluded they shared a common culture. So why did problems arise?

Where the students differed was in reading *cues* of friendliness. White and black students commonly felt they were being friendly—as any American would strive to be in a social context—but they were often perceived instead as being alternately "unfriendly" or "too friendly." Moffatt (1986) writes, "Though blacks' and whites' *definitions* of friendship were virtually identical, friendly styles varied slightly; a cooler or less effusive initial interactive style was favored by blacks than by whites, especially among the males" (166). As well, whites and blacks differed in the estimation of the time it took to extend friendship. In this and several other ways, "a white male and a black male might seriously misinterpret one another's friendship cues: to the black male, the white male might seem suspiciously interactive, trying to be 'friendly' too soon; to the white male, the black male might seem initially hostile and basically 'unfriendly'" (166). That two well-meaning people, striving to be friendly and commonly recognizing it as a social expectation and ideal, would face such difficulties in establishing "friendliness" suggests that this quality, far from being natural, is a cultural form shaped by a combination of conventions and meanings that requires both performative and interpretive work to achieve and maintain. Another point that is crucial here is that we can be doing race in very mundane ways when we make judgments about who is "friendly" or "nice" or whether we feel "comfortable" in a situation—even if there are no explicit or implicit references to racist sensibilities. The way we make these classifications can have racial impacts as well, underscoring how pervasive racial meanings are in our society.

The point that Moffatt draws from this is not that Americans' racial conflicts result from simple misinterpretations of each other's actions and words. Rather, he finds in this setting a deeper problem that Americans face in thinking and talking about race, due to our pervasive belief in and reliance on individualism as a basis for making sense of the world. Whatever its values in political, economic, and social terms, individualism makes it very difficult to recognize and take seriously divergent group circumstances or to recognize and acknowledge group dynamics generally. This put the white students in a difficult position. On one hand, they felt they could not talk about the black students as a group without appearing racist. On the other, they were unable to recognize that they, too, constituted a racial group with a shared set of interests and expectations. Instead, they steadfastly refused to see each other as anything more than a bunch of individuals who just happened to share the same beliefs and expectations.

Individualism and Race

In developing this point, Moffatt (1989) draws on earlier work by Gunnar Myrdal and Louis Dumont, who argued that "racism is a specific ideological corollary of individualism and egalitarianism" (159). The problem lies, partly, in the unstated, implicit assumption of how an individual looks and acts. When **unmarked** individuals encounter difference in another person—that is, someone perceived as not sufficiently or appropriately "individual"—there is no other logical recourse than to assume that something is inherently wrong with that person. In a political system predicated on the notion of equality, this judgment easily leads to viewing that person as something less than human—someone not capable of participating in the social order. Inevitably, this not-quite-human status is depicted in terms of the *individual's* logical opposite—the *group*. The racism here is not a personal quality—as any good individual would be concerned to clarify; rather, it manifests as part of a cultural system bifurcating the world into individuals and groups, with the latter being a somewhat illicit or not fully legitimate status.

Mild social conflicts in the dorm percolated over the course of the year, as students continued to misread each other's friendliness cues. In the face of professed goodwill on both sides of the racial divide, they struggled to find a way to explain the problem. As Americans deeply invested in the notion of individualism, their biggest problem was trying to characterize group dynamics, especially for the white students, who felt that doing so would make them seem racist. What they generally invoked to explain the situation was *culture*. Much to Moffatt's consternation, they did not use the term as anthropologists do; rather, its connotation "was something like individual subjectivism writ large" (1986, 170). Just as we commonly allow that each individual has a right to hold opinions different from ours—within certain unstated boundaries of decorum—*culture* was deployed here to characterize a "natural" set of variation from expected norms. What this usage left in its wake was a sense that everyone else was an individual ("we're all just people"), making it difficult for the students to recognize the deeply conditioned set of expectations that led them to see people of their own race not as a group but as a collection of individuals.

As Moffatt (1986) ruefully concludes, "Notably missing was the idea that culture can fundamentally determine habitual modes of thought and deeply affect behavior, or that it is relativistic in any sense more profound than one person's having a taste for one leisure activity and another for another" (171). Ironically, though we Americans might freely toss around the term *culture*, we have very little familiarity with how to think analytically about that which culture delineates—the arbitrary nexus of conventions and meanings in "natural" objects such as friendliness. Our relative inability to recognize culture and cultural dynamics in these routine settings and practices makes it difficult for Americans to understand how and why race matters. Difficulty in comprehending culture and its dynamics is central to why many whites, in particular, are unable to think critically about race or to grasp its various manifestations and operations. Without some understanding that our experience of the world is culturally contoured, it is difficult to regard racism as more than just an individual failing or a vaguely perceived institutional byproduct.

Without recognition of the interlocking aspects of cultural perceptions and categorical identities, race appears as just another isolated topic of concern. But by starting with basic cultural dynamics, it is easy to show how race both inflects and is shaped by judgments Americans make about whether or not certain people appear to be nice or friendly or hard-working—each reflecting crucial categorical demarcations that ostensibly make no mention of race but that certainly operate at times in racial registers. A cultural perspective allows us to place race simultaneously in the mix of everyday life, shaping perceptions that do not appear racial, but without reductively asserting that everything is about race.

Historian George Lipsitz (1998), in objectifying the "possessive investment in whiteness" that forms the economic, political, and social bases for white dominance, contends

> that the stark contrast between black experiences and white opinions during the past two decades cannot be attributed solely to ignorance or intolerance on the part of individuals but stems instead from the overdetermined inadequacy of the language of liberal individualism to describe collective behavior. As long as we define social life as the sum total of conscious and deliberate individual activities, then only *individual* manifestations of personal prejudice and hostility will be seen as racist. Systemic, collective, and coordinated behavior disappears from sight. Collective exercises of group power relentlessly channeling rewards, resources, and opportunities from one group to another will not appear to be "racist" from this perspective because they rarely announce their intentions to discriminate against individuals. But they work to construct racial identities by giving people of different races vastly different life chances. (381)

The cultural perspective addresses both this inability to grasp the distinctive social conditioning that individualism entails and the attendant ignorance of how collective processes shape our experiences and the very ground of the social order. The power of this view is that it may be more conducive for both thinking about race and recognizing its intersection with other critical categories of social identity.

In developing this cultural perspective, it is crucial to understand that we are examining American culture broadly rather than suggesting that races in the United States represent different cultures. Our respective differences—especially in terms of racial experiences—do not amount to separate cultures to the extent that we are so commonly conditioned to recognize racial meanings. This point matters a great deal because the shift away from explicitly racist public speech was accompanied by an increase in references to racial difference in terms of culture. One particular example is blaming "black culture" for the problems of inner-city life, even though conditions in the cores of decaying central cities are shaped by much larger economic, political, and social forces. This is a matter we will consider in some detail in Chapter 5. But this point of caution about how to reference culture—along with the attention to an overarching American culture—does not preclude the ability to talk about racial differences. Rather, it opens a distinctive way of discussing those associations in relation to whiteness, blackness, and notions of "foreignness" that often confront Latinos, Asians, and other groups in the United States, as we will examine in detail in Chapter 6.

Where Do We Locate Race?

My own fieldwork, in my hometown of Detroit, Michigan, was aimed at analyzing how whiteness works in everyday life. If you know anything about Detroit, you probably know its reputation as the "blackest" city in the country. This characterization reflects the fact that, in terms of raw numbers and majority status, Detroit is the most African American–dominant city in the United States. I chose to study whites there because I knew that their racial identity was not unmarked in any consistent or certain manner. We will consider this in far more detail in Chapter 4. For the moment, I only want to relate one incident that occurred when I had been in the field for just a couple of days. I was living in an extremely poor, inner-city neighborhood—an area that is predominantly white. The whites are largely from the Appalachian states, and they or their parents had migrated to the city during the postwar boom decades. They self-identified as "hillbillies." Interestingly, they stayed in this neighborhood long after white flight gutted the city, with some 1.4 million whites fleeing racial integration for the vastly white suburbs.

I was renting a place next to a large, extended "hillbilly" family. My first night in the place, the three adult brothers—Jerry, Sam, and David—took me to one of the area's remaining bars. We walked there past numerous empty lots where wild grasses grew riotously, since most of the houses had long since burned or been demolished. The next morning, hoping to pick up where we left off in terms of socializing, I joined the brothers outside on the street, where they stood around the open hood of David's Ford LTD. Since I was new in the area, they were still trying to size me up, and they were very suspicious because, though I said I was working on a dissertation, I was obviously not going to school every day. So they had me explain once again what I was up to. Specifically, Jerry asked, "What is it you're studying again?"

I had described my project to them the day before, but I guess it all seemed quite abstract—to them and to me too. So I simplified my reply and just said, "Race relations." They burst out laughing, hooting and whooping it up, as if that was the funniest thing they'd ever heard. "Race relations!?," Sam cackled. "I'll take you over to the bars on Third, and you'll sure learn something." Those bars, I later found out, had been their stomping grounds as much younger men. But that area—and, importantly, the intervening streets—had grown far more black and dangerous. David then added, "Naw, man. You want to learn about race relations, you just walk from here through them projects [across the street] to the freeway on the other side. That's an education! 'Cause I'll tell you what, you won't come out the other side. You walk in there and you're gonna learn more than you can handle what race relations is. You won't come out the other side." Sam wrapped up the topic by affirming, "Yeah, go in there at night, you won't get a hundred yards." Weeks later, when a graduate student from nearby Wayne State University was shot to death by a thirteen-year-old boy while walking past the projects, Sam was quick to point out to me, "See, I told you. That's what happens to researchers."

The housing project to which they referred comprised several massive towers, which loomed over the boulevard that passed in front of their house. All the residents were black. As I learned in the following days, their comments reflected their experiences, as whites, of being mugged or "jumped" by black men. They also recalled the violence that followed in the wake of the city's dramatic racial and economic transformation, in a period when jobs and money hemorrhaged from the city. The experience of these "hillbillies" was hardly surprising or unusual. What did surprise and confuse me was the selective way they referenced these experiences as they mapped out the landscape of race relations.

The night before, I was impressed to see that the crowd at the neighborhood bar was racially mixed, with about an even number of whites and blacks as well as a few Latinos. This interracial pattern remained consistent over the years I spent in Detroit, and it was affirmed by the jukebox, which featured a combination of classic country-and-western songs alongside the latest R&B hits, plus plenty of Motown tunes. Their gesture of placing race relations over there in the projects further confused me over the following days, weeks, and months as I got to meet their black neighbors and friends, who socialized with them at barbeques and baseball games and while drinking beer on the front porch. Three black men even rented rooms in the large house where the brothers lived. As I grew familiar with their extensive interracial networks, I came to wonder why they did not think of these when I mentioned race relations.

There are two parts to this answer, one of which I will only mention in passing now and develop further in Chapter 4. The other part of the answer is much larger and concerns the overall focus of this book on the cultural dynamics of race. The first point is that the brothers did not think of themselves in racial terms, as is frequently the case with whites. Race was something that happened to them when they moved into black-dominated parts of the city. They generally did not regard the ways they walked or talked or socialized as being about race, even though much of what whites do on a daily basis subtly signals belonging to this racial category. Instead, they gesture or assume that *it's over there* somewhere. This is a challenge you will likely encounter as you try to formulate and answer questions about race. But you will also probably find, as I did, that we are doing race in so many ways at once that we hardly recognize it at first. This brings us to the second part of the answer: We generally use "racial" selectively, largely to point to encounters or events that are polarizing or conflictual, as the brothers did here.

When Are We Doing Race?

Such moments are set off against a wide array of mundane instances when we are doing race in ways that draw little or no direct attention. Not surprisingly, the moments we generally label racial are vivid because they are charged and sometimes violent. This is how race relations are often depicted in the media—we reference race when something is going wrong or when conflicts arise. But race is happening around us all the time, in ways we hardly ever consider. Our challenge is to recognize the mundane and pervasive ways that we are continually doing race—signaling belonging to and differing from these categorical identities—in ways that are routine and assumed, that is, cultural. Analyzing race in cultural terms involves moving beyond the spectacular and disruptive moments that we tend to label as racial to attend to the much larger array of moments and settings in which we do race without hardly noticing.

Race is far more than skin color and encompasses much more than forms of social advantage and disadvantage. Race is meaningful, and it is a fundamental part of how we make sense of the world around us; that is, it is cultural too. We move through the world constantly observing and processing the actions and words of others; similarly, we present ourselves to be observed and understood by the people we pass or encounter every day. Race is a register on which we rely in these interpretive interactions. Determining *belonging* and *difference* in social interactions often entails a good deal of speculation and theorizing, which we apply to our presentations of self and our assessments of others. Some behaviors and comments easily conform to deeply held stereotypes and confirm pejorative sentiments; others are not so easily processed, and they raise conundrums.

Culture lies in these alternately confusing and confirming social interactions, rather than just in our interior monologues and judgments. We miss this interactive dimension when we rely solely on the concept of racism to analyze race, because this concept posits attitudes as determining social interactions. This overlooks the contingent aspects of our encounters—how particular settings support or disrupt our classifying assessments, and the ways people may or may not conform to our expectations. Importantly, varied contexts and interactions can differently inflect the ambiguous and contradictory attitudes that people often hold about the world and our categories for it.

The main value of a cultural perspective is that it moves us out of the attitudinal realm and into the domain of *interactions*. I talked with the three brothers a good deal about how they thought about race. As well, I observed them in many interactions with neighbors, strangers, family members, and each other. Over time, I heard them express many varied opinions about black people—some were vicious, others accepting and respectful, and many were simply contradictory. For that matter, they expressed a similar range of opinions about whites—each other, themselves, family members, neighbors, and strangers. How was I to settle on any one as truly representative of their personal feelings? The answer is that I did not. The broad range of their opinions led me away from thinking in terms of trying to fix any one of them in terms of their attitudes. I realized this range reflected their response to particular situations where race, perhaps clearly or ambiguously, mattered. That is, I recognized that they actively thought about race—sometimes using charged stereotypes, but at other times dismissing such stereotypes as ridiculous and distorted. This was not simply because their opinions changed, but because the *social context* in which they were thinking or talking about race influenced their interpretation of how it mattered. This reflects the *interactive, place-specific dynamics of culture*, which are fundamental to how people actively make sense of race.

Making Sense of Race
Jerry, Sam, and David's gesture regarding my interest in race relations reflected an aspect of their view of race that I found very common in Detroit. That is, race took

on a somewhat unfixed quality until someone decided, as the brothers would put it, "to make something out of it." The city's recent history was steeped in racial conflict and animosity; yet, at the same time, those conflicts had so thoroughly transformed the city that it was, at times, not easy to fix how race mattered. The neighborhoods, schools, and property values that whites once vigorously fought to defend had been drastically transformed in the wake of white flight—nowhere more so than this inner-city area. These drastic changes in Detroit's landscape unhinged the meanings of race that were once so keenly linked to battles over segregation and control of municipal power and resources. In the wake of those conflicts, race still mattered, but its significance was more open to question.

In this regard, I found that people in Detroit were often *provisional* in their racial thinking and assessments. This is something that is easily missed by surveys or in polling data that require people to choose from a limited range of possible attitudes to represent their thinking at any one moment. In this regard, too, I found that a great deal of interpretive work goes into sounding out and thinking through the significance of race. The three brothers, for instance, are not simply motivated by a core of ideological beliefs, such as racism. The way they think involves a dynamic between past experiences, current sentiments, and the way these are either confirmed or challenged by the contexts in which they are mulled over or expressed. This links to an additional finding: *the meaning of race varies by location.* This is conveyed by the brothers, in that the significance of their whiteness varied as they moved about the city; as well, racial identities, too, are constitutive of place, as distinctly raced people strive to make their contexts reflect or confirm their racial sense of belonging.

Each of these points led me to underscore the important role culture plays in how we think about or are oblivious to race. The crucial point, again, with culture is that *it precedes and shapes personal experiences and perceptions*—it is the template by which we make sense of all this. So often, with race or racism in particular, we tend to think in very individualist terms—as in assuming that a person either is a racist or is not a racist, as if this was a reflection of personal sensibility. But as we have seen with the evidence of racial discrimination presented earlier in this chapter, race clearly structures the landscape into which we have each been born, differently advantaging and disadvantaging us all by our skin color. But this is hardly an automatic process. Race requires active cultural work for us to continue to sort and subdivide people we meet or know by this system of classification. Though we feel and largely perceive race as natural—a matter explored further in Chapter 3—it is, rather, something that takes a good deal of interpretive work. But how do we think about the way this active dimension of race operates alongside, or perhaps rests on, both unconscious dynamics and the social landscape of racial advantage and disadvantage? The answer, at least initially, is by recognizing and emphasizing *the interactive aspect of race*—that is, the ways we respond to it and project it onto social interactions that either reinforce or challenge those guiding assumptions. This is very much something that is external to our own individual sensibilities, in the way that culture exactly precedes the individual.

The simplest way to encapsulate this is to return again to the concept of interpretive repertoires. These repertoires, remember, are collections of stories and images, expressions and phrases that crystallize certain sentiments, drawn from stereotypes or from real encounters. The point to grasp here is that these are, in a sense, external and shared: they are the common *assemblage of frames* for explaining how we think and feel. They are ways we explain our views and experiences to each other, through common tropes or ideas, and they form the basis of how we listen to what other people are telling us. The remarkably complex task of explaining our experiences of the world and comprehending others' experiences requires a broad array of common categories, images, and shared ways of talking. Such repertoires form the basis for how we do race. These are external social forms—of speaking and listening—that precede our experiences, in much the same way that language precedes us; they are the medium through which we strive to make ourselves understood and to comprehend what others are saying. This is the realm of culture, which we will examine from a variety of angles in each of the following chapters.

CHAPTER 2

Race, Culture, and Ethnography

The role of race in our society is pervasive. For all its import, though, race is neither an obvious nor uniform matter. We can measure its impacts in shaping differential life chances and social worlds, but much debate remains about what actually constitutes race. Is it forms of bias and prejudice, is it a set of beliefs about the superiority of whiteness and the inferiority of blackness, or is it something underlain by another set of dynamics—related to class, for instance—that inform racial thinking as well? These questions are open-ended and subject to ongoing scholarly research.

This chapter focuses initially on the basic elements of racial analysis, highlighting some widely shared assumptions about studying race. Then the focus shifts to seeing racial analysis in juxtaposition with the analysis of culture, in order to consider how racial meanings and relations are shaped by cultural dynamics. You already should comprehend the broad contours of these two analytics from the discussion in Chapter 1. In the following pages, contrasts between these perspectives are initially highlighted, in order eventually to arrive at a clear understanding of how these can be combined effectively. The second half of this chapter examines antiracist research, as seen in conjunction with ethnographic perspectives on race. This discussion is geared toward understanding how both approaches are applied in real-world settings. The overall purpose of this chapter is to sketch possible ways of combining racial analysis and cultural analysis via ethnography.

FUNDAMENTAL FEATURES OF RACIAL ANALYSIS

Racial analysis, as the phrase suggests, is principally about race. The basic starting point is straightforward: race is a problem that has to be solved. The basic task of racial analysts is to explain how and why people continue to think and act in racial terms. Racial analysis generally features two focal points: the facts of racial inequality linked to power differentials, and the role of racism in reproducing that inequality. For racial analysts these are generally the guiding concerns: *inequality, racism,* and correlated *forms of social disadvantage or advantage.* But the study of race is historically deep and varied, so the attention to these primary concerns currently manifests in a variety of forms.

Broadly, race can be studied from a range of angles, sometimes in very detached terms, as a variable in a social analysis, or, instead, in quite personal and political terms, as a series of contestations with the numerous ways race matters in daily life. Sociologists, for instance, have long studied "race relations" as a particular form of generic social conflict. In contrast, the *black radical tradition* combines scholarship with activism as it confronts the various forms of exclusion and repression related to race that arguably form the very basis for this social order (Thomas 2005). Antiracist approaches, generally, also combine critical forms of self-reflection along with an attention to the ways that whiteness can be reproduced in seemingly objective forms of social analysis (Pollock 2008). The basic tools of sociological methods can be quite useful in demonstrating the facts of racial inequality, as illustrated in Chapter 1. But are they effective for getting at the forms of racial bias and belief that may well shape the views of purportedly neutral social scientists? Or are they sufficient for understanding the crucial intersection of different forms of domination in terms of gender, sexuality, and class as well as race?

These questions have generated a variety of ways of analyzing race, most of which we can only touch on here. But they share some key common features that offer a solid basis for at least a cursory characterization of racial analysis. A guiding assumption is that though race is pervasive, it can be difficult for people to recognize, particularly whites, who are generally advantaged by race. This difficulty lies partly in the tension between personal perceptions and beliefs about race and the social conventions that constrain what we can say about it in public. Recognizing a potential gap between "real" and "stated" beliefs about race, some sociologists and psychologists promote the use of *implicit-association tests,* which purportedly reveal the unconscious biases we harbor concerning race. These tests work by asking respondents to match either positive or negative terms (e.g., "nice" versus "scary") with randomly flashed images of people's faces. Researchers find that whites have a tendency to associate negative terms with black images, even while they may profess not to harbor racial views (Blanton and Jaccard 2008).

This approach locates race in the types of adjectives we use to characterize groups of people. Descriptions of a group as "lazy," "violent," or "dangerous," for instance, are key indicators of a racial perception at work. But because today there are strong social sanctions against expressing racist characterizations, these perceptions often undergo a kind of transformation into racial **code words**. These are terms that convey a racial sensibility but, generally, are not as quickly recognized or criticized as being racist. Political scientist Tali Mendelberg (2001) analyzes how some white politicians make "implicit racial appeals" via the use of such code words. Mendelberg explains that "implicit racial appeals convey the same message as explicit racial appeals, but *they replace the racial nouns and adjectives with more oblique references to race*" [emphasis added] (9). By characterizing opponents as "soft on crime," politicians can mobilize racial sentiment without ever explicitly mentioning race.

Such code words speak to the complicated process by which we are socialized into a world of racial meanings, one that has fairly elaborate rules for what one can and cannot say in public (Hill 2008). This speaks to another consistent feature of racial analysis: the recognition of the pervasiveness of race. One way of capturing this dimension is through the concept of *controlling image* (Collins 2000). These images go beyond the generic concept of stereotypes by highlighting the systemic effects of such representations. Powerful, degrading images of black women, in particular—such as the "mammy" or the "welfare queen"—do more than simply distort views of real people. They relationally also provide a generative basis by which many whites constitute a sense of self-image, specifically in contrast to these charged figures.

Importantly, these are not just images in people's heads; they manifest in the media, in school disciplinary practices, and in the policies of government agencies. Sociologist Patricia Hill Collins (2000) explains how this operates in relation to images of poor black women. "The image of the welfare mother provides *ideological* justifications for the intersecting oppressions of race, gender, and class. African-Americans can be racially stereotyped as lazy by blaming Black welfare mothers for failing to pass on the work ethic" [emphasis added] (79). This kind of blaming ignores or is blinded to a host of social and political constraints facing black women in poverty, fixating instead on the image of an uncontrollable matriarch whose way of life seems to threaten white middle-class notions of family and work.

Racial Ideology

Collins' characterization of controlling images features perhaps the most fundamental shared feature of racial analysis, the concept of **ideology**. This focus on ideology also marks something of a point of divergence with the forms of cultural analysis pursued by ethnographers of race, as we will see later in this chapter. The crux of this divergence involves the difference between their respective key concepts—*ideology* for analysts of race, *culture* for ethnographers. These two concepts are not mutually exclusive, and it takes a good deal of effort to keep them distinct. Both make reference to systems of belief and their power to shape (or distort) the social world. But these concepts do have distinctive points of emphasis that are worth fleshing out in order to understand how to combine these respective analytical approaches.

In terms of ideology, the central concern for race theorists, not surprisingly, is **racism**, which involves an elaborate system of beliefs interwoven with material conditions and interests. Racism is construed as both a product and a function of *power* and forms of *inequality* that, in turn, derive from historical practices and social relations. The operations of racism—in its various guises and transformations—stem from a tight combination of material interests and ideological conditioning. This perspective is perhaps best summarized by sociologist Eduardo Bonilla-Silva, whose work on color-blind racism was featured in Chapter 1. Bonilla-Silva characterizes his approach to race as directed toward analyzing the "racial structure," which historically has "awarded systematic privileges to Europeans (the people who became 'white') over non-Europeans (the peoples who became non-white)" (2006, 9). This view regards "a society's racial structure as *the totality of the social relations and practices that reinforce white privilege*" (ibid.). In this perspective, Bonilla-Silva explains, "the task of the analyst interested in studying racial structures is to uncover the particular social, economic, political, social control, and ideological mechanisms responsible for the reproduction of racial privilege in a society" (ibid.). From this array of factors constituting the racial structure, Bonilla-Silva devotes primary attention to the last element, *ideological mechanisms*.

This emphasis on racial ideology is commonplace in sociological approaches to race. But it is also a surprisingly dominant view for race theorists in anthropology as well, who similarly emphasize the role of ideology in rationalizing material conditions related to race. This view is succinctly stated by anthropologist Faye Harrison, who delineates the central problem of race today as the fact that "racist *beliefs* about blackness are embedded in *a system of material relations* that produces and reproduces *taken-for-granted* power and privileges, such as those associated with whiteness" [emphasis added] (1998, 612). In this view, beliefs, or ideologies, are linked to material conditions that then reproduce cultural assumptions about racial hierarchies. From this formulation, it follows that the researcher's task is to devote "sufficient analytical attention to the *ideological and material forces* that categorically mark and stigmatize certain peoples as essentially and irreconcilably different while treating the privileges of others as normative" [emphasis added] (1998, 612). In this perspective, the dual operation of ideology and material interests are mutually supporting, an interlocking system of advantage and disadvantage linked to racial classification and beliefs about race.

For Bonilla-Silva, as for most race theorists, ideology is key because it is the means by which members of a dominant group *rationalize* their material advantages and power. Bonilla-Silva explains: "Since actors racialized as 'white'—or as members of the dominant race—receive material benefits from the racial order, they struggle (or passively receive the manifold wages of whiteness) to maintain their privileges" (2006, 9). In this effort, *racial ideology* is crucial. Bonilla-Silva defines this concept as "*the racially based framework used by actors to explain and justify* (dominant race) or *challenge* (subordinate race or races) *the racial status quo*" (ibid., original emphasis). As we saw in Chapter 1, the pervasive, multifaceted facts of racial inequality support both tenets of this approach—race entails material (as well as symbolic) forms of advantage and disadvantage, and these are reproduced or contested in terms of an ideology of inherent, natural, and indelible racial identities. The enduring power of both racial ideology and race privilege lies in the way these are "rooted in the group-based conditions and experiences of the races and are, at the symbolic level, the representations developed by these groups to explain how the world is or ought to be" (10). Hence, in analyzing color-blind racism, Bonilla-Silva links the various "frames, style, and racial stories" whites produce in explaining "how the world is" back to the continued advantages of whiteness, which pertain even though explicitly racist discourse has receded from public culture in the United States.

Perhaps the most important point about ideology is that it represents a *world-view*. Bonilla-Silva explains that "the central component of any dominant racial ideology" is that it establishes the "paths for interpreting information." These paths, he argues, largely "operate as cul-de-sacs because after people filter issues through them, they explain racial phenomena following a predictable route." But these perceptual paths do not simply limit one's view of the world; they actually quite powerfully "*mis*represent the world" and, especially, the "facts of dominance." This is how, he argues, most whites are so consistently able to ignore "the fact that most people of color are severely underrepresented in most good jobs, schools, and universities" (26). That is, these are not simply neutral features of the social world; these are basic facts that many whites are able entirely to overlook, even if they may feel that they do not harbor any racist sentiments.

ETHNOGRAPHIC PERSPECTIVES ON RACE

This singular focus on the workings of racial ideology is in contrast to the way ethnographers generally approach race in the field. Ethnography is a particular research method, largely informed by the guiding concept of culture. Ethnographers' tasks generally begin with trying to understand how place-specific dynamics both shape and are reflected in peoples' everyday activities. When ethnographers analyze race, they typically do so by trying to understand how it is reproduced or contested in social interactions in particular public contexts. Even when ethnographers focus primarily on race, they are not necessarily pursuing or deploying a racial analysis. This is because, for all its centrality in racial analysis, ideology is not often the focus of ethnographies of race. The works surveyed in Chapters 4 through 6 rarely turn to ideology as a means to explain how and why race matters in the daily contexts studied by ethnographers. This is because, however much ethnographers might share the viewpoint of racial analysis, their task is generally far more diffuse: *to describe the interpretive work of social subjects in particular locales and to appraise how that work is variously supported or undermined in social interactions.* Still, as the ethnographic vignettes at the end of Chapter 1 indicate, this approach is very capable of generating important insights about how race operates. Indeed, as we will see, the type of cultural analysis that informs ethnographic research offers a powerful means of extending and strengthening racial analysis.

Ethnography is a means of producing social knowledge about the patterns of belief and behavior that shape daily life as a meaningful condition. This method was developed by cultural anthropologists in Europe and the United States as an approach to understanding the starkly different lifeways of peoples in exotic locales. But as you have already glimpsed through the ethnographic vignettes in the previous chapter, this method was eventually turned to study Western groups and social problems as well. The basic method involves **participant observation**, a means of comprehending how daily life provides the fundamental cultural template by which people organize their routine activities in meaningful ways. When ethnography was primarily deployed to study native life in other lands, participant observation involved taking part in all manner of tribal practices and ceremonies. Now, as ethnography is increasingly used to study groups such as geneticists and financiers, this focus on participant observation remains central to this method of generating social knowledge. This method is still the principle means for understanding how particular contexts and the details of life in specific settings provide the basis for social relations.

The reason ethnographers of race do not privilege ideology in their accounts is probably that this attention to context and the specificity of social locales predisposes them to a generally more nuanced view of the social world. Despite whatever degrees of nuance the term can encompass, ideology largely entails a reductive perspective. Bonilla-Silva puts the matter succinctly by characterizing ideology as "meaning in the service of power" (2006, 25). By regarding belief systems as chained to the task of explaining and reproducing material interests, particularly forms of domination, ideological analyses render people's thoughts in fairly functionalist terms. As well, a primary implication with ideology is that the "true" state of material relations is "masked from view" by these supporting systems of belief. So Bonilla-Silva characterizes color-blind racial ideology as "an impregnable yet elastic wall that *barricades* whites from the United States' *racial reality*" (47).

An ethnographic perspective, however, involves a rather different orientation, even while sharing a common attention to beliefs and their relation to material conditions. The crux of the contrast lies in the concept of *culture*, which involves a far more unruly notion of meaning. Where "race as ideology" implies that our social practices and beliefs purposely distort or mask basic social reality, a cultural perspective, in contrast, sees culture itself—interpretive work involving the realm of meaning and its embeddedness in distinct locales—as fundamentally constitutive of social life. In this sense there is no absolute or definitive "social reality," nor is there an unimpeded, objective view of it, as an ideological analysis suggests. Rather, culture is a composite of contrasting yet linked interpretive practices that constitute the social, even as culture is drawn from—in the form of conventions of meaning and behavior—to make sense of the world around us. Culture both provides a pattern for our interactions and is reproduced—and sometimes altered— through those very interactions. This makes culture quite dynamic. We learn it but we also perform it; these performance both draw on our socialization and are the means by which the meanings we have learned become transformed.

CULTURAL DYNAMICS OF RACE

The aspects of our daily lives that matter most—identity and conflict, agreement and exclusions—all hinge on the operation of culture. In that sense, we are already very familiar with how it works: We can each state with ease "rules" governing our behaviors and the statements we make, rules that are, of course, not "set in stone" and may be interpreted quite differently by others. But it is important also to be able to articulate in more general terms the particular aspects of cultural dynamics so that we can bring some specificity to our observations about how Americans perform race. The featured operations of culture here all involve the basics of dynamics highlighted in the previous section: the interactional, performative, and associational processes by which we make sense of other people and ourselves. But these additional aspects are broader, in that they involve distinct operations of signification that form the backdrop for our daily experiences.

Culture entails three interrelated, basic operations: **body work**, **spatializing practices**, and the determination of **belonging** and **difference**. Combined, these operations are the means by which we interact with each other, performing a variety of identities and, in the process, reproducing an array of social relations. A glimpse of each of these operations is provided by the ethnographic vignettes in Chapter 1. For instance, body work is what Powdermaker observed on the streetcar in Baltimore, and it is fundamental to the ways we use skin and facial features to serve as markers of group identity. Body work involves the variety of means by which social orders, identities, and behaviors are embodied and "naturalized," in terms of both meanings and comportment, but also includes the disciplinary practices to which bodies are subject. These practices include forms of **etiquette** and decorum, which were also evident in the Powdermaker vignette, as well as the forms of policing and surveillance typically associated with race. Culture, at its most fundamental level, is a means for establishing select ways of being, acting, and perceiving as "natural." This involves our expectations for how people should comport their bodies as well as what qualities—offensive or not—we imagine bodies to possess. In this sense, culture is something that we literally *embody*. This is very relevant to the study of race, since it fundamentally shapes differential sensibilities about bodies—their capacities and dispositions.

But culture also involves an array of spatializing practices—means of organizing space and localities as meaningful sites. We glimpsed these in the type of boundary work around "friendliness" in the dorm that college students pursued in Moffatt's account. The central categories of "individual," "group," and "friend" all manifested in tangible ways for these students as they negotiated both their own personal space and their location in the dorm as a shared collective space. The role of place is also plainly evident in the streets and neighborhoods of Detroit, where whites' sensibilities about race relations are finely attuned to matters of location. These practices range from the ways that particular social contexts influence our interpretations of others' words and actions to the way we articulate our identities via feelings of rootedness in a particular place called home. Spatial practices are fundamental to how race works, as well, as we will consider in Chapters 4 and 5 in relation to segregation.

Culture in Motion

Each of these sets of cultural dynamics—embodiment and location—contributes to the process of sorting out belonging and difference. In the most basic terms, culture is about determining sameness, which is how we establish and cultivate forms of similarity while variously distancing ourselves from (or sometimes being attracted to) forms of difference. As we will see in Chapter 3, perceptions of sameness and difference in relation to nature are powerfully conditioned by culture, just as they also provide the basic fodder for cultural operations such as drawing boundaries in relation to bodies and places. In the Moffatt vignette, white and black students alike are unable to recognize their common form of sameness—a shared, general definition of *friendly*—because they fixate on differences in the social cues by which friendliness was expressed. In Powdermaker's case, she only recognized a form of sameness—smelly bodies on a crowded streetcar—when she shifted out of her cultural conditioning that emphasized only charged forms of difference in skin color. As well, whites in Detroit could alternately emphasize sameness (a shared neighborhood location) and difference (contrary experiences of racialization) when they talked with me about race relations. In each of these cases, the matter of belonging turns on how we learn to sort out copious aspects of the world around us in terms of sameness and difference.

The value of the cultural perspective is that it places a priority on understanding how these various dynamics play out in *interactions* between people. Where ideology primarily implies ideas in people's heads related to somewhat abstract notion of interests, culture fundamentally "takes place" in relations between people. Culture involves an intriguing interplay of behaviors and beliefs that both inform and are influenced by actual interactions among people in particular settings. Culture provides the template for our sensibilities about proper and improper words and actions—that is, etiquette. But that template is also potentially changed or altered by how interactions play out in particular places, which are, themselves, often subject to change. This dynamism is captured in the concept of **performance**. When we perform our identities, we do so with a host of cultural ideas about how such performances should go. But these expectations and assumptions can be revised through the course of other performances—both our own and others—that subtly shift these routines. The plasticity of culture resides in the fact that it is fundamentally about meaning, and meaning is something that is inherently unstable.

This aspect of culture points to another key difference with the concept of ideology. In terms of ideology, culture works as a form of mystification of social relations, as described by Bonilla-Silva. But for ethnographers, culture is not something that principally distorts or obscures real relationships; rather, *it is the very medium of social relations*. Culture is not something that we can simply "see through" to an underlying material reality. Instead, culture manifests in the **expressive forms**—language, certainly, but also styles of dress and ways of eating or making music, and so forth—that we use to relate to other people. Culture combines material and symbolic media into patterned ways of interacting with people in everyday contexts. These interactions may hew closely to long-standing beliefs about how certain types or kinds of people can relate, or they may provide surprising challenges to such beliefs. The focus on such interactions, though, is what makes ethnography the principle method of cultural analysis and why, as a method, ethnography relies on a cultural perspective.

In establishing that culture is about meaning—its various media and the ways we confirm or challenge it—we have to understand that this does not simply involve big meanings, as in the meaning of life. Rather, it is primarily about the manifold unconscious ways *we try to mean what we say and do*. Instead of being about abstract values that we may consciously associate with a culture, the meaningfulness of culture lies in the routine and seemingly unimportant ways we gesture or make references that people around us may understand. In fact, the remarkable feature of culture is that these complex operations unfold without ever attracting much conscious attention from us—much as in the ways we breathe or walk without giving any thought to our lungs or the mechanics of bipedalism. They are fundamental to how we maneuver through the world, even if we perform them unconsciously. This point will become clearer by considering now some of the particular features of American culture.

AMERICAN CULTURE IN THREE WORDS

In aiming to characterize American culture, for instance, it is easy to assume that we would do so in terms of big concepts such as *democracy, freedom*, and *individualism*. But patterns of meaning in American culture are more easily traced via three simple, mundane terms—*friendly, nice,* and *work*. We have already considered friendliness extensively, via Moffatt's ethnography, which illustrated the types of **linkages,** or associations, Americans draw between *friendly* and big-meaning terms such as *individualism* and *freedom* (Varenne 1986). Moffatt's example also points to the kind of racial dynamics that can play out as Americans' interpretations of friendliness cues and gestures. So the main focus here is on the additional terms, *nice* and *work*, that are elements in the larger repertoire of common terms that do dual work of conveying value in mundane situations while also playing a key role in how Americans do race.

What is particularly notable about these terms is that they are somewhat hard to define, because we use them so frequently but also because their meanings are fundamentally *relational*. Think about *nice*. How would you define it? *Nice* is *a way of characterizing people and interactions as well as a range of social activities*. This term seems completely innocuous and even bland, but that only underscores its cultural importance. But what makes someone *nice*? Often we answer by juxtaposing an image of someone who is *not nice* or *not friendly*. It is hard to settle on a definition without just spinning off a series of synonyms, such as *pleasant, polite, good*, and finally, coming back to *friendly*. Parents and teachers endlessly instruct children to *be nice* or *play nice* and use the term to characterize gifts, gestures, and sentiments from other children. Children, in turn, characterize for their parents the people they meet in school or on the playground or at birthday parties as either *nice* or *not nice*. Actually, once we get to *not nice* we start formulating a better sense of how this category works in American culture.

Think of all the ways you could possibly characterize a person you have just met to someone else in generic terms—"He's . . . responsible, rationale, smart."

Yet Americans predominantly rely on *nice* to convey the cultural message that this person is socially acceptable and *belongs* in polite society. Consider the kinds of things that characterize *not nice* people: They are rude, argumentative, mean, spiteful, or dangerous. That is, they are decidedly *not friendly*. With *nice*, as with all major cultural categories, the definition of the term is typically established oppositionally. This is why it is hard to define *nice*. At its core, *nice* characterizes *a person who will uphold social conventions and can be relied on to do so in a fairly pleasing manner*. Someone who is *not nice* is liable to violate cultural decorum. That is why *nice* is so important for children to be able to recognize in other people. They quickly develop a facility with this term and its opposite, *not nice*, that allows them to characterize other children and adults they encounter who either can or cannot be relied on or not to be *friendly*. The systematic way these terms are linked or associated is a key indication that we are dealing with cultural dynamics and meanings.

The really striking matter, then, is the way *nice* operates in relation to race. Anthropologist Setha Low examined this process in her ethnography of gated communities, *Behind the Gates: Life, Security, and the Pursuit of Happiness in Fortress America* (2003). Low forefronts an attention to class in her discussion of race, and she strives to capture the interplay between the discourse of inhabitants and the material settings in places where the well-to-do live. But Low also finds "that 'niceness' and being willing to pay the price of perfection has to do with the defense and maintenance of whiteness" (152). In this finding, Low stresses that whiteness "is not only about race, but is a class position and a normative concept" (18). Residents' decisions about whom or what is nice involved complex readings of race in relation to class and belonging. Furthermore, whites may easily consider it not nice to bring up the facts of racial inequality or discrimination that we addressed in Chapter 1. This is a very powerful way of reproducing white racial identity that does not rely on ostensibly racist ideas about people of color.

Niceness establishes a set of norms pertaining to landscapes and home exteriors as well as to possessions and people. This usage shapes an *unmarked* normative space without ever having to equate any of its individual components as white. But, Low (2003) argues, "niceness—keeping things clean, orderly, homogeneous and controlled so that housing values remain stable—is also a way of maintaining whiteness" (172). This functions by simply and usually implicitly equating *nice* and *white*. "By regimenting the environment, keeping it 'nice' and filled with 'nice' people, maintaining the resale value of one's home, and putting up with increasing privatization and restriction" (173), white residents maintain and foster racial segregation without ever having to think in terms of race. *Nice* is sufficient to the task.

Culture at Work

The third category that is crucial in understanding American culture is *work*. Like *nice* and *friendly*, this term imparts a high degree of value to a variety of activities, but it also provides the frame for understanding a great deal of what we do in our daily lives. The centrality of work in American culture could be established statistically by pointing to the fact that Americans work more hours per week and take less vacation time than do people in any other major industrialized nation. But a cultural analysis aims to get at the dynamics of meanings and processes of interpretation; for Americans, this requires looking at the patterned ways we use the word *work* to bestow meaning in mundane, everyday contexts.

Think for a moment about how often you or others you know use the term. "Whatever works for you," we will frequently say, or "That works for me." *Work*, somewhat surprisingly at first, plays a key role in how we think and talk about our social lives. "I'll try to work you in," we may explain to someone, or we might ask them to "work on her/him" to get another person to join in an undertaking or consent to some social arrangement. If your schedule does not permit, you may have to "work around it" to make some social interaction possible. Most strikingly, *work* is also key to how we talk about intimate relationships. Couples earnestly confront the recognition that "this isn't working," though they may desperately want to or believe they can "work it out." If "working on the relationship" fails, they may each separately spend a long time "working through" the breakup by trying to understand what it all meant.

Work is cultural, in that *it is a pervasive, patterned way of making sense of experiences*, one that we apply in a wide range of settings or with a variety of objects or actions. With food, for instance, we will commonly say "I'm working" on this salad or hamburger or sandwich, as when a waiter asks if we are done yet. We might order a pizza with "the works" and then later "have to work off a few pounds" in a "workout" at a gym. As well, we use it to frame poignant or confusing aspects of our personal lives, as in "I'm working through some personal stuff." But we also use the verb for more casual activities, as in "working on my tan," or reading ("I'm working on this book"). All the while, parents studiously instruct their children to "work at being nice." The striking aspect of all this is that we use a single term that connotes labor to frame pleasurable experiences (eating or reading), emotional dynamics (relationships, manipulating friendships), and recreational activities.

The point here is not that "Americans are crazy" for doing so; rather, Americans are obviously quite culture bound—*in order to value such activities in our culture*, we feel compelled to characterize them all as *work*. Once you recognize the array of places or situations in which Americans deploy *work*, you begin to grasp the extent of our cultural conditioning. We "work up" ideas or plans but might describe unkind treatment from another person with the phrase "he really worked me over." We may say of someone that "she knows how to work the system" or that "he worked the room/crowd," as with a comic or musician, or ask someone to "work the phones." Doing well in any of these activities might result in a person's "working his way to the top." "How do you work this thing?" we may ask while exclaiming "Good work!" when someone accomplishes a task. "Works hard" or "works well with others" are phrases kids love to hear. We might promise someone that "it's in the works" while reminding that person that we can't "work miracles." Movies, novels, and poems are "works of imagination," which we might only have time to enjoy if we can "work it so my weekends are free."

In all these uses, not surprisingly, *work*, like *nice,* plays a fundamental role in how Americans think about race. Importantly, each of these terms is crucial for thinking about ostensibly nonracial ways Americans do race. As survey research indicates, whites have long harbored the view that blacks and Latinos are "lazy," while thinking of themselves as "hard working." This view has been crucial to understanding American politics, particularly around welfare or job-creation programs. Whites are quick to connect *work* to the things that they do while generally refusing to extend that valuation to activities pursued by blacks and Latinos. In the 2008 presidential election primaries, Hillary Clinton described her base of supporters as "working, hard-working, white Americans." Clinton was criticized for this comment, which implicitly sets up an opposition whereby whites are associated with hard work while others are, by implication, simply lazy. But Clinton insisted that there was nothing racist about what she said. Was it a racist characterization?

Thinking about Stereotypes

In a racial analysis, the answer would lie in showing how a particular *controlling image* of people of color as lazy was animating Clinton's thinking when she made the statement. Her comments might even be regarded, in Mendelberg's terms, as an "implicit racial appeal." These views provide a valuable purchase on how such characterizations operate in public discourse. But there is also a certain limit to this kind of analysis. Typically, critical attention to stereotypes is primarily concerned with, first, identifying their role in peoples' words and thoughts and, second, in disproving or deconstructing the stereotype. The cultural perspective being sketched here bears the possibility of carrying that kind of analysis further, because it calls attention to the far wider array of interlocking uses of *work* that remain largely invisible when we criticize stereotypes of laziness. Without bringing that pervasive cultural conditioning around *work* into view, the deeper roots of the racial dynamic continue to be reproduced. Stereotypes may come and go as people become more aware of their racial bases, but unless we are able to think about and engage the larger system of cultural valuation that generates them in the first place, they will likely simply be replaced by other representations—new code words, perhaps—that reproduce similar racial oppositions but in different registers.

Friendly, nice, and *work* are key concepts that Americans rely on to interpret interactions and to characterize people or situations. These terms form a texture of cultural understandings that pattern the ways we make sense of the world around us. Rather than abstract values or powerful symbols or political ideals, culture is generally most readily identifiable through these kinds of categorical judgments or characterizations people make habitually without giving them much thought. These terms precede our particular experience of any situation or encounter, and they are ready-made objects that we deploy in offhand, unconscious ways. These terms are also fundamental to how we articulate sensibilities about belonging and difference, sometimes in terms of race, but at other times in regard to class or gender or various other forms of collective identity we may be loathe to cite explicitly.

In the *multivalence* of these terms, we begin to see how an attention to cultural dynamics expands the scope of racial analysis. As the phrase suggests, racial analysis involves making race the principal focus of inquiry and discussion. This is important, since, as we have seen, race is often purposefully shunted from view in a variety of forums or settings. But perhaps a certain weak point also suggests itself in this phrase: the propensity or potential of making an analysis all or only about race. The problem is that, if "everything is about race," as you may hear social commentators or even some of your friends complain these days, then we lose sight of the ways race fits into larger contexts, shifting in and out of primary relevance, depending on how other, competing issues crowd for attention. Culture brings these contexts into view with all their specificity without treating them reductively. From a cultural perspective, what matters is that terms such as *friendly, nice,* and *work* are **equivocal**—their meanings sometimes are keyed to race, but they could just as easily be ways we contrastingly characterize people in terms of class, gender, or generational differences. By following the play of such meanings, a cultural perspective can show how race slides in and out of reference and relevance in the varying ways people use such important but utterly mundane words.

ANTIRACISM AND ETHNOGRAPHY

After developing this comparative perspective on racial and cultural analysis, it's important now to ask how all this plays out "on the ground" in the ways scholars, researchers, and activists apply these ways of understanding the social world. The goal of the first half of this chapter was to consider racial analysis in comparison with cultural analysis in order to see where they differ but also to think about how they overlap and can be effectively combined. The second half of the chapter focuses on how they can work in conjunction. To do this, we will now consider the principle means by which these two analytics are directed at explaining social relations. For racial analysis, this typically involves antiracist inquiry and activism; for cultural analysis, it is primarily ethnographic research and writing. This last portion of the chapter discusses antiracism as it both overlaps with and is distinguished from ethnography. We will see how antiracist work can inform ethnography and even become the subject of ethnographic analysis (Mullings 2005). In seeing these two approaches in juxtaposition—antiracism and ethnography—we will arrive at a clearer sense of the value of cultural perspective on matters of race.

Antiracism is the term for a movement that covers a broad range (historically and contemporarily) of efforts to counter directly the reproduction of racism in its manifest institutional and personal forms. Antiracism, as a political practice, increasingly also encompasses efforts to generate critical knowledge about whiteness and its operations while also challenging, destabilizing, and short-circuiting the social routines by which white dominance is reproduced. In the United States, antiracist politics has a long and diffuse history, but in the 1970s there emerged a range of "awareness-training" methods and "consciousness-raising" strategies to provoke in whites a realization of their participation in the reproduction of racism.

These initial efforts emerged as *racism awareness training*, a series of techniques deployed in institutional settings to reveal and intervene in racial dynamics.

Antiracism established inroads in various bureaucratic domains in academia and the corporate world in the form of multicultural training sessions. Anthropologist George Sefa Dei characterizes this version of antiracism as "an action-oriented strategy for institutional systemic change that addresses racism and other interlocking systems of social oppression. It is a critical discourse of race and racism in society that challenges the continuance of racializing social groups for differential treatment. Antiracism explicitly names the issues of race and social difference as issues of power and equity rather than as matters of cultural and ethnic variety" (1996, 4).

In this characterization, we can see some intriguing points of similarity between ethnographic work and antiracist practices. The commonalities are that they both recognize and devote their attention to the powerful dynamics of ostensibly mundane interactions in the realm of everyday life. Ethnography—a view onto the lived experiences, social relations, and symbolic dimensions of everyday life—shares with antiracist interventions a recognition that daily routines and practices are fundamental forums for reproducing social relations. As well, both ethnography and antiracism frequently examine and challenge the marginalization of certain voices within society. Similar to the work of ethnographers, antiracists detail the delegitimation or devaluation of the knowledge and experience of subordinate/minority groups. As Dei explains, antiracism "challenges definitions of what can be named 'valid knowledge,' and how such knowledge should be produced and distributed, both locally and globally" (1996, 6). These points of resonance between ethnography and antiracism partly reflect the fact, as Dei further notes, that antiracism developed as "a consequence of ongoing transformations in social science epistemologies that offer alternative readings of how, as social beings, we live our lives in multiethnic, multiracial communities" (4). Given these points of correspondence, it is not surprising that antiracist practitioners turn to anthropology, both for methods and for insights.

Antiracism, as a series of disparate projects, is partly informed by the efforts of anthropologists to understand such processes as transnational identity formation and globalization. Indeed, some antiracist scholars see direct participation in anthropological knowledge production as quite valuable. For instance, *Racism and Anti-Racism in World Perspective* (Bowser 1995) presents an "area studies of racism and anti-racism," in which researchers examine "how racism is expressed in his or her national culture" and "comment on the nature and extent of dominant group anti-racism." Not surprisingly, they find the latter task very difficult, "largely because of the lack of attention to anti-racism from scholars, newspapers, and activists alike" (155).

Still, the researchers are able to suggest a range of goals, tactics, and objects of engagement for antiracists in distinct "national cultures" and specific "world communities" (303–305). Challenges to the false consciousness of workers' attachment to "artificial and inaccurate" representation of national identity are promoted as a starting point in the United States and western Europe, but different tactics are called for in the Caribbean, "where the issues of racism and anti-racism are waged between peoples of color in a micro setting within the larger world economy" (156). And though the use of racism "as a way to maintain group control of the state and the material privileges that are derived from state control" (ibid.) is certainly as evident in Brazil as in South Africa, the contrasting histories and forms of diversity within these national populations makes problematic any formulaic agenda for critical antiracist interventions.

ETHNOGRAPHY OF ANTIRACIST WORKSHOPS

As antiracists employ anthropological approaches in an effort to generate a broad, critical knowledge base to serve their goals of challenging multiple forms of racism, antiracism as a social movement has also become the subject of ethnographic study, with intriguing results. Practitioners and interested observers have usefully applied ethnographic methods to examine both the implicit and not-so-hidden racial dynamics in the social interactions that comprise antiracist interventions. Work by sociologist Sarita Srivastava is particularly interesting, since it combines political criticism with the goal of producing ethnographic knowledge about antiracism as a social movement. Srivastava (1996) regards antiracist workshops—which she observed as a participant, a facilitator, and an ethnographer—as "a privileged site for the performance and inscription of racialized identities." By objectifying workshop practices, she raises "questions about how knowledge of racialized identities, racism and antiracism is produced and circumscribed" (292). Her aim of revealing "the specificity and diversity of these power relations" is directed toward the goal of transforming these relations.

From an ethnographic perspective, Srivastava first identifies beneath the plethora of labels for such practices—antiracist, diversity, cross-cultural, equity, conflict resolution, postequity, and so on—*an underlying social pattern*:

> They have a variety of formats, but share a number of common features: they are events held outside routine schooling, and their participants are usually adults or adolescents. Their goal may be to cause awareness, reduce conflict, or initiate change, often within an institutional context, including schools. They are discrete but often regular events, in contrast to antiracist education, which is part of an ongoing, general educational programme. Finally, they almost always use methods and ideas of popular education, in varying ways and degrees. (1996, 293)

Additionally, this stylized form of social event features a common set of practices. "A variety of techniques—drawing, role playing, body sculpting—are used to discuss and collectively analyse participants' experiences, emphasizing diverse and enjoyable ways of learning. The participant's experience is seen as a valuable source of knowledge, and attention to technique, group dynamics, organizational contexts and physical space promotes a participatory and egalitarian environment to share and analyse experience" (298). *Storytelling* is usually central to the event;

participants are frequently asked to "share personal experiences of racism." Srivastava concludes that this production of stories reproduces, rather than facilitates, the deconstruction of essentialized racial identities, such as whites and blacks. From her ethnographic vantage point, Srivastava is able to analyze—rather than reproduce—generalizations about racial groups.

Srivastava's ethnographic eye allows her to discern the social conventions shaping the stylized interactions in these workshops. These conventions are evident in how stories are solicited in these settings: People of color are circumscribed strictly "as victims of racism or as resources on racism." She relates instances of nonwhite students refusing to relate their experiences as "raw material" for group and social analysis. She suggests that they are rejecting the way the requirement of

> having to present our experiences as knowers of racism, or as people of colour, produces and reproduces those categories. Within this relationship, white participants may speak about their commitment, hope, solidarity, complicity, guilt, lack of complicity, failure to understand and disbelief, and about the hurt caused by accusations. This alternation between confession and *performance of experience produces new racialized representations and corresponding labels.* Constructions such as "angry women of colour" and "weeping white women" surfaced frequently in my initial interviews about antiracist organizational change. [emphasis added] (1996, 301)

Rather than effectively challenging the operation of racist practices within educational or occupational settings, these workshops often reproduce the power dynamics or stereotypes they explicitly intend to counter. "Because of these discouraging, draining, and painful encounters, many people of colour are dropping out of, rejecting, and refusing to participate in mixed antiracist workshops" (1996, 302). Srivastava thus argues "that we should conceive of antiracism and antiracist education not only as objectives to be prescribed, evaluated, and restructured, but also as a place to understand the relations we are seeking to change" (308). That is, "the field," is not just a place where we intervene with racial dynamics; it is also a site that we continually need to learn from in order to understand that changing and varied ways that race matters. This is an important stance, one that may set her apart from many antiracist practitioners but that highlights the valuable role ethnography can play in studying race.

ANOTHER VIEW FROM DETROIT

I found Srivastava's stance on learning from the field as well as some of her findings to be borne out in the course of my fieldwork in Detroit, which I briefly described in the previous chapter and will describe in more detail in Chapter 4, "Understanding Whiteness." In Detroit, Srivastava's observations about the sharply circumscribed role for people of color in antiracist workshops also extended to whites. In addition to working in the aforementioned inner-city neighborhood, I did some contextualizing research in different class neighborhoods. One was a working-class community on the city's far southwest side called Warrendale. Although I did not directly observe such workshops in Detroit, I did hear many accounts from a number of whites who participated in a two-day antiracism session that was developed in relation to a controversy over an elementary school—the Malcolm X Academy. The academy was being opened in a previously shuttered neighborhood school, one that the city's Board of Education had closed two years prior, citing insufficient funding for its continued operation.

Whites in Warrendale protested the school board's decision for a variety of reasons, but their concerns appeared to reporters and city officials to be based strictly in racist sentiment. The concerned and sometimes-angry voices of white residents echoed strongly the history of working-class resistance to the racial integration of public schools. Framed by the background of their small, aluminum-sided tract homes, the image of violent white racism was hard to dispel. The controversy over the academy was protracted but not violent, and there were many nuances to the positions local whites assumed, either in support of or in opposition to the school and its curriculum. In lieu of a full description of this conflict, I will simply focus here on residents experiences in the antiracism workshop, which was sponsored by two local Catholic churches.

The area churches, along with the Warrendale Community Organization, actively tried to calm white residents' anxieties about the academy and its curriculum. Members of these organizations were typically more concerned about the accumulating signs of deterioration in the neighborhood, which they associated with the influx of "renters." They did not want to undermine further the "character" of Warrendale through its depiction as a racist "white enclave." The workshop was conducted and facilitated by two white women, each with lengthy local histories of activism relating to racial conflicts. One runs her own business as a diversity consultant; the other is a dedicated social worker for a Catholic human services agency.

Identifying the Role of Race

I found white residents' accounts of the frustrations they experienced with this workshop to be indicative of the classed confusions over how race mattered in this conflict, where black professionals squared off with white working-class homeowners in a contest over control of civic resources represented in this neighborhood elementary school. In my interviews with whites in Warrendale, the antiracist workshop typically arose as an instance of how they had been confronted with the assertion that blacks could not be racists due to their generally disadvantaged and disempowered status nationally. These whites would easily spout this position for me: racism is equated with power; without power—institutional, political, or social—blacks simply could not be racists. They questioned this assertion by pointing, first, to the local political dominance blacks achieved in the city and, second, to the characterizations of whites by school officials and promoters of Afrocentrism associated, in some manner, with the Detroit public schools.

Whites referred to statements made by blacks in the course of this dispute, which ran the gamut from what might be cast as racial to racist. They pointed to comments by callers on radio talk shows charging that "we have to keep the [City] Council black" or shouts at a school board meeting that "we're the majority now. We'll do what we want." Each of these statements was regarded by whites as blunt assertions of black dominance, creating, for these whites, the impression that blacks were insisting that power operate along racial lines rather than in a "color-blind" manner. But primarily they pointed to statements by advocates or promoters of the Afrocentric curriculum, such as characterizations of whites as "killing machines," "devils," and "ice people," or claims that melanin was actually a basis of black cultural and intellectual superiority. In response to such characterizations, these whites stressed that their opposition to the Malcolm X Academy was not because it was a "black school" (99% of the enrolled students were black) but because of the threat—to them as whites—they perceived in the curriculum that the school promoted.

The workshop leaders were suspicious of whites' claims that they were not opposing the school based on a visceral contempt for or fear of blacks. They dismissed many of these whites' concerns over the Afrocentric curriculum as "smoke screens" obscuring fundamentally racist sentiment. In my interviews with the two women who directed the workshop, they described being confronted by "lots of rhetoric that was really hard to mush through" in order to get at what they believed to be the racist core of the whites' response to the academy. Their view of white residents' comments is very much in line with Eduardo Bonilla-Silva's characterization of color-blind discourse generally. When confronting the "slippery, apparently contradictory, and often subtle" language of color-blindness, he asserts, "analysts must excavate the rhetorical maze of confusing, ambivalent answers to straight questions" (2006, 53). This approach, though, proved ineffective for the Warrendale whites with whom I spoke, because it made the workshop facilitators seem oblivious to the way class and power mattered in this particular situation.

Instead of altering residents' thinking about the academy, the antiracist workshop in Warrendale further strengthened the convictions of opponents of the school. This is largely because the facilitators' stance on racism seemed absurd to these residents, but also because it revealed a broad gulf between antiracist whites and those who were engaged in an emotional struggle over events in their own neighborhood. The contrast was between people mired in a losing conflict and the detachment of others who are trying to enlighten them with a broader view of their predicament. This rift was most evident in the different ways the Afrocentric curriculum was characterized in the workshop. White residents complained that facilitators would not talk about the aspects of the controversy that mattered keenly to them (the Afrocentric curriculum), refusing to examine its implications and ramifications. The facilitators—preferring instead to regard the curriculum as an innocuous expression of multiculturalism—dismissed residents' sentiments and anxieties as being expressed *in terms of* the curriculum stemming from a deeper ideological conditioning about race.

The Elusive Meaning of Afrocentrism

Long after the academy's opening, the school's Afrocentric curriculum remained an elusive, haunting concern for these whites—elusive because school officials were reluctant to address the issue; haunting because this subject led them into a disorienting, powerful assemblage of racial imagery and narratives. Afrocentrism—molten, formative array of assertions, claims, facts, and theories—confronted white residents as a bewildering perspective, challenging, threatening, and certainly racializing "whites," whether or not they contested the academy directly.[1] The dissonance generated in the workshop between the antiracist perspective and the view of whites from Warrendale centered on whether they regarded Afrocentric discourse as "the issue." One participant, Jeff, who ran a lawn mowing service in the neighborhood, described to me how he tried to raise questions with one of the facilitators about the implications of teaching what he and others regarded as religious or spiritual material in the public schools.

> *Jeff*: She didn't really want to hear anything about it. I asked her, "What do you know about this curriculum that you're teaching us about, and the way we're reacting? Do you know what they're preaching?" [He mimics her voice] "Yeah, they've got Kwanzaa." "Do you know what Kwanzaa is?" "Yeah, it's a holiday. I've been to . . ." "DO you know what it is? It's being taught in the schools. Do you know the religious implications, and the political implication behind it? Are you familiar with the libation ceremony in Kwanzaa that's similar to partaking of communion in the Roman Catholic Church, and they're doing this in our schools, except that the children are drinking out of what they call a Timbiko cup, with their dead ancestors. IN SCHOOL! Now that is a religious ceremony."

White opponents of the Academy, as shown in this account, were actually avid consumers of Afrocentric writings and pronouncements. Since they could not get their questions about the curriculum answered by school officials, they cast a broad net, which drew in a range of claims, assertions, and charges that probably far exceeded the scope of the curricular program being developed by the Detroit public schools. But the disparate range of sources and versions also reflected their multifaceted readings of this neighborhood's political and social position in Detroit. The "curriculum" was not simply a euphemism for a racial threat; it was a measure of the range of changes that were transforming the city and making the status of working-class whites increasingly uncertain.

From one perspective, certainly, the version of Afrocentrism they compiled was self-interested—choosing "extreme" over "reasoned" statements—and perhaps naive. But more importantly, the whites' perspective showed their vulnerability to seeing themselves in the "white devil" subject position in this discourse. Although antiracist whites can regard Afrocentric tenets as a benign, balancing addition to

---

[1]Afrocentrism was never a fixed and ratified object in this controversy. When opponents made reference to it and also when they suggested readings for me, they stressed a panoply of authors: Maulana Karenga, Asa Hilliard, Molefi Asante, and Cheikh Diop.

multiculturalism, these whites found that the discourse conveyed a deeper reality, reflecting their predicaments as whites in this Detroit neighborhood. Their political incapacitation in this controversy pushed whites to emphasize the most racially apocalyptic versions of the future preached by some Afrocentrists.

Analyzing White Racial Thinking

Antiracism is fundamentally guided by the conviction that white domination and black subordination define racial dynamics. However well this formula may address race relations in the nation at large or globally, it badly distorts the experience of working-class whites contesting black city officials over scarce civic resources in a city that has been devastated by deindustrialization. In the Warrendale neighborhood (and in Detroit at large), this antiracist perspective also seems askew to the dramatic local shift in political and cultural power. This is partly because it does not recognize these whites as mired in a fundamentally *racial* predicament—trying to regain control of their identifying features, disoriented by the disjuncture between a projected social identity (as white racists) and personal experiences, and feeling the inadequate fit of stereotyped depictions. It is easy to assume that the correspondence between emotional, angry images of working-class whites and public representations of racism in the United States derives from an essentially racist class disposition. But this view ignores the difficult fact that the neighborhoods and jobs being used to rebalance the racial order in this country are predominantly those of working-class whites, who have benefited little from the nation's recent economic boom (Kefalas 2003).

Certainly, the situation of whites in Detroit is unusual. As a racial minority, they confront contradictions and uncertainties regarding generalizations about racial identity that are not widely shared by most whites in this country. But, given the changing demographics in the United States, many more whites will likely face similar predicaments around race. This is where and how the usefulness of ethnography for understanding race becomes more apparent. One of the values of ethnography is that it tries exactly to do more than generalize—*it aims to bring the complexity and ambiguity of cultural dynamics in particular contexts into view so that we can develop a more incisive view of large-scale processes, such as those associated with race.* As anthropologist Harry Wolcott explains, "Ethnography *is* a matter of detail. Ethnographic questions beg for relevant and complex detail" (2008, 5). It was the particular details of social life for whites in Warrendale that the facilitators missed and that point to the value of a different kind of listening to be employed in antiracist interventions.

HOW TO LISTEN TO "WHITE TALK"

Such a listening stance entails more than just a willingness to hear the particularity of whites' racial predicaments; it also involves regarding the "field" not solely as a site of intervention but also as a location for *learning* about the variable operations of racial identity. This orientation, though, clashes with antiracists' view of social contexts principally as sites in which to reveal and disrupt the work of racial ideology. The tension between these two approaches—between generating knowledge and directing effective interventions—may not be easily resolved. But we can use it to gain further insight into the challenges and rewards of combining racial analysis with cultural analysis.

One way of pursuing this issue is by considering Alice McIntyre's research for her book, *Making Meaning of Whiteness* (1997). McIntyre, an education professor, makes use of antiracist approaches to produce knowledge about whiteness and whites but also as a means of challenging the social reproduction of racism. She employs participant observation in her work with education students who are learning about and reflecting on their initial experiences as teachers. In particular, McIntyre develops and applies the concept of "white talk" in a "participatory action research project" with a small group of white student teachers. Her work provides an example of some of the fault lines between antiracist interventions and ethnographic work on race. But McIntyre allows us to see the advantages an ethnographic perspective brings to questions about racial thinking and perceptions.

McIntyre described her work with education students as "a challenging journey of self- and collective reflections about the intersection of whiteness, racial identity, racism and teaching." In sessions with thirteen female students of somewhat ambiguous class backgrounds, McIntyre identified the continual emergence of *white talk*: "talk that serves to insulate white people from examining their/ our individual and collective role(s) in the perpetuation of racism" (1997, 45). As McIntyre further explains,

> during the group sessions, the participants used a number of *speech tactics* to distance themselves from the difficult and almost paralyzing task of engaging in a critique of their own whiteness, some of which served to push the participants to be more self-reflective about being white and some that resulted in the perpetuation of white talk.

These tactics, which she calls characteristic of white talk, consisted of derailing the conversation, evading questions, dismissing counterarguments, withdrawing from the discussion, remaining silent, interrupting speakers and topics, and colluding with each other in creating a *"culture of niceness"* that made it difficult to "read the white world" [emphasis added] (46).

As an educator myself, often teaching about race, I think McIntyre has identified a critical dynamic in the reproduction of white racial identity. I also found this concept of *white talk* to be effective in ethnographic contexts as a way to characterize an aspect of how some whites respond to racial subjects. But in reading McIntyre's study, my ethnographic sensibilities were unsettled by the way her analysis "zeroed in" on the task of discerning how these students were socialized into whiteness. That is because, in the process, she disregards or dismisses much of the ambivalent and "highly contradictory" aspects of these students' experiences.

Any form of analysis that singularly takes race as its basis runs the risk of treating reductively the complexity of people's social perceptions and behaviors.

This type of reductionism certainly is both warranted and useful, particularly in overcoming the obstinate refusal on the part of many whites to recognize that racial inequalities still exist. But in McIntyre's study there is a point of diminishing returns where we begin to miss insights into the more muddled and ambiguous aspects of racial situations as they sometimes develop in everyday life.

Whites Talking about Race

McIntyre has a keen ethnographic ear for her subjects' use of stories. She explains that "the participants told numbers of stories during our project that illustrated the difficulty they had understanding the nature of racism as a system that privileges and maintains the social practices, belief systems, and cultural norms of the dominant group, and beliefs in the superiority of that group over the inherent inferiority of others" (1997, 48). McIntyre takes their stories as examples of racism, as material that reveals racial perceptions and judgments. In a series of exchanges she labels, "waitress stories," students both related and compared observations from their work as waitresses or restaurant hostesses. In particular, the women evaluated their perceptions that "black people tip horrible." The discussion begins with one woman, Elizabeth, describing her thought process as she began to notice this "trend" among her black customers and how it was "confirmed" (in an unsolicited comment) by another waitress who made the same observation. Elizabeth explained:

> It was every time I got a Black party, whether it was a single person or a family of six, whatever. Bad tips. So I just kind of kept to myself, well, you know, said, "Well, whatever," you know? But just thinking that, I was, like, "Well, am I just being racist or," you know? And I'm, like, "But isn't that kind of odd" (laughs), you know? And I just didn't know what to think. And so one day, I was, um, I don't know how it came out but another coworker said this to me. They said, "Oh, I had a bad day of tips. Well, I had a lot of Black parties." And I said, "Well, why do you say that?" you know? And they said, "Well, every time I get a Black party" and so then, now every time, you know, you get a Black party, you think or just everyone there is, like, "Alright, how good is this tip going to be?" You just kind of expect a lower tip and every time I get a Black party I'm, like, "What am I thinking? Did I think this" and I just, its horrible 'cause I say to myself, "I am being racist in expecting a lower tip" or maybe trying to go out of my way to be extra nice and hope for a good tip or whatever. But it kills me 'cause I know that just thinking it is being racist and I also know that I try my hardest not to be. (49)

McIntyre concludes emphatically:

> This story exemplifies how deeply ingrained racism is in "the souls of white folks." Elizabeth seems to "pick up racism" by osmosis. She notices that Blacks don't tip as well as whites "without anyone ever telling me." She describes it as a "trend" and that "you can just expect a lower tip" from Blacks. In addition, "it just about kills" her to be racist—to accept the stereotypes that have been created about Blacks by the white people in her restaurant. The "guilt inside of me" motivates Elizabeth to question her assumptions about Blacks. Her desire to "know if it's racist" to perpetuate the idea that "Blacks are horrible tippers" appears to stem from her need to be free of guilt. (50)

I hear this story differently, though, as an example of the problems inherent in reducing such stories to object lessons on white racism. Elizabeth's "desire to know" may reflect her effort to make sense of an uncertain matter. She may really be striving to think through an ambiguous perception, resisting an unpalatable interpretation, rather than just relieving her sense of guilt. After all, her narrative frames her uncertainty rather than steadfastly insisting that this perception and the workshop folklore it is linked with are true. "Racism" does not seem adequately to diagnose or objectify the interpretive process in which Elizabeth is engaged. Relying solely on "racism" to explain her thinking disregards the forms of ambiguity and ambivalence evident in her interpretations. That is, this story works just as well in suggesting that our critical language may not match the complexity of racial matters—there is no other term than *racist* (or *antiracist*) to be used to make sense of the perceptions shared by the white waitresses.

"Waitress Stories" as an Interpretive Repertoire

McIntyre valuably focuses on the socialization process that racializes this setting and on the exchange of racial observations; this is a great advance over locating racism as an individual failing or as a somewhat abstract aspect of institutions. But her analysis is stymied when the women then proceed to develop this genre of stories—of their experiences as waitresses and hostesses serving blacks—rather than pursuing her questions about racism. Another student, Faith, follows Elizabeth's stories with her own experiences from three years of working in a restaurant, relating similar perceptions of blacks and adding the elaboration of seeing patrons "pull away in their Mercedes" after leaving a meager tip. "It stinks because it's the money that you're taking home, you know what I mean? And it's hard. It's really such a struggle in your head, but, you know, I don't know. When you've been waiting tables for three years and it's like statistics. You can look at statistics. You can look at the numbers and know and lay it out and that stinks" (1997, 51).

McIntyre relates being "disturbed at the direction of this conversation" (1997, 51). She describes waiting patiently

> for one of the participants to intervene in the discussion and highlight the myriad racist comments being made. Instead, the participants revert to a "white-as-victim" stand and rigidify the boundaries that get established when white people talk to white people without self- and collective criticism. Elizabeth states: "It doesn't matter how hard you work." No one disagrees with Elizabeth's comment or, if they did, failed to make it known. Faith expresses her own frustration over not being rewarded by a Black patron for her "exemplary service" and by suggesting there are statistics to prove her point that Blacks are bad tippers. Her indignation that "they" would "pull away in their Mercedes," leaving her "thirty cents on a fifty dollar bill," seemed justified. It appeared to me that the other participants accepted her reporting of such incidents as a common occurrence, thereby facilitating the growth of white talk. (52)

The transcript of this conversation provided by McIntyre is a useful example of how ethnographic data is generated and how it can be subsequently analyzed and reanalyzed. It also offers an opportunity to contrast a concept of racial analysis—white talk—with a term of cultural analysis mentioned earlier: interpretive repertoire. The latter concept highlights the way a collection of stories, incidents, and images congeal as a means for making sense of shared aspects of everyday life. Regarding the waitress stories as an interpretive repertoire allows us to glimpse important, contingent aspects of this exchange that are not so evident to McIntyre. As an interpretive repertoire, such comments stand as an effort to make sense of particular encounters by sounding out potential meanings, rather than simply reflecting ideological conditioning.

For instance, in contrast to McIntyre, I hear primarily the frustrated ambivalence of "you know, I don't know," that "it stinks," and that "it's really such a struggle in your head." Rather than an insistence that there are statistics to back up her claim, I hear Faith saying specifically that "it's *like* statistics," in that "you can look at" them. She can recall "the numbers" of blacks "and lay it out and that stinks." She can make a serial observation and not come up with a better alternative conclusion or interpretation than to confirm and reproduce the stereotype of blacks as bad tippers. What is useful in this context, then, is a keener attention to the interpretive processes in which whites are engaged, instead of focusing solely on discerning the ideological core or belief structure that might be revealed by their comments. Taking these waitress stories as an interpretive repertoire leads us to ask what social dynamics make these conclusions seem obvious and inevitable, rather than solely criticizing this group for "failing to attend to how whites perpetuate racist behavior."

Listening Ethnographically

Antiracism, as evidenced by McIntyre, features an approach that reads "against the grain" of what people have to say. Ethnographers in contrast, generally approach subjects' speech with the goal of grasping the structures of meaning and the forms of interaction that constitutes the speakers' world. Antiracist approaches instead aim actively to challenge the validity of statements, stories, and ideas expressed by subjects. The analytical work of antiracists (their stance as listeners) is geared toward revealing different meanings than those ostensibly intended by speakers, for which they use the concept of *code words*. That is, they read *against* the ostensible meaning of the speaker in order to reveal a true, racist motivational core where whites strenuously claim "not to be racists."

The analytical stance of ethnographers is generally oriented toward understanding how people make sense of the world. What matters is to grasp how people organize their perceptions and prioritize their interests in relation to their position both within a larger social order and in a particular locale. The interpretive work of subjects—the linkages they draw between various events and certain meanings—is important to understand, not simply to "correct" or "deconstruct." The criteria people employ in making sense of ambiguous situations provides a glimpse of the forces that economically and politically shape the places they inhabit, and these criteria reflect peoples' perceptions of the meanings of these forces. Ethnographers aim at grasping how place both shapes and reflects the interpretive work people pursue in everyday situations. This kind of interpretive work needs to be understood in the "waitress stories"—whether regarded as points of intervention in the reproduction of racism or as sources of knowledge production about whiteness.

Such a listening stance still allows us to pose critical questions about race in this context. For instance, one may ask, why is it that these women so easily and readily characterize black customers as a *group*? What about whites who tip poorly? Do they fall from view in this interpretive repertoire because, as whites, these waitresses more readily regard such customers as *individuals*. Are they perhaps more willing to explain how whites tip in individualistic terms? Would such a willingness primarily reflect racial sensibilities, or would they be keyed to class circumstances? Would stories about meager-tipping whites lead so quickly to generalizations about types or groups of people? How do class similarities and differences matter across racial lines? Each of these questions opens a broader examination of the cultural dynamics both shaping and being engaged by this repertoire of stories, while still providing a keen attention to racial dynamics.

COMBINING AN ATTENTION
TO RACE AND CULTURE

The point here is not simply to contrast antiracist interventions with ethnographic approaches. Rather, this is an opportunity to return to the earlier juxtaposition between racial and cultural forms of analysis. A cultural perspective regards these stories not as reflective of a monolithic ideological conditioning but rather as active efforts to make sense of situations that may or may not reproduce categorical racial judgment. McIntyre's approach, though, pursues an opposite course toward the stories that Elizabeth, Faith, and the others are narrating, relying on a view of white racism formed from two critical assumptions: that racism is an absolute or totalizing phenomenon and that only clear thinking can short-circuit its power.

The root of antiracism is the belief that *racism is the problem* and that white subterfuges must be penetrated, and their confusions and contradictions about race clarified in order to reach a point where whites stop reproducing and participating in a social order organized on racial privileges and inequalities. McIntyre illustrates this stance well when she challenges the students' efforts to distinguish between *active and passive forms of racism*. She is upset that, for the these women, "intentionality is equated with 'blatant racism,' thereby, exonerating the participants from racist thoughts and actions *if* those cognitions and behaviors are not premeditated and intentional" (1997, 54). At one point—partly in response to McIntyre's assertion that "we, as whites, have all internalized dimensions of racism" (54)—Faith remarks in confusion, "So everything, every encounter that you have with someone of an opposite, someone of a minority is racist? Every interaction? Whether it's blatant or intentional or whether it's blatant or not? I'm confused" (54). The students want to distinguish between the active production of racism, carried out through intentional acts, and the possibility that there is some state other than racism to characterize their thoughts and behaviors. They also seem to be striving to articulate a view from the position of everyday life where the relevance of race is changeable, shifting from being obviously active to being part of a dense, signifying background. But McIntyre insists on the absolute, all-inclusive power of white racism—they either actively resist its transmission or they unconsciously reproduce its insidious effects.

Along with an insistence on the pervasiveness of racism and the uniformity of whites' participation in its reproductions, antiracists also promote clear thinking about race, relying on sharp definitions to bring this problem into view. Indeed, for McIntyre, ambiguities and confusions expressed by the students were strictly active forms of reproducing racism. McIntyre, in finding that the white women's comments were becoming "convoluted" and "contradictory," echoes Bonilla-Silva in taking this as an indication they are "resist[ing] a critical analysis of the consequences of racism both for people of color and for whites, resulting in these young white females' accepting an ideology in fear and distortion." In particular, McIntyre reads the convolutions in their stories and expressions as signifying either their inability or their resistance to imbibing an antiracist activist mindset, as well as their susceptibility to myth and fantasy. Indeed, "lack of clarity in defining racism and zero-sum thinking contributed to the group's construction of white talk, for they are both strategies for insulating speakers from tackling the underpinnings of whiteness" (59–60).

"Lack of clarity" certainly may be a tactic used by whites for resisting antiracist analyses of whiteness. But it is also worth pondering whether such confusions are hopeful indicators of points where the certainty of racial logic is breaking down. Ambiguous moments could as easily suggest that an ideological conditioning has been ruptured or has exceeded its confident reach. An important question, too, is whether they are amplified or resolved in particular contexts. In Detroit, I found that whites' "lack of clarity" about race was a function of the changing political and social settings in the city; the instability in whites' "opinions" and "views" on racial matters reflected the fact that the ways race operated in the city were often unpredictable. The "racial" features of exchanges and conflicts were typically nuanced and ambiguous; they consistently involved interpretive efforts by individuals who had to decide whether to prioritize *race* in relation to competing frameworks for understanding interaction—*class, family, place,* and so forth. Their responses to "race" were shaped by contingencies in daily life that are not easily acknowledged by antiracist analyses. Recognizing these contingencies may open a point of entry into the realm of whites' everyday experience, offering relevant insights that make sense of their daily routines. This is particularly true in the case of whites whose economic position does not reflect a status of power and privilege. In the case of these waitresses and the working-class whites of Warrendale, a similar anxiety over money and resources is too easily reduced simply to "racism." This reductive approach perhaps undermines as much as it illuminates antiracist interventions.

The first and second halves of this chapter featured two juxtapositions: first of racial and cultural forms of analysis, then of antiracist and ethnographic approaches to studying race. These comparisons highlight an important contrast. These various approaches differ fundamentally on whether their principle aim is *to study* or *to change* particular racial situations. With racial analysis, changing these relations is the imperative. In contrast, people pursue cultural analysis for more varied reasons—sometimes with an implicit or explicit commitment to changing problematic conditions, but, as often as not, out of intellectual and social curiosity. In political and moral terms, it is hard not to privilege racial analysis and antiracist approaches. But the imperative behind ethnography, one that animates much social science research in general, is also one that warrants respect. We may well need to learn more from the field before we can properly effect changes in social contexts. As well, ethnographic approaches aim to understand something of great import: the cultural dynamics that underlie racial relations. An understanding of these dynamics allows us to explain racial matters without reinscribing essential notions about racial identities. In the end, these need not be antithetical stances. These fundamental differences need not mean that the two approaches cannot be combined. They can be, but in so doing we need to take stock of where and how they fit together well and where they do not.

CHAPTER 3

❧

Race and Nature: Culture, Biology, and Genetics

P eople's ideas about "nature" are one of the most effective places to start in trying to comprehend the role of culture. This is because a common feature of cultural identities is the notion that they are, in some sense, "natural." The most fundamental power of culture is the ability to make particular ways of life, habits, or beliefs seem natural. The aims of this chapter are, first, to frame the cultural dynamics that shape our views of nature and, second, to show how these operate in relation to ideas about race—both popular notions and scientific concepts—in the realms of biology and genetics.

The initial stage of this chapter examines the ways we use physical features as touchstones for confirming the reality of **categorical identities**, such as the use of skin color to identify people as belonging to distinct groups. This discussion is followed by a detailed view of processes of racial classification, historically and contemporarily, with a particular attention to the instability of these systems of identification. We then turn to recent controversies linked to scientific claims about a possible biological or genetic basis for racial identity. In each of these topics, you will be able to recognize the prevalent role of cultural dynamics in shaping the very bases of our interest in connecting race to genetic or biological domains. This chapter concludes with a discussion of the role of culture in shaping the genetic structure of humanity, thus pointing to the **biocultural** "nature" of social identities such as race.

WHAT IS NATURE?

The biggest challenge in grasping the cultural dynamics that shape our notions of nature is to bracket off (for a moment, at least) identities that we take to be natural, in order to consider them as "data" for cultural analysis rather than as "facts" about the world. Certainly, this is hard to do, because we know there is a real world out there—governed by physical laws and constituted of physical properties—that we experience every day. But to what extent is that world "natural"? Consider for a moment how much of our environment is either built or affected by humans. Think, too, about how much the air we breathe bears traces of human industry and activities or about the enormous amount of processing that the water we drink and the food we eat requires. Then think, in contrast, about the variety of uses we make of a concept such as *nature*. This word can alternately refer to essential qualities and characteristics and to the sum of inanimate and animate forces that constitute the universe.

We use *nature* to talk about the physical world in contrast to human activities, but we also label some human behaviors as either natural or unnatural. Human achievements in athletics are sometimes attributed simply to *nature*, even though they require immense amounts of training and social support. Human creations, such as society, are also sometimes construed as reflecting a *natural* order—an idea often invoked to legitimate forms of inequality in the social order. Sometimes *nature* is meant in distinction with urban life or industry—think of the country-side, parks, or wilderness areas—but we also use it to characterize underlying dynamics that shape events in the world around us—as in *natural disasters* that menace those very cities. That is, nature stands as something destined to be managed by humans, and then alternately as that which is unpredictable and ultimately unmanageable. This variety of meanings for *nature* indicates the great amount of cultural work this concept does for us in designating a wide spectrum of activities as, in some sense, fixed or given.

However real or given the world around us may be, we still experience and make sense of basic physical processes via the structures of signification and the webs of meaning that constitute culture. This is readily evident when we think about the associations people draw between race and nature. Studying people's ideas about nature is all the more important with race because they are a key basis by which humans came to believe that racial identities are simply given facts of life. The belief in racial identity, though, is hardly natural. We know this because the idea of race emerged rather late in human history. Also, it has hardly been one single idea in its varied history, changing its basic contours and assumptions as politics change and science advances. We will explore the historical, political, and scientific vagaries of the concept of race later in this chapter. But first we need to develop a stronger analytical grasp of how *the notion of nature works in grounding cultural forms of classification and categorical identities.*

The simple fact of human cultural diversity—the wide array of ways people organize work, family, recreation, and reproduction—suggests that there is no simply given or natural way of doing these things. Yet, within any particular culture, the social world feels exactly that—natural. This is a reflection of how powerful culture is in establishing a tight correspondence between its forms of classification and systems of order with some version of the real world. Two general features of this correspondence serve as touchstones for analyzing the cultural aspect of any characterization of something as natural. The first is that these designations are *selective*. Out of the wide universe, we fixate on only a few items or objects to convey the idea of nature, and, in doing so, we consistently focus on only partial or limited aspects of those objects. This selective dimension reflects both the interested use we make out of nature and the fact that such representations are usually developed in relation to concepts that we want to affirm as fixed or given aspects of our culture.

This brings us to the second aspect, which is that references to nature mark an ongoing tension in our thinking between the characteristic of *permanence* or *continuity* as opposed to *change* and *instability*. Nature can easily be characterized by either of these two dynamics—fixity or mutability—though we generally emphasize the former over the latter. Biological systems, such as human bodies, are as much in flux (e.g., growing, aging, and alternating states of sickness and health) as they are stable. The larger point is that we invoke nature as part of an ongoing process of making sense of the world in terms of its forms of dynamism and stability. Anthropologist Sarah Franklin characterizes this way of thinking as the **traffic in nature and culture**, as in the way we use "nature versus nurture" to locate various activities or ideas along a continuum of fixed and unfixed properties. What matters, Franklin says, is to recognize this as a series of interrelated "processes of overlap and opposition, of borrowing from each other and yet remaining distinct" (Franklin, Lury, and Stacey 2000, 9). That is, things are not just natural; we characterize them as such in our ongoing efforts to order the world according to the categories of fixity and mutability. Racial ideology construes racial identities as inherent and static. In contrast, the enormous amount of physical and genetic variation found *within* imagined "races," along with the historical mutability of people's conceptions of race and the plasticity of social groups, suggest just the opposite. The cultural perspective honed in this chapter represents an explanation for both how these conceptions arose and the ways they are perpetuated today.

TOTEMIC IDENTITIES

Culture would have no hold on us if it simply generated classifications out of thin air or if it posited a system of categorical identities that were established only once in the deep recesses of time. Culture works because it is a dynamic way of comprehending the world, first by economically drawing attention to limited features of an object we think of as natural and then by deploying that object to make sense of a range of changing conditions and shifting relations, particularly social ones. This is a feature of social life that extends from the first emergence of **totemism** to our current thoughts on racial identity. Anthropologist David Hess (1995) explains: "Totemism is the process by which social groups achieve coherence and distinctiveness by being identified with natural phenomena" (21). The first images that come to mind with this concept are probably tribes that identified subgroups using animals or birds, as in the bear clan and the eagle clan. But totemism remains a current human activity even in modern society. In an amusing sense, think of how many sports teams we identify in a similar manner: Bears, Eagles, Lions, Tigers, Cardinals, Dolphins, Orioles, Blue Jays, Marlins, and so on.

Another example is *bulls* and *bears* in relation to the stock market. Economists and brokers—very rational people—often describe themselves using these two totemic items. If you are a bull, you believe the stock market is going to go up. Bears believe the market is heading down. These creatures became key symbols because of selective observations people made about their behaviors. When bulls attack something—a bullfighter perhaps—they use their horns to toss that object high into the air. So people use them to imagine markets going up. When bears forage for food, they may well knock fruit off low-hanging branches—an image used to convey how financial interests crash to the ground. Certainly, these sets of ideas are linked to observations of the natural world. But importantly, *they are selective.* Bulls and bears do many more things than these two activities, some of which are completely contrary to selective images for rising and falling markets.

These contemporary totems also reflect the second feature of our ideas about nature. They are used to make sense of the dynamic, often-volatile world of the market and to characterize people's orientations to those conditions. Fundamentally, these identities are *relational.* The assertion "I'm feeling bullish" makes sense because we can contrast it to an opposite view, "I'm feeling bearish," in relation to the same market conditions. As Hess (1995) further explains, "A fundamental attribute of totemism is that social categories and natural/technical categories are *co-constituted as systems of distinction.* In other words, the social and natural become meaningful by being mapped onto each other or translated into each other" [emphasis added] (23). These identifying features represent an active trafficking in nature and culture by which we sort out important questions as to whether or to what degree our identities and the world around us are fixed or fluid, driven by forces outside of our control or very much under and subject to our mastery. The important point is that our assessments can vary as circumstances change, though we can just as easily become fixated on believing all this is immutable.

This is an important aspect of how we do race. With race, we ground our system of racial classification and the *categorical identities* it operates—white, black, and so forth—in the natural realm with biological markers, mostly skin color. Interestingly, various modern societies select from a wider set of markers in addition to skin color—hair textures, facial features, height or stature, eye color, and the shape of one's nose—which we will consider in the next section. Obviously, one of the first things you notice about a person is her or his skin color. This happens quite unconsciously, despite whatever views you may individually hold about the relative importance of race. We learn to do this at a very young age because race has great importance in our society, as we discussed in Chapter 1. This is also easy to do because skin color is a "natural feature" of humans. Even though people's skin color can change through life and is influenced by a variety of physical, cultural, and environmental processes, we still invest it with the ability to tell us something about the people passing before us in the course of a day.

The key issue is how we link these natural features and the categorical identities that organize them to a set of conceptions about what that person is like. Think about it: We actually have very little interest in the particular characteristics of the natural feature—skin tone, in this case—which shows a huge amount of both variation and mutability. Rather, we jump very quickly to the categories that simplify all this physical variation to "black," "white," "yellow," "brown," or "red" and that, in so doing, allows us to move to the relational ideas about human characteristics that we associate with racial identities. That is, we are least interested in the natural component and most concerned with the cultural aspect of concepts we attribute to these categories, even though we generally insist it is the natural feature that makes race "real." But if the natural feature were truly that important, we would deploy a far larger number of labels that would more adequately characterize the huge range of color tones that fall under any of our racial categories.

RACIAL CLASSIFICATION

Once you realize the categorical aspects of race take precedent over the nuances and vagaries of human skin color, it becomes easy to recognize that, first and foremost, race is a system of classification. As with many other forms of classification, we associate it with the real world. But the closer you look at its operation, the more you recognize forms of arbitrariness. This brings us to *the core of a basic cultural operation*—to assign arbitrary features a set of significations that then operate as a system of meanings, as with language. Skin color varies both from person to person and within an individual's lifetime, depending on where that individual lives and his or her social practices. We simplify this natural variation with the set of color terms that Americans quickly recognize. But our skin rarely matches those colors—"whites" range from pinkish to tan and usually do not look all that white. "Black" skin colors have an even wider range of tones, varying from light ginger to quite dark brown hues. The further we consider the skin color continuum, the more stretched the linkages with color labels become. Can you really maintain that Asians look "yellow" or that Native Americans' skin tone is "red"? Rather, we have made selective use of natural features in order to make our categorical identities for people seem commonsensical.

The cultural aspect of all this becomes clearer when we confront the basic challenge in understanding *human variation*. Whatever features you choose to use in differentiating people—hair texture, height, or a variety of facial features, which have all been used in addition to skin color as a basis of racial identification—their rate of occurrence among humans falls along a continuum. In dividing up the human population, there are no points at which any particular natural feature simply stops occurring and another starts. The "common sense" clarity of dividing people by skin color dissolves when you look at the facts on the ground about how skin tones, in particular, lighten and darken as you move geographically toward or away from the earth's magnetic poles. Yet we insist on taking racial categories and identities as real because we can simply see them on people's faces. The point here is not simply to dismiss or dispute such notions; rather, the important task is to see how this thinking about skin color reflects and reproduces a whole range of cultural interests and concerns about *belonging* and *difference*. From this angle, we can see that culture links to "nature" not just as a way of making sense of the world but also as a means of making our cultural ways of thinking about people seem utterly natural.

The unnaturalness of race as a means for making sense of human variation is apparent in the fact that there is so much discrepancy over how we classify people racially. There is little consistency to racial classification, either from country to country or across recent human history. This is illustrated by raising the most basic of questions about race: How many races are there? The answer ranges widely, depending on whom you ask and who is keeping track. In the United States, according to the most recent census, we have at least twelve races—with options allowing respondents unsatisfied with those offerings to fill in their own terms—though as recently as 1980 we had only four (Rodriguez 2000). Compare that to a country such as Brazil, where there are hundreds of terms to designate a person's racial identity. Or compare this to France, which officially has no races because they do not ask people to identify racially in their census—even though the country is riven by racial conflict between natives and African immigrants.

How Many Races?

The question of how many races there are becomes even more complicated when you consider the matter historically. Within Europe alone, answers to this question have varied greatly. One influential race theorist in the early 1900s, William Ripley (1910), discerned three distinct European races, though today we would readily recognize these people simply as white. Using anthropometric measures of skull sizes, Ripley delineated three races in Europe: the Teutonic (northern) race (long-skulled, tall, and pale-eyed); the Mediterranean (southern) race (also long-skulled, but shorter and dark-eyed); and the Alpine (central) race (round-skulled, stocky, and with intermediate eye colors). In terms of skin color, we have no problem today assuming these groupings are all white. But race can just as easily be read as it was by Ripley—in terms of stature and eye color or "carriage" and hair texture. The main feature for fixing the reality of racial classification at that time—skull size, by which people were designated as *dolichocephalic* or *brachycephalic*—is no longer used because this feature clearly varies so much and is so influenced by a range of social and environmental factors that there is little basis for assuming its stability. But that hardly hindered scientists at the time from producing copious empirical measurements of skull size that confirmed, for them, the reality of fixed racial types with inherent mental characteristics.

This tripartite arrangement of racial identity in Europe competed with a contrary model that recognized a huge range of differences where Ripley saw only a few set race types. Amid the anxiety over immigration to the United States in the early 1900s, the Dillingham Commission was convened by Congress to identify the racial dimension of this social development. The commission's report established that there were some forty-five races discernible among the immigrants coming to the United States; thirty-six of these were considered indigenous to Europe.

Albanians, Bohemians, Greeks, Jews, Poles, Russians, Gypsies, and Romanians all were distinguished on a racial basis. The commission emphatically asserted that these groupings were not just "nations." They were considered to be physically, intellectually, and spiritually distinct based on physical features such as hair color, skin color, stature, facial forms, and shape of the head. Though we would not recognize these differences today as racial, people at the time could see them quite plainly.

These differences were most readily apparent in the United States, where the matter of the whiteness of European immigrants was hardly assumed. Whiteness has been a crucial feature of citizenship in the United States since this country was founded. Congress established this in 1790 when citizenship was restricted solely to "free white persons." This category, notably, did not automatically include the three million impoverished Irish that arrived in the mid-1800s. As historian Noel Ignatiev relates in *How the Irish Became White* (1995), the religious and social differences between this mass of immigrants and the dominant Anglo-Saxons, at least initially, made their claims to full citizenship suspect. But through a process of political organizing and adopting racist ideology, as Ignatiev argues, the Irish were able to gain admittance to the ruling American racial class. Other European immigrants underwent a similar process of racialization—particularly Italians and Greeks—whereby they learned simultaneously to despise African Americans and to identify readily with the form of whiteness embodied by Anglo Americans (Roediger 2005). At times, this process was fought out in the courts, where racial identities were established and contested in legal terms (Jacobson 1998). The vestiges of such battles—and the charged political and social developments that animated them— are readily apparent in the history of the census in the United States.

Why Categories Matter

The shifting racial categories featured in the U.S. Census would seem absurd if we did not view them in the context of the political and social concerns from which these categories were fashioned. These categories derive not from biology, though they reflect a concern with that realm but, rather, from ways of looking at the world that both were shaped by and responded to dramatic political and social changes. These developments were fundamentally oriented around the institution of slavery as well as subsequent black emancipation, Reconstruction, and Jim Crow practices. But they also crucially turned on events such as the annexation of Mexican territory, the Indian wars, Asian immigration restrictions and exclusions, along with the annexations of Hawaii and Puerto Rico, and the conquest of the Philippines. For most of the 1800s the census reflected white Americans' obsession with miscegenation. The prevailing racial ideology of this period—one that still influences American notions of racial classification today—was the rule of **hypodescent**, epitomized in the notion that "one drop of black blood" fixed a person's racial identity as black. In stark contrast to other national systems that established racial identity more fluidly, Americans relied on notions such as *quadroon* and *octoroon* to keep track of who carried, however faintly, that "one drop of black blood."

The task of measuring this phantom "one drop" grew increasingly untenable and was eventually relegated simply to the "mulatto" category, which stood alongside "black" in the census categories until both were replaced by "Negro" in the 1930 census. That same census featured the emergence of "Mexican" as a racial category, sifting out peoples who had previously fallen under the white category. As a racial category, this change was a response to Anglo American concerns with the influx of immigrants from Mexico after that country's revolution. "Mexican" awkwardly took its place alongside other nations-as-races, such as "Chinese" and "Japanese"—peoples who were racially restricted from immigration to the United States in the late 1800s and early 1900s—until 1940, when the category was discontinued (Rodriguez 2000). The racial classification "Hindu" was added in 1920, resorting peoples who had fallen under or vied for the white designation via claims to "Aryan" identity. Though obviously a religion, "Hindu" bizarrely included all Southeast Asians from the subcontinent, such as Muslims and Sikhs. This category was dropped in 1950 but resurfaced in the 1980s as part of the generic Asian or Pacific Islander category—a racial category unique to the United States (Skerry 2000).

The varieties of racial classification illustrate an important point: *Their rationale derives from culture, not from nature.* These classificatory schemas shifted not as a reflection of new scientific developments but, rather, from changing anxieties and interests. The shifting categories of race reflect changing political and social concerns rather than a fundamental biological fact of racial identity. Only if they functioned independently of such concerns would we see a stability of categories, which clearly is nonexistent. We cannot settle on the number of races that exist because *our interest in race and the uses to which we put it in talking about the social world are not static* (or uniform or consistent) long enough for the simplest question to be resolved: How many races are there? In fact, far from being settled, the number of races in the United States keeps growing. Gradually, the Asian and Pacific Islander category has opened up into a host of more specific "races," such as Guamanian, Samoan, Vietnamese, and Korean. But for all that increased specificity, the glaring oversight in this system is that these categories fail to capture one of the critical dimensions of racial dynamics in the United States, because "Hispanic" is not considered a race. Even though Latinos are subject to racial discrimination in the United States, as we saw in Chapter 1, there is hardly a rationale in this schema for considering them a race. That is because "Hispanic" or "Latino" includes such a variety of "races"—blacks from Cuba, the Dominican Republic, and Nicaragua, whites from Chile and Argentina, and mestizos from Mexico, who might be categorized as Native Americans if they were born on the other side of the border with the United States.

Categorizing Skin

The issues of classification and the categories relating to Latinos and Asians will be explored in greater detail in Chapter 6. Let it suffice to note that, particularly with Latino, U.S. racial classification conflicts with other schemas for organizing racial identity. In many Latin American countries, for instance, race is more of an individual variable than a uniform type of familial inheritance. Family members can vary in their racial identification according to a host of social factors and life history events. Indeed, people that Americans might view as plainly "white" or "black" could be classified in a variety of contrary ways throughout the world. We see this most strikingly in Africa, were African American travelers frequently encounter situations where their nationality signifies more powerfully than does their skin color. Debra Klein, in her ethnography of drumming traditions in Ghana (*Yoruba Bata Goes Global: Artists, Culture Brokers, and Fans*, 2007), is one of many researchers who note the discordant way Ghanaian usage of the term *oyinbo*—meaning "peeled-back honey," but with connotations that refer to light-skinned status—clashes with U.S. racial sensibilities. "While *oyinbo* literally refers to skin color, it is inextricable from nationality: for example, all U.S. citizens—white, African American, Asian American, Latin American—are considered *oyinbo*. In its most generalized meaning, *oyinbo* comes to stand for all privileged status" (2007, xxix). This usage prioritizes a sameness of geopolitical status over commonalities in skin tone.

Anthropologist Mary Weismantel, working in the Andes, observes a similar dynamic there regarding terms for racial identity. This arose as she recorded Indian stories about a mythic white vampire who lived off of the fat of Indians. The race of such vampires is important, Weismantel finds, because these stories are about how whites exploit Indians. Since indigenous Andeans specified the whiteness of the vampyric *pishtaco*, Weismantel was surprised to find apparently "black-skinned" people being included in the category. The rationale for this inclusion, Weismantel explains, is that racial identity in the Andes is established, first, by a broader reading of physical difference and, second, by the possession (or lack) of certain material forms of wealth—not simply by skin color. First, Weismantel observes, "the color of [the pishtaco's] skin is a less important sign of racial alterity than other features shared by many white and black Americans, such as light-colored eyes, a hirsute torso, and especially great height or fleshiness (2001, 182)." But she recognizes, too (180), that "products of industrial technology . . . also confer race. Manufactured goods—especially those expensive and imported objects fetishized as the epitome of technological sophistication—bestow whiteness upon people," whatever their pigmentation may be.

In the face of such nuanced and complicated readings of racial identity in terms of status, possessions, and a composite of physical features, it is easy to acknowledge the allure of falling back on a strict, reductive emphasis on skin color. The problem with that option is that, in doing so, we get no closer to the "nature" of race, *because skin color can actually obscure more fundamental genetic dynamics*. Take blackness, for instance. Classifying people as "black," globally, based on skin color, would lump together peoples from southern India alongside Australian aborigines and sub-Saharan Africans. Yet these groups are hardly "close" in genetic terms, given how human evolution progressed; as well, many of their facial features suggest contrasting racial identities in other systems of classification.

At the same time, in a contrary gesture, the inherent instability and even arbitrariness of racial classification could as well lead to the opposite conclusion: we should entirely ignore race altogether, adopting something like the color-blind approach discussed in Chapter 1. But for all the ways racial classification may be regarded as arbitrary and distorting, race retains enormous importance socially. The primary reason the U.S. Census records data on race today is an outgrowth of civil rights legislation passed in the 1960s mandating that the federal government use this data to address ongoing problems of discrimination. The challenge, then, is *to approach the problem of beliefs about the natural basis of racial identity from a cultural angle.*

These beliefs have been hotly contested concerns for over a hundred years and promise to remain subjects of debate for years to come. The rest of this chapter examines further the issue of how cultural linkages between race and nature continue to be forged by developing a critical perspective on both historical and contemporary debates about the scientific status of the race concept. The precariousness and mutability of racial classification should make us suspicious about any uses of "race" in science, especially since *most scientific research relies on census categories as the basis for labeling people racially.* Yet there are some pressing concerns—primarily the stark health disparities between whites and blacks in the United States—that are significant enough that scientists in a variety of fields continue to make race a focus of biological and genetic research. The challenge, then, is to understand the ways that race can both be "socially constructed"—as we have seen from the way census categories reflect political concerns and cultural anxieties—and yet also tangibly manifest in differential impacts and trajectories of disease and ill health. This challenge is complicated by the way such concerns are shadowed by increased efforts by some researchers to use genetics to posit that "race exists." The following sections—(Mis)uses of Biology, Race and Disease, Racial Health Disparities, and Understanding Genetics and Culture—approach these complex issues by developing an "anthropology of science" perspective that reveals the cultural dynamics shaping scientific research and findings. This perspective is crucially important to comprehending the continued interest in linking race with "nature" by trying to find race in human biology and genes.

(MIS)USES OF BIOLOGY

Race did not emerge initially as a subject of scientific inquiry. Rather, Europeans gradually articulated the idea of race in the process of their colonial expansion across the globe. Historian George Fredrickson explains, "No concept truly equivalent to that of 'race' can be detected in the thought of the Greeks, Romans, and early Christians" (2002, 17). Racism, as a worldview, "has a historical trajectory and is mainly, if not exclusively, a product of the West" (6). This worldview was fundamental in developing the global trade in human beings from Africa and the extraction of natural resources from Europe's colonies. In Fredrickson's analysis, racism had two components: difference and power. "It originates from a mindset that regards 'them' as different from 'us' in ways that are permanent and unbridge-able. This sense of difference provides a motive or rationale for using our power advantage to treat the ethnoracial Other in ways that we would regard as cruel or unjust if applied to members of our own group" (9). Increasingly, through the 18th and 19th centuries, Europeans turned to science to ratify this sense of difference as both natural and immutable.

Scientific articulations of the race concept emerged at a particular social and political moment. Somewhat ironically, it was a period when the Enlightenment was characterized by two countervailing impulses: to differentiate and classify ele-ments of the natural world while simultaneously promoting universalistic and egalitarian ideals. The science of race arose as one resolution of these contradic-tory orientations. Bruce Baum, in *The Rise and Fall of the Caucasian Race: A Politi-cal History of Racial Identity* (2006), explains, "The concept of race provided a means for eighteenth-century Europeans and Anglo-American elites to reconcile emerging egalitarian ideals with the new and pervasive sources of inequality and social instability. Thus, while Thomas Jefferson declared that 'all men are created equal,' he insisted, in the same breath, that some were 'racially' deficient" (62). Race, in the hands of scientists, became a means of *resolving the tension between antithetical ideas about human identity and capacity* by interpretively grounding the social conditions of increasing forms of inequality as a simple "fact of nature." Perhaps most profoundly, notions of race quickly shifted from a matter of color dif-ferentiation, which was clearly inadequate, into a process of physical measurement, concentrated on skull size.

Scientists devised a variety of means for measuring human anatomy and mor-phology in order to generate findings that confirmed what they already believed—that the world was neatly divided into clearly defined and permanent racial types. This perspective—**racial formalism**—posited racial identity both as a fixed, visible feature and as an innate capacity. This approach—based on preconceived notions that scientists worked to confirm, even to the point of fudging data to make it fit with expectations (Gould 1996)—has been labeled **scientific racism**. Historian Elazar Barkan (1992) uses this concept to highlight the fact "that political beliefs had a greater impact in attitudes toward race than did scientific commitments" (343). This became apparent as, in the face of mounting data pointing to a con-tinuum of human physical variation, scientists throughout the 19th century in-sisted on upholding the notion of pure racial types. The problem is that belief in the concept of race and the powerful uses to which it was applied—purporting to explain that some peoples were naturally inferior to others—warped how scientists approached the study of race (Smedly 1993).

Critiquing Race Science

In response to such nefarious practices, there has long been a very powerful argu-ment that there simply is no scientific basis for using the concept of race. This ar-gument was first articulated by the sociologist W. E. B. Du Bois in the early 1900s. Du Bois surveyed the intellectual wreckage of years of failed efforts to amass physical measurements that would substantiate the notion of racial types—Aryan, Negro, Asiatic, for instance—and concluded in 1915 that "in fact, it is generally recognized today that no scientific definition of race is possible. Differences, and striking differences, there are between men and groups of men, but they fade into each other so insensibly that we can only indicate the main divisions of men in broad outlines" (1915, 7). Du Bois' perspective has been reiterated and buttressed by critics of racial science in subsequent decades, and it is dramatically borne out by genetics as well. The basic point he made is that human variation forms a continuum without any clear or essential forms of breaks or natural boundaries between the groups that we generally perceive. Today this is the prevailing view among geneticists.

Du Bois' critique of race science was buttressed by the work of anthropologist Franz Boas, also in the early 1900s. Boas proved that immigrants arriving from Europe did not actually represent fixed a racial type, which discredited the idea of racial formalism (1912). In a longitudinal study of immigrant children, he showed that they grew larger in stature than their parents in the United States—perhaps as a result of better nutrition in this country for the second generation than their parents might have had in their impoverished homelands. This powerfully demonstrated that race was not a fixed physical characteristic and that the human form is fundamentally varied and elastic. The work of both Du Bois and Boas, as later substantiated by genetic research, provided the basis for the argument that races are *social constructs* rather than natural objects. The notion that race is socially constructed highlights the determinate power of cultural interests in shaping research and discussions on this subject.

Decades after Du Bois and Boas articulated this perspective, biologists and physical anthropologists honed a scientific concept that encapsulated their insights—**clines**. This concept refers to human physical traits, such as the features we use for classifying races, and their tendency to occur along a continuous gradient. These traits reflect the varying impacts of natural selection in particular environments rather than emblemizing the permanence of racial characteristics. Importantly, the features that we tend to combine, such as skin color and hair texture, vary independently of each other—a reflection of the fact that these forms of variation derive not from essential difference but from a variety of local interactions between humans and their environments. Based on these findings, the biological anthropologist Frank Livingstone concluded in the early 1960s that "there are no races, there are only clines" (1962, 279). Livingstone's work placed race decidedly in the social domain, rather than the biological.

This perspective was emphatically ratified by the work of geneticists in subsequent decades. In particular, research conducted by Richard Lewontin (1972) revealed far greater genetic variation *within* what we consider provisionally to be races than exists *between* such groups. Lewontin's finding that roughly 84% of the genetic variety in humans occurs within "races" demonstrates that people who share a racial identity are likely more different than they are similar to each other. Subsequent genetic analysis has pushed the percentage of genetic variation to about 94% within so-called racial groups. Based on his genetic analysis, Lewontin concluded that "racial classification is now seen to be of virtually no genetic or taxonomic significance," and he further argued "that our perception of relatively large differences between human races and subgroups, as compared to the variation within these groups, is a biased perception" (397). This point was ratified by the Human Genome Project, which established that any two human beings commonly share about 99.9% of their genetic material. These conclusions are the basis by which many people today assert that race is socially constructed, because clearly our idea of discrete, pure races does not reflect the biological or genetic reality of human diversity.

Can Science Still Study Race?

Despite the conclusiveness of this research, interest remains active in linking race and genetics. On one hand, this is perhaps not surprising, in that, as we have seen, "nature" remains a powerful human idea and a central topic of cultural concern. Since "race" is such a fundamental aspect of our social world, it follows that people would persist in finding some way to explain this in terms of natural categories such as biology and genetics. On the other hand, it is truly amazing that, in the face of such emphatic findings that disprove the notion that race is natural, so many people remain utterly committed to this point of view. This primarily speaks to an enduring prior commitment to the idea of race that stems from our cultural experiences of socialization. However, as we shall see later, *this urge to maintain a linkage between race and nature continues to be fueled from a variety of sources* that are not as easily characterized. Unfortunately, it may also be fueled unintentionally by the very assertion that "race is socially constructed."

Sociologist Troy Duster, who has spent years critiquing scientific efforts to link race with supposedly inherent characteristics such as intelligence and criminality, frames this problem as reflecting a false belief that domains such as "biology" and "society" are entirely separable. Sometimes social constructionist arguments seem to assert exactly this stance. Though it is crucially important to assail biased efforts to reduce race to biology or genetics—as Duster's work has proved time and again—this must not be accomplished at the cost of instituting an equally misguided belief that social and biological domains are entirely separable. In an article titled "Buried Alive: The Concept of Race in Science," Duster (2003) states that "by heading toward an unnecessary binary, socially constructed fork in the road, by forcing ourselves to think that we must choose between 'race as biological' (now out of favor) and 'race as *merely* a social construction,' we fall into an avoidable trap. It is not an either/or proposition" (272). Instead, Duster advocates for an approach that does not aim to squelch any scientific use of race whatsoever but, rather, makes sure such research fully recognizes the way human genetics and biology are affected by and reflect cultural interests and dynamics. That is, he urges us to recognize race as a "social fact" that has "biological consequences, which in turn has social consequences" (262). From this view, Duster depicts the recently reignited debates over race and genetics not as something that can simply be squelched—"purging science of race," he concludes, "is not practicable, possible, or even desirable" (258)—but, rather, as an *ongoing instance of the traffic between culture and nature* we considered at the opening of this chapter.

RACE AND DISEASE

In order to grasp this traffic better, we turn now to consider the fraught question of how race relates to health. But in doing so, it bears repeating that the very tools we bring to this task—medical knowledge and scientific research—are not independent of the cultural context that generates our initial and enduring interest in *linking* race and nature. This point is underscored by the emergent subfield of the **anthropology of science**, which exactly aims to understand the interplay between social interests and scientific objects. As Laura Nader explains in *Naked Science: Anthropological Inquiry into Boundaries, Power, and Knowledge* (1996), this perspective locates scientific practice—the problems it confronts, the solutions it generates, and the technologies it produces—in its specific cultural milieu.

An anthropological angle on science highlights the political aspects of scientific research, even though we generally imagine science to be a neutral, value-free form of inquiry. But, as Nader observes, "the politicization of science is unavoidable, not only because politicians, corporations, and governments try to use what scientists know, but because virtually all science has social and political implications" (9). Nowhere is this more obvious than in the study of race. There simply is very little basis to regard the recent efforts to establish a scientific basis for the study of race from a neutral stance, because *the prior belief in races*—as in the earlier era of scientific racism—remains a component of current research. This suggests our biggest challenge in getting the "science of race" right is that we come to grips with the cultural expectations we bring to bear on scientific practice and findings.

At stake in all this is our ability to understand properly the powerful cultural dynamics shaping not only our ideas about race but the very pursuit of scientific research. Evelynn Hammond (2006), a historian of science, argues that understanding the connection between race and health depends on first challenging "the power of biology as a naturalizing discourse." Her point is that biology is as much a culturally constituted authoritative discourse on "nature" as it is an objectivist view of the biological dimensions of the world. This matters greatly with race, Hammond relates, because "in the United States race serves as *a dense transfer point between nature and society*. It links our social structure to our individual and group biologies and it links our biological differences back to our social structure" [emphasis added]. In this regard, not only is it important to see how constructions of nature have influenced our thinking about race; one must grasp the importance and centrality of race to the kinds of links we make between identity and biology. The connections between race and disease—those that are frequently discussed and those we barely acknowledge or even recognize—make this quite tangible. As we will see, the clearest indication of culture's role in all this is *the selective way we talk about and acknowledge (or ignore) links between race, biology, genetics, and inequality.*

Visible and Invisible Connections between Race and Biology

The most salient aspects of the possible linkages between race and biology are the stunning racial health disparities in this country. The significance of race for health in the United States is evidenced by the difference of five and a half years between the average life expectancy of whites and blacks. African Americans face higher mortality rates than whites for most causes of death, particularly for heart disease, cancer, diabetes, homicide, and HIV/AIDS. Hispanics and American Indians also face higher mortality rates than whites in some of these same categories (Barr 2008). Why? This is a difficult question to answer, partly because we so easily equate health with a fact of nature. That is, we have a tendency to assume these differences are simply natural. But they are not. Each of these causes of death involves a welter of social factors—particularly the experience of discrimination—that have direct biological impacts. So to think through the association between race and health, we have to see biology as more than a matter of what is "natural."

The easiest illustration of this point is that life expectancies change quite dramatically as social and cultural innovations affect the biological conditions of human life. In the United States, in particular, life expectancy rose dramatically in the last century due to both medical and social advances, from inoculations against infectious diseases and other public health campaigns to improvements in urban infrastructures and efforts to combat poverty and hunger in this country. Despite these dramatic impacts on the conditions of human life, we see a persistence of racial inequality in terms of health. Yet, instead of focusing on the connections between poverty, disadvantage, and health, public discourse about race and biology seems to most frequently fixate on topics of genetic disease. This reflects the selectiveness of how we talk about linkages between race and health.

Typically, when people raise the issue of biology, race, and health, they do so only in relation to a fairly rare set of diseases, such as Tay-Sachs disease, cystic fibrosis, and sickle cell disease. Though these are frequent touchstones in how people think about race and health, they are negligible factors in the health disparities cited earlier. Those differences are affected by where you live, as we saw with environmental racism in Chapter 1, but they also are impacted by what you eat, your daily activities, and what kind of work you do, or whether you have a job. The problem is that, as our attention is drawn to fairly rare diseases that have a genetic component, *we tend to ignore the more complicated, seemingly intractable range of health problems* that are social in nature but more emphatically linked to race.

Cystic fibrosis, Tay-Sachs, and sickle cell anemia are autosomal recessive disorders, which manifest only when both parents of a child contribute a gene that, when paired, produces the disorder. There are more than a thousand such disorders, but these three are frequently cited because they are associated with ethnic or racial groups. This prominence suggests that, in both popular culture and much medical discourse, these diseases have become *totems of race*, representing an apparent proof that "races exist." The surprising aspect of this association is that, in looking closely at who actually develops these diseases, the notion of a biological basis for race becomes highly questionable. That is, on closer inspection, these diseases illustrate the basic point made here about cultural ideas about nature—that *the linkages and associations we make with this realm are inevitably selective and interested.* The basic facts concerning the incidences of these diseases make this apparent. Tay-Sachs is concentrated among Ashkenazi Jews, but one in three hundred non-Jews is a carrier of this genetic trait. Cystic fibrosis is often labeled as a "white" disease because it disproportionately affects white Americans, with a frequency of 4.5%, in contrast to lower frequencies among African Americans (1.5%) and Hispanics (2.1%). Interestingly, though, these rates for blacks and Latinos are actually higher than among Europeans, since only 1% of that population is affected. But the most telling of all is sickle cell, which still is frequently labeled a "black disease," though it ranges from West Africa, throughout the Mediterranean, as far as southern India, and across South America.

Renaturalizing Race

The emblematic status of these diseases in public discourse obscures a great deal of the crucial role that culture plays in shaping both health and human constitutions. First, that we are aware of these diseases at all is a testament to the tremendous social strides made in the last century to lower human mortality rates due to far more prevalent contagious diseases or chronic health conditions. Historian Keith Wailoo (2003) points out that "there is an important therapeutic backdrop to these diseases. All of them were obscure in the early twentieth century but became increasingly central to medical, public health, and public discourse in the last half of the century" (238). Their emergence in public consciousness was predicated primarily on the decline of childhood infectious diseases with the advent of penicillin and antibiotics, but another factor was that they provided an apparent basis for affirming the biological reality of race in an era that saw the dismantling of legal sanctions for social segregation. As Wailoo explains (Wailoo and Pemberton 2006), "since their emergence into broader social discourse, they have served as vehicles for thinking about race and ethnicity in America" (10). Consistently, public discussions have championed the belief that these diseases "prove" that racial identities are simply natural, even though they just as easily prove the opposite point. The problem with all this is that the categorical thinking about race affirmed in these discussions actually leads us to misunderstand and misconstrue both biological variation and disease processes.

Sickle cell anemia shows this well in terms of various concerted efforts to label this disease as race specific. The belief that this was a "black" disease started early and endured even when clinical counterevidence for this thesis began to surface. Why? Historian Melbourne Tapper finds that sickle cell "emerged and reemerged at the intersection of a variety of medical, genetic, serological, anthropological, personal, and administrative discourses on whiteness, hybridity, tribes, and citizenship" (1999, 3). From the 1920s (sickle cell anemia was discovered in 1917) to the 1940s, instances of the disease were used by scientists to question the whiteness of non-African groups, such as the Greeks, Italians, and other Mediterranean peoples. As further cases of sickle cell emerged in the 1950s in Southern India, some doctors tried to claim that East Africans, Sicilians, and Indians all shared a common racial heritage—even though this belief distorts the course of human genetic evolution. That is, the prior belief in racial types and the fierce insistence on regarding them in some sense as "natural" led some doctors to interpret the genetic record badly. By the 1970s, sickle cell anemia played a significant role in questioning the fitness of African Americans as part of the U.S. body politic. In each of these eras, *a prior commitment to and belief in the reality of racial groups* prevented physicians and researchers from recognizing the true extent of sickle cell across a variety of populations.

The overarching point is that genetic diseases get a disproportionate amount of attention when thinking about race and health, though they really represent only a tiny portion of the health problems that humans face. **Genetic diseases** are rare and generally affect only 6% to 8% of a population. Yet they are made the focus of attention when people try to make the case for a genetic basis for race. The very low prevalence of such diseases suggests that they are not a good basis for understanding something as pervasive and socially significant as race. Evolutionary biologist Joseph Graves (2005) characterizes the problem here in a way that brings us back to the question of racial health disparities that opened this section. "It is a much bigger problem to understand how the essential genetic uniformity of the human species can produce the glaring disparities in the ten major sources of death in America, such as heart disease, diabetes, kidney disease, and cancer. We cannot answer this question by discussing genetics as most people think of it" (121). The serious concern Graves raises is that the increasing focus on genetics in relation to race will actually distract us from the major problems of racial health disparities. Importantly, in understanding these disparities, we have to think of biology not as something strictly natural but as something profoundly affected by, and intertwined with, culture.

RACIAL HEALTH DISPARITIES

Grasping the forces at work in generating racial health disparities requires that we shift the discussion from the level of the genes to that of the social context that generates these disparities. We have to do so, though, by thinking about links between biology and race in ways that do not reproduce cultural ideas about nature and identity. The basic point is that *the forms of racial inequality we considered in Chapter 1 have physical and biological effects.* From an epidemiological perspective, the distribution of disease and ill health is hardly natural. Epidemiology, as a science, is predicated on the recognition that we are cultural beings living in social contexts that profoundly influence our health. Simply put, the dynamics of disease and chronic health conditions reflect the impact of differential social conditions on biological organisms. People are biological organisms with cultural identities that are located in social contexts, which reflect or register the impacts of larger political and economic forces. This dynamic is particularly evident with race.

Epidemiologist Nancy Kreiger (2006) characterizes racial health disparities as the "biologic expression of race relations." Her point is that the health consequences of living in segregated areas with high rates of pollution, crime, and lack of access to open spaces, combined with the experience of racism in its many manifestations, takes a physical and psychological toll on bodies. Kreiger asserts that "the arbitrary biological traits conventionally used to delineate 'races' may be conceptualized as *racialized expression of biology*." The value of this perspective is that it moves us away from a simplistic, reductionist contrasting of "culture" and "biology" and shifts us toward the fundamental recognition that our identities inextricably involve an interplay between these respective domains. A double form of attention to the complex interplay between culture and biology is required here, which moves us far away from thinking in terms of "natural" categories in relation to race. In this regard, Kreiger emphasizes "the importance of taking into account both racism *and* biology" when we approach the question of health and illness.

This approach involves more than race, though, and importantly allows us to confront the fundamental fact that health is stratified by class—the poorer you are, the worse your overall health and well-being. Simply put, longevity is related to your position in the social hierarchy. Life expectancy, infant mortality, and incidence of most major diseases are linked to class position (Barr 2008). Though appalling, this fact should really not be surprisingly. Access to health care, good nutrition, and safe opportunities for exercise are linked to relative degrees of wealth and poverty. Inner-city dwellers simply do not have the resources—social or economic—to maintain healthy regimens when they are daily exposed to the various hazards of urban poverty—high crime rates, concentrations of industrial toxins, and lack of access to healthy food or forms of recreation. Conversely, the ability to achieve and maintain good health is greatly facilitated by life in an upscale neighborhood, where an inverse relation pertains regarding access to a healthy lifestyle. When we additionally consider the racial aspect of poverty in this country, it is not hard to see that the correspondences between social inequality and poor health will be reflected in racial differentials in mortality rates.

The Interplay of Culture, Race, and Biology

But there is an additional factor to health disparities: for African Americans, these often crosscut class positions. This is because experiences of racism—which are not limited only to poor blacks—affect mental and physical health (Williams 2003). Racist encounters produce heightened rates of depression, anxiety, anger, and psychosis, each of which potentially affects physical health. Numerous studies report a strong association between experiences of discrimination and poorer health, particularly in terms of chronic conditions and other disabilities. Prominent among these is the correlation between experiences of discrimination and rates of high blood pressure. Encounters with racism are even a factor in the high rates of preterm deliveries and low-weight birthrates among African Americans. A study conducted by Kreiger (2004) found that factoring self-reported experiences with racism alongside a series of other risk factors linked to poverty entirely accounted for the three-times-greater risk black women face of delivering a preterm baby compared to whites. These stark, important findings, though, do not yet factor in the differential experiences people of color face in even initially gaining access to medical care and navigating the medical system.

Epidemiologists have demonstrated a robust relationship between discrimination and higher rates of disease, even though research on this connection is still in its infancy. Many questions remain to be explored concerning the extent of this relationship, the threshold for and persistence of exposure to racism and its impacts, as well as the important question of specific mechanisms and processes that might be involved. As well, there remains the challenging task of separating the variety of meanings and uses of race that people develop in relation to biology.

In the difficult matter of disaggregating the cultural dimension of biological conditions, an interesting example is provided in research by the biological anthropologist Clarence Gravlee (2005), who examined the correlation between race and high rates of blood pressure in Puerto Rico. Gravlee and fellow researchers set out to test two competing hypotheses regarding the relationship between skin color and blood pressure. One suggested that the link reflected a genetic predisposition (associated with skin color) for high blood pressure; the other considered skin color as a marker of exposure to social stressors such as racism, emphasizing the cultural, rather than genetic or biological, significance of skin color. Puerto Rico presents an excellent place to test these hypotheses because the ascription of race is based on more than skin color. There are five primary racial categories on the island: *negro* and *blanco* define opposite positions, with the intermediate categories of *trigueño, jabao,* and *indio,* falling in between. Ascription of these categorical identities hinges on assessment of hair texture and other physical (particularly facial) features in addition to skin color. Wealth and status, family background, and residential location also are factors in attributing racial identity. This study highlights that individuals sharing any given concentration of skin pigmentation may vary in their racial classification. More importantly, the researchers found that ascribed racial identity, rather than skin color, is associated with differential rates of blood pressure. They concluded "that the cultural rather than biological dimensions of skin color" stand out as a key factor in making sense of health disparities related to blood pressure (2005, 4).

The crucial point in these various perspectives on the interplay between culture, race, and biology is that these associations are complex rather than simple, as genetic reductivism mistakenly promotes. The problem with many genetic approaches to these matters is that the focus on genes often ignores the way their expression is affected by cultural and social factors. Yet another problem with the genetic approach is evident in something just as central to health disparities: differential rates of hypertension. Some geneticists seek to explain this by treating race as a series of distinctive physical types. But rates of hypertension for African Americans are twice as high as for urban West Africans and five times higher than for those living in rural areas, which indicates that far more than genes are involved in this condition. For that matter, African Americans have differential rates of hypertension depending on whether they live in the South or the Northeast United States, and these rates are all higher than for people of African descent born in the Caribbean (Daniel 2003). Clearly, there is more at work than genes in affecting these widely varied health conditions within what might be construed as one racial group—continental Africans.

The Challenge of Medical Research on Race

The breadth and depth of these studies reframes the importance of both examining and discussing the interplay between race and health. But it remains difficult to do so without reinscribing the cultural notion that racial identities are simply natural. Gravlee's work is an excellent example of ways to operationalize race as a variable that still allows us to think about cultural dimensions of racial health disparities. But this view has to vie against our tendency to essentialize racial identities in biological terms. This danger is framed by historian of science Steven Epstein (2007), who traces the emergence of what he calls the "inclusion-and-difference paradigm in the medical research industry in the United States." This model results from effective political mobilization over the last two decades targeting the exclusion of women and racial minorities from medical research that relied on white males to represent "the standard human." In challenging these exclusions, activists aimed to achieve two fundamental goals: "the inclusion of members of various groups generally considered to be underrepresented previously as subjects in clinical studies; and the measurement, within those studies, of differences across groups with regard to treatment effects, disease progression, or biological processes" (6). Epstein regards this development "as a victory worth savoring in a long struggle to bring medical attention to the excluded and under-served" (285). But he also cautions that these gains unintentionally resulted in "a truncated understanding of the biological and social production of bodily difference" (204) that make critical political work around race more difficult and complicated in the long term. That is, the goal of trying to assure that minorities groups are represented in medical research produced an approach that reinvests categorical racial identities with notions of inherent biological difference.

Epstein worries that the elaborate political and scientific infrastructures supporting these biological notions of difference will do little to help us grapple with the social problem of health disparities outlined earlier. For one, they are inadequate to the task of addressing "the ways in which inequalities and power differentials in the broader society affects people's exposure to health risks" (299). For another, "they may obscure other aspects of social hierarchy that are highly relevant to health, such as social class." Furthermore, "they may disincline us from recognizing that in many situations the practices one engages in, the networks within which one moves, and the resources one has on hand may be much more immediately relevant to health risks than one's membership in a categorical group" (300). This host of potential problems is an unanticipated outcome of the valuable work of keeping track of the relations between race and health, and they underscore *the continued and even increasing traffic in nature and culture* flowing through the realms of medical research. This traffic, in turn, contributes to the renewed efforts to find and establish a genetic basis for racial identity—even in the face of research that continues to dismiss the possibility of such a basis.

UNDERSTANDING GENETICS AND CULTURE

Despite the crucial role culture plays in both forming our views of the relation of race to biology and the function of biology itself, reductive efforts to construe race as a strictly natural phenomenon continue to arise. Though these efforts have been meticulously and effectively challenged in relation to *biology*, they are now being rearticulated in the domain of *genetics*. We turn now to a major controversy developing among geneticists as to whether "races exist." In certain regards, this controversy reprises the debates over race and biology, with similar stakes over whether our racial classifications can be regarded as natural. Similarly too, the basic facts of human variation—whether highlighted in terms of biology or in terms of genetics—strongly support the position that race is socially constructed. The vast amount of human variation occurs within the groupings we regard as races, and there are so many different ways to parse this variation in terms of populations, with overlapping and contrary criteria. Hence, the notion that genetics will prove that race exists, apart from our cultural expectation that it is real, is dubious. Still, this is a subject that will be keenly debated for years to come, so the purpose of the final portions of this chapter is to orient you to the basic terms and issues in this controversy.

To do this successfully, we have to expand on the perspective we used in the earlier discussion of biology by *delineating the different domains across which claims about race are being made and evaluated*. Reality, in relation to race, has many dimensions; for simplicity, we can limit these to three: culture, biology, and genetics. In scientific terms, different dynamics pertain at each level, though they are thoroughly interwoven and co-constituted. How does this work? Consider, for a moment, a level below, or more fundamental than, any of these—the domain of particle physics. While this level, as physicists would assure us, is the primary "ground" of reality, it is of little use in explaining anything about the other levels, such as patterns in gene mutation or the biological processes involved with stress or the cultural dynamics that shape our interpretation of racial identities. Though fundamentally intertwined, each of these levels involves a distinct order of phenomenon for which particular dynamics pertain. In the same way we would not use the laws of physics alone to explain organic processes (metabolism, for instance), so too the forms of statistical analysis used for detecting patterns of gene flow are of little use in analyzing contests over the public meaning of racial images in the news. Once we recognize that culture, biology, and genetics represent distinct domains—in terms of dynamics and how they are respectively analyzed—the next challenge is how to talk about the ways these level interpenetrate.

Making sense of the interrelation between these three domains is challenging, but we can begin by first differentiating the two levels people often take to be synonymous: biology and genetics. Despite their considerable overlap, biologists and geneticists generally focus on two different units of analysis: **phenotypes** and **genotypes**. Phenotypes are the level of manifest biology—our physical features, anatomy, and physiology—or the outward appearance of an organism. Genotypes, on the other hand, refer to the genetic makeup of an individual. The genotype influences the phenotype, but phenotypes also reflect and are shaped by many nongenetic factors, as well. These contrasting levels are crucial to grasp in terms of race, because the social conception of race was developed initially in relation to phenotypes, which people still rely on in making reference to or thinking about race. When we shift in scale from phenotypes to genotypes we risk misconstruing the disjuncture between one set of physical dynamics and another in relation to race.

The possible confusions that follow are captured well by the evolutionary biologist Joseph Graves (2005), who remarked: "If you try to use [phenotypic] characteristics such as height, body proportions, skull measurements, hair type, and skin color to create a tree showing how human populations are related, you get a tree that doesn't match the measured genetic relatedness and known evolutionary history of our species" (16). That is, the kinds of associations we make with race at the level of manifest biology—where we are so certain that we can plainly see it—misconstrue the genetics of human variation. An example Graves uses is of skin color and hair type. If we posited "dark-skinned people with thick curly hairs as the same race," in terms of phenotype, we would be lumping together sub-Saharan Africans and people from southern India along with Papuans from New Guinea and Australian aborigines. Though this makes sense at the level of manifest biology, it is a distortion of human genetic relations, in that "Papuans and aboriginal Australians are the groups most genetically distant from sub-Saharan Africans" (17). This disjuncture highlights the contrast between the biological and genetic domains in relation to race. It also frames the vastly different scientific connotations of race—in broadest strokes, the racial formalism (based on phenotype) that marked its use by scientists from the mid-1700s to mid-1900s differs greatly from the probabilistic statements about frequencies of genetic mutations to which it is linked now. Yet we are often indifferent to this crucial contrast of connotations.

What Are We Talking About?

Neither the original race theorists, such as Johan Friedrich Blumenbach, who coined the term *Caucasian*, nor Carl Linnaeus nor most people confronting "race" in their everyday lives, would likely recognize the range of variability and complexity in gene frequencies as inherently "racial." That a genetic variant like factor *V Leiden*, which confers an increased risk of venous thromboembolism, occurs in about 5% of white people but less frequently among East Asians and Africans seems strikingly tenuous in relation to the emphatic assertions people commonly make about racial differences. The allele *APOE*—associated with increased risk of Alzheimer's disease and relatively common among all racial and ethnic groups—varies in frequency among white and black populations by 14% and 19%, respectively. This is a modest basis for broad, assertive claims that such variation proves the existence of race. Just as importantly, this genetic perspective is quite removed from what most people in their day-to-day lives think of as race. For that matter, use of *race* in relation to genetics is quite different from the typological formalism that characterized earlier scientific efforts to talk about race. There may be a biological connection in relation to race, as we discussed earlier regarding racial health disparities, but this is not the same as proving races simply "exist" and "naturally" sort human diversity into distinct entities.

This problem of differential scale becomes more pronounced when we shift to the level of culture in order to consider what genetic ancestry-testing companies do when they claim to be able to establish a person's racial or ethnic heritage. Aside from the many complications with genetic analysis that make such assertions dubious (Bolnick 2007), these companies' claims deemphasize the fact that different dynamics establish racial and ethnic identity at the level of culture, where perceptions of relatedness are constituted and perceived in terms of social context, history, and life experiences. Importantly, too, genetic ancestry claims rest on the ill-founded assumption that the cultural ethnicities in particular areas sampled today are identical to those that existed hundreds of years ago, which is highly unlikely.

Populations and Groups

As we think about the relation of genetics to cultural systems of classification linked to race we have to be attentive to the process of shifting scales of reference or levels of analysis between these interrelated domains. While we readily and casually refer to or invoke "genetics" in everyday conversation—and we avidly consume reports, however contradictory, of recent findings from genetics research—we are crossing domains with little thought to the implications or the processes of translation involved in this traffic. One way to maintain an awareness of the distinctness of these domains is to consider how they manifest between two terms we often consider synonymous—**populations** and **groups**. As with any two common terms, there is a good bit of overlap. As well, there are intermediary sciences, such as epidemiology and demography, that may deal in both. And certainly, "races" are frequently characterized by either or both terms. So the contrast between the two terms is not easy to grasp, but doing so matters a great deal in understanding the level of analysis entailed by genetics and how this pertains, if at all, to the level of culture.

Groups are central in the cultural domain and hence are units of meaning. They are the means by which humans sort out matters of belonging and difference. Initially through forms of kinship and then increasingly through various bureaucratic technologies of citizenship and copious expressive media, membership in a group is a cultural matter established by both interpretation and negotiation of forms of sameness and differentiation. Membership in groups can, of course, overlap and vary. A person may belong to more than one group and may move in and out of groups in a lifetime. This often entails dramas over competing or shifting allegiances to and alliances between various groups as well as mutable forms of belonging. In these dramas, the content and boundaries of groups are variously dynamic or constant. The central point here is that cultural dynamics govern these processes:

they may or may not key primarily to biology or genetics, but when they do, it's the cultural dynamics that are determinate, not the biological or genetic ones.

Populations are units of frequency that geneticists use to talk about and analyze human biological variation. Evolutionary forces—mutation, selection, drift, and migration—are highlighted in populations. These units can be defined in local, regional, or global terms, depending on the type of questions geneticists are trying to answer or the varying degrees of precision they bring to their analyses. Initially, the least concern was over individual forms of belonging or difference. Geneticists, though, are now able to deploy what they have learned from population genetics to exactly identify individuals as belonging to a particular racial group, one that matches that person's own self-identification. So have they confirmed the existences of race? The urge to ground cultural categories in nature is evident in translating *populations* (which we often misconstrue to be a natural unit) as *groups* (which we know to be generally in flux). But populations are hardly natural, even though they reference genetic and sometimes biological dynamics.

There are a variety of ways of defining populations in terms of specific dynamics, such as mating propensity, genealogy, or competition. This variety of approaches reflects the fact that these units are not given natural facts; rather, they are particular ways of carving up the enormity of human variations. Philosopher of science Lisa Gannett (2003) makes the case that "populations are not mind-independent objects that scientists discover." Instead, she finds that "populations are pragmatically and variably constituted in different sorts of investigations of species genome diversity" (990). That is, they are "constructed as objects of investigation according to the aims, interests, and values that inform particular research contexts" (ibid.). This is evident by the way they so neatly "satisfy practical needs and theoretical preferences associated with specific contexts of investigation" (989). The point is not that they are, then, simply fictions; rather, populations, as delimited by geneticists, reflect *a selective attention to certain features or dynamics*. The point to bear in mind is that "genes are bounded in space and time in ways that are determined not only by patterns of relations among organisms but by specific contexts of investigation" (993).

The insight that populations are not simply natural, even though they involve natural processes linked to genes and biology, is well illustrated by an example developed by Troy Duster (2003). "It is possible to make arbitrary groupings of populations (geographic, linguistic, self-identified by faith, identified by others by physiognomy, etc.) and still find statistically significant allelic variations between those groupings" (265). That means we could sample all people in any two cities in the United States "and find statistically significant differences in allele frequencies at some loci" (ibid.). This would have nothing to do with race yet would be generated by the same procedure that makes race look real. The point to underscore here is one that opens this chapter: *representing portions of the natural or physical world is always a selective process*, and our basis for *selection reflects the social and cultural concerns and interests that we bring to the natural world* in hopes that it will confirm what we already believe about the solidity and realness of our cultural categories, such as group identity. This prior belief in naturalizing groups via populations profoundly influences our approach to understanding genetic variation.

Consider two basic facts about genetics and race. The first was mentioned earlier, that any two people are about 99.9% similar in terms of their genes. From wherever across the globe humans are sampled, the consistent finding is that we are enormously more similar than different in terms of genetics. Though most genes are exactly the same in all humans, genetic variation results from the process by which individuals inherit a mix of dominant, recessive, codominant, or polymorphic genes from their parents. This leads to the second fact: the biological variability that exists among humans occurs primarily at the individual level. This degree of variability is significant—even at only 0.1%, this can amount to about three million distinct DNA variants between any two individual. But the surprising aspect of these two facts taken together is that we overwhelmingly prefer to talk about genetic similarity and difference in terms of groups rather than individuals. Given that the vast majority of genetic variation occurs *within* what might be posited as racial groups rather than between them, this is even more surprising and bespeaks a strong prior commitment to naturalizing both groups and races, even though, in cultural terms, we know these entities are not simply occurring naturally, apart from the interest we bring to finding them in "nature." These dynamics are critical to keep in mind as we now turn to consider more fully the recent uproar among geneticists over the possibility of establishing a physical basis for racial identities.

THE CONTROVERSY OVER GENES AND RACE

In the summer of 2000, as the initial successful efforts to sequence the human genome were completed, leaders of this massive international undertaking seized the moment to make a few pronouncements about the broad significance of this genetic map of humanity. Prime among these was a basic claim about race, one that only seemed to underscore established knowledge in both genetics and anthropology. Craig Venter, then president of Celera Genomics, the private company that competed with publicly funded scientists from around the world in mapping the human genome, enthusiastically proclaimed that "the concept of race has no genetic or scientific basis" (Venter 2000, 8). This definitive, succinct claim endorsed what physical anthropologists and geneticists who spoke publicly on the subject of race had been saying for several decades (Montague 1942; Livingstone 1962; Lewontin 1972). Hence, the new era of genetics seemed to build seamlessly on the previous order of knowledge.

This consensus view was further ratified by a series of editorial assertions made in premier science journals in the United States. An editorial in the *New England Journal of Medicine* emphatically proclaimed that "race is biologically meaningless" and that "race is a social construct, not a scientific classification" and declared that "instruction in medical genetics should emphasize the fallacy of race as a scientific concept and the dangers inherent in race-based medicine" (Schwartz

2001, 344). As well, an article in *Nature Genetics* arguing that "commonly used ethnic labels are both insufficient and inaccurate representations of inferred genetic clusters" (Wilson et al 2001, 265) was followed by an editorial promoting a "race-neutral" methodology in phase III clinical trials testing drug efficacy in different groups of patients (Editorial 2001). These claims resonated easily with an editorial in *Science* that dismissed "the myth of major genetic differences across 'races'" on the basis both of current genetic evidence and ongoing research (Owens and King 1999, 452). Taken together, these statements worked to affirm a seamless suturing of an earlier era of genetics—before the sequencing of the human genome—with the emergent period, one that features distinctly new techniques and methods for analyzing human genetic variation. At the core of this affirmation was the assertion that the consensus concerning the biological insignificance of race would carry over into the new age of genetics.

But rather than stabilizing this meticulously assembled and widely promoted view that there is no biological basis for race in our genetic code, these assertions instead provoked a series of counterclaims based on a range of examples and evidence that suggested that race indeed has significance in a physiological sense. Not only are race and biology linked, certain geneticists and clinicians boldly argued, but this linkage is also potentially crucial to understanding the widespread racial health disparities in the United States. The foremost figures challenging the consensus view that "race is biologically meaningless" are population geneticists Neil Risch (Stanford University) and Esteban Gonzalez Burchard (University of California, San Francisco), as well as Elad Ziv (University of California, San Francisco) and Hua Tang, a biostatistician (University of Washington). Drawing from recent work on *haplotype variation* (patterns of DNA polymorphisms on a single chromosome that are inherited together) and *linkage disequilibrium* (referring to the nonrandom frequency of two genes appearing in close proximity on the same chromosome), they argue against the view that the greater degrees of genetic variation *within* rather than *between* purported racial groups discounts the usefulness of the concept of race as a reliable, objective means for delineating human populations. Citing the ability of geneticists to generate and analyze discrete clusters of human genetic diversity, Risch and Burchard argue that "two Caucasians are more similar to each other genetically than a Caucasian and an Asian" (Risch et al. 2002, 5). Risch and Burchard additionally argue that "a 'race-neutral' or 'color-blind' approach in biomedical research is neither equitable nor advantageous, and would not lead to a reduction of disparities in disease risk or treatment efficacy between groups" (11).

Terms of the Debate

Since Risch, Burchard, and their colleagues made these claims, a great deal of debate and controversy has followed. This debate was highlighted in the editorial pages of the *New England Journal of Medicine* in 2003. There, the claims by Risch and Burchard were answered by Richard Cooper (Loyola Strich School of Medicine), Jay Kaufman (University of North Carolina), and Ryk Ward (University of Oxford, now deceased). Cooper et al. (2003) raised many technical challenges to the claims about the significance of race that can only be adequately addressed in a fuller discussion of genetic analysis. But they also make a series of important critical points about the way such claims fit a history of misuses of genetics that are worth considering here because they highlight the earlier-raised issues of scale and the prior commitment to race.

Cooper et al. challenge the scientific basis for claims linking race and genetics by pointing to the array of social interests, historically and contemporarily, that form a type of bias warping research practices and findings. The core issue they raise concerns the overwhelming interest in positing "genes" as an explanation for an array of social problems, which extends well beyond topics linked to race. Their point is that

> genes are regularly proposed as the cause when no genetic data have been obtained, and *the social and biologic factors remain hopelessly confounded.* Even when molecular data are collected, causal arguments are based on nonsignificant findings or genetic variation that does not have an established association with the disease being studied. Coincidence is not a plausible explanation of the widespread occurrence of this practice over time and across subdisciplines. The correlation between the use of unsupported genetic inferences and the social standing of a group is glaring evidence of bias and demonstrates how race is used both to categorize and to rank-order subpopulations. (1168)

For Cooper et al., the disproportion between the tenuousness of evidence and the sweeping claims being made—as well as the consistent ease of making such claims against certain racial groups—reflect the determinate impact of power relations and cultural dynamics more than any genetic reality.

For Cooper et al., such claims repeat the mistakes of scientific racism by *the selectiveness of their attention.* Genetic claims are consistently and almost singularly made about black people, striving to posit something that makes them qualitatively or quantitatively distinct. A striking aspect of this tendency—aside from the point raised by Cooper et al., that it reflects a power dynamic of using genetics research against minorities—is that it so frequently plays out in contradictory forms. In the United States, claims about the genetic distinctiveness of African Americans have alternately portrayed them as *inferior* and *superior* in terms of their genes. In the early 1900s, some geneticists postulated that the race would go extinct because their supposedly inferior genes lead to higher rates of mortality; today, similar arguments are made relating to the higher rates of hypertension we discussed earlier. These stand out against antithetical claims made about African Americans' superior strength (for work as slaves) and greater athleticism (to explain their dominance in professional sports). What makes such claims even more suspect than their contrary formulations is that they are made about the population that has the greatest degree of genetic variation. Human life began in Africa, and hence that population features the largest concentration of genetic diversity. We have to ponder why such reductionist claims would be so consistently made against the group that is most difficult to characterize in such terms. The question matters because it gets at the problematic aspect of fixating on genetics to explain, for instance, black rates of hypertension when those rates vary so greatly through-out the African diaspora—a fact that underscores the important role of culture.

Again, How Many Races Are There?

This debate over a possible genetic basis for racial identity will not be resolved any time soon. Surely more intriguing and disputed findings will follow before long. The key point to keep in mind, though, is that genetics research cannot resolve the cultural questions we bring to it, largely because genetics does not operate inde-pendent of these same cultural concerns. This point is evident in the way genetic arguments are made regarding race, but it also surfaces in one of the key studies that Risch and Burchard cite in making their claims. Geneticists Noah Rosenberg and colleagues (2002) developed a study making use of advances in computing power and statistical analysis in genetics to sample a far larger number of micro-satellite loci than had previously been examined. Notably, their results powerfully buttressed a central finding from genetics in the 1970s, which had been crucial to assailing misguided biological thinking about race. With this more advanced ana-lytical power they further demonstrated that there is far greater genetic variation within groups that we think of as races than between them. Indeed, they found even higher rates of this within-group variation than had earlier been reported by Richard Lewontin in 1972. But their findings did not matter as much as the way the study was reported by the media.

The result that drew journalists' attention was the claim that, in their analysis, they "identified six main genetic clusters, five of which correspond to major geo-graphic regions" (Rosenberg et al. 2002, 2383). This finding was picked up and reported by the media as conclusive proof at last that races do exist. But these re-sults were far from conclusive and actually contradicted this simplistic assump-tion. The point that reporters missed about this study is that a variety of results were produced by the computer program (Structure) that the geneticists used to parse the data. The tiny amount of genetic variation they found (3–5%) could ac-tually be structured in any number of ways, depending on how many groupings the geneticists specified for the program to find. Specifying only two groupings produced two "races," one that included sub-Saharan Africa, Europe, the Middle East, along with Central and South Asia; the second comprising East Asia, the Americas, and Oceania. And so it continued. However many groupings they spec-ified, that's how many "races" they found. Targeting six groupings produced a clus-tering that roughly accorded to continental populations, but it also included a grouping solely composed of the Kalash in Northern Pakistan. Journalists totally ignored the study's finding that "individuals can have membership in multiple clusters" (2002). That is, they could belong simultaneously to different groupings—hardly a common assumption about racial identity—depending on any of a variety of ways of structuring the same genetic material. Thus, even with advances in tech-nology and computing power, we remain unable to answer the very basic question with which we opened this chapter: How many races are there? The more geneti-cists study the question, the more apparent it becomes that there are many logical ways to classify human genetic variation into "populations" and that these ways do not operate independently of our prior interest in the question of race.

GENES AND CULTURE: A RESOLUTION

There may be ways to link biology and race, as we discussed earlier regarding racial health disparities, but this is not the same as proving that race simply "exists" in the natural realm. That is because, for all our increasing prowess with genetic analysis, we have a tendency to forget or overlook the crucial role culture plays, even in shaping the flow and expression of genes that geneticists aim to objectify. When Burchard et al. (2003) delineate the "genetic" level of analysis—in countering "social constructionist" claims about race—they hold up an odd entity, "mating patterns," as constituting the ground of genetic reality. "From the perspective of genetics, structure in the human population is determined by patterns of mating and reproduction" (1169). Yet matting patterns are far from simply a matter of nature; rather, they reflect the deepest imprint of the role of culture.

Few matters are more influenced by cultural rules, practices, and beliefs than how people decide whether and with whom to mate. For millennia, structures of kinship have guided the process by which humans reproduce, shaping the gene flows that many are tempted to regard as simply occurring naturally. Nowhere is this impact of culture on basic biological and genetic processes clearer than in regard to race in our own country. As anthropologists Mukhopadhyay, Henze, and Moses (2007) observe, "in the United States, *cultural* processes—especially mating, marriage, and kinship practices—are responsible for preserving biological markers of race" (161). Just as cultural practices were responsible for bringing people of different ancestries together on the continent, strictures against interracial sex and marriage worked to preserve whiteness. That is, "culture was used to shape biology" in ways that preserved the power and status of whiteness.

This is most evident in the cultural rules of *hypodescent*. In kinship terms, hypodescent is a rule of ancestry—stipulating that the child's racial status comes from the lower-status parent—designed to preserve the social status and exclusiveness of the dominant group. As Mukhopadhyay et al. explain, kinship rules linked to race "create a cultural system that ignores biology—a rigid, bipolar, bounded racial system where one is either White or Black. There is no continuum. *Biology is manipulated by culture*" [emphasis added] (170). As a result, Americans have been all too willing to take the outcomes of this process as a proof of the "naturalness" of race, when it is instead a profound example of the power of culture driving us incessantly to invest biological or genetic realms with the capacity to prove the truth of our social order.

At the genetic level, it is more important than ever to leave behind any vestige of the notion of "nature" as the fixed and essential aspects of our world or the concomitant idea that geneticists are simply depicting the world as it is. In the first regard, "culture" plays an active role in shaping genetic structures—it is hardly ancillary to what genes tell us about identity. Second, the unit of analysis matters greatly. Populations do not just present themselves to geneticists; they are selected. Genes may be identifying in terms of individuals, but identity at the next level—groups—is a different matter altogether. These, too, are not simply found existing in nature but are dynamic entities that are always in process. Genetics is central to this debate because it is analytically powerful and because it frames a version of the natural world. But we cannot expect genetics to tell us what we most want to know about race—why it matters so intensely—because race is primarily a cultural phenomenon.

CONCLUSION

The fact of basic human sameness is something anthropologists recognized a long time ago. The basis for our comparative view of humanity is the understanding that the human template is held in common. Anthropologists also long ago noticed that humans across the globe do something similar with our basic commonality—we find ways to use the natural world to develop and inscribe differences that distinguish "groups" of humans—from kin to tribes to nations. Anthropologist Claude Lévi-Strauss established decades ago that people use natural elements making totems in order to create symbolic forms of difference. "The differences between animals," Lévi-Strauss explained, "which man can extract from nature and transfer to culture are adopted as emblems by groups in order to do away with their own resemblances" (1966, 107). The basis for elaborating complex symbolic systems related to kinship, myth, and cosmology is this generation of forms for differentiating remarkably similar human beings into groups. David Hess (1995) updated this insight with the concept of *technototemism*, which specifically takes into account the ways we use science and technology in modern societies to pursue this basic cultural work of differentiating aspects of human commonality.

That we see something similar today with race does not suggest that people have always been "racist." On the contrary, the tribal peoples anthropologists have long studied, while pursuing totemic practices, typically maintained processes for incorporating the very peoples that they differentiated in this manner, often through adoption but also via marriage. The key contrast between ancient forms of totemism and the modern technototemism we deploy in relation to race—indeed the central idea behind biologically based notions about racial identities—is that they are indelible and inherent. But this insistence badly misconstrues the fundamental facts of human genetic and biological variation: Our differences are arrayed along a continuum that bears no such indelible delineations of inherent characteristics based on heredity. In this regard, for all our prowess with techniques of genetic analysis, we may be far more imprisoned by our culture than were our predecessors.

The history of scientific racism and the interested uses of biology to establish forms of racial identity (and importantly their attendant forms of inequality) as "natural" provide powerful cause to be suspicious of current and future efforts to study race scientifically. At the same time, we cannot, out of hand, regard such efforts as illicit or wrong. As Troy Duster (2003) argues, "In the rush to purge com-monsense thinking of groundless beliefs about the biological basis of racial clas-sifications, scientists have overstated the simplicity of very complex interactive feedback loops between biology and culture and social stratification" (258). In-stead of simply replacing biologically determinist or genetically reductivist claims about race with rote assertions about its social construction, Duster counsels that "we should recognize, engage, and clarify the complexity of the interaction be-tween any taxonomies of race and biological, neurophsysiological, social, and health outcomes. Whether race is a legitimate concept for scientific inquiry de-pends on the criteria for defining race, and will in turn be related to the analytical purposes for which the concept is deployed" (258–259). The statement "race is socially constructed" is accurate in terms of the history of the race concept—its origins and primary uses in the social domain—and its array of current uses as people try to link it with nature. But it also has become a kind of shorthand that will not likely be sufficient for keeping up with the ways claims are being made about race in the domains of genetics (Hartigan 2008) or with the interplay Duster mentions between the social and biological. Increasingly, instead, we need ap-proaches to biology and genetics that are able to specify and take into account the particular operations and effects of cultural dynamics. In considering both the history of racial science and current debates over possible connections between biology, genetics, and race, we confront time and again the importance of culture in these matters. Indeed, the discussion here should make it clear that "race" is preeminently a matter of culture, rather than a simple fact of nature. Given the primacy of culture in constituting race, it is time now to turn our attention fully to understanding its dynamics. The first half of this book has provided you with a grounding in the basic workings of culture in relation to race. Now, the second half of the book turns to the task of considering in detail, through the work of ethnog-raphers, how this all plays out in daily life in the United States.

CHAPTER 4

Understanding Whiteness

One of the important recent advances in the study of race has been to render whiteness visible as a subject of discussion and analysis. Whiteness is a crucial starting point for thinking about race for two reasons. First, it typically drops out of the picture in such discussions because of assumptions that *race* refers principally to "people of color"; second, the concept of race begins with notions of whiteness—the cultural construct that Europeans used to articulate their differences from the rest of the world. Understanding how and why race matters involves coming to terms with whiteness in its various manifestations. This is hardly an easy undertaking, but fortunately there is already a great deal of research on this topic, which is surveyed in this chapter.

As with any form of racial identity, whiteness is most easily grasped by working from generalities to specifics. In this regard, there are two broad points to understand about whiteness. The first is **white privilege**; the second is the tendency of whites to disavow the very notion of white collective identity. Not surprisingly, these aspects of this racial identity are interrelated, but for clarity we will consider each in turn. The most important point to acknowledge initially is that whites generally have the advantage of appearing racially *unmarked*, or "normal." In a society so profoundly shaped by race, as we saw in the previous chapters, this is an enormous privilege. Certainly, we can point to poor whites in this country who hardly seem privileged when compared to black professionals in the ranks of the upper class. But the defining feature of whiteness, in the broadest sense, is the privilege of not having to think much about race at all. The second, related point is that whites generally do not see or acknowledge this advantage, and they generally do not recognize this circumstance as a function of either culture or collective identity. Whites, by and large, attribute their successes and failures entirely to themselves as individuals and believe that they rise and fall strictly according to their own merits. Taken together, these two points construe whiteness as an interesting cultural object—as a collective identity that is powerful but largely disavowed or misrecognized by whites. The primary objective in this chapter is to discern and analyze the forms of group circumstance that fundamentally link white individuals within shared patterns of social identity.

OBJECTIFYING WHITE PEOPLE

The challenge in thinking about white people in cultural terms is to get at the racial aspects of their social identities and practices. White people in the United States, like any other social group, are heterogeneous and highly differentiated, so it is not easy to posit something general about all whites. At the same time, whites share a racially conditioned perspective on the world, which reflects experiences in a variety of social arenas where whiteness frames their interactions with others. To grasp the racial dimension of white people's lives, we need to draw on observations and research data on their attitudes, beliefs, and practices as well as social theories that analyze the operation of racial dynamics generally.

As an initial step, consider the popular book *Stuff White People Like*, by Christian Lander (2008), a spinoff from his website of the same name. In both formats, Lander compiled a series of canny observations about white people's tastes and enthusiasms as demonstrated in activities such as shopping, hosting dinner parties, and pursuing outdoor recreation. He offers these in quasi-ethnographic fashion, as if describing some exotic tribe. "Immediately following [college] graduation but prior to renovating a house," Lander intones, describing key rites of passage for this group, "white people take their first step from childhood to maturity by hosting a successful dinner party" (115). Similarly, he advises, "if you plan on spending part of your weekend with a white person, it is strongly recommended that you purchase a jacket or some sort of 'high performance' t-shirt, which is like a regular shirt but just a lot more expensive" (112). From these sarcastic vignettes, a bigger picture emerges of the web of consumerist sensibilities that characterize a certain class strata of white society.

Lander's playfully provocative list is interesting in its breadth, referencing a range of cultural domains, such as food, work, clothing, and music. For instance, he characterizes sushi as embodying "everything white people want: foreign culture, expensive, healthy, and hated by the 'uneducated'" (51). Obviously, favoring sushi does not make you white. For that matter, with the reference to the "uneducated," we see an important fault line in his objectification of whites: He is especially not talking about poor whites. Lander acknowledges that his observations are keyed on mostly left-wing, upper-middle-class whites, a subpopulation that he feels is most anxious to efface their whiteness, often in the pursuit of "exotic," "ethnic" foods, such as sushi. That is, the majority of white people do not count as the "white people" Lander is skewering. This hardly undermines his observations about white styles of consumption and socialization. But it does make obvious the need to be specific when directing attention to the racial dimension of whites' lives.

At first blush, this objective would seem quite easy, since white people have been the subject of so much social research in the United States. Whites have occupied a preeminent space in the study of American culture, starting with works such as *Middletown* (1929) and progressing through *Yankee City* (1941) and *Levittown* (1967). Yet the striking characteristic of this research tradition is that whites were so rarely studied in terms of race. The enormous amount of academic writing by anthropologists, sociologists, and political scientists on American culture has focused on whites as representing the nation, without posing the basic question of how race matters in their daily lives. Simply put, race has largely been neglected or ignored in the study of white people.

A good example of this problem comes from Constance Perin's *Belonging in America: Reading Between the Lines* (1988). Perin's ethnography provides a marvelously insightful glimpse into white suburban life, drawing on interviews with over one hundred people from Minneapolis, San Francisco, Houston, and Dallas. Her focus is on the boundary work Americans pursue in the face of ambiguous aspects of social life. But she neglects to specify the racial aspects of her subjects' daily life, because whiteness in these suburbs is largely taken for granted. In an otherwise admirable analysis of how seemingly generic categories of "friend," "neighbor," "family," and "stranger" generate exclusionary perceptions and gestures, Perin almost entirely leaves race out of the picture. I say *almost* because race crops up at certain odd moments in this book. Explaining her research results, Perin writes, "I found that *Americans* see renters, *blacks*, children, the elderly, people with low incomes, together with signs of them in housing and geographical location, as being culturally unsettling" [emphasis added] (10). Certainly unintended, this distinction between "Americans" and "blacks"—along with the accompanying generationally and class marked "others"—strikes us as glaring now. That is partly because of the ways whiteness studies have identified this exclusionary gesture by which "blacks" are posited in contrast to "Americans" as commonplace of the conceptual routines by which whites in the United States assume an unmarked, normative position and identity.

A White Creed?

One notable exception to this characterization of the previous state of social knowledge about whites is the work of Hortense Powdermaker, mentioned in Chapter 1. Powdermaker, as noted earlier, conducted one of the first ethnographic studies in the United States focused on "modern" (rather than "native") populations. She studied race relations in the town of Indianola, Mississippi (Powdermaker, Williams, and Woodson 1993 [1939]). Her fieldwork was conceived as an "experiment," designed "to apply to a segment of contemporary American society the training and methods of a cultural anthropologist and whatever perspective had been gained through fieldwork in civilizations other than our own" (xliii). Her primary interests lay in the lives and perceptions of African Americans, but, being a good ethnographer, she surveyed the whole social scene in this part of Mississippi. This broad approach led her to generate some interesting findings about white people as well.

In this locale, "typical of the small American town," Powdermaker found that the defining feature of the white community was a creed concerning the significance of race. "Certain articles of faith, constituting a creed of racial relations," she explained, "are held almost unanimously by the Whites in our community" (23). Interestingly, these beliefs crossed class lines. The primary "articles of faith" were easily summarized by Powdermaker:

> "Negroes are lazy and shiftless, and won't work unless forced to do so."
> "Negroes are congenital thieves and born liars."
> "Negroes are like children, incapable of self-discipline and forethought, living only in the moment."
> "The Negro smiles, laughs, and enjoys himself no matter what straits he's in."

The initial value in Powdermaker's findings is that she identified a set of beliefs that are at the root of the stereotypes whites—not just in the South but throughout the United States—held concerning blacks and other peoples of color. The idea that people who worked devastatingly long hours under harsh conditions for meager wages are lazy is stunning in its misconception of the world. For that matter, too, the notion that people who were continuously cheated and deceived by whites in a constant series of legal and financial matters could be construed as "liars" is mind-bogglingly distorted. But a deeper importance of Powdermaker's findings is that this is a *creed*—a set of beliefs that are powerfully interlocking and virtually unassailable from within this worldview. "Like all creeds," Powdermaker wrote, "this one does not depend upon facts and logic for its support, nor is it directly vulnerable to them" (24). But she made an additional point, too: "To say that a creed is unshaken by facts is not to say that it is unrelated to them" (ibid.). Whites were able to point to instances that supported their beliefs, even if they badly misconstrued the reality of a situation. The same remains true of stereotyping today: there are typically enough moments that seem to ratify racial misconceptions that they manage to operate actively, despite all the good research aiming to deconstruct them. This is what makes racial thinking so difficult to assail.

An important question to ask is what remains of this "white creed" today? A great deal of research documents the endurance of such beliefs, certainly through the end of the 20th century. But is this kind of thinking still widespread among whites? Survey researchers encounter an interesting difficulty in trying to answer this question, because there is a widespread recognition that *expressing* racist beliefs is socially unacceptable. So it is difficult for pollsters to be sure whether whites harbor such sentiments while responding with something other than their true feelings. Subsequently, pollsters devised a variety of ways of getting around this type of potential misrepresentation, one of which involves asking more oblique questions about race. This approach was widely used during the enormous amount of polling about race in the 2008 presidential election campaign.

Race in 2008

The big question was whether white racism would prevent Barack Obama from winning in a year when all the major trend lines pointed to an easy Democratic triumph. In order to divine white support for Obama, one approach pollsters took was to ask likely voters to respond to a set of adjectives characterizing black people. An AP-Yahoo poll (2008) conducted in late August and early September found that "one-third of white Democrats harbor negative views towards blacks—many calling them 'lazy', 'violent', and responsible for their own troubles." The use of such adjectives—and others, such as *complaining* and *boastful*—were much higher among white Republicans and independent voters. This finding suggests the creed remains active, at least among segments of white voters. But since it is not commonly shared by all whites, how do we account for its potential relevance and impact in a major event such as the 2008 presidential election?

Survey research offers a valuable glimpse into whites' racial thinking, but it often raises more questions than it answers. The pressing questions here were whether such vestiges of the "white creed" are widely shared and whether they would influence voting behavior. But polls could only offer partial answers at best. During the Democratic primaries, whites responded in various ways to Obama's campaign. When they voted against him in large numbers in states such as West Virginia, Ohio, and Pennsylvania, pollsters and pundits argued that race was a primary factor. But the exact opposite conclusion—that race did not matter—seemed borne out when Obama won white support in states such as Iowa, Wisconsin, Connecticut, Virginia, and Maryland. In the fall election, about 44% of whites voted for Obama, which was a proportion slightly larger than Bill Clinton had garnered in either of his two victories. But did this prove that race was not a factor in whites' decision-making? The question remains difficult to answer because the act of voting involves so many factors and influences. A good example is the phenomenon of "racists for Obama." This group surfaced when pollsters found that, of the significant percentage of whites (20%) who "strongly agreed" with statements such as "African Americans often use race to justify wrongdoing," one-quarter of these voters still planned to vote for Obama. Such findings suggest that white racial thinking is complex, varied, and not easy to characterize.

WHAT IS WHITENESS?

More than a creed or common set of beliefs, white people commonly share a distinctive experience of race, one that allows them generally to avoid thinking about the racial dimensions of their lives and social circumstances. What makes whiteness interesting as a social identity is that it is generally much easier to see its advantages and entailments if you are not white. This is most sharply evident in whites' being typically the least conscious of the pervasive fact of "white privilege." Peggy McIntosh (1989) captures this well in an essay titled "White Privilege: Unpacking the Invisible Knapsack." McIntosh had been very active in antiracist work for some time, but she realized that, as a white person, she had to vie against a certain kind of constant forgetting about the very thing she worked so hard to engage critically: whiteness.

This comprehension began to develop when McIntosh "realized I had been taught about racism as something that puts others at a disadvantage, but had been taught not to see one of its corollary aspects, white privilege, which puts me at an advantage" (1). It is a commonsensical realization: *If race disadvantages some, it necessarily advantages others*. But this obvious fact is not often the starting point in discussions of racism. McIntosh's insight pertains to more than matters of race; she also identifies a key feature of cultural conditioning: simultaneously to make some things obvious and others almost impossible to see. This is captured in the essay's title, which references "an invisible weightless knapsack of special provisions, maps, passports, codebooks, visas, clothes, tools, and blank checks" that comprises whiteness (1).

McIntosh's initial insight led her to write down key aspects of the ways whiteness works in daily life, in terms of the web of social assumptions and conditions that make up everyday routines. She starts by noting how many social situations are near effortlessly navigated by whites. McIntosh observes, for instance, that it is easy for her to be in the company of other whites most of the time, and she does not need to make much effort to avoid people of other races. "I can arrange my activities," she relates, "so that I will never have to experience feelings of rejection owing to my race" (1989, 3) Whites, too, can count on not having their race raise suspicions among clerks or security guards when they enter stores or use checks or credit cards. Whites generally can count on finding a place to live without the color of their skin being a negative factor, and they will typically be at least neutrally or pleasantly received by neighbors in a new locale. White people can be sure of seeing people of their race represented in depictions of our national identity (historically and currently), both in everyday media coverage and in their children's school curricula. "I can turn on the television or open the front of the newspaper," she explains, "and see people of my race widely represented" (3). Importantly, too, whites do not have to prepare their children for encounters with systematic racism, particularly random violence in the form of hate crimes.

The list McIntosh generates is quite long and runs to fifty items. These additionally include the privilege of acting rudely or inconsiderately and not having these failings attributed to race. "I can talk with my mouth full and not have people put this down to my color" (1989, 4). As well, she never has to hear her accomplishments characterized as "a credit to my race"; nor is she ever asked "to speak for all the people of my racial group." McIntosh also enumerates the many things whites take for granted in the workplace, such as generally being afforded professional guidance or having neither their failures nor successes construed in racial terms. But she also points to the advantages in seemingly random circumstances: "If a traffic cop pulls me over or if the IRS audits my tax return, I can be sure I haven't been singled out because of my race" (3). For that matter, "If my day, week or year is going badly, I need not ask of each negative episode or situation whether it had racial overtones" (4). This freedom from doubt or uncertainty related to the potential negative impacts of race is simply an enormous advantage in this society. Additionally, McIntosh notes, "I can be pretty sure that if I ask to talk to the 'person in charge,' I will be facing a person of my race" (3). These elements of white privilege that McIntosh details run the gamut from mundane to major, and they encompass a vast range of largely unconscious, taken-for-granted social activities. This list, then, gives us a glimpse both of the extent that race matters in our society and of the cultural dynamics of not recognizing or commenting on something with so much social significance.

Although McIntosh's list is an invaluable resource in thinking about whiteness, it is important to note that it is also primarily just a starting point. That is because the list is very general, and I suspect that most whites reading the list, like myself, could take exception on one or two matters. For instance, living in Texas, I have been in situations where I asked to speak to "the person in charge" and then was introduced to someone who was not white. As well, I know from my experiences in Detroit that there are places where white privilege is negligible. But we gain little from assuming a nitpicking stance toward this impressive itemization of the advantages that accrue to whiteness generally. Rather, having recognized the larger system of white privilege, we can move now to a more specific and detailed focus on the particular situations of white people in the United States.

WHITENESS AND DISCOURSE

The question of whiteness first became a subject of qualitative field research with Ruth Frankenberg's (1993) study of white women in the San Francisco Bay Area of California in the early 1990s. She interviewed thirty white women, asking them about their childhood experiences (of home and neighborhood, school and friends, etc.) in order to understand how they each "came to conceptualize people of different racial and ethnic groups, and whether [each] saw herself as racially or ethnically identified" (26). The central finding of Frankenberg's approach to whiteness is one she shares with McIntosh: the recognition that it entails a systematic series of advantages. A distinctive feature of Frankenberg's project is that it did not aim to study racism, per se, but, rather, to examine the ways whites come to think of themselves as unmarked or not racial, over and against their racial ways of viewing "people of color." The principle goal of her analysis in *White Women, Race Matters: The Social Construction of Whiteness* (1993) is to determine "the salience or meaningfulness of race in the construction of white experience" (1). This involves moving "well beyond the study of 'racial attitudes,' developing an analysis of how white people's positions in the racial order are produced through the interplay of discourses on race with the material relations of racism" (21). For Frankenberg, the study of whiteness involves grasping how whites' perceptions and experiences of the world are shaped, first, by the long history of racial advantage that contours American social landscapes, which is what she means by "material relations." Second, though, she also sees whiteness as constituted through a variety of ways of talking about everyday life that carry implicit assumptions about who is or is not "racial." For this, Frankenberg uses the term **discourse**.

The concept of discourse has been a crucial development in social inquiry over the last three decades and is initially drawn from the work of Michel Foucault (1972). In simplest terms, a discourse creates the objects of which it speaks.

Neurosis is a good example. Psychologists may debate whether Freud's conception of neurosis is a real clinical phenomenon, but the term now widely serves as a way of identifying and lumping together a range of disparate behaviors and assumptions about human nature. With the discourse of neurosis, it becomes easy to identify friends, strangers, or yourself as "neurotic," whereas, before the term was established, these behaviors did not register as particularly meaningful. Discourse analysis, then, involves the study of how people recognize and reference such objects; but more broadly it entails analyzing what can be said, by whom, and to whom. With *neurotic*, this term allows people to reference an "unconscious" realm, where "anxieties" become manifest in the form of phobic behaviors or beliefs. "You're just being neurotic," as a discursive statement, mobilizes these concepts to dismiss certain concerns or apprehensions. Often there is a particularly gendered dynamic shaping this discourse, evident when men characterize women as being "hysterical" and "overreacting." The concept of discourse lets us consider such objectifications not as simple true or false statements, but as rhetorical acts that both draw on and reproduce certain assumptions about the world and identity.

Frankenberg analyzed the discourses "through which white women seek to describe and comprehend their positions in the racial order" (1993, 20). One of the immediate payoffs from this line of inquiry is that it allowed Frankenberg to grasp the larger social context shaping her white interviewees' thoughts and perceptions. As she explains, "tracking a discursive environment shows us how inhabiting it is not a matter of individual choice, any more than is the case for material conditions" (137). This perspective moves her away from seeing racial thinking as a characteristic of some individuals and, perhaps, not others, and toward a recognition that the ways we speak and think about race are profoundly shaped by social discourses. Through her field research, Frankenberg was able to identify three such ways of talking and thinking about race: *essentialist racism, color- and power-evasive discourse,* and *race-cognizant discourse.* These discourses represent distinctive sets of assumptions and ways of talking about race that are, to some extent, mutually informing.

Ways of Not Saying Race

As we saw in the previous chapter, people invoke the notion that "race is socially constructed" in order to stress that it is a human invention rather than a naturally given way of neutrally sorting people into different groups. We take this insight further with the three discourses identified by Frankenberg, in that these represent distinct modes that render race alternately visible and invisible in relation to social identity. These discourses are the basis by which race is made meaningful in distinctive yet interrelated manners. The first discourse, *essentialist racism*, for centuries was the dominant way of talking about race in this country. This discourse features explicit statements about racial superiority and inferiority. Though it no longer is considered "acceptable" in public, this way of talking about the world remains quite active in private, as evidenced by the way whites continue to get caught making "racial remarks" in settings where they assume themselves to be safe to express such views. Frankenberg found evidence of this discourse in her interviews with white women, but it was far more muted than the other two ways of talking about race.

In contrast to essentialist racism, Frankenberg more commonly found whites engaging selectively with race. In this manner, they referenced race but also dismissed its importance. Consider the following comment from one of her interviewees: "Friends are people that you can talk to, that can understand why you feel a certain way about a certain thing, you have something in common. *And it wouldn't make any difference if they were black, green, yellow, or pink*" (1993, 149). Likely, many readers may regard this as a noble sentiment, and many of you may even have made a similar statement. The problem, Frankenberg points out, is that such statements actually serve as a means for not taking race seriously. In particular, this phrase "shifts attention away from color differences that make a political difference by embedding meaningful differences among nonmeaningful ones" (ibid.). In reality, no one is green or yellow, but people are denied loans, jobs, and places to live on the basis of being perceived as black. Evading such facts of social life may not be "racist," but it has the effect of reproducing a racial position that dismisses the reality and significance of how race structures advantage and disadvantage in society.

A similar dynamic plays out in the ways whites avoid acknowledging the power differentials race involves. Frankenberg points to seemingly innocuous statements, such as "*We are all the same under the skin*" or "*We all bleed red blood*." Both statements are certainly true, but they also function to shift attention away from the fact that social collectives, such as whites and blacks, are differently advantaged or disadvantaged by race. The stress on commonality—certainly to be valorized over blatantly racist expressions—still needs to be examined in terms of its impact on whether we recognize or take seriously the power differentials engendered by race. Taken together, these constitute *color- and power-evasive discourse*, which comprises euphemisms and partial descriptions that skirt around dimensions of race that may cause the speaker to feel uncomfortable. Often these are used to express a desire to overcome interracial hostility; the problem is, by evading direct reference to racial inequality, such gestures dodge the forms of power imbalance that are at the source of racial conflict and animosity.

In much the same way that color- and power-evasive discourse developed as a reaction to essentialist racism, so too does *race-cognizant discourse* respond to ways that whites avoid talking about differences that matter with race. In contrast to expressions of essential sameness, this discourse features an insistence "on the importance of recognizing difference, but with difference understood in historical, political, social, or cultural terms rather than essentialist ones" (Frankenberg 1993, 160). Frankenberg found that the white women in her study who were involved with antiracist work strove to speak this discourse.

Though it may be considered the most "advanced" of these three, it is hardly the case that race-cognizant discourse breaks free of the power of language to shape our social reality. Notably, Frankenberg found that these women "continued to articulate their analyses of racism in dualistic and moralistic terms" (171). The dualism lay in the belief that "either an individual is fully complicit with racism and imperialism or not complicit at all" (ibid.). Such a belief posits an impractical goal of being entirely free from racial forms of signification, which, not surprisingly, ended up generating a good deal of internal frustration for these women. As Frankenberg observed, "The absence of a language with which to analyze in sufficiently complex fashion the relationship between the white self and racism as a system of domination threatened at times to generate not just confusion, but also anger and backlash on the part of race-cognizant women" (169). Even speaking a race-cognizant discourse does not free one from the fact that race matters in ways that we often cannot control.

WHITENESS AS A SUBJECT OF STUDY

Frankenberg's (1993) work demonstrated that it was possible and useful to make whiteness a subject of social science research, even though this requires working against the grain of the cultural conditioning that makes it difficult to see, at least for many whites. Subsequent studies have ranged from attitudinal surveys to ethnographic fieldwork projects. But each was largely informed by Frankenberg's basic finding: that whiteness is "fundamentally a relational category" (231). That is, it is not defined by a certain feature or content as much as it is constituted by conventions for marking and unmarking racial identity. This can be grasped in the way each of the three discourses she identified relates to the other discourses and to established social conventions for talking (or not talking) about race in the United States. In this section we turn first to the attitudinal approach, as mobilized in Melanie Bush's book *Breaking the Code of Good Intentions: Everyday Forms of Whiteness* (2004). The following section will then feature a variety of examples of ethnographic approaches to the problem of whiteness.

Melanie Bush, an anthropologist at Aldelphi University, set out to examine her students' views of race. She did this by surveying and interviewing students at this fairly diverse campus, which is roughly 50% white, 29% black, 10% Hispanic, and 7% Asian/Pacific Islanders. But for Bush it was important to use the surveys to do more than just identify a variety of beliefs or attitudes. Instead, her goal was to understand more fully how a constellation of attitudes on a range of topics is linked to one's position in the social order. The starting point for Bush is "that there is a critical relationship between racial attitudes and social structure" (2004, 2). Beliefs do not just float nebulously about in public space; rather, as we will see, they are typically reflections of social position. For Bush, whiteness is a means of naming the social position that white people occupy in this country.

Bush initially sketches the contours of white racial thinking by pointing to a series of key findings from survey research. These include an enduring though diffuse range of negative sentiments held by whites toward people of color, particularly blacks (as revealed in political polling in 2008), as well as a clearly articulated refusal to live in areas where blacks make up more than 15% of the population. Surveys also show that many whites hold a strong sense of **racial resentment** over policies developed during the past decades to address racial inequality in this country. Perhaps most crucially, whites generally maintain a firm conviction that racial equality has already been achieved in the United States. This is the most interesting belief, in Bush's account, because it amounts to a *misperception*. If whites are strongly certain that they have similar earnings, levels of education, and equal access to health as do blacks—when the opposite has been true for decades—then there must be a social basis for these misconceptions.

Bush brings this social dimension into view by asking a simple question: Why do most whites believe we have achieved racial equality in the United States, while social and economic measures indicate otherwise? Her answer is that an interlocking series of beliefs and practices—namely, whiteness—lead whites away from recognizing the racial dimension of daily life in the United States. She finds this most manifest in beliefs about poverty, a condition that generates intense sentiments for Americans. Bush observes that "mainstream explanations about why certain people are poor tell us it is because 'they' are 'less smart,' 'genetically weak,' 'lazy,' 'angry,' 'greedy,' 'violent,' and 'unmotivated' " (2004, 13). Even though the basic cause of poverty is not having a job (or being born into a poor family), Americans generally reject structural or social perspectives in favor of moralistic views. In her interviews and surveys, Bush finds that "whites more frequently than other groups support mainstream explanations, often because of the material benefits they receive from the system (however small) and because of the belief that they too can one day achieve the 'American Dream' " (123). This finding returns us to the issues of advantage and individualism.

Recall that since we talk about race mostly in terms of disadvantage, it is challenging to grasp the logical correlate that, in turn, others must be advantaged by race. This is made more difficult to grasp by Americans' belief in the "individual" as the basic unit of the social world. These two conditions combined make the collective dimension of white identity hard to recognize or acknowledge. Bush captures this in a variety of quotes from her interviews with white students. Andrew (a white male) complains, for instance, that "people use prejudice as a huge excuse for everything in everyday life. 'This happened to me—I got a grade I didn't deserve.' If they didn't study, people are quick to say, 'He's prejudiced, or she's prejudiced.' It's sick" (2004, 72). Such a view entirely dismisses the idea that race could be a factor in how a professor regards a student. This view also reflects a social position from which one has not likely had to consider the real possibility that race is a factor in how a person is evaluated and judged by others. Another student, Gerda (a white female), insists that "everyone should be individually responsible, but people are always complaining about the system or racism or being poor" (72). This is a rather mainstream view in the United States, one that rules out of bounds any explanatory factors outside the individual. This also reflects a social position from which the idea that one might accrue advantages by race is very hard to imagine or countenance.

Bush argues that "these comments illustrate the sentiment that claims of prejudice are really excuses to avoid hard work" (2004, 72). That is, Americans' cultural conditioning to see "hard work" as the solution to most problems blinds us to the ways that people both succeed and fail, quite apart from their individual effort, as a reflection of the obviously crucial roles of social status, power, and privilege. The important point to recognize here is how our discussion has subtly shifted from a singular focus on race to encompassing the very broad features of American culture discussed in Chapter 2. In order to get at white people's beliefs about and experiences of race, we have to step back and see how these are shaped by a larger set of ideas and discourses about success and failure in the United States. This is what makes racial thinking so difficult to tackle: Often the key terms and dynamics hardly seem "racial" at all, since they have a much wider set of meanings and references. Nowhere is this clearer than with the highly valorized and championed notion of **merit**.

What is Merit?

In considering merit, two fundamental aspects of culture are important to keep in mind. The first is that *culture simultaneously affords us the ability to recognize some things while leaving us oblivious to others*. Second, *culture entails a range of interlocking ideas, sentiments, and behaviors*. Bush captures this well in the following claim. "By incorporating the language of standards, merit, individual responsibility, and civility, racially coded language provides justification for reestablishing more privileged populations as the main beneficiaries of public higher education and for significant de-funding of the public sector" (2004, 10). This claim is quite insightful, but it also requires a good deal of "unpacking" in order to grasp its import. The first point to highlight is that Bush here identifies an interlocking set of concepts and practices—most crucially, *merit* but also *individualism* and *civility*—that at times are racially inflected. She references this with the concept of *racially coded language*. This notion asserts that whites—or other racial groups, for that matter—may obscure the racial intent or meaning of an expression by couching it in seemingly neutral phrases that do not mention race but that do have racial effects.

Merit, for instance, as we will see in detail later, is no doubt an admirable ideal, but its promotion often results in advantaging whites, exactly by directing attention away from their social advantages. This brings us to the second cultural point in Bush's claim, one that expands on her discussion of social position. Whites, historically and contemporarily, are advantaged by the way public resources are redistributed in this country, even while they disparage public spending designed to ameliorate the disadvantages of people of color. This type of position—both in the social sense and in terms of polemics—is predicated on cultural practices of marking and unmarking race that leave whiteness invisible while highlighting blackness.

This all becomes clear when we consider merit as a cultural discourse, that is, as something that *brings certain objects into view and leaves other aspects or dimensions of social reality invisible*. In its most tangible form, merit is often distilled as grades or test scores, accompanied by the idea that these are an objective, neutral basis for ranking those who deserve to be elevated in our society. What typically falls from view is that wealth is a key factor in performance on tests such as the

SAT and ACT. The **wealth factor** manifests in a variety of forms, such as the advantages bestowed on those who attend private schools or those whose parents pay thousands of dollars to send them to expensive test-preparation programs, as recounted by Peter Schmidt in *Color and Money: How Rich White Kids Are Winning the War over College Affirmative Action* (2007).

When we talk about merit in regard to college admissions, we like to believe that test scores should be the deciding factor. But the wealth factor plays a crucial role here as well. What these discussions overlook are the advantages that go to children of the wealthy, in the form of extensive, expert counseling services—which outstrip those available to students in public schools—or the expensive consulting agencies, such as Ivy Wise or IvyLeagueAdmission.com, whose services include writing personal statements or letters of recommendation and personally lobbying admissions officers on the behalf of clients' children. Schmidt explains, "The wealthiest parents generally provide their children so many advantages that it can take sheer determination and a lot of effort—often in the form of years of sustained rebellion—for those kids not to end up qualified for admissions to a decent four-year college" (41).

For a variety of reasons, these advantages usually do not register when Americans talk about merit in relation to higher education. Instead of considering the massive advantages that go to children of wealthy alumni (legacy applicants) or of influential politicians, we generally complain about affirmative action. In this way, the discourse on merit *replicates the marked and unmarked aspects of race* by highlighting a policy designed to counter the disadvantages associated with race but without making plain that this all stems from a prior form of advantage—the very benefits of social class that the idea of meritocracy was designed to counter (see *The Big Test: The Secret History of the American Meritocracy*, by Nicholas Lemann [2000]). The other important aspect of race that drops out of the picture here is the resegregation of American society. After falling for years following the *Brown v. Board of Education* ruling in 1954, rates of segregation in this country have returned to the level when Martin Luther King Jr. was assassinated in 1968. A chief factor in this rise is the decision by white parents who primarily consider the racial composition of neighborhood schools in choosing where to live. Such decisions are not racist, per se, but they do reflect a fundamental contradiction of merit discourse—while we affirm that every individual should rise and fall on his or her own merits, parents will scheme and fight to give their child every possible extra advantage.

With race, this unfolds without white parents' ever having to affirm racist sensibilities. Schmidt (2007) explains, "Few of the people who contribute to segregation of society through their personal choices and political decisions express outright malice toward minorities or people with less money. Rather than talking about keeping people down, they almost always speak in terms of just wanting the best for their own children" (41). In fearing the low test scores associated with minority areas, their decisions have a racial impact without ever being accompanied by racist expressions or sentiments. It is this dimension of race that whiteness serves well to name, as in the concept of a "possessive investment in whiteness" developed by George Lipsitz (1998) to talk about how whites become invested in the social advantages of suburban life that are, in turn, predicated on racial exclusivity.

STUDYING WHITE PEOPLE IN EVERYDAY LIFE

The task of analyzing and understanding whiteness gets a good deal more complicated (and more interesting) when we shift the focus from general attitudes and positions toward a more fine-grained attention to everyday life. This is hardly surprising, since most social dynamics appear much different when examined up-close in commonplace settings. This is a basic premise of ethnographic fieldwork: we obtain a more insightful perspective on how culture works when we consider in detail daily activities in particular places. Not surprisingly, then, ethnographies of white people greatly expand and sharpen discussions about whiteness.

As an analytical concept, whiteness seems to work best as a means of talking about race in broad terms and regarding the nation as a whole. It also is effective in characterizing racial ideology generally. But how does whiteness matter in the everyday lives of white people? We could also ask what kinds of differences exist among whites—in terms of class, gender, and region—that might complicate generalizations about whiteness. This section turns to ethnographers who have gone beyond discussing whiteness in general terms to try to understand how the cultural position of particular whites shape their ability to think about race. What comes to the fore in these accounts is *the interpretive work of whites and the role of performance in understanding racial identity*, rather than seeing it as a matter of ideological conditioning.

Shifting into an ethnographic perspective allows us to maintain an attention to the ways that whiteness is unmarked (thus advantaging whites) while also considering some of the ways the racial textures of white people's lives are increasingly subject to comment and reflection. Leland Saito develops both these angles of analysis in *Race and Politics: Asian Americans, Latinos, and Whites in a Los Angeles Suburb* (1998). Saito's ethnography is set in California's San Gabriel Valley, an area that encapsulates the dynamism of recent demographic transformations linked largely to immigration. In this part of California, Japanese Americans, Chinese Americans, Mexican Americans, and whites all contend with the impacts of two very different streams of immigrants: Chinese entrepreneurs, flush with educational and economic capital, and low-wage Mexican laborers locked into the lower (but absolutely crucial) tiers of the job market. Whiteness is hardly the singular focus of Saito's study, but it is a fundamental touchstone for understanding the ways race is politicized in this fast-growing region.

Building directly on Frankenberg's (1993) study, Saito (1998) examines the "reassertion of whiteness" (39) in civic debates over the redevelopment of a shopping mall, Atlantic Square, in the city of Monterey Park. Heated issues arose in city council meetings over whether the architectural design and the featured business would reflect "Anglo culture" or "Oriental" and "Asian" influences. White residents—but also some Latinos—expressed anxiety over the social transformations that were, in their view, making life in Monterey Park seem "just like being in China" (49). Interestingly, this complaint was often voiced in relation to favored local Chinese restaurants that were changing their offerings (away from "American-style Chinese food") and clientele as many more Chinese immigrants moved to the area. In white complaints about these changes, Saito hears frustration over a loss of familiar places and experiences. Sometimes this sense of loss reflects transformations of the social position of whiteness while, at other times, signaling something more particular, as white people respond to dramatic social changes in their home places.

White Culture

Saito (1998) describes how public commentary on Atlantic Square's redevelopment revealed two types of discourses. The first reflected "a general theme that permeates U.S. society," asserting "that Americanness equates whiteness" (39). This discourse, Saito argues, unfairly "negates the immigrant history of the United States and presence of ethnic places throughout the country" (49). For whites, ethnicity is largely symbolic, something "freely chosen and unacknowledged in most aspects of their lives" (40). From this perspectives, "cultures become ethnic in comparison to whiteness, and what is on the surface an appreciation for the richness of another culture is in reality a reflection of racial hierarchies" (51). The second discourse that Saito detects more deeply reflected the particular dynamics in Monterey Park, revealing "how whiteness is experienced and expressed in culture and language of everyday life when the defense and reassertion of whiteness becomes explicit, challenged by the growing demographic and economic presence of Chinese immigrants" (40). Saito finds much to be critical of in each of these discourses, especially in terms of the way they each rely on unmarked and marked assumptions about race. But with the latter perspective, Saito recognizes a certain understandable confusion and uncertainty as whites "usually for the first time in their lives . . . feel economically superfluous and culturally marginal" (50).

Saito (1998) comes to characterize these two discourses in terms of a distinction between "whiteness" and "white culture." In this contrast Saito both acknowledges and critiques whiteness scholars such as Frankenberg and David Roediger. Through his ethnographic fieldwork, he similarly finds that "whiteness supports racial hierarchies" (51) in Monterey Park. But he argues that "white culture" does something different, performing a role that is unacknowledged in whiteness studies:

> White culture . . . anchors people to what is familiar, comforting, and everyday. The daily routine of leaving the house to engage in conversation with a friendly shopkeeper as one buys thread, dropping by a local restaurant after a city council meeting for a cup of coffee and a rehash of the evening's topics, and a special dinner at a small, neighborhood Chinese restaurant run by a helpful Chinese American family are everyday activities situated in a life enriched by many forms of culture associated with whites. (51)

This observation leads Saito to argue for the importance of distinguishing between the racial dynamics that operate at a general level in the nation at large—reproducing a racial hierarchy defined by white dominance—and the *local experience of place* for white people that mixes and confuses defense of this dominance with efforts to maintain the familiar and routine. This may seem like an apologist position for whiteness, but it actually reflects a considered insight into how antiracist efforts might be advanced. In this regard, Saito criticizes abstract generalizations about whiteness for "underestimating the power, resiliency and the meanings" (1998, 52) that whites attach to place. "To develop strategies to dismantle the racial privileges of whiteness," Saito concludes, "the affirmative and beneficial aspects of white culture might be recognized" (ibid.). In this suggestion, Saito points to a means for disaggregating white people from whiteness.

Whites and Place

We can argue over whether the contrast between *whiteness* and *white culture* is as helpful as Saito believes. For myself, I think the concept of *white culture* does not make the contrast he intuits sufficiently clear. While the term is certainly evocative, I think that it still does something similar to the concept *whiteness* by reifying racial identity. The more important point is to work with the cultural dimension generally rather than trying abstractly to formulate a too-easily generalizable notion of *white culture*. An example of such attention to the cultural dimension of whites' attachment to place is developed by Roger Sanjek (1998) in his study of Queens, New York. As with Saito's ethnography, the backdrop to Sanjek's fieldwork are major demographic shifts related to immigration, but an added element in his account involves the impact of *white flight*. The dramatic changes in the Elmhurst-Corona community of Queens reflect both the arrival of Latino and Asian immigrants and the mass exodus of whites from this part of New York. In 1970 the population of this working- and middle-class community was 98% white; in 1990 whites composed only 18% of Elmhurst-Corona residents. The important aspect that white flight introduces is that it leaves in its wake a residual population of whites who are compelled to think concretely about what joins them to and distinguishes them from their new neighbors.

Sanjek's ethnography, *The Future of Us All: Race and Neighborhood Politics in New York City* (1998), is as much about the dynamics of big-city democracy and the impact of recent economic developments as it is about the role of race in urban America. Because of this, we can see race not as an abstract composite of attitudes and beliefs, but as one texture among many shaping people's perceptions and experiences of place. Notably, in this portion of Queens, which he describes as "an ethnic cross-section of the planet" (1), Sanjek finds that local political structures (particularly city-established boards called *community districts*), with their established forms of public rituals and social interactions, provide a basis by which whites develop relations with immigrant in-movers. Civic political organizations designed to represent neighborhood interests become meeting grounds in which residents begin to recognize and articulate commonalities across racial boundaries. This is striking because such organizations served the opposite function as the neighborhood first began to integrate in the 1960s.

Though white racial identity was not a basis for political mobilization in the 1980s or 1990s, Sanjek stresses that "race *was* an issue when whites mobilized to keep out public housing in the 1960s" (253). The key difference is that, two decades later, as the community's "political field was becoming increasingly multiracial, the established white population now understood that local quality of life was affected as much by white business owners, police, school board members, mayors, absentee landlords, organized crime groups, and developers as by anyone else" (253). In the interim, those whites who stayed in Queens came to think differently about race, placing it in the larger context of the array of economic, political, and social forces shaping urban life rather than identifying with it in an essential sense. This shift allowed whites in Elmhurst-Corona to recognize that many of their problems were not caused by immigrants but by other whites.

One of the values of Sanjek's ethnography is that he frames how this locale was affected by other long-term developments, such as the decline of manufacturing in the city and the concomitant rise of the speculative economy (focused on the FIRE sector: finance, insurance, and real estate) as well as repercussions from the city's massive, ongoing fiscal crises, which generate numerous quality-of-life problems in neighborhood New York. These economic transformations and trends played out in the heightened salience of class identity in the city, which both opened and revealed huge rifts within whiteness. Sanjek (1998) summarizes the outcome:

> The stayers recognized differences between themselves and other groups of whites: the Manhattan elites who formulated economic and governmental policies affecting the neighborhood; local business proprietors, police, and school board members who lived outside of Community District 4 [in Elmhurst-Corona] but influenced its quality of life; recent European immigrants, particularly Italians, Greeks, and (by the 1990s) Russians; upper-middle-class "liberals," mainly residents of Manhattan; and "yuppies," the beneficiaries of the 1980s boom. (229)

Each of these forms of difference among whites undermines the singularity that characterized invocations of white identity in the tumultuous battles over integration in the 1960s. For this reason, Sanjek talks about neither whiteness nor white culture but aims instead to grasp the cultural aspect of whites' relationship to place and to each other.

What Do Whites Have in Common?

Sanjek asks an important question in his ethnography: What is it that the remaining whites of Elmhurst-Corona share in common? Part of what they share is a linked set of interests in the neighborhood, which puts them in direct conflict with whites outside the area. Sanjek relates how resentment "simmered and occasionally boiled over between Elmhurst-Corona whites and white local business owners who resided outside Community District 4, white police who lived outside New York City, and the white School Board 24 members from other neighborhoods who controlled Elmhurst-Corona schools" (1998, 244–245). But more fundamental than these animosities or resentments, whites in this neighborhood shared a common sense of attachment to place, one that was textured by race but not reducible to it. "What white residents shared most was local knowledge, common experience, and lifelong memories. They viewed their streets and neighborhood through layers of reminiscence, which surfaced in everyday conversation" (242). As whites, they once defined that sense of belonging in terms of race; but as whites now, in a place where "people and languages ran into each other in a mix never seen before" (ibid.), the racial associations were dissolving and transforming. Sanjek sees this shift most keenly in the way that "the boundary around 'American' could shift as whites used the term" (254) increasingly in reference to their multi-hued neighbors as well as to themselves.

So how do we name this shared sensibility among whites? Sanjek (1998) tries to locate it in a general notion of culture rather than in a specific form, as with the concept of *white culture*. He explains, "these understandings and routines constituted what anthropologists call 'culture'—a way of life that was reproduced daily along predictable pathways and in ordinary interactions, [which] grew more meaningful over years and decades, and at the same time was continually adjusted to new circumstance" (242). Sanjek's assessment points to a certain bifurcation in the analysis of race in relation to white people: Do we pursue it singularly in terms of race, as with white culture, or, rather, do we try to see how race is constituted and negotiated as part of a broader cultural dynamic by which whites (and people of color) articulate a sense of belonging to place? The advantage of the latter approach is that it offers an opportunity to examine race as it melds with and weaves through the textures of daily life, rather as an abstraction. As well, focusing in on the cultural dynamics of particular places allows us to be much more attentive to the ways racial meanings and identities are susceptible to change, because places are rarely static.

Sanjek envisions these developments as representing "the future of us all," as the demographic changes in California, Texas, and New York come to characterize places throughout the United States. In that regard, it is easy—too easy, actually—to misread aspects of the transformations in Queens. For all that seems laudable in Elmhurst-Corona, it is not the case that "race doesn't matter" there. This is most strikingly evident in the fact that blacks continue to be excluded from housing in the area, certainly by some white landlords but also by recent in-movers. This underscores the point that race in the United States continues to be defined by the polar opposition of blackness and whiteness. But even among residents, race remains an undercurrent, affecting people's daily lives and their differential experiences of the city. This plays out in discussions in community forums, where whites develop an "insistence upon a nonracial discourse among residents" (254). Whites crave this, Sanjek conveys, because such a discourse would "dissolve a racial definition of whites that connected them to whites who supported policies they opposed, especially those that a person of color might label 'racist' " (255). The problem Sanjek points to in this desire is that an inability to talk about race "silences 'minority' expressions of issues affecting persons because they were not white" (255). Even though residents found ways of relating that breached racial boundaries, the significance of race in the larger world all around them continued to matter greatly.

Whites in Different Places

Has Sanjek really glimpsed "the future of us all" in the demographic changes in Queens? This question requires a comparative perspective, one that considers, first, whether these transformations are representative of developing trends regarding race and, second, whether his framing of the cultural aspects of white identity are applicable elsewhere. An excellent place to turn for this comparative perspective is an ethnography by Pamela Perry, *Shades of White: White Kids and Racial Identity in High School* (2002).

Perry's ethnography serves this role well because it is structured comparatively, providing a view of whites in two very different social settings—one where whites are demographically dominant and another where they are a small minority. Perry conducted her fieldwork in the San Francisco/Oakland Bay Area. Her research is part of a significant subfield within cultural anthropology: the ethnography of schooling. This approach is particularly valuable with race because it affords insights into processes of socialization that involve both peer groups and institutional authority.

Perry pursues a comparative approach in order to consider the question of how well generalizations about whiteness or white culture work in discussing the particular social circumstances of white people. The crux of her comparison involves class. The two schools in which she conducted her fieldwork are a study in contrast. Valley Grove High is located in a wealthy suburb with a median household income of $100,000 in 2000. This suburb is also 93% white. Social life in this community, Perry finds, is predicated on white cultural norms and expectations that "saturate" everyday life. She pairs this location with Clavey High, a central-city school where the poverty rate is high. The median income in this area was only $37,000 in 2000. Also, African Americans constitute over half the school's population, with Asian Americans comprising just under one-quarter of the students; only 12% of the students are white and 8% are Hispanic. Juxtaposing these two schools allows Perry to study whites alternately in zones where whiteness is largely unmarked and in a setting where it is hardly normative.

Perry's aim is to understand how social circumstances (and, implicitly, class backgrounds) shape whites' racial thinking. In part this involves observing how race plays out in the daily relations in school, as in how students form cliques, what physical spaces they claim or contest on the grounds and in the cafeteria, and how they interact in the classroom. But her approach also features a good deal of interviewing. Proceeding in comparative fashion, she posed the same basic question to white kids in each setting: How would you describe white American culture? In Valley Grove, the suburban school, white students had a difficult time answering. Basically, they consistently drew a blank. The typical replies were "I don't know," "Nothing," and "It means nothing." Perry finds that this reflects the vast extent to which whiteness was taken for granted and informs the assumptions permeating social life. Whites at Valley Grove, she explains, "fall into a cognitive gap" (2002, 78) when they are explicitly asked to describe white American culture. Because it is assumed to be "normal" rather than "racial," they struggle to name its features.

Specifying White Identity

In contrast, Perry (2002) writes, "every white kid I spoke to at Clavey had something to say about white American culture" (84). "White," like other racial identities at this central-city school, requires and provokes a lot of thought. Sometimes they described white as an arbitrary ascription, as a sort of matter-of-fact characterization of certain people; but some students instead characterized it in detailed terms as a highly heterogeneous identity. Other students construed it as a sort of "lack" or absence, as just an amorphous social aggregation without community, culture, or "pride." These responses reflect a tension between "white" as an impersonal social ascription and as a personal or cultural category with which one can identify. Taken together, they also highlight another contrast with Valley Grove: white students at Clavey produced a variety of elicitations, rather than the consistently uniform replies of the suburban whites.

Perry does not try to overdraw these contrasts. She notes, for instance, that central-city whites also had some initial difficulty in answering this question. The significant comparative points for her lie in the range of variation of whites' thoughts on the subject at Clavey and their tendency not to see whiteness as entirely lacking content. This contrast was mirrored in the respective characterization of "minorities," who, in Valley Grove were largely characterized as a homogeneous mass, whereas at Clavey whites had much more specific responses when asked to describe minority groups. Another point she stresses is that white kids at Clavey were often provisional in their responses: "Just *how* students defined white identity and culture in a given moment depended on feelings and sentiments associated with how they defined racial-ethnic differences at that time" (2002, 121). That is, these whites not only varied from their schoolmates in how they appraised racial identity; their own thoughts on the matter fluctuated, sometimes even in the course of a day, in conjunction with the ways they experienced race in social interactions and in classroom discussions.

The comparison between these two schools and the variation within Clavey led Perry to conclude that white students' sensibilities about racial identity are conditioned by three types of social processes. First and foremost are the *different types and proximities of interracial associations*. Where interracial interactions are commonplace, race becomes the subject of both reflection and discussion in a way that destabilizes assumptions about marked and unmarked forms of identity. "The unconscious construction of white as norm was most prevalent at Valley Grove because whites there had little to no association with racial difference and found their social-cultural milieu to confirm their normalness" (2002, 83). In a related manner, it mattered very much *how white youths constituted their relationships to people of color*. In the suburban school, many whites were into rap and hip-hop, but their active consumption of this music did not lead them to reflect much on what constituted either whiteness or blackness. In the central city, whites' daily interactions with students of color provided frequent opportunities to think about the significance of race in their own lives. The third critical process that shaped their thinking about race operated at *the institutional level and involved the ways racial and ethnic differences were structured by school practices.*

One of the important points Perry stresses is that even though whites at Clavey were a minority, the school, as an institution, embodied broader social assumptions about race. Though whiteness was far from dominant in peer-to-peer interaction, it was inscribed and reproduced in routine ways in the high school. These practices included the tracking of students—a fundamental feature of American education—by separating them according to the perceived likelihood of academic achievement. As in most schools in this country, this resulted in the white kids at Clavey being largely tracked into the high-achievement classes, while students of color were steered toward vocational education offerings. Whiteness, too, was manifest and reproduced in world history courses that focused primarily on Europe and the West. But a more subtle process reaffirming a normative sense of whiteness occurred in the school's effort to promote greater awareness about race through a series of "cultural assemblies." These events, featuring the cultural characteristics of particular racial and ethnic identities, had the effect of making students of color "more culturally visible" (2002, 130) while making the racial identity of whites more difficult to recognize and discuss.

Keeping White Identity in View

With these three social processes, Perry provides us with a developed perspective on how white racial identity manifests and either becomes the subject of discussion or slips into the background of powerfully informing assumptions about normative identities. In at least two of these processes, the particular dynamics and social contours of location matter a great deal, as in the ways interracial associations provide opportunities to make an elusive construct such as whiteness subject to discussion. But it is also clear from Perry's account that locations are always embedded in larger contexts—in this case, the institutional setting of school practices and routines. Beyond the institutional setting, the larger context of the school either can become increasingly nebulous, as when we refer to American society in general, or it can be drawn into quite concrete appearances in the form that students most often referenced—popular culture. As in any high school in the United States, the larger world manifests in the form of styles drawn from the realms of music and fashion, providing enormously varied material from which students performed and played with racial matters.

In both schools, clothing, hairstyles, sports, body piercing, and street language are the means by which "young people claim personal power and mark a multiplicity of identities" (Perry 2002, 104), such as peer group, gender, class, and racial identities. In these media, students cultivated indirect and symbolic forms for exploring and expressing a sense of identity. For whites, these activities were starkly different in the suburban setting and in the central-city school. As just mentioned, white kids at Valley Grove were big fans of hip-hop. But this engagement with racially marked music hardly generated much conscious thought about either whiteness or blackness. In consuming this music, Perry finds, "they wanted the characteristics of blackness, namely to be 'cool,' tough, or hip" (110). Although these symbols are valued and perhaps positive, they serve primarily to reinforce stereotyped notions about race.

The situation was quite different for whites in the central city. "At Clavey, the same cultural forms that Valley Grove youth freely sampled were charged with racial-identity meanings" (112) that were deployed in the form of active boundary construction and maintenance among and between students. These musical forms were not mere symbolic constructs at Clavey, but the material that real people used in active ways to constitute palpable lines around racial identities. Whites at Clavey "faced sanctions that came with crossing racial boundaries and not sticking with your kind" (131), which served to reinforce rather than undermine the sharp lines delineating racial identity. The result is that although white students at Clavey were more articulate about racial matters, they were hardly freed from the strictures that link race to identity.

This finding may seem pessimistic—even whites, in the position of a racial minority, who think consciously about race are not able to escape its incessant significance. But since race is a pervasive feature of our social landscape, why should we imagine that individual cultural activities would simply dissolve that larger context? I will return to this matter of how race informs our social land-scape, particularly with regard to whiteness, in just a moment when I reference my own ethnographic study of white people. But, by way of concluding this discussion of Perry's research, it is worth dwelling on a somewhat surprising finding she de-velops in relation to the question of identity and social context. This finding relates back to the question of culture. Perry (2002) makes the point that "experience is not something outside of culture that is found reflected in it or resonating out of it, but the cultural activity itself" (126). This view leads her to recognize the way students across the racial spectrum constituted a unique "multiracial self" (128) via their uses and deployments of popular music.

Performing Race

Perry (2002) found that at both schools "the cultural identities of white, black, and other students of color were dialogically shaped with respect to one another" (132). That is, these identities are relationally defined, often in discussion of kids' affini-ties for a variety of styles, particularly in relation to music. These dialogues were informed by the type of "competencies" kids developed in relation to racially marked musical genres and styles. At Clavey, "whites responded to external ascrip-tion by either adopting them or exercising self-determination and defining white-ness in their own terms" (129). In the face of characterizations of "indie rock" or "heavy metal" genres as white music, they varyingly respond by affirming the as-sociation or refusing it in search of alternative representations of white identity. This type of dynamic, which also played out with other musical styles, amounted to an "us-them dialogue" about race. This dialogue, in turn, was bracketed by other dialogues, as in one where the "self" is populated by the "other." In such dialogues, carried out through the medium of popular music, "whites carry the 'eyes' of blacks, Asians, Latinos, and others in their views of themselves" (122). Another dialogue featured fluency with the range of racially marked forms of music, where cross-cultural competencies with identifying features amounted to a kind of "multiracial self."

This dialogue worked with the polarizing constraints of racially marked items from popular culture. Perry sketches this landscape as a series of *claims* and *generalizations* that students at Clavey relied on and deployed regarding parallel sets of racially opposed activities:

> Black students speak Ebonics, listen to rap, dress certain ways, play basketball, braid their hair; whites students speak Standard English, listen to rock, dress certain ways, play lacrosse, let their hair go grunge. These distinctions to an extent *forbade* black youth from speaking Standard English, listening to rock, or playing lacrosse, and white youth form speaking Ebonics, listening to rap, and playing basketball. Still these competencies were available to all youth. (130)

The "multiracial self" develops out of the ways students imbibe these stereotypes and variously perform them, at times reproducing them while on other occasions disputing and disproving them. With this concept, Perry discerns how the active practice of identity construction involves racially marked materials that individuals sometimes adhere to and at other times refashion or reposition. Whites, Perry found, "for the most part kept their black and other cultural competencies shelved until the right time or place to bring them forward" (2002, 131). At Clavey, they faced many direct and blunt interdictions from black schoolmates if they seemed to be appropriating "black" expressive forms. So they demonstrated competencies in these realms on select occasions, when there were opportunities for effacing charged boundaries. These were moments when race assumed a tangible form that allowed it to be played with and negotiated, in ways that revealed "racial difference and sameness as interdependent" (132).

LOCATING WHITENESS IN THE SOCIAL LANDSCAPE

Perry's ethnography points to several important aspects about racial identity in relation to whites: *it is dynamic in reflecting social location, institutional practices, and the cultural activity of using expressive media to sound out and explore the significance race holds.* Each of these points moves us away from generalizations about whiteness or white culture and toward a more specific attention to the ways white people in particular social contexts make sense of race. In such a shift, the various discussions about whiteness continue to have bearing, but the relevance of generalizations about race decline in value as analytical aides in understanding cultural dynamics that shape the meaning of race in particular situations. This became apparent to me in the course of my ethnographic work in Detroit, Michigan (Hartigan 1999).

Like Perry, I aimed for a comparative approach by examining whites in three distinct class neighborhoods: an inner-city zone, a nearby area undergoing gentrification, and a working- and middle-class community on the city's far Westside. Each of these neighborhoods variously registers the effects of the cataclysmic changes linked to white flight that have devastated Detroit. Between 1950 and 1990, over 1.4 million whites left Detroit, fleeing racial integration, taking money and jobs with them, and leaving the city's tax base severely crippled. The inner-city neighborhood where I worked, Briggs, once was home to over 24,000 people; today fewer than 3,000 residents dwell on city blocks that have returned to prairie grass, where only scattered homes remain in the wake of fires and the decay that follows abandonment. A similar situation was shaping up in nearby Corktown, until whites from small towns and suburbs began moving in, drawn by the area's proximity to downtown and its somewhat better preserved stock of historical houses. The third neighborhood, Warrendale, survived the worst of the city's riots and industrial decline, but the whites there fear that the demographic changes advancing on their borders will make the community look like much of the rest of Detroit—mostly black and poor.

Places Shape the Meaning of Race

A central finding from my fieldwork in Detroit is that *the meaning of race varies from place to place, reflecting the localized impacts of economic shifts, demographics, and class compositions.* Race matters in starkly different ways for whites in each of these neighborhoods. For poor whites in Briggs, race is alternately mundane or volatile. On one hand, these whites have little invested, economically or socially, in this community; not owning homes, they have little anxiety over property values or maintaining social appearances for the neighbors' sake. So, unlike whites throughout Detroit who fought against racial integration of neighborhoods and schools in the 1960s and 1970s, they literally have little to defend. They lack what George Lipsitz (1998) calls "the possessive investment in whiteness," which is a defining feature of vastly white suburbs. At the same time, as poor people in a desperately depressed city, where rates of crime and violence are high, race is easily and sometime randomly made a flashpoint between themselves and black neighbors, friends, or strangers. Race is waiting there for someone to "make something of it," in a way that reflects the basic uncertainty about life in this blown-out part of Detroit.

For whites in Corktown, race is a very different matter. First, because of their class status (mostly professionals: bankers, lawyers, architects, etc.), they are largely able to avoid the type of random encounters on the street with poor blacks that can become flashpoints for whites in Briggs. They are isolated from the street, too, because they pour so much time and effort into their homes. Then, in contrast to the working- and middle-class whites, they are not concerned that the "quality" of local schools will be affected by its racial demographics. In Corktown, white professionals tend to have careers rather than children; the few who do have children send them to private schools rather than to the Detroit public schools, so they are insulated from racial encounters in the emotionally charged realm of childrearing. This is not to suggest that race was entirely removed as an element in their lives. Many of them told me stories about being "the only white person" in meetings with city officials or in large social events downtown. These whites achieved a certain dexterity around race largely predicated on avoiding talking about it altogether. One resident even explained to me his strategies for changing the subject "when the R-word comes up."

Whites in Warrendale had been somewhat similarly isolated from racial encounters in their predominantly white neighborhood abutting the wealthy, white suburb of Dearborn. But the neighborhood is changing slowly, with rates of home-ownership declining as renters increasingly occupy houses left empty as retirees move out of the city. There is a racial element to this shift, for the numbers of blacks in Warrendale is steadily increasing. But white residents conveyed to me a deeper concern over "white trash" renters than with black middle-class in-movers. This process would have probably proceeded without notice if it had not been for the controversy over the Malcolm X Academy and its Afrocentric curriculum discussed in Chapter 2. The clash of white neighbors against black city officials riveted a city that had thought racial conflicts over schools were long a thing of the past.

The whites in Warrendale who opposed the academy—hardly a majority of the residents—did so for a variety of reasons: They were upset over having no input in the selection process (the city refused to see it as a "neighborhood" school, and their children were not given applications to attend) and over the fact that the school's student base was mainly drawn from wealthy families rather than serving the purported target population of "at risk" inner-city youth. They also felt that the curriculum involved faith-based elements, such as "ancestor worship," which arguably are banned from public schools. They also criticized the school as an effort to "resegregate" black children through the use of a "separatist," "black nationalist" ideology. Regardless of their concerns, in media coverage of the school, residents appeared and were cast strictly as "white racists" opposing a "black school." In their encounters with school officials and reporters, they could not manage to speak over the obvious significance of white racialness.

The intriguing aspect of this media spectacle is that black city and school officials—as well as the issue of the school's curriculum—were *racially unmarked*: They spoke with bureaucratic power and authority and radiated the trappings of professional status. In contrast, white residents—with their angry, emotional voices and unpolished speaking styles that reflected working-class backgrounds—found their comments and actions immediately read as racially significant. Whether they were motivated by racist impulses or not, they could not shift public debate from their *racially marked* position as "white racists." They could not make their views heard over the apparent significance of their racial identities.

Each of these settings in Detroit reflects the crucial role that place and class identity play in shaping how race matters. There is no "white culture" that commonly linked these residents across the stark divides of class, nor does the characterization of "advantaged" apply equally to whites in these neighborhoods. Poor whites in Detroit's inner city have little advantage based on race, though whites in the adjacent gentrifying neighborhood clearly do. In contrast with these groups, Warrendale whites were encountering, for the first time, the dissonance of having their words and thoughts reductively framed entirely in terms of race—hardly a condition of advantage, but certainly not entirely disadvantaged either, at least in terms of racial identity. The fundamental way that *class textures whites' experiences or the role that place plays in shaping the kind of social interactions that feature race* should not be taken as discrediting efforts to talk about whiteness in general terms. Rather, these settings stand as a glimpse of the density of cultural dynamics shaping racial matters in the complicated, nuanced realm of everyday life.

The particulars of place and the role of culture manifest in the *interpretive repertoires* that these white Detroiters fashioned and relied on in making sense of race. These repertoires were somewhat analogous to the ways the high school students at Clavey and Valley Grove made sense of race by drawing on racially marked material from popular culture. In each setting, we can see whites engaged in an active process of interpreting the significance of race. The key distinction is that the repertoires of white Detroiters were largely place specific, reflecting the range of encounters they had in a variety of social settings where racial meanings could alternately be active or fairly muted. These repertoires were filled with gossip and rumors about what neighbors and strangers had done as well as being inflected by incidents that were part of the city's historical and current efforts to come to terms with race. These repertoires—each contoured by class and social position rather than by a common ideological orientation—provided the basis by which whites in Detroit actively considered and made sense of the role that race played in their own experiences and the lives of people around them.

CLASS AND RACE: BRINGING GREATER SPECIFICITY TO WHITENESS

As a subject of social science research, whiteness is still an emergent topic, especially in comparison with blackness, as we will see in the next chapter. Still, there are some clear trends emerging, as described briefly shortly. Generally, this is an area that has enormous room to pursue new questions or to pose again, in new settings, the inquiries addressed earlier.

The following ethnographies feature a primary attention to the ways that class contours white racial identity. But these works largely pursue a detailed attention to the situations of whites in particular class positions rather than refining or extending a comparative perspective on class differences among whites in how race matters. Although some works, such as Lorraine Kenny's *Daughters of Suburbia: Growing Up White, Middle-Class and Female* (2000), pursue further Frankenberg's initial attention to well-off whites, more researchers have turned to studying working-class and poor whites, in part to develop a more fine-grained assessment of relative aspects of racial privilege and racist sentiment. Regardless, these ethnographers similarly find that, as expressed by Kenny, "whiteness is not only about race. Nor is race simply about skin color" (2000, 7). Rather, these ethnographers consistently identify specific dynamics of location that complicate generalizations about white racial identity.

Poor Whites

Sociologist Kirby Moss stands out in this regard for his notable ethnography *The Color of Class: Poor Whites and the Paradox of Privilege* (2003). As the title suggests, Moss made poor whites his central focus as he examined how their marginal social and economic circumstances inflected their racial identities. His ethnography "empirically explores the seldom considered experience of poverty and social class differences through the lives of urban, impoverished, sporadically employed White women, men, and high school students who, in defining their experiences, help deconstruct immutable assumptions of normative Whiteness and class privilege in general" (2). Moss is particularly deft at this deconstructive work because, as a black researcher seeking out poor whites, he was able to confront the various paradoxes of race and class directly. Moss explains, "My goal was to record how people responded not only to my presence but also to the uncomfortable exposure of their own fragmented and contradictory selves within Whiteness" (13). Regarding this latter point, Moss particularly attended to how "poor white students navigate through categories of assumptions" in school as they are alternately included in and excluded from middle-class forms of whiteness and varyingly "believing and disbelieving in the ideals of achievement ideology" (42). This vantage point leads Moss to critique the very starting point of whiteness studies—the assertion that it is an unmarked identity—because it relies on generalizations that practically prevent a detailed attention to the specific contents (especially in terms of class) of white racial identity.

One of the strengths of Moss' approach is that he studies a series of sites—homes, workplaces, bars, and so forth—rather than just concentrating on an institutional setting, such as schools. He also has two chapters on "encounters," in which he conveys a range of reactions to his class status (carrying "a credentialed shield" as doctoral student) in the social realms of poor whites. Some of these are predictably hostile encounters, as when he ventures into a "roughneck" bar. But other encounters are surprising, partly stemming from the fact that Moss, in pursuing this fieldwork, is returning to his hometown of "Midway"—a pseudonym for a midsized, Rust Belt city that has seen better economic days. Given this background, he spoke fluently the local terms of place and belonging, and he was also able to identify "many common experiences low-income Whites and I seemed to share in our paradoxical connection to privilege" (2003, 94). Moss found that "many of the poor Whites and I have an awkward affinity because we share a familiar marginal existence, but under vastly different assumptions" (98). Moss takes as his task in this ethnography to trace out the contours of those shared affinities and contrasting assumptions.

Moss' insights about the marginal status of poor whites in relation to the larger body of whiteness are borne out by Edward Morris' ethnography on white students in a majority-black, urban Texas middle school. In *An Unexpected Minority: White Kids in an Urban School* (2006), Morris highlights both the "surprising meanings" of whiteness at Matthews School and the maddening fact that "the typical rewards of whiteness remain largely intact" (2) in this locale. He assembles this perspective by selecting three foci at Matthews: disciplinary procedures, teacher perceptions of students, and student interaction and peer culture. These respective domains allow him to analyze, in turn, policies that reproduce white privilege, settings in which whites are ostensibly disadvantaged by their race, and then interactions in which students, white and black, actively transform racial meanings and boundaries associated with whiteness.

For all Morris' interest in the possible insights to be gained from studying whites in a minority position, he avoids a crucial pitfall of whiteness studies—relegating peoples of color to the edges of analysis—by attending carefully to the ideas and practices that inform disciplinary procedures in the Matthews School. Administrators and teachers concerned with "ladylike" behavior on the part of African American girls—while being anxious over threatening oppositional behavior and dress from African American boys—"frame these students as inappropriately masculine or feminine" (2006, 86), diverging from norms that, Morris argues, are "subtly centered on hegemonic notions of whiteness and middle-classness, constructing white privilege" (86–87). This argument is intriguingly paralleled by an account of how white and black teachers perceive differently the behaviors and backgrounds of the school's few white students. In contrast to black teachers, who viewed white students generally as middle class, white teachers regarded these same students in highly stigmatized terms as *trailer trash* or *white trash*—a term that loomed large in Moss' research. "The whiteness of these students," Morris reports, "did not act as a form of privilege in the eyes of most white teachers. Instead, they viewed white students in this setting as somewhat anomalous and extended more positive attention to students of other racial groups" (74). The dynamics informing the perceptions held by white teachers are complex, but they hinge centrally on how class distinctions inflect racial perceptions and meanings, even of a dominant form such as whiteness.

His attention to the disparate meanings related to whiteness affords Morris some important insights about race generally. He finds that "the importance lies not in race as an essence, but in how race acquires meanings in different contexts and how people's racialized experiences shape their development and understanding of these meanings" (2006, 77). Even though structured forms of privilege and subordination are formidable aspects of the social landscape, the significance of race still hinges both on the interpretive work of racial subjects and on the varied meanings of race, which can be rendered pliable and novel in certain circumstances. Morris observes these students "performing" racial identities, which in turn "partially transformed many expectations and boundaries that typically distinguish white from nonwhite" (127). This leads Morris to conclude that "the meaning and future of whiteness and race relations in the United States" (14) will be worked out increasingly following place-specific dynamics.

Working-class Whites

Maria Kefalas also pursues a place-specific analysis of class forms of white identity, in her ethnography *Working-Class Heroes: Protecting Home, Community, and Nation in a Chicago Neighborhood* (2003). Kefalas mirrors aspects of "Midway," as described by Moss, but this is a neighborhood fighting against the tide of urban decay that was spreading through southwestern Chicago. Where do these whites draw the battle line? On their lawns. Kefalas describes the class aesthetics of lawn care and interior decorating that evidence "a tangible, material expression of a distinctly working-class sensibility" (96). She astutely relates that, since "it is not possible for working-class homeowners to distance themselves physically or economically from poverty, they create *symbolic* distances and erect *moral* boundaries instead" (100). Compare this to the white residents of gated communities, who are able to erect more powerful material boundaries—and "nicer" ones too—against the threats of poverty and racial mixing.

An important contribution of Kefalas' work is its steady attention to racism. Kefalas depicts nuanced ethnographic subjects as they grapple with the emotionally charged subjects of racial and class identity. She documents their racism, detecting racist sentiments even in comments designed to deflect such charges, yet she doesn't reduce them to being only ciphers for racist ideology. Residents are alternately astute and myopic about race. They critique the class politics that directs racial integration primarily toward working-class communities and away from wealthy white areas; as well, they discern a tight correlation between integration and the decline of property values in this part of Chicago. Yet they are oblivious to their racial privileges as whites and to the institutional forms of disinvestment that have shaped the expanding "ghetto." More profoundly, they are unable to recognize the emergence of a critical mass of alienated, destructive young white people in the neighborhood, because they are so steadfast in equating signs of disorder and violence with poor blacks.

Kefalas' analysis is both sympathetic and critical. She depicts a lively, expressive cultural sensibility that reflects the residents' financial uncertainties, but Kefalas also conveys the fearsome human toll that it produces. She implicates their cultural values in generating a type of urban violence that whites in Beltway mistakenly assume occurs only in "the ghetto." Kefalas links the fragility of their economic position to their racial sentiments without being reductive about racism. Rather, she shows racist beliefs as imbricated in the mundane textures of daily life, requiring very sophisticated forms of political intervention. In conveying nuanced working-class subjects in all their contradictions, Kefalas offers a depiction of the local dynamics that profoundly shape racial identity in this country.

As evident in these various works, the study of white racial identity will benefit from the "multisited" approach to ethnography that has become increasingly practiced in anthropology. A glimpse of this approach is provided by Monica McDermott, in *Working-Class White: The Making and Unmaking of Race Relations* (2006). There are two immediately distinctive aspects of McDermott's study: first, she generated her data by working as a convenience store clerk; second, she worked in stores in two predominantly white working-class neighborhoods (each bordering black working-class neighborhoods), one in Atlanta and the other in Boston. Subsequently, McDermott opens an intriguing window into this particular class strata of whiteness. She directly targets the seemingly contradictory sociological and survey data on race, which points simultaneously to decreasing open racial animosity yet increasing racial segregation and the persistence of racial inequality. Her approach is to rupture the sheen of decorum that she anticipates whites maintain regarding their "true" racial sentiments; she accomplishes this by basically going "undercover," observing white interactions furtively from her station behind the cash register.

Two findings stand out from McDermott's work. The first is that she "discovered that antiblack prejudice is alive and well" (2006, 149). But it is largely hidden by the social decorum whites adopt to keep from revealing that prejudice to the larger world. But McDermott saw it on display—as well as the conventions generally keeping it from view—as she spied on whites in her undercover researcher's role behind the convenience store counter. "Race is rarely discussed by whites when blacks are present," she concluded, "and most whites are reluctant to make racially derogatory statements in front of strangers, regardless of their race" (59). Interestingly, she adds that such expressions largely emerge in "certain situational contexts and conversational topics, such as crime or schools" (149). It would be interesting to know whether such statements were counterbalanced by other kinds of statements about race in home or workplace or recreational settings, but McDermott's observations were confined to exchanges in that particular commercial setting.

The second key conclusion McDermott reaches involves the wide variation in white identity. *Being white had very different meanings in Atlanta and Boston, even though the whites she studied shared a similar class background.* In the Atlanta neighborhood, whites "have no sense of working-class or ethnic solidarity, but are instead aware of others' perceptions of them as individual failures for living in a city neighborhood on the less affluent, majority-black side of town" (2006, 149). In sharp contrast, whites in the Boston neighborhood have a strong collective identity, "not only as whites but as working-class ethnic whites with a strong positive identification with their neighborhood" (ibid.). These contrasts play out as different meanings for whiteness. In Atlanta, working-class whites were distanced from this racial order, because "whiteness meant affluence, power, and privilege, but in the neighborhood being white meant one had failed to live up to expectations" (150). In Boston, whiteness, in contrast, was seen as somewhat bifurcated in terms of class, such that white, working-class ethnic whiteness did not need to be equated with affluence and power. In noting these contrasts, McDermott, though she does not pursue them deeply, points to the importance of posing questions about whiteness not just in terms of class but also in distinct regional locations, in order to get at additional factors shaping the significance of whiteness.

CONCLUSION

Bringing whiteness into view involves a tension between the coherence it possesses at the most general level of society and the various ways whites confront and reproduce racial meanings and identities in particular locales. An effective means of contending with these differing dimensions of white racialness is by paying close attention to the dynamics of marking and unmarking race. Whiteness is not always unmarked, as we have seen in this chapter, but the ability to elude racial markings is a common feature of white social interactions. The key point is to recognize how *cultural conditioning makes some things highly visible (marked) and others fairly invisible (unmarked)*. This will help you recognize the crucial relational dimension of race as we turn now to discussing blackness.

CHAPTER 5

Understanding Blackness

The challenges in understanding blackness are deeply connected with the task of comprehending whiteness. These two cultural constructs are fundamentally related and mutually informing. Blackness, like whiteness, delineates a position in the social structure, one that variously informs or defines the life chances and experiences of people identified as "black." Our sensibilities about race are shaped by an imagined polar opposition of these constructs, but we understand little about racial dynamics if we strive to characterize them simply as contrary positions or social conditions. Rather, blackness, like whiteness, is a **relational identity**. The purpose of this chapter is to examine these relational dynamics in detail, first by reviewing the history of social science efforts to analyze blackness and then by surveying recent ethnographic research on this fascinating, complicated subject.

In considering the relational aspects that constitute blackness, it matters first to recognize the fundamental role marked and unmarked dynamics play in shaping our thinking about this identity. This is apparent when you consider that blackness, in social science research, has been characterized by exactly the opposite condition as for whiteness. Although the racial aspect of whites' lives was long "hiding in plain sight" for sociologists and anthropologists, black people have been obsessively studied in singularly racial terms. Whiteness eluded critical attention while blackness was incessantly construed as a "problem" warranting intensive investigation. This dynamic requires that our first steps in understanding blackness involve thinking critically about how it has been represented and studied by social scientists.

OBJECTIFYING BLACK PEOPLE

The sustained attention to blackness as a subject of study presents both advantages and disadvantages. In the first regard, we have the benefit of an enormous amount of social science research—extending well over one hundred years—on which to draw. This historical depth makes it somewhat easier to grasp the important mutability of blackness. Algernon Austin makes this point in *Achieving Blackness: Race, Black Nationalism, and the Twentieth Century* (2006): "Blackness is about meanings and definitions, and about social practices and social identities informed by those ideas. The meanings and definitions of blackness change over time and from place to place. The racial structures that restrict and shape black social life change with time and place. Black people's identities change with time and place because their sense of who they are similar to, and who they are different from, changes" (19). The variety of historical ways of understanding blackness—as well as the shifting and varied notions about who counts as black at any one moment— makes it much easier not to construe this cultural construct in abstract or essentializing terms.

Yet the disadvantage of this long history of study is considerable and daunting. The crux of the problem is that research on race or race relations in this country has too often focused strictly on blackness, often construing it in pathological terms. Stephen Steinberg, in *Race Relations: A Critique* (2007), refers to this as the **racial optic** of social science, by which only "blacks, not whites, must be the 'problem' under examination and thus the object of inquiry. Indeed, in the vast cannon of studies on race, nearly every aspect of the black body and soul has been scoured in a misdirected search for the reasons for racial hierarchy" (66). In developing this framework, sociological or anthropological approaches to blackness have often reproduced racial perceptions and understandings rather than effectively making *racialization* an object of analysis. In terms of the relational dimension of racial identities, the "racial optic" has denied blackness exactly that which is so deeply associated with whiteness—normalcy.

It is no simple matter to overturn the traditions and tendencies in social science approaches to race that are organized around the notion of blackness as a problem. But it is a worthwhile and necessary endeavor, one that combines critical reflections on how we pursue social science research with a focus on developing innovative new approaches to studying race. This chapter surveys historical and contemporary approaches to blackness and highlights four basic challenges regarding representations of this cultural identity. The first involves discerning the racial assumptions that have informed social science research on African Americans. The second task centers on developing accounts that counter the *pathologizing perspective* and, rather, depict African Americans in ordinary, mundane circumstances that are not solely reducible to race. Third is the keen challenge of seeing African Americans in what Du Bois termed their *doubleness—* simultaneously very American but also black. Finally, it is vital to recognize the social heterogeneity of blackness, particularly in terms of class, and to see that the "black community" is a nuanced and complicated entity, composed of and concealing a variety of communities. Each of these challenges opens a wide array of philosophical, epistemological, and political issues that we will consider only in passing. But the primary goal of this chapter is to present ethnographic approaches to blackness.

WHAT IS BLACKNESS?

As with whiteness, it is helpful to start with some general characterizations of blackness that will guide us as we move toward considering the racial aspects of black people's lives in more specific terms and circumstances. There are two primary or initial conceptualizations of blackness that are most crucial in thinking about how to approach it via social science. First and foremost, blackness can be regarded as a *form of consciousness* and experience that develops from both historical and contemporary conditions of *racialization* resulting from discrimination and domination. This form of blackness was made a subject of study by some early social scientists, such as the sociologist W. E. B. Du Bois (*The Souls of Black Folk*, 2000 [1903]) and anthropologists such as St. Clair Drake (*Black Metropolis*, 1945, and *Black Folk Here and There*, 1987). But blackness can also be recognized as a collection of images that whites have projected onto people of African descent. Paul Gilroy, in *Against Race: Imagining Political Culture Beyond the Color Line* (2000), describes this as a series of historic associations of blackness with violence, crime, idleness, and excessive threatening fertility. These associations referenced by Gilroy resonate strongly with elements of the "white creed" discussed in the previous chapter. Toni Morrison, in *Playing in the Dark: Whiteness and the Literary Imagination* (1992), characterizes this version of blackness as a compilation of "views, assumptions, readings, and misreadings that accompany Eurocentric learning about these people" (7). In this view, blackness is construed relationally to whiteness as a form of **otherness**, via a selective vision that only recognizes aspects of black life that seem antithetical to whites' self-conceptions.

In each of these conceptualizations—and similarly to whiteness—it is crucial to see blackness as not simply equivalent to the lives of black people or as condensing, in abstract form, a characterization of black lives. *Blackness informs and shapes the everyday settings where African Americans negotiate the significance of race*, but it is neither totalizing nor absolute in its effects and relevance to these various situations. The complexities of blackness highlight the challenge of understanding the significance of race in the lives of African Americans. On one hand, there are the material conditions of racial disadvantage that were highlighted earlier in this book, for which "blackness" provides an apt means of identification. On the other hand, this term has always encompassed a wide range of **social heterogeneity** that strains against the confines of one generic identifying label or characterization (Gwaltney 1980). The tension between these two poles has become manifest in a variety of ways in the United States.

One example may suffice. In the fall of 2007, the Pew Research Center conducted an intriguing poll, with the aim of identifying the extent of a divergence of views between whites and blacks on the question of racial progress. It was hardly news that, indeed, whites and blacks do see this issue differently—whites were twice as likely as blacks to answer "yes" to the question "Are blacks better off now than five years ago?" Interestingly, a majority of both groups took a more neutral stance, concluding that social conditions for African Americans were "about the same" as five years prior. The striking finding of the poll—which drew by far the most media attention—is that "African Americans see a widening gulf between the values of middle-class and poor blacks, and nearly four-in-ten say that because of the diversity within their community, blacks can no longer be thought of as a single race" (4). The question the poll posed is quite important: *"Are blacks still a single race?"* A majority of African Americans (53%) answered in the affirmative, but 35% expressed the contrary view, which suggests that the answers to this question are far from simple.

At its root, this question seeks to understand whether divergent class circumstances among African Americans are developed enough to create a palpable divide within what has long stood as a fairly unified racial condition and identity. Apparently, the much-noted rise of the black middle class over recent decades—as well as the increase in the number of black professionals (or "blue-chip blacks," as we will see later)—has produced this result. The poll asked African American respondents to answer an additional question: "Have the values of middle-class and poor blacks become more similar or more different?" A large majority, presumably crossing class lines, asserted that the values of these respective groups have indeed diverged. Whether this is an accurate perception remains an open question and will be considered in detail in the ethnographic portion of this chapter. But this finding suggests that the effort to understand blackness requires a clear, initial sense of how it can be glimpsed on the social landscape.

Position of Disadvantage

As we saw in Chapter 4, whiteness entails a range of systematic advantages in our society; concomitantly, blackness encompasses a variety of related disadvantages. Sociologist Thomas Shapiro captures this well in his book *The Hidden Cost of Being African American: How Wealth Perpetuates Inequality* (2004). Shapiro echoes the findings of people such as Peggy McIntosh and George Lipsitz, who make the basic point that disadvantages related to racial discrimination necessarily imply advantage for those unmarked by race. Shapiro similarly finds that "many whites continue to reap advantages from the historical, institutional, structural, and personal dynamics of racial inequality, and they are either unaware of these advantages or they deny they exist" (13). Importantly, Shapiro carries this insight further, finding that "Black Americans in particular pay a very steep tax for this uneven playing field and outcome, as well as for the denial of white advantage" (13). In his study of the racial differential in how wealth is passed between generations—in the form of inheritances but also, crucially, in the financial support extended by living parents to their adult children—Shapiro outlines the process by which whites' gains equate to higher costs for African Americans.

Shapiro (2004) finds in housing markets, for instance, that "it is harder for creditworthy black families to qualify for home mortgages, that blacks receive far less family financial assistance with down payments and closing costs, that black homeowners pay higher mortgage rates, and that homes in African American communities appreciate less in value" (13). This badly tilted financial terrain is one of the key ways that blackness continues to be linked to racial disadvantage in this country. While discrimination remains a cultural factor in this form of disadvantage, the more subtle but arguably more profound impact turns on economics. This begins with the earnings differential between whites and blacks in this country: Black households typically earn fifty-nine cents for every dollar earned by typical white households. This difference in wages compounds the wealth differential by race that developed in the United States throughout the 20th century, which was discussed in Chapter 1. This disparity is increased as one generation passes its wealth on to the next: inheritances received by white families are on average seven times larger than inheritances that black families receive. These factors work together to make it much more difficult for black families to provide the head start, in terms of economic and social advantage, that whites receive from their families.

As we saw in the last chapter, whites are not likely to recognize these advantages. Nor do blacks necessarily grasp these disadvantages with ease or view them in racial terms. They are such a deep part of our social landscape that they often pass without comment. But consider how these factors play out as racial disadvantage. First, Shapiro points to "the legacy of grandparents of black baby boomers, who lived and toiled under harsh discrimination and glaringly different conditions" (2004, 72), resulting in much lower levels of wealth transfer within black families. This makes it more difficult for these families to offer their children assistance in the two most crucial points of entry into the middle class: a college education and homeownership. The majority of white families Shapiro interviewed received substantial assistance from their families in paying for college, though this was not often the case with the black families in this study. Interestingly, no one Shapiro interviewed considered such financial assistance as a form of inheritance, though this indeed amounts to a generational wealth transfer. The main point, though, is that blacks who do not receive such familial support with college costs are at a subsequent disadvantage in the goal of achieving homeownership.

The Middle Class in Black and White

Shapiro illustrates this dynamic by drawing on the stories of two middle-class families that emerge from his extensive interviews: the Conways (white) and the Barzaks (black), families that "both fit the American middle-class picture neatly: educated; good incomes; white collar, professional, or self-employed; and homeowners" (2004, 93). The combined income of the Barzaks ($84,000) is actually higher than that of the Conways ($70,000), but the Barzaks' position in the middle class is more precarious. The Conways are not burdened by student loans because their parents paid their college bills; as well, they benefited from a gift of $10,000 from their parents for a down payment on their house; furthermore, they have inherited close to $100,000 and expect to receive more after their parents die. In all, given their limited amount of debt, the Conways' net worth is about $140,000. In contrast, the Barzaks faced difficult hurdles in moving out of Compton, a city with a high poverty rate and mostly black population. Burdened with hefty student loans of tens of thousands of dollars, they had a difficult time obtaining a mortgage. They only did so by wiping out the husband's 401(k) retirement account, which resulted in huge fines and depleted savings. Given their debt levels, the net worth of the Barzaks is about $10,000.

Surely many readers will consider both of these families advantaged; they are, after all, solidly ensconced in the middle class. But that is what makes these portraits all the more valuable, in that they illustrate how *the disadvantages associated with blackness persist even with movement up the class ladder.* The other crucial point to see in this portrait is the tight association between community, schooling, and parental assistance in buying a first home. Whites, we know from Lipsitz's work, typically raise families in wealthier neighborhoods, with schools that offer students greater advantages because of that wealth differential. They often would not be able to afford houses in such neighborhoods without their parents' help with down payments. Blacks typically pay a much steeper cost for gaining access to such neighborhoods—when they can find realtors to show them such homes—and they draw on less familial support in making such moves, which leaves them disadvantaged in the competition for access to a good education and higher home values. This dynamic plays out regardless of whatever role overt forms of racism may or may not play in the lives of black families.

Blackness in the Public Sphere

Though disadvantage is a significant aspect of blackness, it is hardly the only way of characterizing this cultural identity. Blackness, too, refers to a distinctive aspect of the public sphere in American life. Perhaps this is most obvious in the realm of popular culture, where blackness is evidenced in expressive traditions that permeate and texture music, media, and entertainment. But it is also manifests in what Melissa Harris-Lacewell labels the "black counterpublic," a loose collection of people in an array of social sites—churches, political organizations, and mutual aid societies, for example—where class and gender diversity crosscut racially homogeneous gatherings. In *Barbershops, Bibles, and BET: Everyday Talk and Black Political Thought* (2004), Harris-Lacewell describes how this counterpublic takes shape in three broad arenas: black organizations, black public spaces, and black information networks. The defining feature of such arenas is that they provide forums for black people to talk back to dominant narratives and beliefs in the culture at large. "**Black public spaces** are unique," Harris-Lacewell explains, "because African Americans come together in these arenas *because* of their blackness" (8).

Harris-Lacewell's research is interesting both for her findings and for her methods—she layers in an ethnography of an urban barbershop and a case study of a southern, black Baptist church alongside statistical analyses developed from national surveys and experimental data, as well as textual analyses of the writings of key black public figures. In particular, the Truth and Soul: Black Stars barbershop on Chicago's Southside, provides a glimpse of how "everyday black talk" articulates a distinctive perspective on American culture. In this site—"a black public space where black men, through everyday discourse, shape and reshape their political attitudes and worldviews" (2004, 202)—conversations about blackness unfold that are shaped by copious implicit distinctions of class and gender identity. Regarding the latter, Harris-Lacewell finds the men drawing certain boundaries around racial identity, "where blackness is narrowly defined and concerns of gender and sexual orientation are seen as potentially divisive agendas that should be subordinated to heterosexual, male-centered, racial goals" (188). This observation is just a glimpse of the *important lines of cultural difference within blackness that are often covered up in generalizations about racial identity*. For that matter, Harris-Lacewell notes that these men "shared no single vision of blackness" and "they did not always agree on the ways race articulates itself in the lives of individuals and communities" (181). What they shared, though, was common participation in such social settings and an interest in talking about "definitions of blackness, black people, and the position of black people in U.S. society" (ibid.). While such conversations are reflective of these racially defined arenas, they also evidence broader cultural discourses through which "American blackness is constantly subject to redefinition both within and outside the group" (175).

BLACKNESS AND DISCOURSE

The foregoing discussion—on the facts of black social and economic disadvantage, the particular sites of black public space, and contrary opinions on whether African Americans still constitute one race—underscore the value of a discursive perspective on blackness. Remember, the concept of discourse moves us away from simple questions of whether statements are true or false, toward an attention to the enabling conditions of basic assertions—*what they allow us to see or what they obscure from view*. This stance matters a great deal with blackness because it is the subject of so much public discussion, quite in contrast to the status of whiteness. In Chapter 4 we saw that, for the most part, whites have a difficult time characterizing or even recognizing whiteness. In contrast, black people frequently find themselves in the situation of discussing and reflecting on blackness. This is because, as either a referent to a historical and contemporary social identity or as a projection of whites' anxieties, blacks regularly encounter blackness in everyday life. Approaching blackness from a discursive perspective lets us consider how the contours and contents of this construct are mobilized and assessed in public exchanges and everyday speech.

The Meaning of Obama

There is likely no better place to start from in developing this perspective than by considering the debate among African Americans over the racial significance of Barack Obama. The question of whether or how well "blackness" characterizes something fundamental about the experiences of African Americans was percolating long before Obama made his successful run for office. The debate was driven, in part, by the success of a host of African American politicians, in addition to

Obama, who won elected offices in campaigns across the country that were not primarily centered on redressing racial inequality. This phenomenon has been labeled *postracial politics* and will be considered in detail later in this chapter. Such developments, though, led social commentator Debra Dickerson to declare "the end of blackness" in 2004 in a book whose title featured this declaration. Dickerson argues "that the concept of 'blackness' . . . is rapidly losing its ability to describe, let alone predict or manipulate, the political and social behavior of African Americans" (3). Her conclusion gained increasing support in the debates concerning the significance of Obama's victory.

Obama's candidacy for the presidency fueled passionate debates about the meaning of blackness and the significance of race. Strikingly, public figures took opposite stances on these questions. John McWhorter, author of *Winning the Race: Beyond the Crisis in Black America* (2005), asked pointedly "whether Mr. Obama would elicit this swooning buzz if he were white" (2006, 12). In answer to his own question, McWhorter concluded, "The key factor that galvanizes people around the idea of Obama for president is, quite simply, that he is black" (ibid.). The relevance of race could scarcely be put more bluntly. But other black commentators and politicians antithetically questioned whether he was "black enough" to warrant their support or even whether he was black at all. Dickerson asserted this latter position. When his candidacy first seemed imminent, Dickerson relates that she resisted appeals for her to write about Obama. Why? "I didn't have the heart (or the stomach) to point out the obvious: Obama isn't black." That is, she explained, he is not "politically and culturally black." "Not descended from West African slaves brought to America, he steps into the benefits of black progress (like Harvard Law School) without having borne any of the burden, and he gives white folks the plausible deniability of their unwillingness to embrace blacks in public life" (2007). But if he isn't black, what race is he? Jesse Jackson criticized him for "acting like he's white" when Obama did not actively rally to the cause of the "Jena Six."[1] Obama's studied, race-neutral response—"outrage over an injustice like the Jena 6 isn't a matter of black and white. It's a matter of right and wrong"—was enough for Jackson to question his racial identity altogether.

At the crux of this questioning of racial significance is *a basic uncertainty over whether Obama's race is a disadvantage or possibly an advantage.* The long-standing assumption in American politics has been that being black is a disadvantage in a national election. Yet in the campaign for the presidency, two forms of advantage seemed to emerge for Obama: one from not being black and one from not being white. In the first frame, Dickerson asserts his advantage lies in not being black, to

---

[1]This case involved six young black men in the town of Jena, Louisiana, who were charged with attempted murder in a brawl with a white man. The case drew attention because a similar attack by whites on black youths in the same town largely escaped punishment. An account of these incidents and the massive civil rights rally they inspired is featured in my book *What Can You Say?: America's National Conversation on Race*, Stanford University Press, 2010.

the extent that he presumably had not suffered the historical effects of discrimination, though perhaps he has potentially benefited from their forms of redress. In the other frame, he is advantaged, as McWhorter (2006) argues, because not being white allows him to stand, in McWhorter's words, as "a ringing symbol that racism no longer rules our land" (12). These two commentators' questioning of Obama's blackness reflects their uncertainty over whether this racial identity still constitutes a disadvantage in national politics. The idea that this equation may be even slightly destabilized is enough to provoke the widespread questioning of racial identity that Obama's rise to public prominence has provoked.

The questioning of Obama's racial identity runs much deeper than this issue of disadvantage, though, because of the fact that his father was an African and his mother was a white woman from Kansas. In American parlance, this makes him alternately *racially mixed* and *black*. The difference between these two labels is important and marks a developing rift in the racial landscape of the United States. Less than two decades ago, Obama's identity would not have been a question—he would simply be regarded as black. This is a reflection of the ideology of *hypo-descent*, a notion that reflects certain beliefs about racial purity in relation to "blood"; just "one-drop" of "black blood" was considered enough of a genealogy to make a person "black" (see Chapter 1). This ideology operated for centuries in the United States, when whites were adamant about preserving the privileges of race in terms of lineage and beliefs about biological substance (see Chapter 2). Evidence that this thinking is changing—and along with it a range of ideas about interracial "mixing"—comes from the 2000 U.S. Census, which for the first time allowed people to mark more than one race. By 2010, around nine million people, almost 3% of the population, chose more than one race on the census—a 32% increase from 2000. This development reflects an evolving sensibility about the static or given aspects of racial identity (see Chapter 8). The fact that there was a debate at all as to Obama's racial identity underscores another important point about blackness: it is increasingly construed as an *achieved identity*, reflecting the kinds of social history and experience Dickerson itemized rather than simply a given characteristic or feature.

Rethinking Blackness

The questions about blackness generated in the run-up to the 2008 election only increased after Obama's victory. The hallmark of the concept—a certain elasticity that allowed it to encompass great degrees of social heterogeneity within one collective identity—seemed suddenly precarious. Could blackness stretch to encompass the enduring forms of disadvantage in America's desperate inner cities while also characterizing the identity of the man holding the highest elected office in the country? This remains an open question, but some tentative answers have emerged that suggest blackness has fundamentally altered. Charles Johnson (2008), noted African American philosopher and novelist, argues that Obama's success heralds "the End of the Black American Narrative." The concept of *narrative* here is similar to that of *discourse*, in that both point to the cultural forms that organize our perceptions of events and their meanings. Johnson characterizes the "black American narra-tive" as encompassing the types of historical and contemporary experiences high-lighted by Dickerson. "This unique black American narrative," Johnson writes, "is quietly in the background of every conversation we have about black people, even when it is not fully articulated or expressed. It is our starting point, our agreed-upon premise, our most important presuppositions for dialogues about black America" (32). This narrative structures the discourse on blackness by aligning new experiences or events with a long-standing framework for contextualizing and explaining their meaning. But this structure, Johnson argues, has buckled and collapsed.

The focal point in Johnson's claim is not simply Barack Obama but, rather, all the social and political transformations of the last forty years that laid the ground-work for his success. Prime among these developments is the emergence of a sizable black middle class. We know from the work of Shapiro (2004) and others that this class remains in a precarious position relative to the white middle class. Yet it represents a substantial shift in the social landscape of race. A reflection of its impact, Johnson (2008) suggests, is the fact that "well over 10,000 black Americans have been elected to offices around this country" (38). This is an important point, but it also bears noting that Obama was the only black senator at the time of his election; although much has changed, many racial dynamics remain unchanged. But the other development Johnson highlights is the rise of the foreign-born black population in this country. "In America's major cities," Johnson observes, "15% of the black American population is foreign born—Haitian, Jamaican, Senegalese, Nigerian, Cape Verdean, Ethiopian, Eritrean, and Somalian—a rich tapestry of brown-skinned people as culturally complex in their differences, backgrounds, and outlooks as those people lumped together under the all-too-convenient labels of 'Asian' or 'European'" (40). What strains the black narrative framework to the breaking point are these two developments taken in concert: the rising social and political status of African Americans and the changing cultural content that falls under the label of *blackness*.

The developments to which Johnson points do not suggest that blackness is simply going away or no longer relevant. Rather, the crucial matter is that the cul-tural complexity of both blackness and racial identity generally are exceeding our prior ways for making sense of them. "No matter which angle we use to view black people in America today," Johnson concludes, "we find them to be a complex and multifaceted people who defy easy categorization. We challenge, culturally and politically, an old group narrative that fails at the beginning of this new century to capture even a fraction of our rich diversity and heterogeneity" (41). His point is that the way Americans of all colors have talked and thought about black people is changing rapidly, as a reflection of the ways that the content of blackness is chang-ing. But it is important to remember that Johnson is referencing here the level of national discourse. What remains to be seen is whether or how these claims relate to circumstances in daily life in particular social settings. For this we turn now to ethnographic perspectives on the subject of blackness and black racial identity.

BLACKNESS AS A SUBJECT OF STUDY

As we saw with whiteness in the previous chapter, by shifting the focus from the level of general discourse, our questions and answers about race become more interesting and nuanced as we move to the ethnographic level and glimpse people in their everyday lives in particular social settings. This is the case with blackness too, but, as noted in this chapter's opening, this subject also requires an additional task. Before we get too far in considering current ethnographies of African Americans, let us reflect on the history of their objectification by social scientists. This is a twofold process: first, looking back in history for basic models of how to approach this subject of study and, second, considering the role of the *racial optic* in producing distorting images of black people. This is a more difficult undertaking than the case of whiteness presents, because this effort requires a simultaneous attention to the useful potential of social science approaches—for instance, in countering stereotypes of African Americans—while being cognizant of how these representations may reflect the influence of racial thinking.

There is no better place to start in both regards than to consider the work of W. E. B. Du Bois (1868–1963), who remains one of the foremost authorities on the subject of race in this country or in the world for that matter. It is difficult to overstate the breadth and depth of Du Bois' intellect and the incisive quality of his research on race. He authored over twenty books and thousands of articles, essays, and editorials. Du Bois' areas of expertise ranged from history—his dissertation on the slave trade was the first volume in the prestigious Harvard Historical Studies series—to sociology—he played a pioneering role in establishing this discipline in the United States—to economics, where his classic work, *Black Reconstruction in America, 1860–1880* (1992 [1935]), continues to be mined for insights, such as the *psychological wage* that he posits working-class whites gain from identifying racially instead of in terms of common class interests. His active career of intellectual work extended well over six decades and is far too broad in scope to be adequately covered here. We will only dwell on his initial effort at applying social science to studying race in the United States, which resulted in his impressive book *The Philadelphia Negro: A Social Study* (1996 [1899]).

It is a sobering matter to consider the example Du Bois set for the study of race more than a century ago. First, it is impressive that he was able, so early on, to deploy the tools of social analysis so effectively in framing the problem of race. But it is a somber realization that the racial dynamics he strove to objectify remain a tangible force in our society. Second, it is saddening to consider that his excellent work was so thoroughly disregarded for years by white social scientists, who failed to follow the path that he so clearly blazed. In the end, though, the quality of his vision of how race matters retains the power to animate researchers who today strive to devise effective means of analyzing racial dynamics.

In his study of black people in Philadelphia's seventh ward, Du Bois (1996 [1899]) spent 835 hours interviewing members of roughly 2,500 households; he additionally tabulated social and economic data on some 15,000 households in the city, developing a stunningly detailed and expansive picture of black urban life in the late 1800s. Du Bois chose the seventh ward because of its class heterogeneity. Amid the area's poverty there also dwelt, "the best class of Philadelphia Negroes, though sometimes forgotten or ignored in discussing the Negro problem" (7). This social strata was composed of "a class of caterers, clerks, teachers, professional men, small merchants, etc., who constitute the aristocracy of the Negroes" (ibid.). His aim in bringing this group into view was to challenge the fundamental misunderstanding that whites held about black people—that they constitute a homogeneous group occupying a largely impoverished social position. As he cautioned in his study, "There is no surer way of misunderstanding the Negro or being misunderstood by him than by ignoring manifest differences of condition and power in the 40,000 black people of Philadelphia" (310)—a reminder that remains pertinent today, though our racial nomenclature has changed. This assertion reveals Du Bois' basic assumption, in his initial foray into social research, that the best way to challenge racial thinking is by developing objective and empirical attention to the diversity that we misconstrue with stereotyped perceptions and generalizations about blackness.

Identifying the Role of Race

By highlighting the black middle and upper classes in Philadelphia, Du Bois aimed to draw the racial dynamics shaping their lives into greater relief. Among these classes, Du Bois (1996 [1899]) explained, "are social problems differing from those of the whites of a corresponding class because of the *peculiar social environment* in which the whole race finds itself, which the whole race feels, but which touches upon the highest class at most points and tells upon them decisively" (8). In these classes, Du Bois found lives that extended furthest beyond stereotyped perceptions of blackness; yet they continued to be reductively misconstrued in whites' characterizations of black people. Experiences of this group, Du Bois decided, amounted to a "complicated mass of facts" that presented "tangible evidence of a social atmosphere surrounding Negroes, which differs from that surrounding whites" (ibid.). Through his empirical research on this group, Du Bois aimed to depict and understand what constituted this racial dimension of black lives.

Regarding the power and influence of this "peculiar social environment," Du Bois (1996 [1899]) addressed his research to prevailing public opinions, which somewhat resemble today's debates about race. He summed up the dominant views on the relevance of "color prejudice" succinctly: "Negroes regard this prejudice as the chief cause of their present unfortunate condition. On the other hand most white people are quite unconscious of any such powerful and vindictive feeling, and . . . they cannot see how such a feeling has much influence on the real situation or alters the social condition of the mass of Negroes" (322). Du Bois regarded these antithetical stances—that racism was a principle influence or a negligible factor—with equal suspicion. To resolve these competing views, he turned to social analysis as a means to get beyond these racially polarized views on the matter.

"It is time now," he wrote, "to reduce this somewhat indefinite term to some-thing tangible. Everybody speaks of the matter, everybody knows it exists, but in just what form and how influential it is few agree" (322). Du Bois, then, impres-sively deployed the primary quantitative and qualitative tools of social science (surveys and interviews) to establish with great precision and insight the ways race mattered in the daily life of blacks in Philadelphia's seventh ward. His research stands as an exceptional statement of the value of a social science approach to race, as captured in his assessment: "That such a difference exists and can now and then be seen, few deny; but just how far it goes and how large a factor it is in the Negro problems, nothing but careful study and measurement can reveal" (ibid.).

Du Bois' (1996 [1899]) specific findings in *Philadelphia Negro* also arguably retain their relevance today. "As a matter of fact, color prejudice in this city is something between these two extreme views: It is not today responsible for all, or perhaps the greater part of the Negro problems, or of the disabilities under which the race labors; on the other hand it is a far more powerful social force than most Philadelphians realize" (ibid.). Du Bois meticulously reported his findings, which documented systematic and sustained forms of discrimination in hiring, housing, and health, which remain active today in the United States. He correlated the force of this prejudice with fluctuations in the local economy—rising in hard economic times and relenting some when resources were plentiful. This dynamic led him away from depicting the role of "color prejudice" in absolute terms. Yet his careful, objective analysis generates an undeniable picture of differential life chances based on race. "Presumably the first impulse of the average Philadelphian would be to emphatically deny any such marked and blighting discrimination. . . . Everyone knows that in the past color prejudice was deep and passionate" (325). This state-ment bears an uncanny resemblance to the ways people today are quick to dismiss the ongoing presence of racism. This should provoke a shudder of recognition of how little may have changed regarding people's ability and willingness to confront the enduring significance of race. At the same time, this recognition, more impor-tantly, underscores the continuing relevance of Du Bois' initial application of social analysis to the question of race.

Race from Many Different Angles

Du Bois continued, over his long career, to analyze race from a variety of other angles. His most well-known work, *The Souls of Black Folks* (2000 [1903]), is a notable example. This book combines sociological writing with personal and public history, fiction, autobiography, ethnography, economic analysis, and poetry in a manner that anticipates many "postmodernist" attempts today to capture the complexity of social life. He used these varied styles of writing and analysis in order to reveal the "many things which if read with patience may show the mean-ing of being black here in the dawning of the 20th century." The book contains some of his most oft-quoted statements, such as "the problem of the 20th century is the problem of the color line" (10). Here he also articulated the notion of a black "double consciousness": "One ever feels his two-ness—an American, a Negro.

Two souls, two thoughts, two unreconciled strivings" (3). But Du Bois rarely rested on any single formulation of the significance of race, because he found its operation to be so mutable and evolving.

This perspective is perhaps best captured in a conclusion he developed about "the race concept" in *Dusk of Dawn* (1980 [1940]): "It had as I have tried to show all sorts of illogical trends and irreconcilable tendencies. Perhaps it is wrong to speak of it at all as 'a concept' rather than a group of contradictory forces, facts, and tendencies" (133). Such contradictions were, and remain, manifold. For instance, in this one book he alternately regards blackness as an arbitrary designation and as a fundamental form of global solidarity. In the former sense, this racial identity is a product of a legal structure that sanctioned white dominance: "The black man is a person who must ride 'Jim Crow' in Georgia" (153). In this same vein, he defined race as "a matter of conditioned reflexes; of long-followed habits, customs and folkways; of subconscious trains of reasoning and unconscious nervous reflexes" (172). But in the latter sense, he viewed blackness as a "social heritage" binding together "the children of Africa," in "a common history . . . of a common disaster" (116). Today this view is articulated in terms of the **African diaspora** (Wright 2004), which we will examine further later.

It would be difficult under ideal circumstances simply to follow the lead Du Bois set for analyzing the racial dimension of black people's lives and experiences, because he pursued so many different approaches to this subject. But the challenge of drawing from his example today is compounded by three additional factors. The most important of these is that Du Bois' work went largely ignored by sociologists and anthropologists for decades. Simply, whites, who dominated these disciplines, failed to appreciate or accept the analytic strength and depth of his research. A compounding factor that follows from this disciplinary disregard of Du Bois is that, in the intervening years, social scientists adopted a largely myopic racial optic that singularly viewed race in terms of blackness. This allowed whiteness to escape attention while anthropologists and sociologists increasingly construed black culture in pathological terms. The third factor forming this challenge is that throughout the last three decades of the 20th century, the daily lived textures of race were fundamentally transformed. We glimpsed part of this transformation in the previous chapter, which looked at the situation of whites who stayed behind when massive numbers of whites fled from the nation's central cities. In fleeing, these whites exacerbated the race problem that was unfolding with the emergence of an urban underclass in the deteriorating space of inner cities.

Misuses of Culture

Taken together, these factors present a significant but not insurmountable challenge to social scientists' efforts to study race in general and blackness in particular. The way forward involves both critically assessing some of the approaches to race that dominated in the 1960s to the 1980s while attending to other efforts in this same period that did not receive as much attention initially.

Fortunately, much of this critical work has already been done, and a variety of excellent critiques point the way toward better-formulated approaches to race. One example is Robin Kelley's work in, *Yo' Mama's Disfunktional!: Fighting the Culture Wars in Urban America* (1997). Kelley reviews urban sociology and anthropology in these decades in order to assess the distorting effect of social scientists' accounts of black lives. The principle problem he discerns is one of focus: from the wide swath of African American life, sociologists and anthropologists singularly fixated on black ghetto dwellers. Their attention was largely framed by the politics and policy debates sparked by Daniel Patrick Moynihan's 1965 study *The Negro Family*, which identified a *tangle of pathology* in the rise of black female–headed households. Research responding to these debates quickly coalesced into a tight focus on inner-city black communities, a view that directed attention away, first, from the heterogeneity of black life that Du Bois studied and, second, from the larger economic and social forces—such as deindustrialization, segregation, and white flight—that were hollowing out central cities, creating massive new forms of social dislocation. Within this framework, the most common adjectives used to describe urban blacks were *nihilistic, dysfunctional, pathological,* and *underclass.*

Kelley finds that these problematic depictions all turn on a basic conceptual error made by social scientists: *They deployed a reductive notion of culture to explain very complicated and nuanced settings and life circumstances.* "The culture concept employed by social scientists," Kelley (1997) states, "has severely impoverished contemporary debates over the plight of urban African Americans" (16). The crux of the problem lies in equating *behavior* and *culture* in static and essentialist terms. Instead of seeing behavior as situational and changing—a set of responses to particular circumstances rather than hardwired conditioning—social scientists depicted it in essentialized terms as both normative and representative for urban blacks. As well, this depiction misrepresented class dynamics—which fundamentally involve economic relations and social status—in behavioral terms. Even sympathetic ethnographic accounts of ghetto life, which strove to interpret black behavior as a response to racism and poverty (as a set of "coping mechanisms"), functioned in a similarly reductive and determinist fashion. As Kelley observes, "Ironically, while this work consciously sought to recast ghetto dwellers as active agents rather than passive victims, it has nonetheless reinforced monolithic interpretations of black urban culture and significantly shaped current articulations of the cultural concept in social science approaches to poverty" (19).

The conceptual error of reducing *culture* to *behavior* was compounded by trying to represent this culture in singular terms, as a uniform *black culture*. Kelley (1997) explains, "by conceiving black urban culture in the singular, interpreters unwittingly reduce their subjects to cardboard typologies who fit neatly into their own definition of the 'underclass' and render invisible a wide array of complex cultural forms and practices" (17). Arguably, the most interesting and nuanced dimension of this wider array of cultural practices is that of *expressive culture*, which is shaped by aesthetics, style, and pleasure—dynamics that did not jibe well with social scientists' efforts to analyze these forms as "expressions of pathology, compensatory behavior, or coping mechanisms dealing with racism and poverty" (18). Even when researchers considered expressive forms, they too often distorted these practices by trying to make them fit into a notion of an "authentic Negro culture." The problem again, as Kelley observes, is that this conceptualization of culture further ensconced the pathologizing focus on "the young jobless men hanging out on the corner passing the bottle, the pimps and hustlers, and the single mothers who raised streetwise kids who began cursing before they could walk" (20). This search for "the real Negro" and "authentic culture" ignored "the men and women who went to work everyday" in numerous occupations that keep the city operating.

Kelley's critical assessment of the misguided search for "black culture" echoes some of the key problems highlighted with "white culture" in the previous chapter. Both concepts lead toward *abstract generalizations about these racial groups or orders, which end up actually directing attention away from where we most plainly see cultural dynamics at work*—in the realm of everyday life as experienced and reproduced in a particular social setting. As in the previous chapter, the critical point here is similar— we need to approach *culture* not as an abstraction but as the tangible practices and imaginings of people who work actively at making sense of race in their daily routines and encounters. A better deployment of culture to talk about race lies in using it to identify the host of *dynamics related to meaning that shape the significance of racial matters*, instead of trying to label a distinctive set of cultural norms. As well, rather than trying to typify a singular "black culture" or "white culture," the point of ethnographic analysis is to highlight the multiple interpretive practices by which race is performed and revised in everyday life. These practices—which always involve the work of establishing and negotiating boundaries and which require active work of interpretation—are the focus of the following section.

STUDYING BLACK PEOPLE IN EVERYDAY LIFE

The shift away from using sensationalistic scenes of inner-city life as a basis for understanding the cultural dynamics shaping black identity began in the 1990s and continues to develop. Sociologist Elijah Anderson made an important early step in this direction with his ethnography *Streetwise: Race, Class, and Change in an Urban Community* (1990). While still located within or on the cusp of a devastated inner-city area, Anderson turned his focus toward black and white middle-class residents of an adjacent area that was beginning to gentrify. Rather than trying to study an "authentic" urban culture, Anderson cast a broader net by analyzing "how individuals come to interpret and negotiate the public spaces in the community" (6).

Anderson concentrated his attention on the ways residents read local codes of *racial conduct* in the clothing and mannerisms of people they encountered on the street. Among black middle-class residents, he found "at least two often competing, highly complicated racial perspectives" (40), both contoured by class identity. One view is largely informed, first, by a fundamental conviction that whites are primarily racist and then, second, by an anxiety over "retaining their racial identity, or 'blackness,' in a predominantly whites socioeconomic class context" (41). Blackness for these residents seemed to be primarily associated with black working and lower classes. For another group, though, class mobility and identity outweighed concerns over racial identification; these blacks felt "reasonably at home" in predominantly white settings and generally leaned toward deemphasizing the importance of race. These various stances toward blackness emerge because Anderson was not bound by notions of depicting an authentic, singular form of black identity. Instead, he was able to examine how ideas about racial identity and its significance shape the types of attention residents paid to neighbors, friends, and strangers. Anderson's approach opened the way for far more nuanced ethnographic accounts of the class textures of black racial identity.

Another ethnography that solidified the shift away from framing blackness in terms of an "authentic culture" is anthropologist Signithia Fordham's *Blacked Out: Dilemmas of Race, Identity, and Success at Capital High* (1996). The high school Fordham studied is 99% black and is located in a historically black neighborhood in Washington, D.C. Her research examined black students' ideas and images of success. Specifically, Fordham aimed "to determine whether, as a cultural symbol, blackness was imagined as a barrier to academic achievement" (23). Much of her focus turned on rhetorical uses of the notion of "**acting white**" to police or to maintain a bounded sense of black identity over and against the larger white society. Fordham found that students used the phrase to sound out the possible difference between black individuals and "an imagined Black nation" (23). Fordham's research contributed to a larger, vociferous debate initiated by the work of her mentor John Ogbu. The contested issue is whether the accusation of acting white adversely impacts black students' academic performance.

The significance of acting white continues to be debated and studied, with somewhat contrary findings. Sociologist Karolyn Tyson conducted an ethnographic study of eleven schools in North Carolina and found that black and white students largely share similar attitudes about achievement in school. Tyson's study ("It's Not 'a Black Thing': Understanding the Burden of Acting White and Other Dilemmas of High Achievement," 2005) dismissed the idea of substantive racial differences regarding success. Another study, by Angela Neal-Barnett, argued that the basic focus of the charge of acting white really has little to do with white society and is *largely oriented toward competing versions of black identity*. She explains: "When the accusation is made, what is being said is that your definition of being black does not meet my definition of being black. Indeed, your definition is wrong" (quoted in Pluviose 2006, 6). In these varied findings and conclusions, what stands out is the fact that black racial identity, rather than being simply given or assumed, is *actively assessed and articulated by youth immersed in the process of formulating their own social identities.*

Class Textures of "Community"

The ethnography that most deeply ratified the shift away from the approach to black racial identity criticized by Kelley is Steven Gregory's *Black Corona: Race and the Politics of Place in an Urban Community* (1999). Gregory did his fieldwork in Queens, New York, initially working on a team of researchers with Roger Sanjek, whose ethnography *The Future of Us All*, was discussed in the previous chapter. In selecting his site and subject matter—predominantly black portions of Queens known as Corona and East Elmhurst—Gregory explicitly rejected dominant approaches that concentrated on the black poor and "ghetto life" in favor of examining "the process of black class formation and, more generally, the social complexity of black urban life and identities" (17). Gregory states in his introduction, "This is not a book about a 'black ghetto' or an 'inner city' community. Whatever service these categories might have once rendered toward heightening recognition of the ferocity of racial segregation and urban poverty, they today *obscure far more than they reveal*" (10) [emphasis added]. Notably, Gregory draws this contrast not just to distinguish his work from the traditions of social science scholarship that generated distorted and stereotyped views of black urban life. This contrast is one that is also drawn and debated by some of his research subjects—black middle-class homeowners in a fast-changing corner of New York City. In this regard, Gregory neither treats class identity as a given—he sees it as in flux and variably shaped by an array of economic and social factors—nor assumes that racial identity and interests are predetermined. The focus of *Black Corona* is on the processes by which black residents of these neighborhoods actively develop, remake, or reject ties with lower-class blacks in adjacent areas of Queens.

Gregory identifies the racial component of his subjects' lives in an interesting manner. "Corona is a 'black community,'" he explains, "not because its residents share a common culture or class position. Rather, it is a black community because, through much of its history, its residents have been subjected to practices of racial discrimination and subordination that inextricably tied their socioeconomic well-being and mobility to their racial identity and to places where they lived and raised their children" (10–11). This delineation of race is important because, as Melanie Bush does with her surveys of students in Chapter 3, it allows us to see the connection between racial perspectives and social location. Racial identity, in this approach, is hardly something that is simply "authentic" or essential; rather, it derives from particular social practices and circumstances. In this light, Gregory also warns against assuming that "community" implies social and economic homogeneity. Rather, "community," in this part of Queens, encompasses discrepant class circumstances and conflicts.

Making Sense of Black Identity

Gregory's (1999) ethnographic work draws into view "the diversity of black urban experience by directing attention to the political struggles through which Corona's black residents have contested the practice of racial exclusion and, in the process, negotiated multiple and shifting meanings of race, class, and community" (145). This diversity is sharply rendered in the competing interests and claims regarding place between low-income black residents of a large public housing complex and those of middle-class black homeowners. These groups, Gregory shows, have contrasting sensibilities regarding political practices and objectives, rather than sharing a unified racial identity. But one of the values of Gregory's approach is that, rather than depict this diversity as an inert social fact, he examines "the social processes through which that heterogeneity has been produced, negotiated, and contested in the everyday lives of African Americans" (156).

Even though his work covers a spectrum of black class positions, Gregory (1999) primarily examines "how the identities, interests, and political commitments of black homeowners are formed and negotiated through struggles over the built environment that pit residents against a medley of public authorities and private sector interests" (177). Black homeowners in Queens—much like their white counterparts throughout the city and the country at large—often articulate and act on their interests through block associations and other local political organizations. These interests tend to crystallize in opposition to social service projects (such as a group home for foster children in this case) or in support of "quality-of-life issues" linked to property values. Such interests are fundamental to what George Lipsitz characterizes as the possessive investment in whiteness. But what kind of racial charge do they carry for members of the black middle class? Anticipating Shapiro's work on the "hidden costs" of being African American, Gregory finds that black homeowners occupy a generally more tenuous position than their white counterparts, in part because dominant institutions tend to read the racial concentration of blacks in Corona as making these neighborhoods less valuable. These homeowners read these racial stakes both vis-à-vis state institutions and regarding the clientele assisted by such programs. As a result, they actively aggregate and disaggregate the racial dimension of their "interests" in the process of articulating their stakes in this middle-class neighborhood.

In each of the varied class sites Gregory (1999) depicts, *he maintains an overarching attention to the interpretive work of his ethnographic subjects*—that is, to how they actively make sense of these situations by drawing on an array of class and racial discourses, narratives, and symbols. This approach allows Gregory to reveal "not only the range of positions within the African American community concerning the goals, methods, and social base of political empowerment but also the multiple and conflicting interpretations of black experience, needs, and identity that informs them" (176). In this regard, Gregory's fieldwork provides more than a portrait of the *social heterogeneity of blackness*. He uses ethnography to explain the recursive process by which place is both informed by and constitutive of racial identities that, in turn, are recursively deployed and revised in local political actions in support of neighborhoods and tenuous class positions.

Class Conflicts within Blackness

The kind of attention Gregory directs toward the varied class concerns and social contexts shaping black racial identity is affirmed by an array of subsequent studies, such as Mary Pattillo-McCoy's *Black Picket Fences: Privilege and Peril Among the Black Middle Class* (1999). Similar to Gregory, Pattillo-McCoy articulated the rationale for her work by stressing that "the black middle class and their residential enclaves are nearly invisible to the nonblack public because of the intense (and mostly negative) attention given to poor urban ghettos" (1). Pattillo-McCoy followed her study with a deeper ethnography of the same Chicago neighborhood featured in her earlier work. Importantly, in this later work, *Black on the Block: The Politics of Race and Class in the City* (2007), she explores political rifts within blackness by examining the contentious process of gentrification of the North Kenwood-Oakland area. *Black on the Block* examines "the conflicted but pivotal frontline role that middle-class African Americans play in the process of transforming the neighborhoods of poor African Americans who are sometimes dismissed and disparaged, while at the same time battling *on behalf of the race*, including the poor of the race, for the rights and resources that citizenship and municipal residency should, but do not always, automatically entail" (21). In this fascinatingly complex dynamic, Pattillo-McCoy finds that "the black position becomes many positions, split along lines of seniority in the neighborhood, profession, home ownership, age, and taste" (3). These forms of differentiation within blackness are hardly new, but they are clearly growing and becoming subject to greater forms of investment as a reflection of the processes changing urban America.

The expanding ethnographic record on African Americans is generating more than just increasingly detailed views of the class heterogeneity and competing interests internal to blackness. Greater attention to the social dynamics in particular locales makes it much easier to recognize the important role that culture plays in shaping racial identities. Karyn Lacy makes this point in her study *Blue-Chip Black: Race, Class, and Status in the New Black Middle Class* (2007). This ethnography continues the trajectory of more detailed attention to the role of class dynamics in shaping the significance of race, but Lacy additionally attends to the difference place makes in how racial matters are experienced and perceived. Lacy's starting point is *black suburbanization*, In contrast to both Gregory and Pattillo-McCoy, she wants to look at the higher end of the black middle class, "whose socioeconomic circumstances more closely resemble the white middle class" (1). To do this effectively, Lacy chooses three distinct suburbs for her field sites: Lakeview, a middle-class, majority-white suburb in predominantly white Fairfax County, Virginia; Riverton, a predominantly black suburb in mostly black Prince George's County, Maryland; and Sherwood Park, an upper-middle-class, majority-black community within Riverton. This closer attention to place makes cultural dynamics quite apparent in shaping the significance of race.

Lacy (2007) explains, "*Blue-Chip Black* focuses on differences by residential location in how middle-class blacks think about and make use of their social identity" (5).

In contrast to general sociological survey research on attitudes or beliefs, foreground-ing the role of place in an ethnographic perspective makes it apparent that *the mean-ing of race varies a great deal and usually requires or provokes a considerable amount of interpretive work*. Lacy observes of the people she interviews, "their conceptions of what it means to be black and middle class vary widely, from perceptions of eco-nomic stability, to the optimal way to prepare black children to traverse the color line, to attitudes about the collective interests of their respective community" (5). The initial points she makes here—that class is a primary factor that contours and informs their sensibilities about race—supports established findings. This is appar-ent in the ways that black residents in these sites differ, not just from each other but also from the situations of members of the black middle class in the central cities. But the larger finding in Lacy's research is the substantial amount of cultural work that is required to make sense of race in everyday contexts.

Boundaries within Blackness

Lacy develops this finding by deploying the anthropological notion of *symbolic boundaries*. Such boundaries may be materially concrete, as with a fence or a road or a wall, but more often they are subtle and ephemeral—a facial or hand gesture, perhaps just a "look" that warns someone they have transgressed a social line. With this concept, Lacy (2007) explores how "some class boundaries within the black community may be more impermeable than those between blacks and whites" (12). Lacy articulates this point by referencing the "**black middle-class toolkit**" (13), a concept that "draws attention to the material and nonmaterial forms of culture that help people to negotiate everyday life and to make sense of the actions of others" (ibid.). Lacy characterizes this "toolkit" as an interpretive repertoire composed of a host of items: "black cultural capital," "public identities," inclusionary and exclusionary boundary work, as well as "improvisational pro-cesses and script-switching" (73, 77, 84). With this toolkit, middle-class blacks navigate white-dominated social spaces, maneuvering to circumvent potential dis-criminatory treatment while ensuring that they reproduce a class identity in their children that keenly differentiates them from blacks of a lower-class standing.

In material terms, clothing and posture play a crucial role in the overall presenta-tion of self that asserts belonging in the social world. Middle-class blacks "eschew clothing associated with urban popular culture" while "relying on mainstream language and mannerisms" (Lacy 2007, 76) in order to ensure that their public interactions—shopping trips, dealing with subordinates at work, or buying a house—are not marred by encounters with white stereotypes about poor blacks. This requires a two-pronged effort at presenting a "public identity" that differentiates them through exclusionary boundary work from lower-class blacks while they also "engage in inclusionary bound-ary work in order to blur distinctions between themselves and white members of the middle class by emphasizing areas of consensus and shared experiences" (75). These material gestures are accompanied by a set of nonmaterial practices.

Lacy finds middle-class blacks deploying improvisational tactics and script-switching strategies learned during childhood and their socialization in integrated or white-dominated settings. Improvisational tactics are means of managing interactions with whites where racism is evident; these involve indirect ways for circumventing foreclosed opportunities or possibilities. Script-switching is a more complex process of recognizing and rejecting racially limited or predetermined roles in any type of social interaction. Lacy explains, "because public interactions are governed by mainstream scripts, middle-class blacks are compelled to switch from black scripts to white scripts in public space" (88). Taken as a whole, this black middle-class toolkit represents a complex interpretive repertoire for negotiating public life in a variety of social settings and encounters.

A point that Lacy (2007) makes in describing these as "public identities" bears emphasizing. Unlike a psychological or an essentialist notion of identity, this formulation prioritizes the active symbolic work of asserting identities and contending with whether they are recognized, refused, or ignored. These are not simply achieved or given identities; they require performative work for them to be acknowledged. "Middle-class blacks employ these identities instrumentally to establish their position in American society relative to white strangers, their white middle-class neighbors, lower-class blacks, and one another" (14). These identities must be honed and wielded in very common settings—shopping in a mall, getting a table at a restaurant, finding a hotel while traveling: situations that rarely seem challenging to middle-class whites but that are often perilous for blacks of a similar class background. The problem, as Lacy points out, is that "the public perception of who is middle class in this United States does not include black people" (14). Given this fact, members of the black middle class are continually in situations where they must try to make the markers of their class identity sound out or shine more brightly than the features that identify them in terms of race.

But the cultural perspective developed by Lacy also valuably points in a contrary direction: the work that black middle-class parents undertake in guiding their children in formulating a racial identity as "authentically black." These parents express a common anxiety that their children will "forget they are black"—an anxiety that turns on very complex class dynamics. "The parents I interviewed," Lacy (2007) conveys, "aim to help their children become skilled in moving effortlessly across the black-white color line, but they also strive to help them forge meaningful connections to the black world, to a racial community where they can reconnect with other blacks after spending the bulk of their day in the white world" (156). The problem is that there are so many different classed versions of "the black world." Lacy reports that "for the parents in this study, helping their children to maintain a black racial identity requires as much thought and effort as nurturing a middle-class identity" (157). That is, acquiring blackness hinges on observing and reinforcing certain intraracial class boundaries. "Indeed, they prefer to interact with certain kinds of blacks, and they actively exclude others" (184). Not surprisingly, these different preferences are a reflection of place.

The primary difference is between the two majority-black neighborhoods (Riverton and Sherwood Park)—where "the neighborhood serves as the construction site for black identity" (Lacy 2007, 152), with black neighbors playing a prominent role—and the majority-white area (Lakeview), where black children spend most of their time in white-dominated social milieus. In Lakeview, parents seek out black religious and social organization, where their children can experience and cultivate a common racial identity. But in all three places, the class dimensions of race remain a sharp concern. "Just as residential location structures the construction of racial identities, proximity to the black lower class influences the kinds of class-based boundaries that middle-class blacks erect against their poorer counterparts" (173). In Sherwood Park, the wealthiest and most exclusive of these three communities, black parents drew "marked symbolic boundaries between their immediate neighbors and residents of the less exclusive subdivisions located close by" (ibid.). In Riverton, intraracial class boundaries were drawn against the black poor, largely as represented in forms of popular culture associated with "ghetto life." In Lakeview, though, these black poor were tangibly present in a community on the other side of a major highway from the upscale suburb. In each setting, though, this boundary work involved drawing moral distinctions that set apart members of the black middle class from lower-class blacks.

Lacy's study powerfully illustrates the analytical advantage we gain through an attention to cultural dynamics in relation to race. Most crucially, this approach allows us to move away from generalizations about black people—or white people, or any other racial group, for that matter—and move, instead, toward much more specific experiences and forms of interaction. We can then consider how these stem from or relate to very basic human processes of creating meaning and establishing a sense of belonging and difference. The cultural perspective Lacy develops on suburban, black middle-class people affords us the ability to recognize class-based commonalities in how whites and blacks of a certain status recognize and convey aspects of a shared social standing. We can also then see *how these commonalities disrupt or complicate intraracial similarities*. This type of symbolic activity would be difficult to grasp with only a race-based form of analysis, because it involves such highly varied, intraracial activity. The other important value to note here in the cultural perspective is that, with its emphasis on the active performative and interpretive work racial identities entail, we affirm a very basic point that anthropologists have been making for some decades now: race is socially constructed. While this point is typically made in reference to dismissing efforts to link biology and race, as we saw in Chapter 2, arguably it is of equal or greater value in revealing the dynamics that shape the significance of race in the social landscape.

LOCATING BLACKNESS IN THE SOCIAL LANDSCAPE

The surge of current studies of the black middle class is providing a long-needed corrective to the singular emphasis social scientists placed on studying "ghetto life." At the same time, though, it bears remembering that the growth of the black middle class over the past few decades is only one aspect of blackness. Black households earning over $100,000 a year—similar to the families that

Lacy studied—still represent something of a rarity, as less than 10% of the African American population in the United States. Compare that with 40% of black families earning less than $25,000 a year or the 25% poverty rate for blacks.[2] In many ways, the problems of race remain entangled with the conditions of poverty in this country. This should prompt us to consider some possible limits to Kelley's critique of anthropological and sociological efforts to study concentrated poverty in the inner city. For that matter, perhaps another corrective to the way anthropologists and sociologists misconstrued blackness in the United States may come in the form of ethnographies that reexamine social life in inner cities.

Where earlier studies produced findings that conformed to white fears and misunderstandings, as detailed earlier by Kelley (1997), contemporary ethnographic works show that social science research can also be used powerfully to counter distorting racial stereotypes (Mullings 1997). Arguably, this approach has long been a feature of the best ethnographies on urban poverty. Judith Goode (2002) makes this point, asserting that "the ethnography of the urban poor enables us to see up close how people struggle to make the best choices under dreadful conditions" (291). An excellent example of a work that set the standard for this approach is Carol Stack's ethnography *All Our Kin* (1974). But the motives and direction of returning to this type of fieldwork arguably should be principally guided by what Adolph Reed, in "The Underclass Myth" (2000), describes as an "imperative to reject all assumptions that poor people are behaviorally or attitudinally different from the rest of American society" (99). Indeed, studies of urban poverty, such as Jay MacLeod's *Ain't No Makin' It* (2009)—a comparative ethnography of white and black youths in a public housing project, discussed in Chapter 1—increasingly stress this very point. McLeod, for instance, finds that the black kids in this project are characterized by a zealous commitment to an "achievement ideology" that reflects a belief in and commitment to the American Dream. So powerful is their participation in this mindset that they are largely blind to the effects of racism on their personal lives and opportunities; indeed, they are, rather, quite American in insisting that they "do not see race" at all.

McLeod's findings effectively frame the challenge of taking back up or pursuing questions about blackness in relation to inner-city poverty. Can this be done without reinscribing an image of black otherness that is more distorting than it is insightful? There is no simple, general answer to this question, but we can turn to some particular ethnographies in order to think this matter through. Reexaminations of inner-city populations are hardly uniform in their analytical approaches, but two ethnographies stand out: Elizabeth Chin's *Purchasing Power: Black Kids and American Consumer Culture* (2001) and João Vargas' *Catching Hell in the City of Angels: Life and Meanings of Blackness in South Central Los Angeles* (2006). Where Chin stresses that residents of inner cities participate in a common American identity, Vargas emphasizes the distinctiveness of blackness

---

[2]These figures are from the 2007 Pew Research Center study cited earlier.

and strives to read it in terms of a global, diasporic view of race. Their contrasting views present important additional considerations in trying to understand blackness from an ethnographic perspective.

Elizabeth Chin's (2001) ethnography, *Purchasing Power*, "is primarily about the world of ten-year-old poor and working-class black children . . . and their entanglements with the world of consumption" (18). Conducted in a high-poverty neighborhood in New Haven, Connecticut, Chin's fieldwork challenges pervasive assumptions that the black poor—because of class and racial segregation—are not active participants in American culture:

> Kids like Natalia and Asia are aware of the connections, and this awareness can be seen most clearly in the area of consumerism and popular culture. These kids see and know about nearly all the same TV programs, stores, and goods that most other American kids do. Their relationships to these commodities, and to the process of consumption itself, are distinctive and characterized by complex and contradictory circumstances. (107)

Chin examines these "contradictory circumstances" by observing the various sites where these young people pursue consumerist activities, both in literal places, such as neighborhood stores and area malls, but also in more figurative engagements with media representations of the American dream.

Chin (2001) describes how young, inner-city blacks face a barrage of interdictions to their consumerist pursuits. Sometimes these take the form of media depictions of them as "anticonsumers" or "combat consumers"—distilled in images of welfare moms with several Cadillacs or drug dealers loaded down with gold chains. But more often these interdictions are very material, involving policing tactics and strategies in consumer settings. "Being poor at the mall," Chin writes, "shapes and directs the form and content of most of their time there, either as a sort of specter haunting others' suspicions about them, or as a painful reality forcing their simultaneous admission that such suspicions are true, while asserting that their status as human beings should not be diminished on the basis of their inability to buy" (92). But Chin's emphasis lies not in these structural constraints, rather in the active cultural work these kids do as consumers and as Americans.

Chin illustrates this dynamic by describing how they play with both white and "ethnically correct" dolls. The girls Chin studies display an "impressive ability to adroitly disparage or mobilize the social and geographic dividing lines between white and black" (164) in their imaginative play with racially inscribed dolls. Notably, Chin observes that the children "transform whiteness in very complex and subtle ways" as *they reconfigure and resignify the racial markers* on Barbie dolls, often through styles of braiding and dress. In such play, "these girls did not allow their dolls to remain white" (172), which reflects, Chin argues, a recognition of the plasticities of race that accompany its more emphatic dimensions of segregation and discrimination.

João Vargas (2006) bases his ethnographic work in the highly combustible terrain of South Central Los Angeles, which has been a vortex of racial conflict in the United States for decades. The well-known riots of 1965 and 1992 were merely flashpoints in the protracted conflicts over race and space that have given South Central a central place in Americans' thinking about race. Like ethnographers such as Carol Stack (1974) and Leith Mullings, Vargas strives to depict "the inventiveness of the survival strategies" (26) developed by African Americans in the face of hypersegregation, massive economic disinvestment, and militarized forms of policing. Contrary to previous social science accounts that found dysfunction and chaos in the inner city, Vargas details social practices that counteract the perils of urban violence and uncertainty while providing a basis for both hope and pleasure in a desperate setting.

Where Chin's work directs attention to overarching aspects of a common American identity at work in inner cities, Vargas' analysis instead points toward understanding these racial predicaments in terms of distinct forms of blackness developed within the larger African diaspora. Vargas interestingly finds blackness as constituted in several distinct registers simultaneously. First, blackness is shaped by *forms of exclusion and isolation* that have constructed the landscape of racial inequality in Los Angeles. This condition of imposed marginality informs a second dimension of blackness, one experienced as a sharp *sense of sorrow* but that leads to a shared feeling of *solidarity*. This dimension, though, must vie against an almost-overwhelming recognition of blackness as a form of *liability and powerlessness* in terms of the politics and policies shaping inner-city life. Still, some residents of South Central, Vargas explains, are able to turn each of these dimensions of blackness toward activities of *political mobilization* that seek to challenge the forms of racial domination evident in police violence and restricted forms of social movement based on race. In the end, Vargas emphasizes that blackness manifests, too, in forms of *artistry and affirmation* that derive from a larger sense of communal identity linked to global experiences of race, historically and contemporarily. Vargas becomes attuned to these distinct forms of blackness, with the different sensibilities about race they each entail, through the course of his wide-ranging fieldwork in Los Angeles. Living in a low-income, drug-ravaged neighborhood allowed him to glimpse the shared social life linked to race; pursuing participant observation with local activists opened a view into the ways blackness took shape in forms of political organizing; and participating in the artistry generated in a South Central cultural center revealed creative dynamics that inform distinct notions of black identity. Each of these settings also led him to recognize the role of gender, class, generation, and social in producing "distinct modalities of blackness" (219).

CLASS AND RACE: BRINGING GREATER SPECIFICITY TO BLACKNESS

Questions about the cultural dynamics of blackness are burgeoning today. Once ethnographic approaches in anthropology and sociology began reorienting away from the fixation on "ghetto life," the possible ways of examining the significance of race in the lives of black people became numerous. This closing section of this chapter offers just a snapshot of the plethora of perspectives open to ethnographers by way of considering the research trajectory pursued by anthropologist John L. Jackson. Rather than surveying a variety of approaches that extend the lines of analysis discussed earlier, it seems worthwhile to look closely at one ethnographer who, in the course of devising several different ways of studying blackness, began to investigate racial dynamics more broadly.

Jackson's research trajectory is notable because it begins with the same kind of fine-grained attention to class-based differences within blackness that were highlighted in this chapter—indeed, his work importantly influenced Karyn Lacy's approach. But he moves beyond this focus to ask philosophical questions about how we imagine the realness of race, constituting it between the discursive poles of "*authenticity*" and "*sincerity*." Eventually, this focus on discourse leads him to examine "racial paranoia" as a central aspect of American culture. Jackson presents us with a model of studying race that he has developed in several distinct contexts and that will have bearing on how race is studied in the future.

The Work of Racial Identity

Jackson's work begins with his ethnography *Harlemworld: Doing Race and Class in Contemporary Black America* (2001). The title bears two features that delineate the contours of his distinctive approach to race. The most easily recognized of these two is the hip-hop neologism *Harlemworld*. Jackson uses this term to characterize "a Harlem that is both a world unto itself and absolutely unintelligible without recourse to the outside world, from which it can never shake itself loose" (10). This place embodies an "exemplary blackness" not just in the United States but also globally. Where we glimpse black spaces in the ethnographies by Gregory, Pattillo-McCoy, and Lacy, in Harlem blackness is writ large, making its symbolic dimensions uniquely plain and tangible. This symbolism both informs and is affected by the unwieldy power and circulation of entertainment media and global popular cultures. "This state of affairs," Jackson confides, "demands a peripatetic anthropology that attempts, however vainly, to keep up with the lightening-fast speed of cultural transmissions and transmutations at the very beginning of the twenty-first century" (10). In this formulation Jackson challenges ethnographers to *regard their fieldwork sites not as bounded, pristine locations but as places shot through with widely circulating arrays of images that people actively and often unconsciously use in making sense of race.*

The second feature of Jackson's title is hardly as flashy and easily passes without much comment, but it marks a most significant assertion about race. In Harlem, Jackson studies people "doing" race; he sees race as a performance played out in everyday life. With this formulation we are far removed from the kind of essentialist notions about race that were examined in Chapter 2. Jackson takes as his central focus the "folk theories" of race that people develop and deploy in Harlem. This allows him maximum latitude, from questions of whether race is real or, rather, constructed, neither of which is adequate, to the ways that people engage race in everyday life. Jackson (2001) argues "that folk theories posit race as a kind of 'achieved' characteristic, claiming that racial authenticity is often achieved through performances and practices—usually, although not exclusively, through class-marked performances and practices" (13). This notion is usefully considered in contrast to constructivist assertions about race, which we may cognitively comprehend and accept but which hardly seem adequate to the realness by which race is lived.

In developing this idea, Jackson further explains, "*racial identity takes 'work'* (even hard work) and is therefore, in a sense, achieved or not achieved *based on one's actions and how they are interpreted*. Folk theories of race discover race in the doing, arrived at through specific actions and not only anchored in one's epidermis and morphology" [emphasis added] (149). In this formulation, Jackson does more than gesture toward a constructivist view of race; he points to the process by which this construction takes place. But he also sees in this **performative model of race** a similar potential to jar people out of their investments in race. "This performative notion of race creates a space for people to challenge arguments about what particular behaviors connect to which discrete races" (187).

"Post-Afrocentric Blackness"

How does this dynamic play out in everyday life in Harlem? Jackson (2001) finds it by attending to one of the most basic operations of culture—determining belonging. In Harlem he finds that racial belonging depends on far more than skin color. "Such is the power of Harlem and its symbolism," he observes, "that it helps determine who 'belongs' and who does not, and this issue of belonging begins to show rips, cracks, and holes in any ironclad notion of blackness" (185). The link between belonging and notions of place makes evident both the contestations over race and the interpretive work these contests impel. "The blackness of black Harlem has always been fought for and fought over: a blackness that was only for the civilized, well-to-do northerners as opposed to the newly arriving southerners or for African Americans and not for West Indians criticized for stealing the best jobs" (31). When blacks contest over who counts as a "Harlemite," they do so with an understanding that phenotype is not the deciding feature; rather, competing claims around class, region, and nationality are all more decisive. This is particularly notable in "important distinctions between blackness and brownness" (40), involving contrary ways of reading race in relation to "black Latinos" (whom we will examine in the next chapter) and in hostile reactions to African immigrants that belie notions of a common diasporic identity. In this latter regard, Jackson finds in Harlem "a kind of post-Afrocentric blackness, a black identity that does not need Africa to authenticate and ground its legitimacy. It is a blackness that can invoke the African continent as an icon of heritage and history in one context while disavowing personal connections to other parts of the African diaspora in another" (43). This variability and instability in residents' efforts to designate and identify with blackness leads Jackson to underscore the performative dimension of racial identity.

Jackson (2001) delineates this dynamic succinctly: "Race, like class, makes sense in people's daily lives in terms of performances, practices, and perceptions" (161). We read other people's behaviors and postures, clothing and facial expressions, gaits and reposes—just as we ourselves are read—for indications of how to place them in the racial and class categories that inform our social life. We read these daily, routine performances in order to have these categories confirmed but also to glimpse where or how they might be becoming cluttered and confused. In these readings, we glimpse again the relational aspects of racial identity, in that, as Jackson reports, Harlemites "use white people as a foil for a discussion about black cultural difference" (170). The point Jackson stresses is that "black bodies can be read as white bodies once behavioral specificities are added to the discussion. It is the slippage between identity and action that allows black bodies (and their actions) to be theorized along symbolically white lines" (180). This brings us back to the charged accusation of "acting white," a topic to which Jackson devotes attention.

Jackson (2001) criticizes the social science literature on acting white because it downplays "the multiple performances and practices that constitute the category white" (186). The problem lies in not recognizing that whiteness, too, is performed and enacted behaviorally, often in relation to symbolic designations of blackness. "Race as performance is about jostling for certainty over which particular behaviors are labeled black or white—a certainty that is never fully finalized outside of particular social contexts. The behaviors themselves only have racial value once they are placed within explicit frameworks organized to make claims about the connection between behavior and racial authenticity" (187). With the charge of acting white, blacks in Harlem contend with the racial coding of activities such as "social climbing" or certain ways of speaking and language use as well as styles of dress and physical comportment. Notably, Jackson finds that "this mixture of variables is so complex that specifically black actions . . . are often useless against accusations of whiteness. Acting white (the connection between behavior and racial identity) is more intricate and entangled than that" (185). More than anything, this charged accusation reveals the unfixed aspects of racial significance: "No behavioral gesture is going to allow unproblematized access to black authenticity" (ibid.). This is why we rely so heavily on watching closely people's performances of racial identity to understand how to place them.

Inside the Realness of Race

In Jackson's conclusions from his initial fieldwork in Harlem, the pressing philosophical question that surfaced for him was the matter of racial authenticity. He recognized that the "realness" of race fundamentally depends on notions of authentic forms of identity, which, as anthropologists know, are highly contingent and often contested. In order to analyze such an unstable but highly valued notion such as authenticity, Jackson approaches it via the ways we often counterbalance it with efforts to read and project sincerity. In *Real Black: Adventures in Racial Sincerity* (2005), Jackson sets about "bending the genre of ethnography to flesh out some of the most important conceptual elements we use, individually and collectively, to craft our conflicting responses to the enigmatic workings of race" (9). Jackson finds the dynamics he observed in Harlem pervading American culture in the range of "authenticitytests" applied in racial matters. "Here, race is seen as the restrictive script we use to authenticate some versions of blackness, whiteness, brownness, yellowness, and redness while simultaneously prohibiting others" (13). In contrast, he cultivates an attention to the less noticed ways we observe and project racial sincerity.

Where authenticity turns on objects and objectification, sincerity implies sub-jective states that we cannot presume to know or discern with the same kind of authority we summon in judging the authentic. Sincerity is more nebulous, involv-ing questions of interiority and subjectivity, in the face of which we fall back ever again on an investment in the realness of objects. Hence, *Real Black* is "an ethno-graphic portrait painted with the quixotic brushstrokes of anti-essentialism, brushstrokes that indicate how race is overimagined as real (and really slippery) in American society" (11). His portraiture takes off from his previous fieldwork in Harlem and expands to consider an enormous range of popular cultural represen-tations of race in relation to bodies, music, movies, and conspiracy theories, all of which he finds people talking about and responding to in various everyday con-texts. Jackson uses these encounters to elaborate on his performance model of race. Racial subjects possess "an interiority that is never completely and unques-tionably clear" (15)—hence both the importance and uncertainty of our perfor-mances. "We cannot take racial performances at face value," he explains because "performers can lie, misrepresent, cheat, backstab—even as they fool us all the while with perfect inflections and intonations. Sincerity is another way to talk about these racial concerns and uncertainties" (18). In this impressive work, Jackson defines racial sincerity as an attempt "to explain the reasons it can feel so obvious, natural, real, and even liberating to walk around with purportedly racial selves crammed up inside of us and serving as invisible links to other people" (15). Sin-cerity brings to the fore the vagaries and uncertainties of the racial selves we gen-erate and animate, which, like the "multiracial self" described in the last chapter by Pamela Perry, condense elements of the social world in the interior spaces of identity. In this sense, "sincerity highlights the ever-fleeting 'liveness' of everyday racial performances" (18).

The Uncertainties of Race
Jackson's focus on the subjective dimensions of racial identities led him to his work *Racial Paranoia: The Unintended Consequences of Political Correctness* (2008). This important concept addresses the distinctive ways race matters in the 21st century, a time when acts of blatant racism are infrequent and yet forms of racial inequality proliferate. **Racial paranoia** results from the peculiar situation of both having too much knowledge and lacking it at the same time. Americans are very knowledge-able about the ways racism used to work (up through the victories of the civil rights era) and the ways it is signified today in racial remarks, often evidenced by the "gaffes" of white celebrities. But with the rise of "political correctness," which polices racist expressions in the public sphere, it becomes more of an unknown what people are *not saying* about race in the face of imagined or perceived racial

animosity or contempt. "It is that fear of the hidden vis-à-vis race and racism," Jackson (2008) writes, "that racial paranoia breeds upon. It is about not knowing, not being sure. . . . Racial paranoia for African Americans is the fear that whites aren't saying what they really feel" (212). The result is a state of near-constant distrust that amplifies the possible racial meanings present in any utterance or exchange.

With the concept of racial paranoia, Jackson (2008) is able to analyze a significant force shaping interracial relations in the United States today. As an anthropologist, Jackson strives "to examine racial paranoia ethnographically: as a behavioral and ideological repertoire that creates (and is created by) complex cultural forces" (14). The prime force at work here is the disjuncture between the profound forms of racial inequality—such as the hidden costs of being African American discussed earlier—and the relative absence of obvious expressions of racist sentiment. Jackson sums up the situation simply: "We promote racial paranoia when we combine discussions about color blindness with silent acceptance of continued structural differences in racial realities" (206). That is, it is not so much what is "said" as what goes "unsaid" that fuels this form of paranoia.

To name this "unsaid" racial dimension, Jackson coins the term *de cardio racism*—an unarticulated racial sentiment "of the heart," in contrast to the well-established *de jure* (by law) and *de facto* (in fact) forms of racial discrimination. *De cardio* racism exactly occupies the subjective realm of racial sincerity Jackson examined in *Real Black*. Importantly, though, he finds that this anxiety is not exclusive to one race. "Fears about *de cardio* racism are prevalent among all Americans, not just African Americans, and they demand a different discussion about racism than we are trained (by civil rights activists and policy analysts) to have with one another. These nonfalsifiable suspicions about secretly racist hearts also further highlight the fact that race isn't just an intellectual idea that we can persuade people to disavow" (201). Rather, Jackson reminds us that "race is about emotion, affect, and intuition" (ibid.), powerful forces that often exceed the bounds of social reason of conventions.

In leading us into this intriguing realm, Jackson, as an anthropologist, stresses that these dimensions, though subjective and interior, are still shaped by culture. Jackson (2008) specifically defines racial paranoia in terms of "social and cultural terms over psychological and intrapersonal ones" (14). The important distinction lies in the way we personally feel our subjective sensibilities are either validated or denied by social conventions. These powerful forces shape our understanding of what it is that we intimately feel. There are few better examples of this than racism itself, which manifests in profoundly emotional ways, capable of driving people into murderous rages, yet is something that we learn to feel as we are socialized into a culture where race already matters so greatly.

From this perspective, the concept of racial paranoia "represents a useful way to define some of what is most important about contemporary racial antagonism in American society" (21). In describing "racial paranoia as a distinct analytical lens for understanding contemporary America" (4), Jackson characterizes our current predicament: "America's racial logic has changed dramatically in the last

200 years, and mostly for the better. But our analysis of it lags far behind, especially in terms of the issues we emphasize, the questions we ask" (21–22). But with concepts and analytical frames such as those examined in these chapters, students today are becoming better prepared for advancing research on such issues and concerns.

CONCLUSION

The ethnographic projects reviewed here delineate a variety of lines of research that open up discussions of blackness via a fine-grained attention to class distinctions and the specificities of place. These promising lines of inquiry allow researchers to jettison the *racial optic* in favor of perspectives that reveal the varied ways race matters in the lives of black people. The contrast here is between a tradition that tried to objectify blackness (largely in pathological terms) and new approaches that ask, instead, what counts as blackness. More to the point, these researchers examine the criteria people use—as well as the boundaries they assert and recognized—as they decide on who and what counts as black.

This shift reflects a critical transformation of social science research on race by turning to forms of analysis that attend to basic cultural dynamics shaping racial significance. As we saw with whiteness, these approaches highlight both the immense amount of interpretation race requires and the elaborate repertoires people assemble and rely on in making sense of racial matters. Whiteness and blackness stand as opposite conditions when we consider society at the level of greatest generality. But within each of these social formations, the deeper we move into the realm of daily life the more we glimpse similar processes: interpretive work in the face of routine performances of racial identity that are informed by and reproduce the excessive meaningfulness of race. These common cultural processes are crucial to keep in view as we strive to do more than generalize about racial groups and identities.

CHAPTER 6

Beyond Black and White

The questions about race we have been pursuing become more challenging and interesting as we move beyond the white/black framework for explaining racial matters. This frame is dominant because the constructs of whiteness and blackness are the defining poles of racial meaning in the United States. But the manifold forms of difference that exceed this polar opposition are a plain indication that *white* and *black* are hardly sufficient terms alone for understanding the meaning of race. Too much else is going on with racial identity these days. This chapter aims to extend and further develop our perspective on race by focusing on two very broad, panethnic identities: Latinos and Asian Americans.

These groups encompass an enormous amount of social and cultural diversity, such that they belie the very idea of race as a homogeneous, natural identity. Yet, as we will see, a critical view of racial dynamics is fundamental for comprehending the distinctive experiences of people that fall within these categories in the United States. The crux of the matter is that, though these groups have historically and contemporarily, to varying degrees, been subject to racial discrimination, there is little basis for considering either to be a "race," given the social and phenotypic heterogeneity within each category. The point of this chapter, then, is to discuss the *processes of racialization that peoples of Asian and Hispanic origins have encountered in the United States* while also considering how their experiences lead us to question further our cultural assumptions and beliefs about race.

You will find much familiar in this chapter, at least at the outset, since most of the conceptual tools we will need here have been explained and developed in previous chapters. *The fundamental dynamics remain marked and unmarked cultural forms, along with the relational dimension of racial identity.* Thinking of racial identity as a continuum between marked and unmarked positions, the social features of Latinos' and Asian Americans' lives can be varyingly construed in racial or nonracial terms. There is an additional complicating factor, however, involving **ethnicity** and the role of ethnic discourse in the United States as a form of mediation between marked and unmarked identities. Crucially, as well, the dynamics of marking difference from an implicitly white American "mainstream" are changing quickly. We see this most clearly in references to the **Latinization** or **Asianization** of U.S. cities, cuisine, and popular culture. These terms reflect the degree to which the cultural and social content of representations of American identity are shifting away from the white Anglo image. Still, whiteness and blackness remain the defining poles. Latinos and Asian Americans can alternately be construed as participating in or being distanced from whiteness, and, to some extent, people within these groupings frequently articulate their identity in opposition to blackness. But in each of these regards, more nuance and variation is involved than we have seen in considering the social situations of whites and blacks in general.

The major new development you will find in this chapter is that, as we move away from a focus on whiteness and blackness, the centrality of advantage and disadvantage as a means of determining the relevance of race begins to recede. These conditions or positions were fundamental to discussions of race in Chapters 4 and 5. A considerable portion of the discussion of blackness in Chapter 5 focused on bringing into view the disadvantages in the "hidden cost of being African American" that many Americans do not easily recognize. Concomitantly, in order to grasp the racialness of whites in Chapter 4 we had to recognize the logical correlate that conditions of disadvantage necessarily entail forms of advantage. But Chapter 4 also conveyed that white racialness is not simply equivalent to social advantage—a matter that was examined in ethnographic detail regarding the situations of whites as local racial minorities. Similarly, while Chapter 5 initially focused on making evident the manifold forms of disadvantage that confront African Americans, that chapter also featured ethnographic situations of upper-class African Americans and the performative views of race of Harlemites from a variety of class backgrounds. From this view, black racial identity involves far more than a generic condition of disadvantage.

Now, as we move beyond the "white and black" framework for race, we increasingly need to *recognize racial dynamics that are not reducible simply to forms of advantage or disadvantage.* The role of cultural dynamics—primarily involving ideas about belonging and nature as well as the types of linkages or associations people develop in relation to these ideas—that we examined in the previous chapters becomes increasingly central to understanding how and why race matters. To be sure, racial advantage and disadvantage remain central concerns; a primary marker of the racial aspects of the lives of Latinos and Asian Americans is the extent to which they are disadvantaged by forms of discrimination and racism. But as we will see in this chapter, the social circumstances of peoples of Asian and Latin descent are so varied that we would miss a great deal of how race matters in their lives if we looked for it only in terms of discrimination or the expression of racist sentiments. This social variety makes it even more critical that we examine the role of basic cultural dynamics in shaping the significance of race. What matters in this chapter is that we recognize how *the experiences and perceptions of Latinos and Asian Americans are prompting a reevaluation of what counts as racial identity in the United States.*

RACIAL GROUPS?

If you filled out a U.S. Census form in 2010, you would have been asked to indicate what race you consider yourself to be. The question on the form directed respondents to "mark one or more boxes" from the following options: "White," "Black, African American, or Negro," and "American Indian," along with "Asian Indian," "Chinese," "Filipino," "Japanese," "Korean," "Vietnamese," "Native Hawaiian," "Guamanian or Chamorro," and "Samoan," followed by "Other Asian" and "Other Pacific Islander" and finally "Some other race." Discussions about race in relation to the census largely have focused on the novelty of the directive to choose "one or more." In acknowledgment of the increasing complexity of racial identity in the United States, the Census Bureau finally allowed people to identify as other than monoracial. In 2010, around nine million people (about 3% of the population) chose this option, certainly a strong indication that we are developing a sensibility about race that exceeds the black/white framework. As well, over nineteen million respondents chose the option of writing "some other race," strongly indicating that many Americans find our historical terms of racial identification insufficient.

This development has generated a great deal of commentary and discussion about the changing status of "mixed race" identity. But as interesting as that topic is, further attention needs to be directed to the "commonsense" notions of race that remain dominant in this country, as captured in the racial identifications chosen by the vast majority of Americans. It is important to recognize these options as *cultural artifacts that provide us a powerful perspective onto U.S. history as well as contemporary politics*. Consider for a moment how someone not born or residing in the United States for some time would think it odd that so many nationalities—Chinese, Filipino, Japanese, and so on—are so naturally construed in this country as distinct races. For that matter, if you were born into the U.S. racial system or have dwelt here for a long time, you must find it strange not to see Hispanic or Latino as a race. Both of these oddities are means of reacquainting ourselves with the fundamental point that race is a shifting cultural construct.

The 2010 census question about race is a reflection of long-developing social and political processes in this country—processes that promise to continue to be quite dynamic in the future. Primarily, these racial options stem from federal requirements to track the continuing operation of discrimination and prejudice. If it were not for the discrimination confronting members of these groups, there would be little basis for considering these categories in racial terms. But the complications of recording this information are immediately apparent. The group that most consistently stands alongside African Americans in terms of disparaging treatment is Hispanics (as we saw in Chapter 1), but their case makes the absurdity of racial classification most apparent. "Latino" can hardly be considered a race because it encompasses "whites," "blacks," and "Native Americans." A similar absurdity has been addressed with the previous census category "Asian or Pacific Islander," which was a racial category unique to the United States. But does subdividing this category into discrete national "races" really resolve that problem?

Racialization in Progress

Why we persist in characterizing these groups as races is because of their ongoing experiences of being "marked" in relation to whiteness. This process of racialization, or marking, is historically deep and contemporarily varied. Key events in U.S. history—particularly the annexation of Mexican territory, Asian immigration restrictions and exclusions, the Hawaiian and Puerto Rican annexations, and the conquest of the Philippines—constituted the basis for this racialization. Each of these moments brought a variety of peoples into direct confrontation with the racial strictures limiting citizenship to "white persons" established by Congress in 1790. But these events also contributed to the current moment, when *questions of citizenship*—whether in cultural or legal terms—grow increasingly complex and uncertain. This uncertainty is best captured in the question of whether "whites" in the United States are soon going to be a minority.

Beginning in the mid-1990s, demographers and social commentators predicted that trends in immigration and birth rates suggested that whites are becoming a minority and that soon the United States would have no racial majority. This narrative was based on the declining number of "non-Hispanic whites" in this country. However, the actual results of the 2000 census suggested a different storyline. Instead of declining, as widely anticipated, the number of whites held constant at about 75% of the population. For that matter, current census projections are that the number of whites will increase by about 80 million by mid-century. In 2010, over 14 million more people identified as white, a 6% increase from the previous census. This all becomes more perplexing by considering that the Census Bureau also projects that "people of color" will become a majority in this country by 2042. That is, "whites" may be simultaneously losing and maintaining their majority status (Roberts 2008). At root in these contradictory trends is that the social content of whiteness is changing rapidly.

White identity, as we saw in Chapter 2, has never been a fixed or essential quality. As a result, the question of who was white at any historical moment has been answered quite differently. "Mexican," for example, emerged from the "white" category on the census in the 1930s, reflecting Anglo anxiety over immigration from Mexico following that country's revolution in the 1910s. But they were folded back into white again in the 1940 census, and "Hispanic" did not become a category until the 1970 census. Currently, almost half of Hispanics identify as white. This choice is heavily influenced by class. Latinos living in affluent, suburban zones of Los Angeles, for instance, tended to label themselves white, while Latinos living in the region's barrios generally racially identified as "other" on the 2010 census. This divergence in responses indicates that class is crucial, but it also shows the importance of regional dynamics and *the enduring relevance of place in how people make sense of identity*.

The ambiguities concerning who counts as "white" hardly become clearer when we turn to the criteria used by the Census Bureau to identify races. The bureau defines "white" as "the original peoples of Europe, North Africa, or the Middle East." Not only does this obviously include Spain—and hence people of "Hispanic" origins—but it also encompasses Arabs and Arab Americans, who are frequently subject to racial discrimination by other "whites." The basic points to grasp here are that race is hardly a natural, fixed identity and that white is a far more polyglot category than we might have expected. White continues to be an uncertain matter, as it was in earlier periods in U.S. history, when Irish, Italian, Greek, Slavic, and Jewish immigrants were perceived as not belonging to this category (Roediger 2005, Jacobson 1998). The number of whites in this country is projected to grow, not because of increased births among Anglo Americans, but because so many people immigrating to this country or born here of immigrant parents are identifying as white.

Who Is Foreign?

This underscores a point made in this chapter's opening: Whiteness and blackness continue to define the landscape of racial meaning. Hopefully this is apparent with regard to whiteness, given these demographic trends, but it may take a bit more work to grasp this in relation to blackness. People continue to identify as white because it is advantageous to do so; fundamentally, this is a reflection of the continued disadvantages associated with blackness. In this chapter we will explore how these perceptions of advantage and disadvantage play out in the experiences of Latinos and Asian Americans. But before proceeding, we must *grasp the distinctive racial dimension that links these two groups, over and against readily assumed ideas about blackness and whiteness.* The enduring racial perception that peoples of Hispanic or Asian descent are subject to, by most whites and even many blacks, is that they are foreign. This perception of **foreignness** is both racial and cultural. It is racial in that it is a form of markedness, particularly in relation to whiteness, that has had powerful social, economic, and political effects. It is cultural in that it makes important features of American life alternately *visible* and *invisible,* regarding matters of *belonging* and *difference.* The projection of foreignness onto Latinos and Asian Americans combines both race and culture in a charged dynamic concerning belonging in the United States.

People of Asian or Hispanic descent can be construed as foreign, despite the fact that members of these groups have resided in this country through many generations, because Anglos have made such tenacious claims to representing American identity. The fundamental distortion in this view is that so many peoples in the Pacific, the Caribbean, and northern Mexico were engulfed by the United States in its pursuit of Manifest Destiny throughout the 19th and early 20th centuries. America came to many of them, rather than the implied notion that they all immigrated to America. But however peoples from Asia or Latin America came to reside in the United States, the notion of foreignness operates as *a fundamental means by which these groups were varyingly deprived of rights, property, and access to public resources.* Whether in terms of explicit legal or implicit social means, these peoples were racially excluded from basic rights of citizenship in this country (Haney-Lopez 2006). In some ways, this situation parallels the conditions African Americans faced following emancipation, but it is also important to recognize the distinctive aspects of these situations.

The common dimension of racialization for "peoples of color" broadly is the condition of being marked in relation to whiteness. But similarities in the experiences of racialization for Latinos and Asian Americans involve a crucial difference from that of African Americans, a distinction that is embodied in this notion of foreignness. Mia Tuan, in *Forever Foreigners or Honorary Whites? The Asian Ethnic Experience Today* (-1998), explains that "for Asians, nativism and the stigma of foreignness further compounds racial marginalization. Blacks may be many things in the minds of whites, but foreign is not one of them" (8). Similarly, Suzanne Oboler, in *Ethnic Labels, Latino Lives: Identity and the Politics of (Re)Presentation in the United States* (1995), observes that "Chicanos and Puerto Ricans—regardless of race, class, birthplace, or citizenship status—were explicitly excluded as foreigners from the style in which the white Anglo-Saxon public was encouraged to imagine the national community of the United States" (42). Latinos, as do African Americans, suffer from a lack of recognition of their participation in the historical process of forming the United States as a nation, but this lack additionally extends to denying their native-born presence within this country. As Oboler notes:

> The exclusion of blacks has not been couched in distortions stemming from xenophobic portrayals of them as foreign born. Indeed, the experiences of Mexican Americans and Puerto Ricans in the United States (legally fellow citizens since 1848 and 1917, respectively) exemplify the ways that xenophobic nationalism and domestic racism have been conflated since the early 19th century. This fusion has forged a public self-image of the "American people" in relation to racially perceived foreign "Others" not only in the United States but in the hemisphere as a whole. (32).

Specifically, *this projection of foreignness has operated as a means of exclusion from the privileges of whiteness.*

The construction of Latinos and Asian Americans as "foreign" has additional sources beyond its historical uses to delimit their claims to citizenship. As we glimpsed earlier in Chapter 4 with Leland Saito's ethnography of Monterey Park in California, continued immigration from Asia and Latin America also fuels this perception. This continued influx of new Asian and Latino residents, though, simultaneously pushes in two different direction with regard to U.S. racial categories, both of which we will explore in some detail in the ethnographic portion of this chapter. The first involves the way these immigrants compound or reinforce the image of foreignness. Typically funneled into racially segregated neighborhoods and excluded from whiteness, these groups are highlighted symbolically in a way that makes other members of these categories—Latinos and Asian Americans who have lived in this country for generations—seem invisible. The other direction that this points to is captured by the terms *Asianization* and *Latinization*, which each reference the ways these groups are distinctly transforming the cultural and social content of American identity. Each of these processes, as well as those in relation to racial identification on the census and projections of foreignness, make it clear that the distinct processes of racialization that inform Latino and Asian American identities warrant close attention.

ETHNICITY AND RACE

The crucial element in this distinction is the concept of ethnicity. As with the concept of race, ethnicity is used to categorize groups of people based on notions of similarity and difference as well as on common history, culture, and social ties. But ethnicity plays a particular role in how Americans talk about race, and it functions specifically *to mediate the kinds of contradictions that might disrupt notions of race linked to the maintenance of whiteness.* "White ethnics," as a category, is a good example. This is used to label people who may seem to match a phenotypical notion of whiteness but whose language use and lifestyle seem far from the generic middle-class norms of white belonging. Ethnicity, in this sense, is a means by which we talk about the internal social heterogeneity within racial groups that generally operate as categorical identities. But ethnicity also plays a fundamental role in both mediating and maintaining the dynamics of marked and unmarked racial identities.

Anthropologist Brackette Williams (1989) construes race and ethnicity as linked ways of talking about difference within racially marked identities or social positions, over and against the dominant, unmarked racial identity, whiteness. In this schema, ethnicity allows for a bifurcation of marked forms of difference; although race is used to characterize difference of a threatening nature, the *difference encompassed by ethnicity appears potentially appealing and consumable.* Bonnie Uriciuoli (1996) builds on this analysis and points out that "race and ethnicity are both about belonging to the nation, but belonging in different ways. When people are talked about as an ethnic group, as Italian-American, Polish-American, African-American, Hispanic-American, Asian-American, the ideological emphasis is on national or cultural origins. This emphasis gives them a rightful place in the United States" (19). However, she continues, "when people are talked about as a race (and every group now seen as ethnic was once or is still seen as a race as well as an ethnic group), the emphasis is on natural attributes that hierarchize them, and, if they are not white, make their place in the nation provisional at best" (28). For both Williams and Uriciuoli, at the core of American uses of ethnicity is an equation of the normative American with white identity, which maintains the projection of foreignness onto "ethnics" who may have belonged in this country for generations.

Work and Race

The concept of ethnicity involves an enormous field of inquiry that extends well beyond the scope of this discussion of race. We can hardly consider its more nuanced and intriguing dimensions in this book. But we can look more closely at the dynamics that link race and ethnicity, as discussed by Williams and Uriciuoli. At the core of this connection is the simple but fundamental distinction in *the ability of groups to control and profit from their own labor.* This point is easily grasped if you consider the central role slavery played in developing the idea of race. Europeans rationalized their enslavement of Africans on the basis of notions that they were inherently racially inferior and just a step above animals or beasts. Slavery is the starting point in establishing a polarity between racially dominant and subordinate groups, with the latter having no ability to control their own labor. From this view, as Uriciuoli explains, people are racialized to the extent that they have minimal control over their position in the labor force and in the nation. So long as a labor force remains cheap and highly controlled, it is likely to stay racialized. This is an incisive means, not only for comprehending how poverty and unskilled labor are racialized in this country, but also for grasping the basis for both the similarities and differences connoted by ethnicity and race in relation to Latinos and Asian Americans vis-à-vis African Americans.

As just noted, today's "ethnics" were initially viewed in racial terms upon their arrival to the United States, to the extent that they arrived poor and largely unskilled, prey to exploitative labor practices. This condition of racialization was touched on in Chapter 2 with the case of Irish and Italian immigrants being construed as racial others, even though today they generally assume an unproblematic whiteness. Latinos and Asian Americans underwent a similar but more extreme process, in terms of the types of racial exclusions to which they were subjected upon entering this country. The key question here is to what extent they were able to shift from being perceived in strictly racial terms to being viewed increasingly in terms of ethnicity. The answer is complex and fundamentally involves contrasting dynamics facing African Americans in the same era as well as the various forms of internal social differentiation within these larger panethnic identities. In this sense, the goal in trying to answer this question is *not to establish emphatically which groups are racial or ethnic* but, rather, to *recognize how the relational dynamic that plays off this contrast is linked to changing economic and social positions of groups within the larger U.S. society.*

Restricting Immigration

Without going into a great deal of historical detail, it is easy to see that early immigrants from China and Japan, for instance, were perceived by whites as racial others and subject to racially exclusionary practices. Chinese immigration was initially encouraged to fill the need for cheap labor in building the transcontinental railroads. Excluded from citizenship in racial terms, they had very little control over their work condition or wages, so they remained racialized as a group. Indeed, as they began to establish their own businesses and communities, thus gaining more control over their labor and profits, whites felt extremely threatened and pushed the Chinese Exclusion Act in 1882 banning further Chinese immigration. A similar ban (the "Gentlemen's Agreement" of 1907) prevented Japanese from immigrating to this country, and a whole series of legal restrictions followed in the early 1920s barring southern and eastern Europeans, who, at the time, were also perceived as racially different from white Americans.

Two major interrelated developments followed from these restrictions on immigration. The first is that new pools of cheap labor were required to replace these immigrants and to fill the nation's surging industrial capacity in the early to mid-1900s. Manufacturing operations were compelled to recruit from other racialized populations internal to the United States: southern blacks and Puerto Ricans. Second, in the wake of this development, the relatively small groups of Chinese and Japanese in California were able to continue developing their businesses, gradually achieving greater economic control over their communities. The legal restrictions on Asian immigration kept Chinese and Japanese populations small and relatively stable. But the incessant demands for cheaper labor brought ever-increasing numbers of blacks and Puerto Ricans to neighborhoods already overcrowded due to racial restrictions in the industrial Midwest and East Coast cities. The economic situation facing members of these groups was made doubly precarious—first by the devastating boom-and-bust cycle of industrial labor that made jobs alternately plentiful and scarce and then by the destabilizing process of the constant influx of poor migrants into urban ghettoes.

The upshot of these processes of immigration restriction and labor recruitment is that these racialized populations gradually began to be characterized by very different economic situations. The smaller and fairly constant numbers of Asian Americans allowed these groups to develop stable communities that increasingly controlled their economic resources. This did not entirely transform their situation of being marked in relation to whiteness, but it did profoundly alter the significance of that perception of difference. The basis of their economic control translated into a kind of neighborhood-based tourism, where the restaurants and markets of Asian Americans began to appeal to whites as a "safe" and consumable form of difference. Think today of the pervasiveness of Chinese restaurants and their thorough imbrication in American life, as we glimpsed through Leland Saito's ethnography of Monterey Park, California, in Chapter 4. Similar processes occurred for most ethnic groups in this country. A vestige of this process can be seen today in lower Manhattan, where the neighborhoods of Chinatown and Little Italy continue to draw large crowds of hungry tourists looking for something a little foreign.

The examples of "ethnic restaurants" affords us another angle on the dynamic relation between ethnicizing and racializing, which is evident as we consider key categories for food in this country. Americans speak with ease and unselfconsciousness about *ethnic food*, but we would be loath ever to characterize something as *race food*. You can grasp these contrasting forms of markedness by considering the unique status of *soul food* in the American culinary landscape. Is it an ethnic food that draws white tourists from the suburbs to urban neighborhoods as does Mexican, Chinese, and Thai food? (French cuisine, notably, isn't ethnic food; rather, it is "high class.") Not yet, though its popularity is somewhat on the rise in some East Coast cities, such as New York and Washington, D.C. But the marketability of soul food has to contend with the significant white anxiety about predominantly black neighborhoods. A similar contrast can be seen in the dearth of Puerto Rican restaurants, especially compared with the pervasive presence of Mexican food, both in markets and in eateries. These contrasts highlight the fact that the position of blacks and Puerto Ricans in the labor force remained far more tenuous during the past century, which contributed to their ongoing racialization as threatening others.

Making It in America

A good deal is made in American popular discourse about *the narrative of European immigrant success*, in which all groups are assumed to start from the same point and move onto success or failure depending on each group's "value system." *But this narrative hides from view the crucial matter of race in shaping labor markets and access to capital in this country.* When the overall numbers of these European groups were capped by immigration restrictions in the early 1900s, blacks and Puerto Ricans were actively encouraged to migrate to cities in the industrial Midwest and East Coast. This led to starkly different abilities of these groups to develop and cultivate job networks and capital in their respective neighborhoods. These differences were compounded by racism, certainly in the housing sphere but also in the labor market. European immigrants were allowed to join increasingly powerful unions in the 1940s and 1950s, giving them greater job security and higher wages. In contrast, Puerto Ricans and African Americans were racially banned from unions, restricting them largely to "unskilled" positions. "White ethnics" became key players in unions and urban politics, whereas blacks and Puerto Ricans were consistently excluded from these institutions. Similar processes of exclusion confronted Mexicans and Mexican Americans in the agricultural sector, but with one notable difference for Puerto Ricans—as a former colony of the United States and now a "territory," they occupy a deeply ambiguous position on the cusp of the racial/ethnic divide in this country.

The purpose of this comparative discussion of ethnicity and race is not to fix which groups are ethnic and which racial; rather, the goal is to see these as related forms of markedness in a continuum that is defined by the overarching categories of whiteness and blackness. These identities are dynamic and related. For instance, achieving some degree of economic control over their situation did not entirely relieve Asian Americans of the burden of being marked in relation to whiteness. This is evident in the fact that many Japanese Americans were stripped of their financial resources and incarcerated in labor camps during World War II—a devastating ordeal that German Americans almost entirely escaped. But the relation of identity to position in labor markets does help us begin to specify what is distinctive about differential aspects of the ways groups have been and continue to be racialized in this country.

The crux of the matter is that ethnicity and race constitute two conditions of markedness, in symbolic terms. Where *ethnicity can seem safe and appealing, racial difference is largely construed as dangerous and threatening*—racialized people are depicted as out of control and not belonging to or participating in the nation. Uriciuoli (1996) explains, "marked Americans either succeed as good ethnics or fail as members of a raced underclass" (38). The central point she stressed is that "ethnicization does not negate racialization but perpetuates it" (ibid.). This dynamic defines social meaning for peoples occupying the "racial middle" in the United States.

RACIALIZATION OF LATINOS AND ASIAN AMERICANS

Sociologist Eileen O'Brien (2008) defines the **racial middle** as a complex social landscape dominated by the fastest-growing panethnic groups, Latinos and Asian Americans, whose numbers are expected to double by 2050 (then constituting about 25% and 9% of the nation's population, respectively). *A defining feature of life in the racial middle is the experience of marginalization in U.S. society.* This is illustrated simply by the striking underrepresentation of these groups in national politics relative to the size of their respective populations. At the same time, O'Brien points out that by certain key demographic indicators—"educational levels, marriage patterns, residential choices"—these groups are "more white than black" (200) in terms of the continuum between social advantage and disadvantage associated with race.

The challenge in understanding their situation in regards to race is twofold. First, as O'Brien explains, their experiences sometimes "mirror African American historical experiences in the United States, while others are more reflective of white experiences. . . . They defy simplistic categorization in a society that has insisted on operating along such dichotomous lines for the greater part of its history" (2–3). People within these categories, though, are hardly passive in the face of this lack of fit with the dominant binary terms of racial identity. They make choices regarding how they identify that either seek to undermine this binarism or perhaps reproduce it. The second part of this dimension of racialization involves the question of whether or how Asian Americans and Latinos position themselves in relation to either end of this continuum, that is, toward whiteness or toward blackness.

Sociologist George Yancey makes this question the center of his research in *Who Is White? Latinos, Asians, and the New Black/Nonblack Divide* (2003). As the title suggests, Yancey concludes from his survey research that Latinos and Asian Americans, by and large, are beginning to constitute, alongside whites, a common "nonblack" racial majority, against which blacks remain largely disadvantaged. That is, rather than further undermining the terms of racial identity, Yancey sees these two groups as gravitating toward whiteness and, to increasing degrees, largely finding acceptance in this shift. The evidence for his claims derives from survey data that shows Latinos and Asian Americans "are not only assimilating into the dominant group residentially and maritally, but are also beginning to identify with whites by adopting attitudes similar to those of majority groups members" (20). That is, "nonblack minorities are not just living next to and marrying whites, but are also *thinking like whites in that they are dismissing the importance of race in the United States.* In many ways they are on their way to becoming white" [emphasis added] (10). For Yancey, the telling indicator lies in whether Latinos and Asian Americans opt for a color-blind sensibility that refuses to see race as a significant factor in society.

Social Heterogeneity within Panethnic Identities

Yancey's work initiated a developing line of inquiry regarding racial identity in the United States. By offering an incisive, well-argued thesis, supported by solid and meaningful data, Yancey set the terms for a debate that has been enjoined by researchers such as O'Brien and Arlene Dávila, an anthropologist whose ethnographies we will consider in some detail later. But before diving into the details of this debate, we should revisit a point raised at the beginning of this chapter. The categories "Latino" and "Asian" both reflect and belie the bases of racial classification in this country. We have examined the former point at length but have yet to devote much attention to the latter. Both categories encompass such social variety that it is absurd to consider either of them as representing a single, homogeneous race. "Asian" includes all of East Asia (Japan/China/Korea), Southeast Asia (Vietnam/Thailand/Cambodia), and South Asia (India/Pakistan), countries with enormously varied—and often conflictual—histories, politics, and social relations. "Latino" comprises the enormous ethnic diversity of Latin America, collapsing under one label Argentines of European descent; Mexicans with indigenous as well as Asian and African ancestry; Cubans with Lebanese, African or Chinese heritage; Peruvians with Anglo, Slavic, or Incan lineages; and Brazilians with Asian or Mediterranean forbearers; all with varying degrees of African and American Indian ancestry thrown into the mix. As we move toward trying to say something general about panethnic identities in racial terms, we have to keep in mind that these groups are highly differentiated and varied, which makes such claims consistently tenuous.

This range of variation matters a great deal for Yancey's thesis. Consider the case of Latinos and whiteness. While more than half of "Hispanics" identified as "white" on the 2010 census, that option was contrastingly chosen by members of the distinct nationalities within this ethnic category. The range is captured by the difference between Cubans, with over 85% identifying as white, and Dominicans, of whom less than 30% chose that racial identity. Mexicans and Puerto Ricans fell in the midrange, with just under half of each group selecting the "white" option. Then there were noticeable regional differences, too, with South Americans, broadly, checking the "white" box about 65% of the time, while about 52% of Central Americans, cumulatively, made this identification. These differences in racial identification among Latinos raises the caution that, as we strive to understand something about the broad dynamics of race in the United States, we have to keep in mind that overarching trends—though important to grasp—potentially obscure as much as they reveal. This is why ethnography plays such a central role in these discussions, as we will see in the second half of this chapter.

The Whitening or Browning of America

But before we get to the ethnographic level of detail, there is more to be drawn from broad-level surveys, particularly work responding to Yancey's research. Eileen O'Brien, in *The Racial Middle: Latinos and Asian Americans Living Beyond the Racial Divide* (2008), characterizes the debate Yancey engendered as being divided by two major, antithetical schools of thought on the processes of racial identification for these groups: "I will call them the '**whitening thesis**' and the '**browning thesis**.'" (12). Parsing Yancey's findings, O'Brien explains that "the whitening thesis defies the idea of a smooth assimilation for all groups, and instead asserts that access to such privileges only comes to those who are allowed to step into the nonblack side of the black/nonblack dichotomy" (12). In contrast, the browning thesis, evident in the work of Eduardo Bonilla-Silva (2006), posits the emergence of a collective identity as "people of color" that reflects both a rejection of whiteness and an insistence by whites on maintaining a delimited form of racial dominance. Regarding these antithetical views, O'Brien (2008) makes an important observation: "Rarely has in-depth qualitative ethnographic data been brought to bear on the question of both Latino and Asian Americans' perspectives on whether they are whitening, browning, or remaining in a distinct middle, as a group" (17). O'Brien does not undertake such ethnographic work herself, but she did pursue this basic question via a qualitative approach that yielded interesting results.

Based on in-depth interviews with fifty self-identified Latinos and Asian Americans, O'Brien (2008) found aspects of both theses confirmed, which suggests that the processes of racial identification for members of these groups are quite complicated and nuanced. Indeed, these seemingly contradictory findings suggest "that whitening and browning theses do not necessarily allow for the complexity present in the racial middle" (205). This complexity begins with the type of ethnic heterogeneity represented in the "variety of ethnicities within the two racial groups" (22) in her study. O'Brien relates that "nine different ethnicities are represented among the twenty-three Latino respondents: Mexican, Puerto Rican, Dominican, Cuban, Honduran, Guatemalan, Brazilian, Salvadorian, and Guatemalan. Likewise, eleven different ethnicities are represented among the twenty-seven Asian American respondents: Chinese, Taiwanese, Indian, Filipino, Japanese, Korean, Thai, Bengali, Vietnamese, Cambodian, and Macanese" (22). This diversity forms the basis by which O'Brien finds "that racial and ethnic categories operate more as sliding scales or continua in the minds of respondents rather than as hard and fast classifications" (30). *This continuum makes racial identity a matter of active interpretive work* on the part of both these subjects and the people they encounter in everyday life.

The complexity of this process of identification extends further with the matter of internal hierarchies within these panethnic groups. Though respondents related that they were often misperceived by outsiders—"members of Latino and Asian American groups are often mistaken for other ethnicities within their own racial group" (O'Brien 2008, 205)—in contrast, they evidenced a tendency to see differences in prestige or dominance of particular nationalities within the broader racial categories. Asian Americans distinguished the relative status of Japanese, Chinese, and Koreans, reflecting in part the standing of those nations—and particularly the fraught history of Japanese colonialism—but also the success of peoples of those nations in the United States. Similarly, O'Brien found that "some Latino respondents assert that there exist status hierarchies within their own panethnic racial category. For Latinos, interestingly, at least two status hierarchies are identified across the interviews—one is organized by the particular ethnicity/country of origin (like that of Asians) while the other follows along skin tone, with the lighter the better" (36). This skin-tone hierarchy, or **colorism**, reflects both the enduring impacts of slavery, which was predicated on exactly this basis of differentiating humans, and the fact that the U.S. racial order is not the only one active on the

North American continent. O'Brien finds in her studies vestiges of a similar black–white continuum that turns on the concept of *mestizaje* in Mexico, as well as throughout Latin America. This concept construes racial identity as somewhat more fluid or plastic than in the United States, but one that is still shaped by the dominance of whiteness and the subordination of blackness.

Thinking through Skin

The issue of internal differentiation and status hierarchies within these panethnic identities highlights the complex dynamics of racial identification and differentiation, which in turn underscores the fundamental work of interpretation that race impels and requires. Colorism is one crucial example because we see the attention to a physical feature freighted with enormous cultural significance as operating not in blunt categorical terms but along a diffuse continuum within categories of "black," "Latino," and "Asian."

Margaret Hunter researches this dynamic in *Race, Gender, and the Politics of Skin Tone* (2005). Hunter makes the important point that "resources are allocated unequally to light- and dark-skinned women and beauty is constructed to elevate the status of light-skinned black and Mexican American who most closely resemble whites" (5). In her study of colorism among African Americans and Mexican Americans, Hunter places the emphasis on how meanings are associated with physical features, providing interpretive touchstones for how people "do" race in perceiving others and themselves. "Skin color and features associated with whites, such as light skin, straight noses, and long, straight hair, take on the meanings that they represent: civility, rationality, and beauty. Similarly, skin colors and features associated with Africans or Indians, such as dark skin, broad noses, and kinky hair, represent savagery, irrationality, and ugliness. The values associated with physical features set the stage for skin color stratification" (3). Hunter's research demonstrates the incredible depth of our racial conditioning, that we actively read racial meanings into so many physical features.

The concept of colorism is a useful way for thinking about the continuum of meanings that constitutes the "racial middle." But this concept also reflects that the closer we examine this middle ground between whiteness and blackness, the more it opens up as a highly differentiated terrain. Hunter (2005) makes the important point that "white racism is the fundamental building block of colorism, or *skin-color stratification*, among Mexican Americans and African Americans" (2). But a somewhat different dynamic pertains for Asian Americans, as Joanne Rondilla and Paul Spickard explain in *Is Lighter Better? Skin-Tone Discrimination among Asian Americans* (2007). Rondilla and Spickard also see a dimension of white racism in the notion of colorism evident in the racial thinking of Asian Americans, but they additionally stress that Asian countries "all had long-standing preferences for light skin, especially in women" (3). They explain:

> The feature of Asian American colorism that immediately stands out as being somewhat different from the Black and Latino versions is that Asian American colorism seems not to be mainly about Whiteness as its point of origin. For Asian

> Americans, color hierarchies seem to be as deeply rooted in old-country class distinctions—in the desire to look like upper-class Asians who did not have to work out in the sun—as in U.S.-generated desires to look like White people. (15)

This point of contrasts illustrates the importance of shifting away from making broad generalizations about the panethnic groups, as represented in the whitening thesis or the browning thesis, and move instead toward understanding the specific textures of racialization and interpretations of racial meaning for people within these panethnic categories.

Racism within the Racial Middle

O'Brien's work is a good example of how to pursue this type of focus. She criticizes race scholars for deploying surveys that reproduce a biracial framework, as with questions that try to substantiate these contrary theses by asking whether Latinos or Asian Americans identify more strongly with whiteness or blackness. She asserts that "as scholars continue to focus on the question of whether blacks or whites will become the reference group of Latinos and Asian Americans, they risk missing the possibility that their reference group might actually be found in the racial middle" (2008, 205). She sees this risk most starkly when researchers try to gauge the presence of antiblack racism among these groups. What they miss is "racist discourse about the racial middle, [as] some respondents seemed to be casting a negative light on *those* groups in the same way that whites tend to target African Americans in other studies. Ecuadorians were seen as too close to blacks, some Filipinos were seen as too 'ghetto,' certain Latinos were seen as too 'hip-hop'" (205).

The point she stresses is that *racial interpretations operate at many levels and can be directed at groups within a shared, larger categorical identity*. O'Brien concludes that "the complexity of the way this racism is discursively practiced would most likely be missed by the conventional survey methods of other studies" (205–206). Following up on O'Brien's conclusion and particularly her call for more ethnographic work that can examine the distinctive aspects of experiences of racial discrimination and projections of racial difference within these broad panethnic categories, we turn now to more detailed research on the everyday-life racial dynamics within these larger racial categories, first for Latinos and then for Asian Americans.

ETHNOGRAPHIC PERSPECTIVES ON LATINOS

Ethnographers studying the cultural significance of race for Latinos face a challenge similar to one we considered in the previous chapter on blackness. They commonly contend with the task of undoing some of the stereotypes about this group that have been reproduced by other social scientists. But, on the other hand, ethnographers also confront an additional, fairly unique challenge of not reproducing a *highly attractive depiction of Latinos that would cater to the intense interests of marketers who covet these growing, appealing markets*. Arlene Dávila encapsulates the difficulties entailed in such an undertaking in her ethnography *Latinos Inc.: The*

Marketing and Making of a People (2001). Applying ethnographic methods to advertising firms that specialize in objectifying, promoting, and selling "the Latino market," Dávila generates an astute reading of how "Latinos are repackaged into images that render them pleasing to corporate clients, such as in the garb of the traditional and extremely family-oriented and stubbornly brand loyal consumer" (2001, 4). Attuned to the various processes by which this heterogeneous population is rendered in homogeneous images, Dávila demonstrates that research on Latinos—whether in focus groups, marketing surveys, or ethnographic participant observation—involves complicated and conflicting issues of representation. The critical concern is that these efforts at representation, though largely producing positive images, when keyed in terms of ethnicity run the risk of obscuring the racial dynamics at work in shaping Latino identity. For instance, Dávila underscores a point raised earlier concerning the process of racialization of Latinos (and Asian Americans as well) as she finds that they are "continually recast as authentic and marketable, but ultimately as *foreign* rather than as an intrinsic component of U.S. society, culture, and history" (2001, 4).

Such issues of representation are further explored in Dávila's more recent book *Latino Spin: Public Image and the Whitewashing of Race* (2008), which "maintains that Latinos are simultaneously subjected to processes of whitening and racialization" (12). These processes are not dichotomous but, rather, "need to be seen as constitutive of one another" as means of simultaneously "strategically including and excluding" (ibid.) Latinos from America's mainstream public cultures. This is a dynamic that Dávila unearthed in her earlier ethnographic work on advertisers and marketers but that seems to have grown more extensive and developed. The point to emphasize, at least initially, in Dávila's research on these complicated processes is that *"Latino" is being produced in ways that simultaneously whiten and darken this multihued and socially heterogeneous category*. This recognition leads Dávila not so much to deconstruct stereotyped depictions, but, rather, to reveal their *multiple layers of mediation*. She summarizes this perspective by arguing, in *Latinos Inc.*, that "we must examine culturally specific marketing as a site that simultaneously serves the multiple interests of those who profit from difference as well as the interests of those subordinate populations whose attainment of representation is essential to contemporary politics" (2001, 9). This nuanced, multiangled perspective that Dávila develops is one that we will examine in stages. But before proceeding, we need to step back for a moment to consider in more historical depth the process of conducting ethnography on Latinos.

Revising Stereotypes

As is the case in ethnographic approaches to blackness, ethnographers studying the lives of Latinos often must first contend with the task of undoing distorted representations from a previous era of social science research. José Limón's *Dancing with the Devil: Society and Cultural Poetics in Mexican-American South Texas* (1994) pursues exactly this task in his ethnography of "expressive activities" in the "working-class Mexican-American popular culture in Texas" (14). Limón's work is innovative, because he combines a review and a critique of the ways "the folklore of the people of Mexican descent in southern Texas" (ix) has been analyzed by Anglo scholars alongside his own fieldwork observations in Texas dancehalls.

Limón's ethnographic gaze is eclectic, attending to diverse forms of male humor and styles of meat consumption, forms of popular dancing, and a devil legend shared by women, concluding with a discussion of folk healing practices. This range of topics is linked, in that these expressive practices reflect both "a history of race and class domination" (15) and a *cultural poetics* by which Mexican Americans interpret and respond to this domination. But more than uniform acts of solidarity and resistance, Limón sees in these activities "also seduction, anxiety, internal conflict and contradiction" that reflect the impacts and shifting evaluations of an ever "changing 'Anglo' capitalist political economy" (129). Limón insists that understanding the folk practices of working-class Mexican Americans requires a recognition that they are not simply "authentic" forms that represent a people but, rather, sophisticated responses to that people's position and representation in larger worlds of racial domination.

In this undertaking, Limón consistently encounters and rebuts stereotyped depictions of working-class Mexican Americans, similar to those critiqued by Robin Kelley concerning African Americans (see Chapter 5). Limón (1994) proceeds by challenging the scholarly literature's misinterpretation of these people. "Macho" lower-class and working-class humor is stereotyped in academic studies as deriving from sexual obsession and anxiety, and it is characterized in reductive terms as directed singularly toward humiliating other males. Limón finds many examples of such humor in "*chingaderas*," but because he is able to place them in an ethnographic context, rather than a clinical analysis, he sees these jokes as mobilizing "multivocal symbols possessing *several* meanings and not reducible to one that fits a preconceived psychoanalytic scheme" (129). This multiplicity of meanings is deftly mobilized in subtle forms of joking that encourage and require sophisticated interpretive work on the part of coworkers, friends, and strangers in a range of social settings in central Texas.

Limón concludes that, rather than being informed by an "infantile concern" with sexual status, "the themes of anality, pollution, and bodily penetration may also be symbolic expression of an essentially political and economic concern with social domination" (132). As marginalized workers, their forms of humor comment on and critique their "socially penetrable status," as in using the verb *chingar*, "to also express social violation." What previous researchers missed is that such exchanges are "dynamic forums that interactionally produce meaning, mastering anxiety by inverting passive destiny through active play" (ibid.). Anticipating similar criticisms by Kelley, Limón argues that ethnographers depicting Mexican Americans as pathological for their distinctive style of humor were tone deaf to the "emergent cultural performance" (137) of racialized identities in the face of a dominant culture that similarly pathologized them.

Mexican Chicago

Limón's work stands as an example of how to shift representations of Latinos *out of folkloric frames*—as authentically ethnic, pastoral, and implicitly primitive—*into a racial analytic*. But as suggested by the preceding discussions, the racial position they occupy is in many ways more multifaceted than the black/white model suggests. For instance, although Latinos are often subject to similar forms of racial domination and stereotyping as African Americans, they also, as racial subjects in the United States, find themselves engaged in charged competition with blacks too. This complex dynamic is examined by Nicholas De Genova's ethnography *Working the Boundaries: Race, Space, and "Illegality" in Mexican Chicago* (2005).

De Genova's notion of "Mexican Chicago" aims to capture the ways that city "is practically and materially implicated in Mexico" through the extensive ties fashioned by migrants. With this coinage, though, De Genova aims to formulate a different kind of ethnographic object from previous studies of migrants by seeing this Chicago as "not merely an 'ethnic enclave' or an 'immigrant ghetto' " but rather "a conjuncture of the national and the transnational" (7). That is, he depicts Mexican Chicago as a node in a variety of trajectories that, in crossing and recrossing national boundaries, makes the operation of racialization both tangible and tenuous. This formulation interestingly echoes further work by Limón in invoking "Greater Mexico" to refer "to all Mexicans, beyond Laredo and from either side, with all their commonalities and differences," in his *American Encounters: Greater Mexico, the United States, and the Erotics of Culture* (1998).

De Genova (2005) finds in Chicago a process of racialization that seems to collapse the ethnic designation *Mexican American*. He argues that, at least in the city's many factories, *Mexican* obliterates distinctions of birthplace and citizenship status "and comes to be *racialized* as specifically 'Mexican' in relation to the hegemonic polarity of whiteness and Blackness." This category manifests "in everyday practice of the resignification of Mexicanness as a specifically *racialized* category within the U.S. social order" (3). De Genova's findings are based on two and a half years of research as a teacher of English as a second language (ESL) and basic mathematics to workers in ten factories (mostly metal-fabricating) in Chicago. From this vantage point, De Genova relates how Mexican immigrants "negotiated their own racialization as Mexican, always in relation to both a dominant whiteness and its polar opposite, a subjected and denigrated blackness" (8). The "boundaries" these immigrants work involves the fraught discursive divide "between 'Americans' and blacks" (48).

Similar to Limón, De Genova keys in on the work of humor and joking relations. Strikingly, the Mexican immigrants in his classes respond to their own stigmatized depiction in American jokes by turning the same charges of "laziness" and "stupidity" onto African Americans. Are these instances of racism toward African Americans? De Genova (2005) finds, somberly, that the "intermediate racial location" these Mexicans occupy "seems to be already ensnared in a hegemonic denigration of the Blackness of African Americans," even though "there was no act of racial contempt that would accomplish their transformation into entitled whites" (198). De Genova's ethnographic account provides something of a counterpoint to Limón's, in that he sees the structures of racial domination as somewhat more powerful in the face of the performative work of Mexican humor in Chicago. Yet, together, both ethnographies highlight the crucial role of interpretive work in the face of processes of racialization.

Marking Puerto Ricans

De Genova's perspective on the "racial middle" in Chicago is insightful but needs to be juxtaposed with other ethnographic accounts of how Latinos navigate the color line between blackness and "brownness." A rather different view of this dynamic is produced by looking at particular neighborhoods where Latinos and African Americans live side by side in shared urban settings (Modan 2007). Both Uriciuoli and Dávila conducted such studies, in New York's Spanish Harlem and the Lower East Side, respectively. Their ethnographic accounts feature the interpretive efforts of Puerto Ricans, in particular, to assess the significance of race in their everyday lives.

In *Exposing Prejudice: Puerto Rican Experiences of Language, Race, and Class* (1996), Uriciuoli analyzes practices of *code-switching* (between Spanish and English) in a variety of informal and formal settings—from children's talk to neighborhood gossip to workplace and institutional interactions. She develops an enormously powerful analysis of how "marking" dynamics play out in speech, as people are "marked" by grammar and accents while they also struggle to become "unmarked" through an often-futile effort to achieve "correct" English usage. The futility lies in the ways phenotype often "colors" perceptions of language usage—even using perfectly correct English, Puerto Ricans are still perceived as speaking poorly or improperly based on impressions linked to their skin color. In developing this analysis, Uriciuoli pays particular attention to the interactions between black and Puerto Rican residents of Manhattan's Lower East Side.

The point Uriciuoli stresses is that an enormous amount of interpretive work goes into making sense of race, via nuanced readings of speech and behavioral stylistics keenly attuned to place. Uriciuoli (1996) explains, "Puerto Ricans and African Americans are not seen as racially the same, but they have had similar experience of racialization. They are often ambivalent about each other in everyday life, yet points of sympathy constantly emerge" (65). Both this dimension of *ambivalence and the attendant forms of ambiguity require the steady cultural work of reading and assessing racial significance* in the media of talk and narrative because, as Uriciuoli observes, "they share a great deal of what they do, how they talk, and how they define themselves" (ibid.). Since these commonalities also encompass numerous points of difference, Uriciuoli found that residents continually have to work at determining where boundaries lie and how durable or permeable are their forms of interdiction.

Strikingly, Uriciuoli finds that blacks and Puerto Ricans face similar conundrums in countering moments of markedness in language. Uriciuoli (1996) observes that, in both groups, "People try to control prejudiced perceptions of themselves by editing the ways in which they may be seen as marked, through their hair, name, or skin color" (144). But Puerto Ricans do have an option that is not generally available to blacks, and that is to *ethnicize* by striving to make their public persona (including language use) match the ideal of the "model minority." This is a risky undertaking, as Uriciuoli points out, in that "ethnicizing oneself creates a dilemma: One cannot be a worthy ethnic without acting in ways that appear 'American,' but how does one keep those ways from also appearing 'white'?" Contending on one hand with the perception of foreignness and of "acting white" on the other, Puerto Ricans trying to ethnicize their racial markedness face many perils.

Dávila develops a somewhat similar perspective on the construction and negotiation of racial boundaries in her ethnography of Spanish Harlem. In *Barrio Dreams: Puerto Ricans, Latinos, and the Neoliberal City* (2004), Dávila studied a neighborhood undergoing the process of gentrification, one that was riven by competing visions for the area's future. By one set of contrasts, these competing visions fractured along racial lines, with distinct black, white, and Latino interests vying to shape these city streets according to competing development interests. But Dávila relates that while "blacks and Puerto Ricans share important points of interaction, activism, and collaboration at the level of cultural creation and political activism" (17), they also are often in competition for control of local resources and over how to represent the area's "culture" in marketable ways. The key fault line is in the development of local cultural resources—art and heritage museums, in particular—that are racialized in fairly absolute terms in ways that undermine cross-racial alliances or even the racial heterogeneity of residents. Locally, residents that identified as "black Latinos," "Afro-Boricuas," or "black Puerto Ricans" confronted competing views that insisted on **Latinidad** and blackness as mutually exclusive identities.

Contesting Latinidad

For that matter, *Latinidad* was itself the subject of much contestation, among both Puerto Ricans with long-term ties to the neighborhood and increasingly with recently arrived Mexican immigrants. A variety of divisions emerge for Puerto Ricans, largely in terms of class status: Middle-class residents were far more likely to favor forms of gentrification than did poor or working-class residents. In a manner similar to Mary Pattillo-McCoy's analysis of gentrification in Chicago (see Chapter 5), *intraracial class dynamics often prove to be the significant fault line* in residents' assessment of development plans and narratives. In both settings (Chicago and New York), middle-class residents are precariously perched on the line between those who would benefit and those who would lose from the neighborhood's "revitalization." But *differential experiences of racialization also create rifts* within a larger notion of Puerto Rican identity. Dávila (2004) notes, "Educated Puerto Ricans from the island enjoy greater advantages here, having been exempted from the prejudice and discrimination" (81) in the United States, which contributes to contrasting sensibilities about how best to promote or preserve the neighborhood.

The other important division of life in Spanish Harlem derives from the impact of recent Mexican immigration and how this reflects the large-scale process of "Latinization" in U.S. cities. This dynamic is far broader than the particular case that Dávila examines, but her ethnography offers an excellent glimpse of the complexity of purported Latinization. As in her work on ethnic marketing of Latinos, Dávila sees in Spanish Harlem this identity as being mobilized both as a means of selling or promoting the neighborhood and as a grounds for resisting these very encroachments by outside economic interests.

The area could be marketed as "hot" for its ethnic flair, but residents also invoked a sense of shared ethnoracial identity as the basis for their claims of ownership to the neighborhood. But this latter invocation was, in turn, subject to contestation in the form of competing versions of Latinidad developed by Puerto Ricans and Mexicans. Dávila (2004) documents numerous "tensions between Mexican and Puerto Rican populations, traced to their different histories, citizenship status, and/or self-conception as residents, racialized minorities, or temporary immigrants" (17). This produced a certain torsion as Mexicans and Puerto Ricans confronted competing "ethnic-driven demands for rights and entitlements" (ibid.) along with appeals to and invocations of a broader notion of Latinidad.

Interestingly, in this "contested terrain of Latinization and of Latino politics" (Dávila 2004, 164) Mexican immigrants were able to assume the status of "model minority" over and against racialized perceptions and characterizations of Puerto Ricans in this area. That is, in a variety of ways, *Mexicans were able to "ethnicize," in contrast to Puerto Ricans, who are typically racialized in New York*—in much the same way De Genova describes Mexicans being racialized in Chicago. Partly, this dynamic turned on marketers' enthusiasm over the arrival of Mexicans, because they seemed to represent a revitalization of the New York City Spanish-language market "long considered a more 'acculturated' market because of the great numbers of Nuyorican and older generations of English-dominant Latinos" (2004, 176). But this differentiation also hinged on the ways Mexicans negotiated their "uncertain position as new arrivals into already established hierarchies of ethnicity and race formed primarily around Blacks and Puerto Ricans" (2004, 173). Mexicans would as often seek to distance themselves from Dominicans and Puerto Ricans, in racial terms, as they would recognize or strive to articulate some shared Latino identity. Preferring to be viewed in ethnic terms, as "model immigrants" rather than racially, Mexicans in Spanish Harlem developed very different sensibilities about the area's development.

Varieties of Racial Hierarchies

Dávila's ethnographic research opens a window onto the considerable diversity and differences that fall under the "Latino" category. Even the more singular identity of "Puerto Rican," on closer consideration, opens several forms of differentiation, primarily in terms of class and experiences of racialization. Though we have yet to glimpse it in the ethnographies surveyed so far, "Mexican," too, as a category, contains manifold forms of social distinctions that are obscured with invocations of "Latino." This may not come into view in accounts like Dávila's, which highlights the points of contrast between ethnicities, or in De Genova's account of the racialization of Mexicans in Chicago, which frames their experiences in fairly homogeneous racial terms. We get a better angle on these forms of social difference among Mexicans by attending to the racial dynamics within this category.

Lynn Stephen, in *Transborder Lives: Indigenous Oaxacans in Mexico, California, and Oregon* (2007), brings these forms of diversity into exact view by examining the differential experiences and sensibilities of Mixtec and Zapotec immigrants working in the United States. There are several key aspects to highlight regarding Stephen's ethnography. First, she primarily examines the history and current operation of immigrant farm workers that are drawn into and sustain the increasing economic integration of the United States and Mexico. This economic circuit, which is the basis on which U.S. grocery stores feature such a wide array of fresh fruits and vegetables, had been concentrated in the southwestern states but has now expanded considerably, for Mexican immigrants are noticeably affecting social worlds in the U.S. South and Midwest as well. Second, Stephen is interested in the experiences of indigenous peoples from Mexico, because they both follow and establish somewhat different routes of travel and work than their fellow nationals do in the United States.

An important feature of this distinction is the experience of racism that indigenous peoples face, first in Mexico as *inditos sucios* ("dirty little Indians") and then in the United States as they are racialized generically as Mexican. This second feature flows into Stephen's third concern, and that is with the process of identity formation for transnationals. The notion of **transnational identity** has become a well-established subject of study in cultural anthropology, but Stephen adds a new dimension to this focus with her articulation of the concept of *transborder* identity.

In each of these three regards, Stephen aims to keep pace with the fast-changing but deeply historical forces that shape migrant labor practice *within* both the United States and Mexico but also importantly *between* these two countries. These require an understanding of the larger political economy linking Mexico and the United States but also depend on grasping the personal and social experiences of the people drawn into these circuits of labor. As Stephen explains, *"The challenge for ethnographers is to both conceptualize the larger structural conditions framing migration and work*—such as the emergence of consumer markets in the United States for fresh produce and domestic services and the effects of neoliberal economic policy in Mexico—as well as to *capture the human relationships and lived and remembered experiences of cross-border workers"* [emphasis added] (2007, 142). Stephen responds to this challenge by collecting life histories and stories of people's experiences crossing a variety of borders—within and between nations—and of laboring in these different circuits of production.

The overarching point Stephen makes with the concept of *transborder* concerns the shifting scales of experience and identity that all this movement entails. *Transnational* is adequate for conveying the impact that movements between countries has on processes of identity formation, but it is not sufficient to convey the variation in work and life experiences of fellow nationals that Stephen sees as increasingly significant. In tracing the disparate routes of Mixtec and Zapotec peoples from the same Mexican state of Oaxaca, Stephen recognizes substantial points of contrasts. As she conveys:

> The borders they cross are ethnic, class, cultural, colonial, and state borders within Mexico as well as the at the U.S.–Mexico border and in different regions of the U.S. Regional systems of racial and ethnic hierarchies within the U.S. are different from those in Mexico and can also vary within the U.S. Thus the ways that "Mexicans" and "Indians" have been codified in California and Oregon can differ from how they have been historically built into racial and ethnic hierarchies in New York or Florida. (6)

Stephen makes an important point here that helps bring into view an implicit aspect of the ethnographic research surveyed throughout this book: *The dynamics shaping racial identity vary a great deal*, reflecting the "regional systems of racial and ethnic hierarchies" (6) that derive from specific historical, economic, and social dynamics. These are the forces that make the situations of "Latinos" different in Chicago and New York from those in Los Angeles and Miami, for instance. For all the important attention we devote to recognizing commonalities, it is also critical, as Stephen asserts, to *recognize the distinct patterns that develop in particular regions or even cities*, for that matter.

Indigeneity and Race

In terms of Stephen's ethnography, the central dimension of experience on which she focuses the concept of *transborder* involves the different racial orders that indigenous Mexicans pass through in their migratory routes. Her approach references De Genova's account of the racialization of Mexicans in Chicago, but she contrastingly places her "focus more on how indigenous in the United States have become and continue to be a racialized category *within the Mexican immigrant community* and how Mexicano systems of ethnic and racial classification are influenced by and overlap the historically and regionally situated racial hierarchies in southern California and western Oregon" [emphasis added] (212). In the life stories of indigenous migrants, Stephen documents the stigmatization they face in Mexico and the ways in which their words and bodies are marked in relation to the dominant Mestizo population. Even terms referencing their state-based identity as "Oaxaquitos" (little people from Oaxaca) carry a racial charge, with the point of differentiation linked to their frequent monolingualism in indigenous languages and subsequent limited or lack of ability with Spanish. "Oaxacans are racially marked in this system of difference in ways that groups from other states are not" (2007, 214). Indigenous peoples encounter this stigmatization and discrimination as they migrate for work within the national borders of Mexico, and they find it continues in their experiences with Mexicans in the United States as well.

From their vantage point, indigenous migrants have a distinct perspective on the variable ways racial identity is coded, perceived, and articulated in the various regions of these two countries. Stephen tracks their disparate uses of U.S.-based categories of "Latino," "Hispanic," and "Chicanos"—apart from "Oaxaqueños," their frequent form of self-designation—and the way these terms mark important distinctions that get collapsed in Anglos' racialized use of Mexicans. In the reckoning of these migrants, "Latinos," in contrast to "Americanos," can distinguish between Mexicanos born south of the border and Spanish-speaking Americans. Notably, "Chicano" involves an interesting point of transnational contrast, as well. In the United States, as Stephen explains, "the Chicano understanding of *mestizaje* and subsequent popular cultural manifestations of Chicanismo that draw on symbols of Aztec indigenous culture come from profoundly different understandings and experience of 'being indigenous' than that of many Mixtec and Zapotec migrants" (2007, 225).

For that matter, indigenous Mexicans confront another contrasting sensibility about race in a different set of U.S. Census terms for the racial option "American Indian or Alaska Native." Since this category specifies "the original peoples of North and South American (including Central America)," it encompasses people who identified themselves as both "Spanish/Hispanic/Latino" and "American Indian." As Stephen points out, "In other words, self-identified Latin American indigenous migrants could identify both ethnically as Latinos and racially as American Indians" (229). This choice for identification is complicated by the additional option to list "tribe." Stephen notes that "most did not write in the name of a tribe, as this is a U.S.-based concept that makes no sense in the Mexican and Central American context, where until the 1980s and 1990s panethnic identities such as 'Mixtec,' 'Maya,' and others were not commonly used" (229). This variation in racial identification between countries, accentuated by internal, regional differences, should both underscore the constructedness of race and point to the increasing complexity of grappling with the ways this construct matters intensely. The complexity suggested by this variation is evident as well in the disparate experiences of peoples who fall within the "Asian American" category in the United States.

ETHNOGRAPHIC PERSPECTIVES
ON ASIAN AMERICANS

"Asian American," like the category "Latino," easily reveals a variety of social distinctions that are often overlooked or conflated in references to this identity in racial terms. At the same time, people within this category are racialized in profound ways in the U.S. context. Looking more closely at the dynamics of racialization shaping the lives of Asian Americans, we will consider how this category alternately stands as a racial or as an ethnic identity—even while, like "Latino," this identity strains the very logic of racial categorization. However, the ethnographic record on Asian Americans is not as extensively developed as it is for the other racial groups we considered earlier in this book (Manalansan IV 2000). Hence, portions of the following account will be developed via discussions of qualitative-based projects that feature in-depth interviews, such as Tuan's (2001) study, *Forever Foreigners or Honorary Whites? The Asian Ethnic Experience Today*, cited earlier.

In Tuan's analysis, Asian Americans face a conundrum over the distinction between "ethnic" and "racial" identities in a manner similar to Latinos. Both groups share a common dimension of racialization in the perception of their "foreignness" over against both white and black Americans. But the "ethnic" option appears to be somewhat more easily assumed by Asian Americans, partly due to the broader level of economic success of people within this category. In this regard, Tuan points to similarities between Asian Americans and "white ethnics," while she also draws into view key points of contrast, largely relating to the salience their perceived racial identity has for other people. Broadly, Tuan relates that her respondents "maneuver between a maze of choices and constraints in constructing an identity for themselves" (2001, 151).

The Maze of Ethnicity and Race

Tuan and her research team interviewed ninety-five "third-generation or later Chinese- and Japanese-Americans" (1998, 9) in Los Angeles and the San Francisco peninsula area. These respondents are generally successful economically and socially; Tuan explains, "The majority are white-collar professionals in fields such as medicine/health, banking, law, engineering, publishing, computer technology, education, finance, insurance, and real estate" (9). Her interviews involved questions concerning "1) early memories and experiences w/ Chinese/ Japanese culture; 2) current lifestyle and ethnic practices; 3) ethnic identity issues; 4) experiences w/ racism and discrimination; 5) attitudes toward current Asian immigration and also the social status of Asian-Americans today" (2001). With these questions, Tuan aimed to understand whether the material gains made by these Asian Americans equated with "social acceptance" by allowing "for an abundance of ethnic as well as racial options" (7) as they articulated their individual and collective identities.

Anticipating the debate over the whitening and browning theses, Tuan explored whether or to what extent Asian Americans may be seen as moving closer to whiteness or, rather, as constituting an interim racial identity. She found that some Asian Americans "have embraced the model minority label and see it as their ultimate ticket toward gaining social acceptance, while others reject it altogether" (-1998, 31). Generally, though, she reports that her interviewees "prefer to *define themselves* in ethnic terms . . . but may find themselves *being defined* in generically racial terms as Asian Americans" (21). In a manner similar to white ethnics, she sees her respondents as *choosing to deemphasize ethnicity but finding themselves racialized by others.* "The irony, however, is that Asian ethnics are probably more similar to than different from white ethnics in terms of lifestyle preferences and general values" (19).

In broad terms, Tuan argues "that ethnicity's role in my informants' lives has changed in much the same way it has for middle-class white ethnics. They exercise a great deal of choice regarding the ethnic practices and values they wish to integrate or discard from their *personal lives.* Nevertheless, ethnicity is far from an optional facet of their public lives because others continue to define them in racialized or ethnic terms and to impute significant meanings to these differences" (18). Notably, this experience of racialization varies, depending on a variety of factors linked to socialization, primarily in terms of the racial dynamics of their childhood neighborhoods and their parents' sensibilities about the relative importance of ethnic and racial identity. Asian Americans growing up in predominantly white neighborhoods found that, in their childhood experiences, "their racial rather ethnic identity was salient" for white neighbors, friends, and strangers. In contrast, those "raised in Asian-centered communities enjoyed the greatest degree of freedom from thinking of themselves in racial or ethnic terms" (104). These latter respondents, Tuan relates, "had the luxury of racial privilege, of being 'normal,' within the context of their community" (ibid.). That is, they grew up in *a context in which their identity was largely unmarked in racial terms.*

These contrasting early life experiences of being racially marked or unmarked contribute to the development of what Tuan identifies as two "parallel processes of dissolving boundaries." On one hand, some Asian Americans can be seen as "merging with members of the racial majority," either in terms of intermarriage or integration of previously predominantly neighborhoods. On the other, Tuan points to a trend of "choosing partners who share a common panethnic or racialized identity as Asian Americans" (35). In this latter process, the boundaries dissolving are those linked to the distinct national/ethnic identities within the larger category, Asian American. This trend is fueled, in part, by parents who encourage their children "to associate with coethnics, and be part of a larger Asian American or coethnic community of friends" (56). This encouragement reflects the parents' personal experiences of racism in the workplace and in neighborhood settings. These processes of socialization, Tuan concludes, indicate "the development of a racialized identity for Asian ethnics" (7) that runs against the parallel but countermovement toward a greater embrace of the "model minority" ideal. An interesting point that Tuan returns to repeatedly is that these linked processes mirror the dynamic by which the salience of ethnicity declined in this country for white ethnics in the last century as they increasingly came to identify and be accepted within categorical whiteness.

As was the case for immigrants from southern and eastern Europe in the 1900s, today "Asian ethnics exercise a great deal of flexibility regarding the cultural elements they wish to keep or discard from their personal lives. What they have retained by way of cultural tradition is largely symbolic and a novelty" (Tuan 1998, 74). But they are not free to regard their ethnicity as entirely "symbolic," because they experience pressure to identify in ethnic or racial terms by people for whom these remain salient markers. In particular, "despite their generational longevity in this country, an assumption of foreignness stubbornly clings to them" (155).

As is the case for Latinos, this racialized perception—one that crystallizes in questions such as "Where are you *really* from" and "What are you?"—is additionally fueled by continued immigration from Asia. The fact of these immigrants' "concentration in a handful of states has magnified the intensity of their presence" (158). Tuan explains, "The influx of unprecedented numbers of immigrants has complicated the lives of native-born Asian ethnics because most non-Asians are unable or unwilling to recognize generational differences" (ibid.). Again, much as for Latinos, this inability or unwillingness to acknowledge or recognize significant social differences between Asians and Asian Americans forms *a primary basis for the ongoing racialization of peoples of Asian descent.* One important point of contrast, though, between members of these panethnic identities is the distinct range of class identities among their respective immigrant streams.

Racialization and Immigration

As was illustrated in Leland Saito's ethnographic account of life in Monterrey Park, there is a sharp contrast among newly arriving Asians and Latinos in terms of class and economic status. Most Mexican immigrants are confined in the low-skills/low-wage jobs sector, a situation that certainly contributes to their ongoing racialization. The situation is different for Asians, some of whom arrive from China and Taiwan with enormous amounts of cultural and economic capital. For these immigrants, their situations and experiences in the United States clearly point to a destabilizing of the dynamics of social advantage and disadvantage linked to race. Their somewhat more tenuous ties to forms of belonging or citizenship in the United States also bring us back to the concept of **diasporic identities,** raised first in the previous chapter. But before exploring that form of identity in detail, we need to look more closely at the class dimension and divides in Asian American identity.

Anthropologist Aihwa Ong opens a view into how differential class positions for Asian immigrants leads to divergent forms of racialization in her ethnography, *Buddha Is Hiding: Refugees, Citizenship, the New America* (2003). Ong primarily examines the everyday travails of Cambodian refugees in Oakland as they struggle to adjust to life in the United States. In particular, she attends to their experiences of navigating social services and citizenship procedures that amount to a long process of "learning to belong" in America. But she is also interested in understanding the starkly differential outcomes from the processes for Cambodians in relation to Vietnamese refugees.

The contrast Ong finds is between two waves of immigration, both stemming from U.S. military engagements in Southeast Asia, with two starkly different outcomes. The first wave comprised primarily Vietnamese in 1975, many of whom were urban professionals that networked quickly into high-wage jobs in California. For Cambodians and Laotians arriving in 1980, the situation was quite different. Mostly rural people, coming from long stays in refugee camps, they arrived at "a time of greater anxiety over ideological, health and economic threats to American identity" (2003, 84). Entering the country just before the deep recession of 1981–1982—amid a great deal of political anxiety over the "urban underclass" and alongside political refugees from Central American civil wars and conflicts—Cambodians and Laotians faced very different circumstances and racial dynamics.

Ong's ethnography follows "Cambodian refugees in their transition through different modalities of government—the Buddhist absolutism of modern Cambodia, the policing state of the Khmer Rouge, the mediating world of refugee camps, and the advanced liberal democracy of the United States" (19). Each of these modalities compels different choices concerning the categories of "citizen-subjects" open to these Cambodians. Once in the United States, Ong explains, "for the refugees in this study, the tension between the American stress on individualism, pragmatism, and materialism on the one hand, and the Khmer-Buddhist ethos of compassionate hierarchy, collectivism, and otherworldliness on the other, is a central dynamic in the ethical project of becoming citizens" (6–7).

This process is complicated further by *American racial sensibilities regarding citizenship and belonging.* "The concept of the American nation as a specific, racially homogeneous identity has been and continues to be the measure by which all potential citizens are situated as either integral or marginal to the nation" (Ong 2003, 10). For Cambodians arriving from desperate, destabilizing situations in the refugee camps—with far fewer forms of the social, economic, and political capital than Vietnamese refugees possessed—they rapidly found themselves slotted into the racial position of marginality. Drawing partly on the work of Brackette Williams (1989) cited earlier, Ong finds this outcome to be a function of the "**racial bipolarism** [that] has historically been part of a classificatory system for differentiating among successive waves of immigrants, who were assigned different stations along the path towards whiteness" (2003, 11). According to this bipolar racial order, "newcomers are located along the continuum from black to white" (ibid.) by more than phenotype.

Race and Citizenship

Instead, Ong argues, these evaluations are far more complex, involving economic and social calculations regarding the relative worth of potential citizens. "They become racialized not simply because of their skin color, and ethnicized not simply because of claims of a particular ancestral culture, but because they have been assessed as belonging to a category inscribed with racial indeterminacy in the game of becoming self-motivated, self-propelling, and freedom-loving American citizens" (2003, 14). The outcome Ong documents is that this "racial classificatory logic has placed poor Asian immigrants such as Cambodian refugees at the black pole: They are identified with inner-city African Americans and set off clearly not only from whites, but also from other Asian groups such as Vietnamese and Chinese Americans" (14). This classification keys off of the high rates of mental illness and poverty among Cambodian refugees, as well as social workers' perceptions of them as having an "affectively oriented viewpoint." Ong's finding leads her to a rather different conclusion than Tuan reached concerning dynamics of racialization.

Instead of a shared "racial consciousness," Ong argues, to the contrary, that the Asian American category is *too riven by class and racial distinctions to amount to a homogeneous social identity.* She explains, "many newcomers from the Asian Pacific and from a variety of classes cannot be easily fitted into an overarching Asian American identity, and their presence has made even more untenable the claims that Asian Americans can be constituted as a single community of adversity and racial oppression" (2003, 257). For Asian entrepreneurs in Silicon Valley, immigration to the United States has largely been a success story. Ong asserts, regarding these immigrants, that "the paradigm of citizenship in contemporary America—the self-reliant, flexible, and capital-accumulating individual—has now incorporated the Asian American elite" (267). For that matter, even diasporic Asians who retain their national identities are favorably received. As Ong concludes, "In the current age of globalized capitalism, the process of earning honorary whiteness continues, and Asians have come to represent ideal citizens who not only embody economic and intellectual capital, but also possess the transnational networks and skills crucial to American expansion" (266). What these success stories hide from view, Ong points out, is "the Southeast Asian woman seated at her sewing machine" (ibid.) in an overheated factory receiving only sweatshop wages.

In calling attention to the enduring bipolar racial order in the United States, Ong is able to highlight the divergent positioning of Asian immigrants who are concentrated alternately "at the top and bottom levels of production networks— as in the male Chinese contract manager, the male Indian engineer, the Southeast Asian female pieceworker" (2003, 265). At the bottom of the job structure, Cambodian women locked in the low-wage garment, electronics, and food industries are racialized in ways that position them as far closer to blackness than to whiteness. In contrast, East Asian capitalists and professionals, or "South Asian techno-magnets," with "their capacity to transfer value transpacifically, have transformed American thinking about Asians" (267). In the process, to use a term from Uriciuoli, they have achieved a certain "escape velocity" in relation to racial markedness. Rather than constituting a racial middle, Ong sees the experiences of current Asian immigrants as reproducing U.S. racial polarization between whiteness and blackness. That is, "Regardless of their racial origins, peoples form different parts of Asia can be consigned either to the whiter or to the blacker end of the continuum of worthiness" (270).

Diasporic Identities

Ong discerns this same bifurcated identity structure operating in conceptions of the **Asian diaspora**—increasingly cosmopolitan elites' interests dominate the meanings and invocations of diasporic identity. Where the term used to refer to ethnic "trading minorities" or to name distinct forms of nationalism throughout the Pacific, Ong criticizes a developing trend among academics and activists to use it to materialize a more homogeneous rendering of "Asian" identity. In *Neoliberalism as Exception: Mutations in Citizenship and Sovereignty* (2006), Ong remarks that "given its currency in the age of transnationalism and multiculturalism, diaspora should be considered not an objective category but, rather, an *ethnographic term* of self-description by different immigrant groups or publics" (2006, 62).

Privileging ethnographic perspectives in this way allows Ong to examine various "fields of political action" in which, for instance, "transnational ethnic Chinese" articulate the diaspora, first as an "extension of the Motherland, but then also as a "re-Sinization" (62) of previous, widely dispersed areas of settlement across the

Pacific. Based on the perspective she derives through her transnational fieldwork in a variety of locations across the Pacific, Ong remarks in *Buddha Is Hiding* that "it is both eerily familiar and temporally disconcerting that the racially segmented industrial network spawned in Asian developing countries has returned to the United States and become a centerpiece of the IT industry" (2003, 265). Through such processes, the rendering of diasporic identities clearly requires the same fine-grained ethnographic attention to particular and differing circumstances as do the other racial identities featured in this book.

Another angle on such diasporic identities is provided by Shalini Shankar's ethnography *Desi Land: Teen Culture, Class, and Success in Silicon Valley* (2008). Shankar relates that *Desi*—from the Hindi word for "countryman," and "the newest in a long line of names used to refer to South Asians living outside the Indian Subcontinent"—"marks the inception of a particular type of diasporic, racially marked, generationally influenced consciousness at the beginning of the millennium" (1). A striking aspect of Shankar's assertion is that it illustrates how far we have moved from efforts to define and characterize racial and ethnic groups in strict, static terms, for "Desi," like "Latino" and "Asian" (of which it is a subset), comprises so much cultural variety that its coherence clearly lies in a larger system of racial meanings as much as in any shared social circumstances.

Shankar explains, "Desi teens in Silicon Valley encompass a wide range of religious, linguistic, and ethnic backgrounds, including Punjabi Sikhs, Pakistani Muslims, Gujarati Hindus, Indo-Fijian Hindus and Muslims, Bangladeshi Hindus and Muslims, and a handful of Tamil, Telegu, Malayalee, Khanada Hindus, Sri Lankans, and Nepales" (2008, 4). These disparate social identities converge through processes of immigration and settlement that extend well over a century in California and that remain active today. "Desi" is a *categorical identity* with an excessive, tangible content, whose coherence lies in dynamics of marked and unmarked racial identity.

For such an easily designated and recognizable identity, it is striking how much effort it requires of those it labels to grasp its significance. "For Desi teens in Silicon Valley, the uncertainty of what it means to be of South Asian descent is evident in how they align themselves with the culture of their school and with other racial groups, as well as how they are positioned in neighborhoods and communities" (Shankar 2008, 14). Shankar makes this open-ended and uncertain process of positioning the focus of her research, as she examines Desi teens' engagements with popular and academic cultures and their various experiences of socialization in their home lives and among friends.

Following their articulation of "style" in a variety of media and their consumption of media and other forms of fashion, Shankar traces out *the distinctive process of racialization that forms the larger context of Desis' articulation of social identity*. One path they have open to them is to achieve "model minority" status, much as many of their parents have done. This path grows easier with the support of multicultural discourses that allow them to "celebrate aspects of their cultural background through food, dance, and costume and speak their heritage language in social sanctioned spaces" (14). But deviating in any of a variety of ways from these "acceptable" expressions makes their model minority status ambiguous and their marked forms of racial difference more pronounced.

Larger Fields of Race

Shankar sees this dynamic as broader than the experiences of Desis in Silicon Valley. As she explains, "Within the category of 'Asian American,' differences of race, class, and ethnicity are obscured by the model minority stereotypes but are absolutely crucial to understanding the specific subjectivities that make this collective heading meaningful" (2008, 13). Shankar examines these multiple forms of difference, particularly as they manifest in styles of language use, media consumption, and consumerist practices. Part of her attention is focused on the matter of "whitening" or "browning," as she observes "some Desis continue to seek a place in upper-middle-class society alongside Whites and other more upwardly mobile minorities, while others share more economic, academic, and professional similarities with working-class Latinos and Whites and white other working-class Asian Americans" (14). But Shankar is additionally interested in another broad process: the reconstitution of diasporic identities for Desis—as well, too, for other Asian Americans—as they "shift from South Asian immigrants longing to return to a homeland to public consumers and producers of distinctive, widely circulating cultural and linguistic forms" (4). In this development, Shankar sees a fundamental transformation in the articulation of diasporic identities for South Asians as the frame of cultural reference increasingly is oriented toward the local circumstances and dynamics or particular locations within the larger diaspora.

Though the importance of the local is clear in Shankar's work, keep in mind that "local" need not be restricted to one particular place. Rather, as we have seen in ethnographies such as *Blue-Chip Black* and *Working-Class Whites*, multisited approaches are of great value in understanding the variety of ways place matters. A good example is Rebecca Chiyoko King-O'Riain's (2006) ethnography, *Pure Beauty: Judging Race in Japanese American Beauty Pageants*. King-O'Riain pursued her field work in four cities—Los Angeles, San Francisco, Seattle, and Honolulu. Intrigued by the explicit racial dimension of these pageants—participation requires being of 50% Japanese ancestry—and the problem posed by "mixed race" contestants, King-O'Riain examined how debates about who can participate played out differently in each city. Each of these pageants, and the festivals which they are a part, are products of the particular histories and politics of these Japanese American communities, "reflecting their cultural, geographic and historical specificity" (2006, 11). In turn, these communities all have "developed relationships to each other and all had sister cities ties to communities in Japan" (ibid.). By taking a multisited approach, King-O'Riain draws into view the variety of "race work" these pageants involve as they stage community forums that "determine the content and form of racial categories and meanings" (7). The significance of being mixed race varies in these settings, even as the contests commonly operate as "highly racially charged arenas in which debates about authenticity and representativeness abound" (3).

CONCLUSION

The complex social and political dynamics shaping life in the "racial middle" underscore the importance of developing an attention to underlying cultural processes that crosscut and inform the circumstances of specific groups. This cultural landscape makes clear both the centrality of categorical identities to racial matters and the way internal forms of heterogeneity within those categories can challenge basic American assumptions about race. Broad debates over the whitening or browning of this middle terrain in American culture are intriguing but hard to resolve, given that there are so many levels of group circumstances at which to consider these questions. What is clear, though, is that race operates at each level, shaped by fundamental cultural dynamics involving interpretive work linked to basic operations of determining belonging and difference. Perhaps here more than anywhere, the importance of an ethnographic attention to specific interpretive practices should be apparent. Understanding the racial middle requires careful attention to place-based dynamics, even as they reflect large-scale processes that invest diasporic identities with a range of contradictory meanings.

CHAPTER 7

Ethnography of Race

The ethnographic approaches to race surveyed in this book, taken cumulatively, present an intriguing range of findings concerning, first, the enduring significance of race and, second, ways to think critically about how we reproduce and possibly challenge racial meanings and practices. This chapter features an overall assessment of the findings of ethnographers studying race in the United States. Moving beyond particular questions of what we learn about whiteness, blackness, and the "racial middle" from ethnographers, the focus here is on what we learn about race and racial dynamics in general by considering these research findings taken in concert. This chapter then develops a comparative reflection on how forms of racial analysis and cultural analysis are combined in ethnographic studies. *Race in the 21st Century* has relied on both forms of analysis. But they are not simply equivalent, and the distinctions between their respective forms of attention offer an interesting basis for assessing the future of race.

The initial concern of this chapter is to establish what the findings from these ethnographies of race commonly reveal about racial dynamics. The shared points of orientation and conclusions from these ethnographies make clear the contours of cultural analysis in general, as well as the distinctive methodological aspects of ethnography. The question, then, is what does a cultural analysis via ethnographic methods allow us to comprehend about race matters generally? In answering this question, we will consider various points of contrast and overlap between cultural analysis and racial analysis as two distinctive ways of framing and making sense of social problems. The point in this comparison will be to make clear how racial analysis and cultural analysis can be combined productively in order to generate new insights about the enduring significance of race. Along the way, this chapter additionally addresses questions of how to organize and undertake research on race. This portion of the chapter features a review of the methods, theories, and questions related to the ethnography of race. The purpose of this section is to provide concrete guidance in how to formulate your own ethnographic research projects concerning race.

WHAT DO WE KNOW ABOUT RACE,
BASED ON ETHNOGRAPHIC RESEARCH?

The ethnographies of race surveyed in this book, though focused on various, distinct groups, reach some important common conclusions about racial matters. Whether these ethnographers studied whites, blacks, or peoples in the "racial middle," they commonly demonstrated *the dynamismand complexity of race at the local level.* For all that we can posit generally about whiteness and blackness, the relevance and meaning of racial formations hinge on the contingencies of local dynamics in particular places. These ethnographies also similarly highlighted *the role of social interactions as the locus where people perform, project, and respond to racial identities.* In this regard, the ethnographic perspectives surveyed here show that *these identities take a great deal of effort to maintain and reproduce efforts that hinge on material supports, public discourses, and cultural conditioning.* As John L. Jackson (2001) explained, "racial identity takes 'work' (even hard work) and is therefore, in a sense, achieved or not achieved based on one's actions and how they are interpreted" (149). The *crucial role of interpretation*—the active process of making sense of racial performances—is another point similarly stressed by each of these ethnographers, who share a recognition that racial meanings are often ambiguous or unstable; hence, our near-constant need to sound out their potential, continued relevance, or significance.

Taken together, the findings of these ethnographies can be construed in terms of a somewhat general formulation about how race operates. From a cultural vantage point, racial matters hinge on an interrelated set of elements: *place, social interaction, material and discursive supports* for racial identity, and the ongoing work of *interpretation*. In the first regard, these ethnographies depict a series of processes that comprise the daily, located operation of race. *Places* serve as both settings for social encounters and feedback loops between broad structures of belief and personal sentiments. We do not encounter racial others on a nebulous landscape of the social order; rather, we cross paths with other people in conveniences stores, in restaurants, in parks, and on streets as well as in workplaces, on vacations, or in our neighborhoods. Second, race is more than a set of beliefs or attitudes in our heads; it manifests in how we respond to others and present ourselves in these various places. Through *social interactions* we engage in various forms of boundary work, drawing inclusive or exclusive lines with gestures, looks, and comments, which either affirm or suspend a sense of common belonging. Third, these social interactions are importantly shaped by how or whether they receive *reinforcement and support from the particular setting or social discourses at large.* For instance, it is much more likely that whites will respond to a black person as "not belonging" in a social scene that is almost exclusively white (such as a segregated neighborhood) or when public narratives are circulating that link blackness to crime. Finally, all these matters involve the *interpretive work* of social subjects—how we read bodily cues and postures, how others hear certain words or comments, and how we register all this in correspondence with the features of a particular setting or context.

Perhaps the most crucial aspect of this cultural perspective on race is that it regards each of these elements as working in concert; indeed, *it views race and racial identity as products of active, interrelated social processes.* For example, these places all reflect some aspect of the material supports of race, whether directly in terms of exclusionary or inclusionary practices, or indirectly via the various forms of social investment and disinvestment that race supports. Social sites also provide frames of reference or prompts for the stories in our heads about types of people and encounters that constitute our cultural knowledge. Places form stages where age-old dramas over belonging and difference unfold and where our inchoate understandings of the world are tested, to be either reproduced or challenged. Some places may affirm racial narratives and discourses or may provide the opportunity for people to rupture their cultural conditioning. *Race both shapes the places where we meet each other and is recursively shaped by the outcome of those interactions.* From a cultural viewpoint, the dynamism of race stems from interactive processes between these distinct elements. Racial attitudes and beliefs can be seen as fairly static or "hardwired" when approached through survey research. But on the ground, up close, in people's daily lives, through ethnography it is easier to grasp that racial viewpoints range from fairly fixed to largely contingent, depending on how each of these aspects works in concert. This is a rather distinctive perspective compared to other academic approaches to race.

The core dynamic linking each of these elements is the work of interpretation. For all that we may stipulate about the significance of race in general terms, it remains a cultural matter—*an array of meanings that both inform yet remain contingent on the outcomes of social interactions in particular locales.* As with any cultural matter, race involves interpretation, and our interpretive dispositions cohere in forms that range from fairly plastic to stubbornly obdurate. However deeply embedded racial meanings may be in the landscapes around us—arguably most legible in forms of residential and institutional segregation, but also discernible in most public and private places—they still remain to be recognized, either explicitly or implicitly. This process of recognition certainly hinges on *interpretive repertoires* and *public discourses*, as we have seen repeatedly in these chapters, but it also importantly rests on *the selective apprehension of the real that cultural conditioning establishes.* Whether in terms of the properties of bodies or expectations for certain kinds of behaviors in particular locales, what we notice and respond to rests on *the perceptual line that culture maintains between the visible and the invisible—*that which we recognize immediately and that which passes from view entirely. The interpretive work of racial subjects consistently rests on what we can and cannot see as well as on the explanatory structures on which we rely in sorting out what everything around us means and how it matters.

Considering Racism

The crux of this difference is most apparent with regard to racism. Ideological approaches primarily construe racism as the central subject of concern. This is not the case with ethnographies of race, which focus on a far more diffuse range of signifying practices. Ethnographic approaches, in contrast, depict the problem of race in terms of the interplay between structures of meaning and meaningful practices—that is, as something more varied and indeterminate than ideologically-conditioned sensibilities. Consider, first, the ethnographies of whites covered in Chapter 4. Leland Saito, in applying Ruth Frankenberg's analysis of whiteness, found that, though the concept of whiteness is useful for talking about racial hierarchies generally, it was not useful in describing the cultural forms of attachment to place that whites developed in Monterrey Park—ties that could certainly be "racial" in some cases but not so in others. Pamela Perry, in her comparative study of schools in the San Francisco Bay Area, placed a primary importance on examining whites' contrasting abilities to identify the racial textures of their own lives. Rather than trying to determine which group of whites was more or less racist—in the two schools, one vastly white and the other where whites were a small minority—she examined the contrasting experiences of place that lead them to be either more or less astute about racial matters. As well, she was interested in how kids in *various racial groups* articulated a "multiracial self" by knowingly sampling and referencing racially marked music.

Even ethnographers of whites that did make racism a principal focus of study, such as Monica McDermott and Maria Kefalas, did so without relying on ideology to explain its operation. McDermott, who worked undercover as a cashier at a convenience store, was just as interested in the very different sensibilities of whites and different meanings of whiteness in the two sites she studied—Boston and Atlanta. Kefalas' ethnography framed the racism of working-class whites in south Chicago via a cultural lens, demonstrating how it is embedded in a broader cultural orientation that grants heightened visibility to some social situations while hiding others from view. These whites can plainly "see" a connection between black in-movers' arrival in neighborhoods and those areas' subsequent deterioration. But they importantly *cannot "see" the fundamental role that institutional and civic disinvestment plays in causing that deterioration.* They can "see" the specter of black violence on the edges of their neighborhood, but *they cannot "see" how their own children are succumbing to similar forms of urban pathology* right under their own noses. And they certainly *cannot see the contrary situation of the black middle and upper classes in gentrifying Chicago neighborhoods* such as North Kenwood, as depicted by Mary Pattillo-McCoy. More than just exposing racism—as in prejudiced white views of blacks—Kefalas sketches a broad cultural conditioning that *makes crucial dimensions of the social world invisible to whites while heightening their awareness of other social processes.*

The lack of a central reliance on racism is even more evident in considering ethnographies of black people and blackness. Racism, surely, is evidenced and registers as a factor and concern, but it is hardly the principal focus, since these ethnographies aim to examine and convey the full gamut of social life. For Pattillo-McCoy as well as for Signithia Fordham (*Blacked Out*) and Steven Gregory (*Black Corona*), a key dynamic of the social worlds they convey involves how blacks in different class positions make sense of racial identity and forms of racial solidarity. For both Gregory and Pattillo-McCoy, this involves depicting the conflicted position of members of the black middle class, who feel ties of solidarity for the black poor and working class but whose interests are often at cross-purposes with these same groups. Fordham additionally places a primary focus on the charged term *acting white*, because of the powerful boundary work it performs in *establishing or challenging common understandings of blackness.*

Racism is hardly absent from view, since these ethnographers pay meticulous attention to the construction of places, such as neighborhoods and schools. In doing so, the record of white disinvestment and practices of segregation are plainly legible. As well, there are plenty of examples of how blacks encounter racism in various social interactions. But the role of racism is consistently depicted as something of a social backdrop, as best exampled by Karyn Lacy's *Blue-Chip Black*. Lacy takes the "black middle-class tool kit" as one of her principal subjects of analysis. This toolkit forms an interpretive repertoire for "impression management," much like the one similarly operated by middle-class whites. The difference is that it is also composed of "improvisational processes and script-switching" tactics on which members of the black middle class rely to preempt potential racial assumptions of white coworkers, shoppers, or strangers. This toolkit provides a means of navigating the white-dominated world by deflecting possible perceptions of them as members of the black poor while "emphasizing areas of consensus and shared experiences" with whites of a similar class background. That is, the toolkit is the basis for boundary work, drawing distance from some blacks while establishing commonalities with whites. These tactics are components of a sophisticated interpretive repertoire for negotiating public life in a variety of social settings and encounters.

The breadth of the cultural perspective on race, which extends beyond a singular focus on racism, is further evident in these ethnographers' accounts of how black social worlds are cultivated and reproduced. Lacy draws this into focus with her observation that "middle-class blacks travel back and forth regularly between black and white worlds. They do not exist exclusively in one or the other" (2007, 151). Lacy highlights the social practices they engage in as they cultivate forms of black identity and ties to black social circles. Not surprisingly, this is most apparent with regard to parenting or the task of socialization. "For the parents in this study," writes Lacy, "helping their children to maintain a black racial identity requires as much thought and effort as nurturing a middle-class identity" (157). And while her subjects "all believe that racial identity is constructed primarily through social interactions in the black world" (166), they also recognize how substantial class fault lines starkly differentiate that social world. Thus the process of learning to identify racially hinges on learning to identify in terms of class as well. Lacy's work is an excellent example of the basic point that anthropologists have long argued: race is socially constructed. She extends this basic insight much further by showing the cultural breadth and depth of that construction process. This view is similarly underscored in John L. Jackson's attention to how "it can feel so obvious, natural, real, and even liberating to walk around with purportedly racial selves crammed up inside of us and serving as invisible links to other people" (2001, 15).

The scope of the racial landscape that a cultural perspective reveals becomes even broader as we consider the "racial middle." Here the questions of racial identity and processes of racialization grow so much more complicated. In part, this is because of the ambiguity of this terrain "in between" whiteness and blackness, where issues of "whitening" versus "browning" remain palpable and fraught. But it is also complicated because of the sheer range of social diversity that escapes encapsulation in terms of "black and white" racial dynamics. Issues of panethnic identity—over and against the plethora of intraracial and intraethnic distinctions— stand out as some of the most complicated. Racism, of course, is a central factor in how ethnic distinctions, say, between Mexicans and Puerto Ricans or between Vietnamese and Cambodians, collapse into racialized representations of Latinos and Asians. But it is not a sufficient means for analyzing the dynamics of establishing belonging and difference within these categories that hinge on a welter of additional factors, such as citizenship status, generation, region, religion, and class.

Ethnographers working with Latinos and Asian Americans do bring racism into view. But they also highlight a range of racial forms of interaction that are not easily explained by racism alone. Nicholas De Genova, for instance, examines the process of racialization confronting Mexican immigrants in Chicago, where "Mexican" operates as a racial identity that collapses distinctions in terms of citizenship or generational status. He also documents the racist sensibilities many of these Mexican immigrants hold regarding African Americans. In De Genova's account, adopting racist views is part of the process by which Mexicans in Chicago establish themselves as belonging in this country. In contrast, both Bonnie Uriciuoli and Arlene Dávila, in their ethnographies of New York, depict neighborhood settings (in Harlem and the Lower East Side) where African Americans and Puerto Ricans often live side-by-side and develop social ties across shared spaces. These ethnographers note *the ambivalent views people on either side of this "color line" hold of each other*, particularly in the fraught matter of competing for similar civic resources. But as Dávila points out, the matter of racial identity is hardly clear-cut, given the fact that "black" and "Latino" identities converge within a variety of individuals. For that matter, people in these areas "share a great deal of what they do, how they talk, and how they define themselves," as Uriciuoli (1996, 65) observes, much of it in the form of racially marked social practices.

These ethnographers are as interested in the *forms of contestations and conflict that occur within panethnic identities* as they are concerned with the processes that produce or assert racial difference. In Dávila's work, we get an insightful view of the dynamics of the *Latinization* of major cities in the United States. This term references the complex interplay of valorizing and demonizing aspects of "Hispanic culture" by mainstream interests in New York, which combines with ongoing forms of displacement (through gentrification) and cooptation (through marketing practices) to create certain kinds of ethnic subjects. This is a dynamic Dávila first examined in her ethnography of advertising agencies that produced favorable but "traditional" images of Latinos. But Dávila's attention also includes the contests and conflicts in the neighborhood public spaces of East Harlem, where Mexican immigrants gain ground and status through Latinization, whereas the very same processes adversely affect long-term Puerto Rican residents.

These complexities are paralleled, as well, for those who fall under the "Asian" or "Asian American" category. Through the work of ethnographers such as Aihwa Ong and Shalini Shankar, we see a similar range of distinct processes of racialization, many of which turn on *similar aspects of socialization linked to neighborhood residence and class position*. One important parallel is the question of ethnicity and how it matters or is articulated vis-à-vis the charged matter of "whitening" or "browning." As Mia Tuan concluded, "Asian ethnics are probably more similar to than different from white ethnics in terms of lifestyle preferences and general values" (2001, 19). But, like Latinos, Asian Americans confront an enduring racial perception of themselves as "foreign," despite however many generations they have been in this country. At the same time—and also like Latinos—Asian Americans have a capacity to identify actively with aspects of whiteness, as in claiming the status of "honorary white," usually marked in terms of class position. We find yet another parallel between these groups, in that Asian and Asian American identities comprise a wide variety of ethnic differences, some of which turn on issues of citizenship and immigration status, but that also amount to differential processes and experiences of racialization.

Aihwa Ong called attention to these contrasting textures of ethnic and racial identity in her comparison of the differential experiences of Vietnamese and Cambodian refugees in the United States. Arriving only five years after the primary wave of Vietnamese refugees, Cambodians faced a starkly different process for achieving citizenship. Shifts in the economic and political situation in the United States— along with contrasting forms of the cultural capital between the two groups—led the "racial classificatory logic" in this country to place "Cambodian refugees at the black pole: they are identified with inner-city African Americans and set off clearly not only from whites, but also from other Asian groups such as Vietnamese and Chinese Americans" (2003, 14). As well, Ong points out another set of contrasts with the experiences of Chinese nationals who bring enormous amounts of social, educational, and financial capital with them in their business endeavors in the United States. In each case, the issue extends *beyond basic questions about racism to an attention to the differential processes of racialization and the complex intraethnic or intraracial cultural dynamics that develop and unfold between groups*.

In this latter regard, we also return to the issue of *diasporic* and *transnational identities*. These ethnographers consistently focus on the immense cultural work that goes into maintaining social relations and elements of identity construction that extend beyond national boundaries. For Ong, this involves a landscape that is broader still, composed of a variety of trans-Pacific zones that both cross and compromise a variety of national spaces, held together by flows of people, capital, and products that follow historically deep networks of trade and migration. Racism in the United States is, then, one of many elements in a *complex interplay of regulatory practices and techniques of differentiation that further animate these networks.* This complexity is similarly glimpsed in Lynn Stephen's account of the experiences of indigenous Mexicans as they migrate for work in the United States. Stephen uses the term *transborder* to specify that these people cross an array of borders in addition to national ones, borders that demarcate regional differentials and distinct regimes of racialization in both Mexico and the United States. With Stephen, as well as with Ong, the central question concerns the cultural practices by which these people on the move maintain social ties to far distant homelands.

To echo Jackson once again, all this entails a great deal of cultural work. Shankar captures this well for "Desi" teens in Silicon Valley, who face the challenging task of coming to terms with the shifting meanings and fault lines of this fast-changing identity. As Shankar relates, "The uncertainty of what it means to be of South Asian descent is evident in how they align themselves with the culture of their schools and with other racial groups, as well as how they are positioned in neighborhoods and communities" (2008, 14). The meaning of "Desi" varies in each of these contexts, underscoring once again the crucial importance of place and the active process of making sense of meaning-laden categories in relation to a highly differentiated social structure. *Culture matters as much because it informs this landscape as because it provides the medium—in language use, expressive cultures, and consumption practices—through which these processes of sense-making unfold.* For "Desis," the matter of diasporic identity hinges on shifting or alternate frames of cultural reference that contrastingly highlight the values of local ties with those of an increasingly distant or largely imagined homeland.

CULTURAL ANALYSIS OF RACE

What are we to do about race? In answering this question, two basic points should stand out from the preceding pages. The first is that race is deeply embedded in both our social structures and our psyches; it profoundly shapes the ways we view and experience the world, and it makes for drastically differential life chances. Clearly this is a central problem facing Americans in the 21st century. The second point, though, is that race is exceedingly complex. For all the clarity the problem presents at the broadest level of social description—in terms of whiteness and blackness—the closer we look at it in the frames of everyday life, the more convoluted and intricate its operations appear. These two points are in tension—*the clarity with which race stands as a problem to be solved is sometimes complicated by the facts "on the ground,"* suggesting that simply challenging it is not an entirely straightforward matter. Add to these points a third consideration: in addressing the problem of race, we risk reproducing the very structures of thought that we are trying to critique and deconstruct.

Paul Gilroy, a cultural studies scholar, framed this problem in his work *Against Race: Imagining Culture Beyond the Color Line* (2000). Following from his considerable and incisive scholarship on race in England and across the "Black Atlantic," Gilroy reached the conclusion that one of the most important steps in doing away with race is to stop reproducing it through what he calls *raciology*—basically, the study of race. This is a very difficult task. In order "to liberate humankind from race-thinking" (12), we must be able simultaneously to jettison approaches tied singularly to race while remaining informed about and alert to the relevance of race, historically and contemporarily. He acknowledges that this will be most difficult "for people who have been subordinated by race thinking. . . . 'Race' and the hard-won, oppositional identities it supports are not to be lightly or prematurely given up" (ibid.). This is because, out of the categories and "ideas of racial particularity," "oppressed groups have built complex traditions of politics, ethics, identity, and culture" (ibid.). But Gilroy sees this as the moment to make such a bold move, particularly because of what he diagnoses as the current "crisis of raciology."

He explains, "It is a crisis because the idea of 'race' has lost much of its commonsense credibility, because the elaborate cultural and ideological work that goes into producing and reproducing it is more visible than ever before, because it has been stripped of its moral and intellectual integrity, and because *there is a chance to prevent its rehabilitation*" (Gilroy 2000, 29). That "cultural and ideological work" has been the primary subject of this book. Primarily via the lens of ethnography, that work has been rendered legible and tangible. We can see from these studies the manifold ways that we do race in everyday life, responding to and sometimes challenging its embeddedness in our social structures and cultural landscapes. But it seems that the very depth and pervasiveness of race that these projects reveal stand as almost a counterpoint to Gilroy's confidence that the current moment "offers a welcome cue to free ourselves from the bonds of all raciology" (15). For that matter, would not such a gesture come perilously close to reproducing the problem of "color-blind" racism or discourse, as analyzed by Eduardo Bonilla-Silva?

Bonilla-Silva's conceptualization of the "new racism" specifies that it works via "the increasingly covert nature of racial discourse and racial practices; the avoidance of racial terminology in racial conflicts by whites; and the elaboration of a racial agenda about political matters (state intervention, individual rights, responsibility, etc.) that eschew any direct racial reference" (2006, 94). Basically, he sketches a dynamic whereby whites think racially but manage to avoid explicitly referencing race. As does any dominant group, Bonilla-Silva argues, whites still rely on "very complex ideological formations that provide them rhetorical ammunition to account for social inequality. They also cultivate a moral framework to deal with dilemmas arising from maintaining domination" (137). While in the past, "white privilege was achieved through overt and usually explicitly racial practices, today . . . it is accomplished through institutional, subtle, and apparently *nonracial means*" (12). This complicated matter of distinguishing "racial" from "nonracial means" marks the points where the contrasts in Gilroy's and Bonilla-Silva's stances are most sharply drawn and where the rationale for the cultural perspective on race sketched in this book most clearly emerges.

The crux of the matter is this: though race continues to affect discrepant life chances and alternately to limit and to open access to social resources, it is increasingly difficult to find explicitly "racist" components in much of what whites say and do. Instead there is a profusion of "nonracial" discourses that seemingly strive to obscure the real racist sentiments, perceptions, and interests of whites, who now cautiously and conscientiously police their public comments to efface any mention of race. Using concepts such as *new racism* and *whiteness*, analysts of race strive to make the implicit racial aspects apparent by linking the "nonracial" discourses to racist ideological constructs. But this approach potentially skews as much as it reveals regarding the copious, often novel, ways race matters in our current circumstances. As well, if the ethnographies in this book have demonstrated anything consistently across the board, it is that "racial," in local contexts and social interactions, slides in and out of view and is contingent on the alternately active and passive ways people *perform* racial identities and respond to or *interpret* explicit or implicit racial meanings. From this perspective, developing ever more sophisticated ways of rendering "nonracial" instances or comments as "racial" is not the only or even the best solution for addressing or understanding the enduring significance of race.

The point where the line between "racial" and "nonracial" becomes so amorphous is exactly the point at which to revamp racial analysis and to do so along the lines Gilroy suggests. Rather than confidently subordinate the "nonracial" to an ideological obfuscation of the truly "racial" interests at work in contemporary society, an arguably better option is *to examine how "racial" subjects, interests, and identities derive from fundamental cultural dynamics that also shape class and gendered social terrains.* Cultural processes of interpreting, performing, and locating social identities, as this book has shown, explain a great deal about how race keeps changing and the way racial identities both play into and are supported by other social dynamics.

In Bonilla-Silva's delineation of nonracial and racial, two distinct stances on race emerge. One assumes we know with certainty what race is—how it works and matters or how its effects can be recognized and ameliorated. This approach draws on both a substantial knowledge base and a wealth of critical political practice to update and demonstrate the enduring relevance of *racism* as an explanatory principle regarding current social conditions. The other stance considers that *what counts as race today* is perhaps far less certain and more negotiable than it has been in the past. This perspective is easy to glimpse but somewhat hard to hold in view, especially for people who confront the inequalities of race on a daily basis, as Gilroy acknowledges. But it is an important view because it is oriented toward both the current tumultuous moment and the onrushing future as—whether you scan popular culture or immigration trends—the significance of race grows daily more fluid and dynamic. The fact that nearly seven million Americans classified themselves as "multiracial" in the 2000 census suggests that the meaning of race is no longer stable or uniquely defined by the polarized frame of black and white. This speaks to the need for circumspection as much as certainty about the significance of race today.

The approach developed in *Race in the 21st Century* posits, first, that we do indeed have a good deal more to learn about how race matters. But, second, that in doing so, we should strive not to reproduce the very structures of racial thinking that are a problem in the first place. *Racial analysis of the differential impacts of social dynamics must not reproduce racial thinking about essentially differentiated groups.* One way it reproduces racial structures of thought exactly is by designating one set of analytics for whiteness, another for blackness, and then yet another for the racial middle. Certainly, substantive intellectual and political reasons for making such delineations remain. But it would be unfortunate if racial analysis, in so doing, follows a path similar to that of ethnic studies programs in academia—where each group becomes the focus of distinct, specialized knowledge practices, all of which are ensconced behind a wall of intellectual segregation, allowing the larger knowledge practices of academe to proceed unaltered in substantive ways. This risk can be forestalled and possibly averted if racial analysis is developed in conjunction with the analysis of culture, because the latter takes as its aim processes of drawing boundaries, first around humanity in general and then between distinct social groups that variously pass in and out of coherence and relevance.

The approach suggested here is that we find a means, first, of locating racial analysis in such a broader framework so that it is not "only" about race; then, second, we develop analytical means of examining relational dynamic across the racial spectrum, allowing the basic fact of *the continuum of racial meanings and identities* to be properly grasped (Drummond 1980). Cultural analysis of race allows each of these goals to be met. As well, it involves an approach that does not reproduce racial thinking by positing essentially differentiated orders, with one mode of analysis applied separately to each. Cultural analysis presents the possibility glimpsed by Gilroy of moving beyond "raciology." This is not a total breach but, rather, a first step. But by framing race in terms of cultural dynamics, we avoid explaining *everything* in terms of race and can show *how race is produced and, most importantly, reproduced through fundamental cultural processes.*

Cultural analysis allow us to frame race differently—not as something that essentially differentiates people or as a strict matter of ideology and inequality but, rather, as something that people actively do as they conduct their daily lives, perceiving and responding to others while projecting themselves in a range of manners. A cultural analysis also allows us to follow race as the ways it matters become less obvious. One thing seems certain about race: its meanings will keep changing. Increasingly, our task is to investigate these meanings in order to gauge where or how older meanings linger and new ones are emerging. Our present knowledge about race is weighted heavily toward how it has mattered in the past, but it is equally important to be attentive to the new or developing ways that race matters or signifies. New forms of inclusion and exclusion will develop, varyingly keyed to race; new forms of boundaries will be generated, affecting perhaps also the reanimation of old ones; and, of course, new forms of transgressing these boundaries will also emerge. Because this is fundamentally a matter of "meaning," ethnography is the preeminent method or means for examining these developments.

CHAPTER 8

Postracial America?

An intensely disputed question about race today is whether the United States has entered a postracial era. This phrase attempts to characterize fundamental changes in this country that may be epitomized by the election of Barack Obama, the country's first African American president. In a longer view, "postracial" also references the rise of multiracial identities that seem either to portend or realize the collapse of **racial bipolarism** in this country. But plenty of indications suggest that there is hardly anything "post" about race in America today. For instance, extensive polling of potential voters' racial attitudes, in advance of the 2012 election, revealed that racist sentiment among whites had actually intensified during the first four years Obama was in office—to the point that a majority of whites (51%) expressed antiblack opinions. That majority grew (to 56%) on surveys that measured implicit forms of bias rather than explicit expressions of belief. And just as many whites harbored similar negative assessments of Latinos, as well. The impact of such attitudes is quite evident in statistics on disparate rates of incarceration and higher unemployment rates for African Americans and even in the differential life expectancies for whites and blacks. By all these important measures, "post," in relation to race and to the racial order that produced these disparities, seems premature or even, perhaps, delusional.

And yet, for all that, when Obama was reelected in 2012, he became the first president in fifty years to garner more than 51% of the popular vote twice. His predecessor, George W. Bush, by contrast, lost the popular vote to Al Gore in 2000 and only gained a little over 50% in 2004 against John Kerry. Another point of historical context for Obama's victories: in the decades since Dwight Eisenhower was president, just one Democratic candidate, Lyndon Johnson, won a majority of white votes; Obama attracted a higher percentage of white voters in 2008 than nine of the previous Democratic nominees, and he still bettered the white support of four nominees with his victory in 2012. Whatever heightened forms of racism were operating around the country, they were not able to keep Obama from winning a second term. What does that tell us about the significance of race in the United States today?

Because of the importance of race in producing differential life chances, and because of the resistance of many Americans to recognizing the impact of racial disparities, there is a powerful desire and impetus among race scholars to formulate emphatic and certain claims about racial dynamics. Hence the disparagement of the word *postracial*. Yet, as this chapter will show, arguably more is changing about race each day than remains the same; and, given the dynamism of race, its mutability and its relentless transformative capacity, we need to be attentive to not just how it has mattered but also to the bearing it will have as it adopts new forms and adapts to changing social situations. Postracial exactly marks that shift in focus. Postracial is potentially an apt characterization for our current moment, not because it suggests that "race is over," but because it indicates the assumption that race constitutes a unified, coherent, independent form of reality is coming unmoored.

Why use the term "postracial"? Because it signals a significant break with the previous order, one in which it was practically inconceivable that a black man could be elected president. "Post," here, works much like "postmodernism," a word scholars used to characterize a broad rejection of modernism but one that acknowledged its enduring presence or relevance in architecture, the arts, urban design, and social theory. Postracial does not signal the end of race; rather, that its fundamental logic and codes, its unity and singularity as a form of identity, and its power as a master narrative have been knocked off-kilter and disrupted in profound ways. The term "postracial" arose to characterize the changing dynamics of urban politics as a rising class of black politicians purposefully crafted cross-racial campaigns, with rhetoric that emphasized common economic predicaments. The success of these campaigns is reflected in the estimated 10,500 black elected officials across the country in 2011, compared with only 1,469 in the 1970s (figures from Joint Center for Political and Economic Studies, 2011). Many of these politicians were able to run not as the black candidate appealing strictly to the black community but, as Martin Luther King Jr. envisioned, on the "content of their character." You can well imagine that voters from across the racial spectrum, regarding each of these candidates, had to pose and answer the question: does race matter here? In this question and the varied answers it generates, postracial serves as a reminder that our assessments of the relevance and significance of race remain ensconced within dense cultural sensibilities and their attendant dispositions toward the past, present, and future.

Postracial also suggests that race matters require a great deal more specificity; that generalizations about race warrant more scrutiny and circumspection. References to "white America" and "black America," for instance, are increasingly susceptible to counterpoint examples that may complicate or even entirely undermine sweeping statements about whites and whiteness, blacks and blackness, or any of the identities across the racial middle. The confusions and uncertainties in the racial middle may be the most characteristic glimpses of how forms of racial identity are rapidly changing. For that matter, it's not just a question of groups and their relative standing, but also which locations and places are the most representative of racial matters. Instead of a single racial order in the United States, it is increasingly important to talk about multiple formations—such as the cities where minorities are the majority and the regions of the country that feature very distinct racial voting patterns.

This chapter considers the case for postracial. First, by reviewing emerging cultural developments and recent claims made by some researchers who are following these trends; then by considering ways that whiteness and blackness—the formations that define racial bipolarism in the United States—seem to be changing. Bear in mind that the contentiousness of postracial encapsulates the widely disputed significance of a variety of trends in relation to race, which will be surveyed here in some detail. The overall stance in this book is that the uncertainty over how to characterize racial dynamics broadly, across the nation at large, underscores the importance of paying attention to particular, concrete situations on the ground in everyday life. The valuable role of ethnography in providing such a perspective is borne out in the last third of this chapter, which draws from a range of recent projects that provide detailed portraits from a range of settings across the United States.

WHAT IS CHANGING WITH RACE TODAY?

In current commentaries on race, the year 2043 looms large. This is the date the U.S. Census Bureau estimates that non-Hispanic whites will no longer be a majority in this country. But that moment has already arrived in many parts of the country; for people living in those areas that future is now. As of 2010, four states already featured minority-majorities, including the two most populous ones: California and Texas. At a more local level, over 11 percent (353) of the nation's 3,143 counties reached majority-minority status in 2012. Then there are our nation's urban areas: 22 of the 100 largest cities are home to minority populations that comprise the majority. In the 2000 census these included San Francisco, Los Angeles, and San Jose in California, as well as Miami, Florida, and Houston, Texas. In 2010, the following cities joined their ranks: New York, Washington D.C., Las Vegas, San Diego, and Memphis. Not only are these cities central players in defining and showcasing American culture, they are absolutely fundamental drivers in the nation's economy. And the "face" that they depict of the United States is one where our nation's strengths and power lies in diverse populations, particularly featuring immigrants who are sustaining our economic growth.

Within all this census data and demographics, we can glimpse another aspect of why it matters now to affix "post" to "racial": the categories that we use to characterize and tabulate racial identities are beginning to burst. A key innovation in the design of the 2010 census is that it let people opt to select multiple racial identities. For a variety of political and social reasons, the Census Bureau did not offer a single "multiracial" option. Some federal officials feared that it would "add to racial tensions and further fragmentation" of the nation (Saulny 2011). But the census did allow respondents to mark "two or more" racial categories. Some nine million people, almost 3% of the population, chose more than one race on the census—a 32% increase since 2000. The possible combinations of racial identities are many: respondents could combine any of the five major race categories—white, black or African American, American Indian or Alaska Native, Asian, and Native Hawaiian or Other Pacific Islander—with the option of "some other race"; then with additional response categories, many of which are Asian nationalities, amounting to fifty-seven possible multiple-race combinations. Of these, the most frequent (20%) are black and white, followed by white and "some other race," white and Asian, and American Indian and white, which we will consider more closely below.

Much of this churning of racial categories is the outcome of increased intermarriage across racial lines. Today about one in seven new marriages are between people of different races (Pew Research Center 2012). This varies by region. Such marriages are increasing in the Midwest but surging in the South, a region where such unions were illegal until 1967 when the Supreme Court ruled such prohibitions unconstitutional. There is also a generational shift underway: race is experienced, interpreted, and conceptualized differently for people born either before or after the 1990s. Among children today, multiracial identities increased by about 50% from 2000, to now number around 4.2 million people. These young people give an additional glimpse into the changes happening in cities today, where slow-developing trends at the metropolitan level are accelerating far more rapidly for the youngest generation. In 2012, the majority of Americans less than one year of age were minorities, meaning that the demographic trend associated with the year 2043 has already occurred among babies born in this country. Nine of the ten largest cities are already majority-minority, in terms of this youngest cohort. The percentages range from almost 84% in Los Angeles to 63% in New York—cities with total majority-minority populations of 63% and only 51%, respectively, when all residents are tabulated.

The key point here is not that demography is changing, but rather that our classificatory system is increasingly viewed as inadequate to the task of recording and gauging the significance of race. Remember: race is a system of classification. That the categories are beginning to implode indicates that the coherence of that structure is being undermined. From a system that has been steadfastly insistent on maintaining whiteness and blackness as polar opposites—such that "one drop of blood" was enough to construe someone as black instead of white—we are moving toward far more uncertainty about what constitutes race and how it should be accounted for and recognized. This destabilization of racial classification is key to what some scholars see as an emergent, transformed racial landscape in the United States. Sociologist Jennifer Hochschild, in *Creating A New Racial Order: How Immigration, Multiracialism, Genomics, and the Young Can Remake Race in America* (2012), argues that "the United States is undergoing yet another transformation of its racial order through increasing heterogeneity and interactions, underlain by demographic and legal changes" (10). In addition to changing definitions of race and ethnicity, both at national and personal levels, and shifting relative positions of racial groups in the social landscape, she points to "changes in social relations among individuals and groups so that stereotypes, daily encounters, political coalitions, and social norms are less predictable and more interactive than they have heretofore have been" (11). Hochschild discerns four transformative forces driving these changes: "the entry of large numbers and new kinds of immigrants into American society, the rise of multiracialism understood as a political movement and public identity, the growing impact of genomic science on American medicine, law, and society, and the way in which the current cohort of young adults is reconfiguring Americans' collective racial memory and racial interactions" (13). None of these forces is inexorable, and the changes they presage may well yet be co-opted into reinvigorated support for the previous racial order. Yet, taken together, they identify key dynamics that will be central in understanding race today and tomorrow.

But one important matter to keep in mind is the reason *why* the Census Bureau asks these questions and generates this data in the first place. Principally, they are a means of tracking discrimination, which remains widespread in American culture. Census data is generated for the federal departments of Labor, Education, Health and Human Services, as well as the Equal Employment Opportunity Commission, for monitoring civil rights compliance and to detect covert and institutional forms of discrimination, especially in hiring, education, and housing. These new approaches to categorizing race, which can be sources for enthusiasm for people who feel most labels do not match their racial experiences, also potentially make it harder to discern and address discrimination. This issue was highlighted in 2011 over a policy change in the Education Department that placed students identifying with more than one race into a special "two or more races" category. This classification could include white students who also mark "American Indian" but may encounter few overt forms of prejudice, along with "black and Latino" students—identities that do continue to be subject to discriminatory treatment. Data related to "two or more races" will possibly obscure the impacts of the categorical identities that have and continue to be the focus of racial animus and injustice.

And there is plenty of evidence of ongoing racial discrimination. On the fiftieth anniversary of Dr. Martin Luther King Jr.'s famous "I Have a Dream" speech—delivered during the historic March on Washington that propelled the passage of key civil rights legislation—much about the country looked unchanged, from a racial perspective. In 2013, black families earned sixty-six cents for every dollar whites earned; in 1963, the ratio was fifty-five cents to the dollar. To be sure, the black poverty rate had dropped from 40% to 27%, but that is still substantially higher than for whites (10%) or Asians (12%). As is the unemployment rate, which has stubbornly stood at more than twice as high for blacks as for whites since the 1960s. African Americans with some college education today are less likely to find a job than white job-seekers who dropped out of high school. But the truly disturbing statistics are on differential rates of incarceration: blacks make up 44% percent of the prison population, while they represent only 14% of the nation's population. This point is highlighted in Michelle Alexander's important book *The New Jim Crow: Mass Incarceration in the Age of Colorblindness* (2010). In raw numbers, there are more blacks cycling through the prison system (currently incarcerated, on parole or probation) than there were slaves in 1850. This shocking and disturbing fact will be discussed at length later, but initially, it serves as a reminder of why postracial can meet with such derision and dismissiveness.

Yet the starkness of these facts should not suggest that there is a simple explanation, such as racism, that explains *everything* about how race matters today. Tempting though it is to diagnose so succinctly the cause and problem here, there may well be more complex dynamics at work. This is the stance Nancy DiTomaso takes in *The American Non-Dilemma: Racial Inequality Without Racism* (2013), her follow-up study to Gunnar Myrdal's famous and influential work *The American Dilemma: The Negro Problem and Modern Democracy* (1944). DiTomaso's project arose from her personal and scholarly frustration "with the content of the training provided by diversity experts, both in the university and in corporations" (xx). She recognized these experts' emphasis on eliminating stereotypes and prejudice by combating racism was missing crucial dimensions of how racial inequality operates and is reproduced. She noticed this particularly with her students, who like the vast majority of Americans are convinced that they, as individuals, are not racist. "Most of the students in my classes fit a typical profile: everyone was nice, no one discriminated, everyone believed in equal opportunity and supported civil rights, but most everyone got irritated if not mad when the issue of affirmative action was raised" (xxi). Perplexed, DiTomaso posed the question: "*if there are no racists and no racism, then why is there still a problem with racial inequality?*" There are a variety of ways to answer this important question (see Chapters 2 and 7), which underscores a key recognition that comes with the use of postracial: there is no one, absolute approach to analyzing and explaining race, because there is no unified phenomenon we can characterize as racial.

DiTomaso's specific answer stems from her critique of prevailing approaches to race that emphasize racism; she writes, "almost all of the social science literature on race is organized around a framework of discrimination" (xxiii). Instead, she finds that whites reproduce inequality through forms of favoritism extended to other whites that have little directly to do with disparaging or "othering" people of color. "Rather than racism or discrimination being the primary mechanisms by which racial inequality is reproduced, I argue that it is the acts of favoritism that whites show to each other (through opportunity hoarding and the exchange of social capital) that contributes most to continued racial inequality" (6). From this perspective, "attitudes" and "beliefs" toward racial others have less significance than understanding notions of belonging and sameness—fundamental cultural dynamics. DiTomaso explains, "Whites seek out—and many of them find—ways to protect themselves from the increasing volatility of markets. They can do so, most of the time, without doing bad things to racial minorities. Instead, they do good things for one another, and the net result is the perpetuation of white privilege in an environment of racial liberalism" (8). This approach is specifically formulated in contrast to the idea of *color-blind racism*, but it may be equally effective at calling attention to the reproduction of racial identities. Importantly, it reframes discussion of privilege and advantage, in a similar manner to historian Ira Katznelson's *When Affirmative Action Was White: An Untold History of Racial Inequality in Twentieth-Century America* (2006), which documents the multiple financial and social resources that flowed to whites from the federal government throughout the previous century.

FRACTURING WHITENESS?

DiTomaso's work raises basic questions about how whiteness operates today and suggests that the ways it has been framed by race scholars—as constituted in relational contrast to blackness—may not be adequate to the ways it is currently transforming. A basic tenet of racial theory is that whiteness is an unmarked identity, meaning that white speakers or images are not generally identified by their race. This is arguably the greatest source of privilege available to many whites: the ability to not have to think about race, to not have to wonder if race is countervailing against one's ability to be regarded simply as an individual. Remember Ruth Frankenberg's research (discussed in Chapter 4) revealed that many of her white subjects claimed to never have thought about race as they were growing up. The possibility of being so unaware, of not ostensibly thinking about race, for whites, seems to be changing, though, for a variety of reasons. This development is encapsulated in a finding by veteran pollster Stan Greenberg in a study of GOP voters (2013). Greenberg concluded succinctly: "They are very conscious of being white in a country that is increasingly minority." The roots of this consciousness are varied, but centrally it suggests the claim that whiteness entails freedom from having to think about race needs to be recalibrated.

As Greenberg's formulation indicates, an important factor here is the shifting racial demographics in this country, as summarized in the opening of this chapter. Certainly, for some whites this is producing a heightened anxiety, in that they seem to glimpse for the first time that their race may be a source of disadvantage. This perception is evident in another survey, conducted by psychologists (Norton and Sommers 2011) who found that many whites are convinced that antiwhite forms of racism are more widespread than antiblack racism. This is a remarkable perception, given all that we know about discrimination today, evidenced by the racial disparities in who gets hired, offered a place to live, or obtains a financial loan. But it does speak to the fact that many whites are growing anxious over the potential—real or imagined—to be negatively marked by race. It should be noted, though, that this perception is not commonly held by all whites; it is far more prevalent among the working class—60% of whom think whites are discriminated against more than blacks—than among college-educated whites (39%), who are rather more economically secure. The role of class here importantly raises the broader issue of the drastically altered financial landscape of the United States and who is most vulnerable to these changes.

Since the Great Recession began in 2007, the middle class in this country has been greatly undermined. The kinds of jobs that allow for homeownership, that support buying a reliable vehicle and taking an annual vacation, along with the ability to pay for a child's education and even sock away some savings—hallmarks of middle-class identity—began disappearing after high-paying manufacturing jobs left the country in droves in the 1970s and 1980s. In this financial environment, very few people feel expressly privileged and most harbor heightened economic anxieties. This leads to questioning long-held assumptions about the connection between whiteness and privilege, but, importantly, these developments also open rifts *within whiteness*. Certainly, such rifts are not new, and terms like "white trash" and "redneck" have long been deployed to internally police belonging to whiteness (Hartigan 2005; Wray 2006). But what is different today is the extent to which poor whites are experiencing the forms of ill health that have historically been associated with racial inequality.

There is perhaps no more damning data indicating the enduring significance of race than the differential life expectancy between whites and blacks. But the surety of this racial advantage to whiteness has notably fractured. A stunning report published in the journal *Health Affairs* (Olshansky et al 2012) reveals that life expectancy for whites who lack a high school diploma is sharply declining. In a country where lengthening life spans has been a characteristic feature for decades, this is hard to comprehend. Especially given that, in the period between 1990 and 2008, life expectancies of blacks and Latinos with less than 12 years of schooling actually improved. But white men who did not complete high school saw their average lifespan decrease by three years within the scope of one generation. The picture is far more stark for white women in this cohort; their life expectancy dropped by five years. White women with a college degree live an average of ten years longer than these women (83.9 to 73.5); the gap is even larger for men—those who graduated college live an average of 80.4 years compared to only 67.5 years for white men without a high school diploma. The study noted, "blacks and whites in this educational category were living with unacceptably high mortality risks that were up to a half-century behind their better-educated counterparts" (Olshansky et al. 2012:1807). The study also found "that on average, blacks and Hispanics with sixteen or more years of education lived 7.5 years and 13.6 years longer, respectively, than whites with less than twelve years of education" (1806). There are many formal and informal advantages to whiteness, but in this most crucial class characteristic, the privileges of whiteness are clearly extending over fewer white lives.

At the other end of the class spectrum, the equation between whiteness and "success" in this country also may be coming into question. This is most evident in the changing complexions and ethnicities in places like Silicon Valley, as glimpsed in Chapter 6 through Shalini Shankar's ethnographic research. More recently, sociologists Tomás Jiménez and Adam Horowitz conducted fieldwork in Cupertino, California, "a high-skilled immigrant gateway, where an Asian immigrant-origin population has established and enforces an amplified version of high-achievement norms." Their finding suggested an important rupture has occurred in relation to whiteness. "In Cupertino," Jiménez and Horowitz write, "Asianness is intimately associated with high achievement, hard work, and academic success. Whiteness, in contrast, stands for lower achievement, laziness, and academic mediocrity. This understanding of ethnoracial categories in relation to academic achievement is widespread" (2013, 850). In contrast to notions of Asians as a model minority—an idea that "does not challenge the meaning and status of whiteness" (851)—these new articulations about race not only undermine the unmarked status of whiteness, but they also generate stereotypes of whites as less academically able; even to the point of being labeled as "acting Asian" (861) when they do excel. In this regard, connotations of laziness and ignorance long associated only with poor whites now may be spreading to color whites in the upper classes, as well.

POSTBLACKNESS

If one pole of racial bipolarism in the United States is fragmenting, what is happening at the other end with blackness? Touré, a journalist and cultural critic, captures this with the term "postBlack." What does this mean? "It clearly doesn't signify the end of Blackness; it points, instead, to the end of the reign of a narrow, single notion of Blackness. It doesn't mean we're over Blackness; it means we're over our narrow understanding of what Blackness means" (2011, xv). This term marks a frustration with punitive judgments, such as "too black" or "not black enough," that imply "the idea that there is a correct or legitimate way of doing Blackness." In contrast, Touré imagines a "modern, *individualist* Blackness," one where the vast variety of black cultural identities are not bound to tight, delimited notions of authenticity. But opening up black identity this way, Touré allows, makes some people nervous. "The sheer plasticity of Blackness, the way it conforms to such a bewildering array of identities and struggles, and defeats the attempt to bind it's meanings to any one camp or creature, makes a lot of Black folk nervous and defensive" (xii). The fault lines here are largely generational: African Americans coming of age in this millennium face very different circumstances than those born in the previous century. Touré frames this in quite personal terms: "I've never lived a typical Black experience. My father did—he grew up in the projects in Brooklyn rooting for Jackie Robinson and the Dodgers, and in the slums of Harlem, sometimes eating at the church of the legendary minister Daddy Grace" (53). In contrast, Touré attended prep school and played on the tennis team, earning him the pejorative label "oreo." He argues, though, that his experiences now fit as well within blackness as do those of his father.

Such changes are more broadly, even somewhat sociologically, sketched by Eugene Robinson, a columnist for the *Washington Post* and author of *Disintegration: The Splintering of Black America* (2010). Robinson describes "four black Americas," each "increasingly distinct, separated by demography, geography, and psychology. They have different profiles, different mind-sets, different hopes, fears and dreams." He acknowledges there are moments when these separate "nations" may coalesce, yet, "more and more, we lead separate lives" (5). Robinson's point is not simply about class diversity among blacks, something that has long been a characteristic of African Americans—a fact first documented by W. E. B. Du Bois at the close of the nineteenth century. Rather, he points to something closer to entirely different social worlds. Two of these groupings are familiar to social scientists, just differently named. Robinson identifies one group as the Abandoned, a term that replaces the pejorative label "underclass" in identifying blacks mired in the country's decaying central cities. Then he offers Mainstream as an updating or perhaps popularizing of the "black middle class" (see Chapter 5). With this group, drawing a sharp boundary with whiteness is quite difficult; Robinson observes, "the black Mainstream is now woven into the fabric of America, not just economically but culturally as well" (194). For this group, "There is no cultural gap between black children who grew up in suburban, middle-class settings and their white classmate from down the street" (183). But for the other two groups the situation is somewhat different.

Perhaps most recognizably, in terms of popular culture, Robinson characterizes the Transcendent as "elites with such enormous wealth, power, and influence that even white folks have to genuflect" (5). In these ranks are the luminaries, such as President Obama and Oprah Winfrey, certainly, but also CEOs of Fortune 500 companies and wealthy politicians. There is a generational aspect to this grouping—they largely are not old enough to remember Jim Crow America. This entails a profound historical change that Robinson captures succinctly: "Forty years ago, remember, only 2 percent of African Americans had incomes of $100,000 or more. Now more than 10 percent earn at least that much—and a small but growing number of black Americans earn many times more" (76). This wealth is indeed a world away from members of the Abandoned, whose problems "begin in the womb," because of the lack of adequate prenatal care received by poor black women, and are amplified through underfunded schools, violent urban life, and the general absence of extensive social networks connecting to jobs and civic resources. It may be too reductive to formulate a generalization about race that encompasses both of these worlds.

The fourth group, the Emergent, is where racial notions are being most deeply challenged. There are two parts to this group: "individuals of mixed race heritage," such as those discussed in the opening pages of this chapter, and "communities of recent black immigrants." Taken together, they "make us wonder what 'black' is even supposed to mean" (5). About 8% of black U.S. citizens are foreign born. Predominantly, they come from Caribbean countries, such as Jamaica, Haiti, and Trinidad, but currently there is a significant increase of immigrants from Africa, with the largest contributing countries being Nigeria, Ethiopia, and Ghana. The contrast to the era of slavery is stark: "today, Africans coming here voluntarily on wide-body jets are the best-educated immigrants in the United States—better educated than Asians, Europeans, Latin Americans, or any other regional group" (165–166). Black immigrant children carry forth this legacy: their rates of enrollment in elite, U.S. colleges are higher than that of white Americans. "Immigrant black students also had the highest rate of overall college attendance, including non-elite as well as elite school" (169).

This group similarly draws the attention of another journalist, Ytasha L. Womack, who also tries to define the term "postBlack" (2010). Like Touré, she highlights the generational divisions within blackness, but Womack as well points to the diversity of immigrant experiences of blackness. Black immigrants from Nigeria and Jamaica, for instance, bring contrasting, distinctive sensibilities about what success looks like and how identity should be articulated. In the United States, they surely encounter the fierce investments in whiteness that inform decisions about hiring and who can live in which neighborhoods, but they also challenge American-born citizens' notions of what blackness entails. For that matter, these immigrants also highlight the particular cultural assumptions that inform "African American," a racial category that reflects a particular history and politics of ethnicity and assimilation in the United States. But such immigrants increasingly generate new ideas for asserting or eluding racial identities, rather than simply conforming to American assumptions about race. Often this involves appropriating that key American category—the individual. This is a point that Touré highlights as well, quoting visual artist Kehinde Wiley: "the *cult of the individual* is something that is going to be a rescuing point for Black people" (8). In this view, Obama's accomplishment—to lodge himself squarely and firmly within the category of the individual—is an option that Touré and other black commentators see as increasingly open to others, as *individual* comes unmoored from its unmarked racial associations with whiteness.

WHAT REMAINS THE SAME?

But if so much about whiteness and blackness may be changing, why are the forms of racial inequality highlighted previously so enduring? In particular, thinking of the transformations in blackness, why does so little seem to have changed substantively about racial disparities despite the historic election of a black man to the presidency? There are two basic answers to this question, each of which eventually lead to the ethnographic approaches discussed in the final portion of this chapter. The first is that race in not just in our heads; it fundamentally informs the spaces in which we live, work, go to school, and recreate. Historian George Lipsitz makes this point very clearly in *How Racism Takes Place* (2011). Whiteness, he demonstrates, is as much a spatial arrangement as it is a mindset or collections of attitudes about social groups and identity. Lipsitz shows that "a **white spatial imaginary** based on exclusivity and augmented exchange value forms the foundational logic behind prevailing spatial and social policies in cities and suburbs today" (28). This concept references and condenses the history of discriminatory housing practices—along with the massive federal and state subsidies that fueled white flight and suburbanization—to help us grasp how concern over home investment achieves exclusionary effects quite as powerfully as explicit racial animosity. In this perspective, whiteness "has an enormous cash value" (36) as "a structured advantage subsidized by segregation" (37), which whites will strive to maintain even without holding expressly racist ideals. Lipsitz explains: "It is not that suburban whites are innately racist and consequently favor land use policies that increase the racial gap, but rather that prevailing land use policies produce a certain kind of whiteness that offers extraordinary inducements and incentives for a system of privatization that has drastic racial consequences" (35). The fact is, these consequences operate as part of the landscape and can actively reproduce with little ever expressly said or thought about race. And, much as DiTomaso suggested earlier, they can continue to be reproduced without whites ever having to consider their active role in this dynamic, because it functions independently of explicitly racist assertions or arguments.

The second answer follows, in part, from the first, but it also links back to the particular question posed concerning the impact of Barak Obama's presidency. It turns on another basic question: what did not change when Obama was elected? The answer is: the underlying cultural dynamics that inform racial thinking; these have not changed, nor are they easily altered. "Individualism" is still the dominant ethos in the United States and "groups" are still its categorical antithesis (see Chapters 1 and 4). *Individual* is frequently racially unmarked, simply because it stands apart from all social trappings or contexts; relationally and in contrast, *groups*, as a category, is commonly racially marked: "whites" and "blacks," for instance are groups. Race fundamentally binds us to groups, to categorical identities that assert we are more like people of a certain hue of skin than we are similar to lighter or darker phenotypes. The most common expression of this in American culture is via "community": as in references to "the black community" or the "Latino community." Note, though, how infrequently white gets associated with or characterized as a community. This reflects the enduring capacity of whiteness to be an unmarked identity or formation. The real challenge with race is that our very terms for discussing it reproduce some of this logic, by formulating "people of color" as a *group identity*, one which many Americans, as *individuals*, are going to view with some suspicion and ambivalence. More than heightened racism—or at least alongside it—those surveys cited in the chapter's opening show an intensified association of blacks with *group* and very little progress on seeing whites as more than a loose assemblage of *individuals*.

This basic point is underscored by turning again to the work of Lipsitz and DiTomaso. In relation to the discriminatory government-supported mortgages in the 1940s and 1950s that fueled white flight, along with the massive federal highway and water/sewer subsidies that promoted suburbanization, Lipsitz points to a key reason why whites would not recognize this as a form of "white affirmative action" (Katznelson 2006). Because, "instead of recognizing themselves accurately as recipients of *collective* public largesse, whites came to see themselves as *individuals* whose wealth grew out of their personal and individual success in acquiring property on the 'free market'" (27). DiTomaso similarly sees profound racial implications flowing from the ways occupying the category of *individual* keeps whites from recognizing their racial advantages. She, too, argues that "the ideology of individualism in U.S. culture hides from whites the group-based nature of their advantage or privilege" (2013, 11). Its greatest power lies in obscuring the fact "that social resources are group-based, not individually based. These are ties that develop within communities, within residential neighborhoods, within school districts, through churches, friends, and through other social connections" (10)—resources that are fundamental to how people get their first job, get socially networked, obtains car loans, and buy a home. But when whites in her study talked about their social position—how they got where they are today—they only mentioned "hard work," "personal effort," and "talent." They consistently overlooked or even discounted the importance of networking or "knowing the right people" or of the social capital that comes from being provided with a financially stable home life and a good education.

Now, let's return to the question about Obama. The racialization of *individual* and *group* in American culture is something that President Obama has given a great deal of thought. In his autobiography, *Dreams of My Father*, Obama grapples with understanding the contrasting ways whites and blacks are positioned in relation to these key cultural categories. He describes, first, how wearisome it is for blacks, socialized as racially marked, to be defined by a group status fundamentally equated with race. Obama relates how he "stumbled upon one of the well-kept secrets about black people: most of us weren't interested in revolt; that most of us were tired of thinking about race" (2004, 98). Then he pointed to the contrasting condition of white people, who did not have to think about race because "only white culture could be nonracial, willing to adopt the occasional exotic into its ranks. *Only white culture had individuals* (100) [emphasis added]." Obama's point is not an empirical one—at a basic level, all racial groups are comprised of individuals. His observation, rather, is cultural, about the categories that dominate American culture: the default assumption is that whites are individuals and nonwhites are, rather, identified as belonging to groups or communities.

This realization profoundly informed Obama's campaign for the White House. His strategists knew full well, as Cornell Belcher, a pollster for Obama, explained, "It would be difficult for an African-American to be elected president in this country. However, it is not difficult for an *extraordinary individual* who happens to be African-American to be elected president" (Nagourney, 2008). Suspecting that McCain's campaign was "going to try to make Barack Obama the other," as staffer Daniel Carol remarked, Obama's team countered by posing him as someone personable and distinctive, through direct modes of address to the camera in commercials with pictures of his white grandparents in the background. "He had to be *an incredibly individuated figure*, [emphasis added]" Belcher further explained, and this was clearly the result Obama achieved. It worked, in that Obama was perceived as an individual rather than as representing a group.

This accomplishment underscores the fundamental role of the categories *individual* and *group* in American culture. In electing Obama, a majority of Americans ratified the view that Obama is an individual, rather than primarily being identified with a group—African Americans. The evidence was in the survey data, particularly an NBC News/*Wall Street Journal* poll just before the 2008 election that showed 80% of whites felt that he would not "favor the interests of blacks over other Americans." That is, he would not be bound by *group* interests or identity. It was also evidenced in a *New York Times* poll in early September that found almost 70% of Americans expressed the view that Obama shared their values, a higher score than his opponent, John McCain, received. Clearly, whites could look at him and see a shared sense of identity, one that transcended the cultural boundary demarcating blackness from everything else. But these perceptions, it has to be stressed, are views regarding only one man, which is exactly how the campaign presented Obama.

Returning to the opening question of what changed with Obama's election, we have to ask more specifically: what impact this individual accomplishment has had on the great mass of racial folklore and cultural conditioning that leads whites, perhaps still, to view blacks primarily in terms of the group category rather than as individuals? In this regard, he achieved escape velocity from the racial perceptions that view blacks as a group rather than a composite of individuals. But it is important to underscore: *individual* and *group* are not racial categories; the contrast they draw also operates marked and unmarked forms of gender and class identities, as well. Rather, racial socialization leads toward assuming the valorized category—individual—is associated with the unmarked, normative condition of whiteness. That is why Obama's opponents, from Hilary Clinton to John McCain or Mitt Romney, were not characterized as a "white candidate." This is not a racist perception, per se—it does not stem from any explicit articulation that whites are superior and blacks are inferior. This perception and categorical dynamic arises from something more pernicious and difficult to disrupt: the play of marked and unmarked identities in relation to race and to the fundamental categories of American culture: individual and group. For all the optimism that Obama's example would go a long way toward reconfiguring this racial perception, the social data on prejudice and disparities suggest otherwise. His success in becoming "incredibly individuated" has had limited impact on altering the racialization dynamics around individual and group in the country at large.

COLORING RISK

We get a better sense of this broader, continuing racial dynamic by considering how we color or racialize the categories of individual and group via notions of risk. Everyone's life entails some elements of risk, but exposure to risks—such as environmental hazards, high crime rates, exposure to toxins in food and water, and so forth—are powerfully stratified by class. Wealthy people are able to shelter themselves from the vast majority of risks; conversely, poor people living in an impoverished neighborhood are prone to risks on many fronts. Race, of course, is also a key factor. Environmental racism, as discussed in the opening of Chapter 1, refers to the fact the black and Latino neighborhoods are frequently the locations of noxious industries or their contaminating waste products. So it is notable when any group takes on unnecessary risks, and particularly when they do so for fun and recreation. Bruce Braun, a cultural geographer, writes about just such a group in his article "On the Raggedy Edge of Risk" (2003), which looks at the depictions of white rock-climbers and sea-kayakers in adventure magazines. These are activities that individualize encounters with nature. For these whites, taking on risks, as in extreme sports, is a powerful way to individuate themselves.

This symbolic dynamic is particularly evident in corporate management training and motivational exercises, where risk taking activities are often encouraged. Braun explains the symbolic associations at work: "Climbing the corporate ladder is akin to climbing a mountain: it is about skill, ability, and ambition, not politics, economy, or power" (2003, 199). As the phrase "office politics" suggests, though each of those latter components *are* crucial factors in who rises and falls within a corporate hierarchy, they often appear unseemly and improper ("not nice") in meritocratic terms. Culturally, then, participants are physically performing and imagining a status ideal they hope to achieve; and in motivational or training contexts—highly symbolic, ritualistic domains—the cultural emphasis is on a heightened idea of the individual. So how does race factor in, then, to the coloring of risk? Especially given that whites, as a group, are able to keep so many social risks at bay. Braun acknowledges, "Middle-class whites face risk like everyone else, but they constitute themselves as middle-class and white precisely through the *externalization* of as many risks as possible (locating socially undesirable land uses elsewhere or sending children to private schools) and through barricading themselves from many others (through gated communities or purchasing insurance)" (199). This point is borne out by Setha Low's work on the whiteness of many gated communities (discussed in Chapter 4), where much of the appeal and certainly the selling point is insulation from risks of crime and threatening others.

The question is answered, though, in that the ability of many whites to actively distance themselves from social forms of risk is matched by their capacity to take on *recreational forms of risk as a matter of choice*. Braun explains, "Within mainstream American culture, *taking* risk is understood as an individuating activity associated with whiteness. One takes risk when one chooses to" (198). We can clearly see this in extreme sports—competitions that involve inherent dangers, often associated with uncontrollable natural forces or conditions, such as wind, snow, water, and mountains. These sports feature solitary exertions and individual, rather than team or group, competitions. They also directly draw from and reproduce the idea of white adventurers and explorers, who were foundational figures in European colonization and in the conquest of the American West. So it is hardly surprising that the vast majority of their participants, enthusiasts, and spectators are also white.

But, as we have seen consistently, wherever there are individuals, groups are often lurking in the background in a relationally contrasting position. This is evident in who gets designated as "at risk" in this country. Whether it is due to neighborhood violence or underfunded schools that undermine young learners' education, the phrase "at risk" is consistently associated with people of color. Braun notes, "Being *at risk* is commonly viewed as a property that belongs to someone else, the *racial* subject. It is associated not with agency or choice but with a kind of passivity, helplessness, or deviance" (198). That is, being at risk is an identifier of group status, as in "at risk youth" who face gunfire from urban gangs on their way to school or who lack social and economic capital to take advantage of what education they are able to access. In contrast, individuals freely chose risks. Whites who participate in the X Games are not acting out inherently racist impulses, but their participation in such events with the aim of individualizing themselves definitely plays into and supports a racialized perception of people who cannot or who are unable to do so. This point is underscored when we consider the additional contrast here between naturalized settings, where extreme sports take place, and urban contexts, where the social risks of crime, pollution, and poor health are rampant.

Braun points to the contrary image often offered to depict America's ongoing urban crisis: "the poor black whose degeneracy is a guarantee of his social position, whose natural proclivity is to watch TV, eat junk food, take drugs, who has no work ethic, is overweight, unhealthy, and unmotivated. The black subject simply can't be this 'active' climber" (199). This *imagined figure is a product of many social forces*: from high crime rates that make any outdoor activity potentially life-threatening to the near total absence of grocery stores in the "food deserts" of the inner cities. But often, in American popular discourses, it is hard to grasp or take seriously the social forces that lead to racially disparate life chances—such as the high rates of infant mortality, due to lack of access to good prenatal care, and forces which create a five-year shorter life expectancy for African Americans compared to whites. Instead, we tend to view this figure of the "poor black" simply as a problem of "failed" *individuals* who do not take on an active life.

The social aspect of urban blight, though, is more legible if we carry the coloring of risk one step further. The Great Recession that started in 2007 was precipitated by risky financial practices undertaken by mortgage banks that offered subprime loans to people who were often unable to afford the properties or the terms for which the loans were made. Disproportionately, these loans were marketed and sold to African Americans and Latinos in precarious urban neighborhoods (Rugh and Massey 2010). The failure of many of these loans caused a massive foreclosure crisis across the United States, but the impact was most palpable in deteriorating inner-city communities, where many neighborhoods were undermined as people lost their homes. These practices, though, were actively encouraged and promoted in the boardrooms of banks and mortgage firms, where they were seen as a form of risk taking that could individuate an up-and-coming loan officer or financier. As we would expect from Braun's account, the vast majority of these officers were whites, taking risks that might promote their individual careers; while the people they targeted were financially at-risk African Americans and Latinos, many of whom ended up losing their homes. Underlying the distinct racial codings of risk is the fundamental import of different valuation and perceptions Americans have of the key categories: individual and group.

With the role of individual and group clearly in mind, let us return to the shocking statistics on racial disparities in our penal system. Think about who goes to jail for taking risks and who does not. Two facts are fundamental to understanding the role of race in how incarceration works in this country. First, whites and blacks use drugs in roughly the same proportion, and blacks are not more likely to sell drugs than are whites (Alexander 2010). But blacks are far more likely to be jailed on drug charges. The racial disparities are stunning and depressing, but their national aspect is particularly disturbing. The United States jails far more people than any other country in the world, in terms both of absolute numbers and proportionally. With more than 2.3 million adults imprisoned, the United States is far ahead of China, with 1.5 million prisoners, and Russia, with 890,000 inmates. In rates of incarceration, the United States is also well ahead of nations like South Africa and Iran. Why don't most Americans get upset about this? Why is this not considered a national scandal? Why is this situation allowed to persist while its terrible consequences go unabated?

There are two ways of answering these questions: one strictly in terms of race, and the other in cultural terms; and these contrasting explanations are useful for highlighting the way race rests upon underlying cultural dynamics. Returning to Alexander's book, *The New Jim Crow*, she depicts a racial system that is profoundly powerful and self-reinforcing. "In the system of mass incarceration, a wide variety of laws, institutions, and practices—ranging from racial profiling to biased sentencing policies, political disenfranchisement, and legalized employment discrimination—trap African Americans in a virtual (and literal) cage" (179). The title of her book asserts that "the new caste system . . . may prove more durable than its predecessors" (179). To the important question of why there is not more outrage over this situation, Alexander concludes, interestingly, that "most Americans *know and don't know* the truth about mass incarceration" (177). That is, we recognize the racial disparities but do not acknowledge the role that racism plays in this system. She characterizes this as a state of "racial denial."

In this situation, Americans may not grasp the thoroughgoing nature of this racial system for the simple reason that our social worlds are so sharply divided by race. As Alexander explains, this "denial is facilitated by persistent racial segregation in housing and schools, by political demagoguery, by racial media imagery, and by the ease of changing one's perception of reality simply by changing television channels" (177). But just as importantly, to the extent that Americans are made aware of these disparities, there is a powerful cultural discourse that keeps us from taking it seriously or regarding it as something that needs to be ameliorated. And that is the **discourse of choice**. This meritocratic discourse is particularly pronounced and active in relation to moral and ethical concerns, such as with justice, and it very stridently insists that the focus must be on *individuals*. Alexander sees this as central to the disregard many Americans may feel toward this predicament. "The current system invites observers to imagine that those who are trapped in the system were free to avoid second class status or permanent banishment from society *simply by choosing not to commit crime*" (179). The contradiction, though, is that "we tell ourselves they 'deserve' their fate, even though we know—and don't know—that whites are just as likely to commit many crimes, especially drug crimes" (177). Alexander concludes, "It is far more convenient to imagine that a majority of young African American men in urban areas *freely chose a life of crime* than to accept the real possibility that their lives were structured in a way that virtually guaranteed their early admission into a system from which they can never escape" (179). To avoid this conceptual trap, Alexander wants us to emphasize race instead of "choice" in thinking about who does or does not go to prison. Her argument is that we have to overcome the racial denial and instead see the presence and power of racism behind these disparities in rates of incarceration.

But an aspect of this "denial" goes beyond race and reflects the importance, again, of the categorical centrality and power of *individual* in American culture. In this regard, keeping an attention on "choice" leads us to the underlying cultural dynamics at work in Americans' fundamental *misunderstanding* of how justice operates in this country. As a cultural discourse *choice* highlights some dynamics and obscures others, makes some situations highly visible while rendering other operations practically invisible. Culture lets us see some things quite clearly while we ignore a vast array of other phenomenon. *Anytime "choice" is invoked, you can be certain, as a cultural articulation, it is providing a selective view of the world*. As a collection of individuals, Americans idolize choice and see the individual as characterized by a series of choices they make, rather than a product of social conditions and circumstances. Very often, as Alexander asserts, choice is invoked to explain away the disparate rates at which blacks are incarcerated in this country. On talk radio, online blogs, and discussion groups, it is easy to hear the view expressed that "they just made bad choices," or "they are only in jail because they made a choice to commit a crime." Listen for that "voice" or opinion in your own thinking. As an American, it is very hard to resist; it percolates powerfully even in the face of quite damning statistics. When we are asked to care about the shocking number of people of color in jail, it is easy to fall under the sway of a discourse that says *those people* are undeserving because of the choices that they made.

But the key point here is that, through many forms of racial profiling, young black and Latino youth are consistently not viewed by police as individuals: they are perceived in dependably superficial terms as members of a group, identified not just by skin color but also by neighborhood. These policing practices are well-documented across the country, in big cities and on rural stretches of highways, where "driving while black" can be a sufficient cause for a patrolman to make a traffic stop. The pattern here can even produce self-fulfilling statistics that seem to suggest people of color are more likely to commit crimes, when they are being disproportionately targeted for activities, such as drug use, that they are no more likely to pursue than whites. Furthermore, this group identity carries over into disparate sentencing of offenders based on race, which is widespread in the United States. In cultural terms, black and Latino youth are burdened by a perception that only sees their *choices* and not the social circumstances in which they were made. This view does not encompass the social context of policing tactics targeting minority neighborhoods, while allowing suburban whites practically unfettered opportunities to consume and distribute drugs.

Conversely, the racially unmarked status of whites as individuals goes a long way in explaining why they are not arrested as *often for making the exact same choices*, or, when they are arrested, why they often receive far more lenient treatment. It is easier for police, prosecutors, and judges, generally, to consider whites' choices in relation to the culturally valorized category of individual: someone worthy of redemption or a second chance; someone who "just made a mistake," and not someone predisposed to a life of crime. What this cultural view of the individual exactly obscures is the powerful group dynamics shaping white perceptions that afford leniency to other whites or the patterned way white police may differentially view suspects by race. Much as DiTomaso pointed out earlier, whites making the same choices to do drugs as blacks and Latinos are recipients of favoritism on the part of white officials functioning within the judicial system.

Back to our basic question: why does race not simply end or go away? First and fundamentally, because it is part of our social landscape: it is inscribed in segregated neighborhoods, which are reproduced through the differential choices made by realtors about which properties to show people; it is reinforced through school segregation and the powerful disparities in educational funding and resources, as well as through the decisions made by human resources staff about who to hire or by loan officers concerning who should get access to loans. Discourse of "merit" and "choice" exactly disguise these powerful, enduring forms of racial inequality. In this, they are assisted by the central category in American culture, that of the *individual*. When we talk of whites as meritorious, in academic terms, we obscure the fundamental role of the wealth effect in influencing higher test scores and miss an important group circumstance associated with whiteness. Conversely, dismissing black and Latino youth for making bad choices that land them in jail, also conceals important social patterns: the heightened surveillance of people of color by police and the relative liberties whites experience when they consume illegal drugs. In this regard, though, it is not simply a case of racial denial, as Alexander argues, but the impediments that the basic categories in American culture present when trying to recognize and understand the relevance of race to our contemporary inequalities.

What we end up with, when we think in cultural terms, both about racial disparities and the nonchalance or resignation many Americans demonstrate toward this terrible situation, is a recognition of the powerful role of fundamental, underlying categories of group and individual. It seems that rather than recognize the racial disparities, many Americans resort to individualism to explain away or ignore the profound racial disparities in our justice system. This is not just "racial denial" as Alexander suggests, because, again, the categories individual and group are not inherently racial. Instead of considering the group aspects of this predicament, many Americans will say: those individuals just made bad choices; race is entirely beside the point. This position is very hard to counter, and it exactly frames why it can be so difficult to engage racial dynamics in the United States. It is not just racism at work, but a deep cultural resistance—borne out in the powerful belief in individuals—to see the social aspects of race: whether it is the advantages that flow to whiteness or the disadvantages that accrue to blackness. That these key categories are frequently racialized speaks to the enduring relevance of race in American culture. But as the term postracial suggests, taking cognizance of these racial dynamics requires more than an attention to race. We need to attend increasingly to the underlying role that culture plays in shaping racial situations. And for that, we have no better tool than ethnographies.

RECENT ETHNOGRAPHIES

The advantage of ethnographic research is that it lets us move from generalizing about race in terms of national discourses and problems, to considering what is happening in everyday life in particular settings. From this vantage point, we can return to one of the central discussions in this chapter: what is happening with racial bipolarism in this country? What is going on with whiteness, blackness, and the racial middle from an ethnographic perspective?

With whiteness, importantly, we gain a sense of how limited some of its fractures and stress points may be. On the ground, it appears as if whiteness remains quite durable, as evidenced in recent ethnographies by Matthew Hughey and Circe Sturm. Hughey, a sociologist, developed a truly innovative project: he conducted a comparative ethnography on two seemingly antithetical groups: a white nationalist organization and a white antiracist collective. Stunningly, the two share far more in common than one would imagine or hope; what they share is exactly whiteness, even though one of the groups is actively committed to both disavowing and challenging white privilege. "Located just a short distance from one another on the East Coast of the United States, the members of these two groups inhabit incredibly different social worlds. Yet they rely upon similar racial and cultural meanings to interpret and navigate those worlds" (2012, 3–4). Hughey split his time between the white nationalist and the antiracist organizations, observing their work routines and informal socializing, then arranged semistructured, in-depth interviews with core members. His observations and interview data revealed that, despite their antagonistic political orientations, members of these organizations "make meaning of whiteness in strikingly similar ways" (4). Most tellingly, "both white nationalists and white antiracists see themselves as autonomous *individuals making independent choices* that reflect authentic desires and true selves. Yet these choices, desires, and selves are anchored to racial categories and meanings that structure how they negotiate the world" (3). That is, as whites, thinking very consciously about the collective aspects of whiteness as a *group*, they still uniformly see themselves as radically defined, instead, as unique *individuals*. This socialization into individualism highlights the principal dynamics of American culture operating across intense partisan divides; such that, even when people vehemently disagree on an issue, they share an understanding of what is worth disagreeing about. The question is how this common sensibility relates specifically to the operations of whiteness?

In the cultural "common sense"—normative ideas, rules, and expectations— that similarly informed interactions of members of the respective organizations, Hughey identified a shared set of assumptions about whiteness. "Members of both groups valorized certain performances of whiteness that they strove to attain but of which many fell short. This resulted in a great deal of variation in white racial identities, but it was a variation cohesively bound by their shared understandings and expectations" (14). How could these two groups—one dedicated to white supremacy and the other to assailing the privileges and power associated with whiteness—have so much in common? "In both groups, the pursuit of an ideal whiteness is paramount, and while different strategies are used, these strategies often result from or draw on similar understandings of race" (17). This ideal of whiteness invariably operated over against people of color, on one hand, and then "other whites thought inferior or lacking," on the other.

Hughey discerns an overarching white ideal, one that is articulated in relation to people of color in at least five different, interrelated modes: (1) drawing contrasts to the perceived dysfunctionality of nonwhites; (2) asserting a status as racial victims; (3) imagining themselves as "white saviors" to people of color; (4) claiming to possess "color capital" via interracial friendships; (5) and by construing themselves "as all-knowing subjects of racial information" (172). Some of these modes are easily recognizable. It is not news that widespread stereotyping depicts of people of color as the products of broken homes and prone to drug use or crime. What is surprising, though, is how easily antiracist whites trafficked in this imagery. While they asserted "that the pathologies of people of color are the result racist maltreatment and discrimination," the activists still invested heavily in promoting a view of "the existence of immoral, flawed, and unfit group-level characteristics among people of color" (75–76). As well, in both groups, there was a strong sense of being racially stigmatized, of "suffering because they are white." For the white nationalists, this reflects a view that mainstream society is somehow antiwhite; the antiracists, instead, felt they bore the brunt of social condemnation for challenging white privilege. For both, these sensibilities translate into "claiming persecution because of their whiteness." Hughey finds, "they collectively purse an ideal image of the white martyr who suffers greatly *yet makes the choice* to 'keep up the good fight'" [emphasis added] (80). In each organization, this ideal white identity functioned similarly: "both memberships reproduce an interracial boundary. They claim a double standard in which white actions are unfairly stigmatized while similar nonwhite actions are praised" (112). Whether directly challenging or promoting whiteness, this racial formation has the power to reproduce an idealized form that draws adherents across radically distinct political lines.

Three additional modes of whiteness operated commonly in these organizations: patronizing and paternalistic behaviors toward people of color, stemming from a "white messianism"; "a shared sense of white racial emptiness" paired with "a desire for racial otherness," linked to feelings of "white normativity" (150); and a feeling of "either entitlement to, or trivialization of, knowledge deemed racially important and significant"—they commonly assumed and asserted their status as "race experts," even if that meant dismissing knowledge claims of people of color. These commonalities highlight two points about whiteness. First, as a racial formation it is powerful enough to operate across seemingly incompatible, antagonistic political agendas. Second, it does so because of underlying cultural dynamics. Hughey notes, "political orientation does not provide escape from social expectations" (190). However fully immersed they may be in political activism, members of these groups still have to navigate social settings and circumstances, relying on a cultural common sense that is broadly shared. The "structured patterns of white racial meaning making" (168) that Hughey finds reflect how "these meanings assist whites in meeting everyday accountability obligations across an array of settings and contexts" (192). But more keenly, their activism in pursuit of "ideal whiteness" is powerfully fueled by highly individuating performances and evaluations, which members clearly achieve through the choices they make in relation to race. The rhetoric of "choice" and of "individualism," which helps these activists distinguish themselves from other whites, is what links them across lines partisan lines but also to their fellow Americans, generally. These are the foundations of sense making in the United States that render whiteness all the more difficult to assail, because it so subtly blends into assumptions about self and belonging that inform everyday life.

This *discourse of choice* also informs shifting expressions of racial self-identification, specifically in the movement from whiteness to American Indian-ness. Anthropologist Circe Sturm studies "racial shifters," whom she defines as "individuals who have changed their racial self-identification on the U.S. Census from non-Indian to Indian in recent years" (2011, 5). Between 1960 and 2000 the number of people who claimed Native American status jumped 349 percent. Including those who additionally claimed another racial identity, this growth amounts to an increase of 647 percent over forty years—a radically unusual demographic development, since neither immigration nor reproductive dynamics can account for such an enormous rise. The vast majority of these racial shifters are white. What is going on here? Why would so many whites, who generally have the status of being unmarked in terms of race, decide to adopt a marked racial identity? Sturm answers these questions by examining "the deeper social and cultural values that lie behind this movement" in her ethnography *Becoming Indian: The Struggle over Cherokee Identity in the Twenty-First Century* (2011). Initially, Sturm observes "that many racial shifters readily admit their siblings and parents do not identify as American Indians and that their last Indian-identified relatives may have been a great-great-great-grandparent" (7). This sudden change in identification, then, reflects a highly individualistic pursuit, a "personal quest," rather than being a product of changes in familial relations or ideals. If not much is changing in the family, is something changing in how Americans think of race?

Evidently not in this case, since these whites maintain very traditional U.S. notions about race. This astonishing shift in racial identification hews closely to the underlying logic of race in the United States—hypodescent. Similarly to how blackness is imagined in this country, these shifters reproduce dominant under-standings of race by maintaining that "one drop of blood" is sufficient to establish their new-found Indian identity. They also stridently assert that race is evident in certain physiological features (cheekbones, eyes, hair, and even teeth), and they maintain that racial identities are relatively exclusive, such that "Indianness" displaces more complicated, "mixed" forms of race. Sturm observes that "when racial shifters gloss over their own multiracial histories by privileging their Cherokee ancestry over their white ancestry, they fail to acknowledge the power that attends whiteness and the ways that this might also be embedded in their own histories, life experiences, and bodies" (42). As Sturm listened to the personal narratives of these whites, stories that appeared to be about Cherokee identity turned out to be more telling about the enduring cultural power of whiteness.

In terms of whiteness and American culture, Sturm highlights the dominance of the rhetoric of choice among these whites-turned-Indian. Her ethnographic analysis tracks "how race shifters use the language of choice to deny and to articulate their links to whiteness and white skin privilege—without realizing it, race shifters have the luxury of choice that comes with an 'unmarked' appearance" (50–51). In this sense, belonging to a group is construed largely as a personal preference, a chosen form of association, rather than something socially ascribed or assigned at birth. This dynamic cuts two ways, both indicating a great sense of entitlement. The first step involves a disavowal of whiteness, "despite having appearances that would be read as unambiguously white in most social contexts" (51). They often simply chose to deny any relevance to their whiteness. More astoundingly, though, choice discourse allows them to assert a superiority over "physically identifiable Cherokees who have always been Cherokee because they had no other option" (52). *Choice* stands out, for the racial shifters, as a moral standard that valorized their assertions of identity. Sturm explains, "The idea here is that race shifters are somehow better Indians because they chose to be Cherokee rather than have that identity ascribed to them at birth, as if voluntary association is superior to accidents of love and history" (52). Certainly, this sensibility reflects the enormous privileges afforded to whiteness, such that some whites are able to purposefully *mark* their racial identity and lose little social standing in the process. But just as importantly, this dynamic is a function of the profound belief in the power of individuals in American culture—they can make group membership a matter of voluntary election and individual preference, rather than a mere accident of birth, physical appearance, or social classification.

Given the powerful way the category of individual plays in the reproduction of whiteness and white privilege, is it the case that this category is fundamentally racist? No. The category, like any underlying cultural unit, operates in multiple registers at once: the individual is also fundamental to how Americans make similar distinctions in terms of gender and class, and it is key to how we think of ourselves over and against people of other nations—even those that share the fundamental tenets of individualism. Look back over the discussion of terms like "work," "nice," and "friendly" (Chapter 2), if you need a refresher on how American culture operates through such generic categories. The connection between individual and race, or whiteness, turns on dynamics of marked and unmarked identities, which also are not specifically racial matters. The problem, again, is the way whites can stand as unmarked individuals, with the tapping of their group-based privileges obscured from view. Another dimension of this problem is that people who are racially marked in this country have a much greater difficulty occupying this important category. We see this clearly in relation to blackness in Erin Winkler's ethnography *Learning Race, Learning Place: Shaping Racial Identities and Ideas in African American Childhoods* (2012), set in Detroit, Michigan.

Winkler's study is important for a number of reasons; connecting each of these, as in any ethnography, is a thoroughgoing attention to cultural dynamics. Focusing on black children of middle school age, Winkler develops a distinctive attention to what she calls **comprehensive racial learning**. This concept opens up a significant space between the family and the media as sites of socialization. Much of the academic literature on how we are socialized into racial thinking focuses alternately on one or the other of these two important social institutions. But Winkler recognizes that children are not simply passive receptacles of social messages; they actively strive to make sense of the world around them, and that includes race. In their basic cultural capacity to interpret everyday life, "young people *actively develop their ideas* about race and racism by *negotiating, reframing, and making meaning* of all of the racialized messages they encounter" (145). Two important features stand out in their interpretive efforts to make sense of race. First, as the book's title suggests, is the fundamental role of place in shaping racial meanings. Just as my ethnographic work in Detroit demonstrated (see Chapters 1 and 2), Winkler shows that the significance of race varies a great deal by location and context, especially as these are shaped by class circumstances. Second, though, is the central but precarious impact of the concept of the individual.

In the first regard, Detroit plays a palpable role in providing these children both social encounters and material objects with which to think about race. Similar to Karyn Lacy's ethnographic work in suburban Maryland and Virginia (see Chapter 5), Winkler finds that the city offers manifold "procultural messages" about blackness, such that the parents often do not feel an expressed need to teach their children about this aspect of their identity. Positive examples of African American history, culture, and heritage are ready at hand for youth growing up in this city, and parents are able "to highlight the greatness of African American heritage in and of itself" or to model "normal Black behavior and consciousness" (78), without qualifying or contextualizing all this as a response to racism in the larger society. In fact, the notable contrast Winkler draws with Lacy's work is the scale at which blackness is normalized or unmarked in Detroit. The entire city operates as a "construction site for black racial identity" (79) rather than being limited to particular black-dominated neighborhoods. But poignantly, the power of place extends beyond the city, to the highly segregated and racialized regional level of the city-suburban divide.

In this broader sense of place, the role of race is stark: Detroit's resources have been massively depleted, initially through white flight and then through subsequent, systematic practices of disinvestment in the city. The resulting poverty and violence become subjects that black parents must address through direct forms of racial socialization—in contrast to less focused, self-activated, racial learning—rather than allow implicit associations regarding blackness to form in their children's minds. But more directly and painfully, they personally encounter racism either when they venture outside the city or when they consume national media. These children travel beyond Detroit to compete in statewide sporting events and to shop or to pursue any number of recreational activities. These trips often feature direct experiences of racism—"racialized hostility, exclusions, and expectations" (52)—or they may provide more indirect glimpses of the operation of structural racism in the plight of Detroit. What stands out in these instances is the grave difficulties these children face in asserting a status as an individual, which is commonplace and easy to access for most whites.

Winkler explains, "While many of the children in this study argue that the *individual* and not his or her race is primary, in practice the *group* experience often emerges as primary" (48). Though thoroughly schooled in the ideals of color-blind discourse, as are white Americans, the black youth in this study encounter more complicated forms of racial identifications. In addition to experiencing racism, they weigh whether to identify wholeheartedly with "black pride" and other forms of racial consciousness. This is where Winkler's focus on interpretive cultural dynamics is quite revealing. The children in her study can lurch quickly from "the colorblind rhetoric of race-neutral meritocracy" to comfortably "expressing a race-conscious point of view" (47). Notably, these discourses sometimes clash or create confusion and deep ambivalence over how to talk about the significance of race. "The ambivalence comes through in their discussions of racial pride, whether it is ever acceptable to take race into account, and whether or not race has any impact on them as individuals" (35). The children thoughtfully mull the various aspects of group/racial identity open to them but consistently orient these to a basic American sensibility about and desire to stand simply as individuals. This stance, though, is rendered tenuous when they are subjected to racist ascriptions, statements, or images.

Poignantly, though, their ability to deploy and claim the category of individual stands as one of the strongest counterweights to racism. Winkler observes that the parents "recognize the necessity of preparing their children for racism but also want their children to recognize people as individuals. This serves as a critique of racism, showing it is neither logical nor humane to generalize too broadly about people based on race" (139–140). They preach individualism and messages of common humanity accompanied by "direct discussion about racial identity and racism" (140). Rather than being the fundamental vehicle by which whiteness operates, as we might have concluded from the ethnographies discussed earlier in this chapter, *individual* provides a critical counterpoint to racial thoughts and perceptions. "By encouraging their children to refute racial stereotypes, resist absorbing racist ideas, think critically about racialized representations, and treat people as individuals and with fairness, all of the mothers engage in a critique of racism as an aspect of responsive racial socialization" (142). The problem of race does not lie solely in the concept of the individual. African American parents strongly espouse the concept when socializing their children to avoid internalizing or promulgating racist ideas and perceptions. The problem lies in the views of whites they encounter in various circumstances who are unwilling to extend the recognition of individuality—upon which they lay their own claims to personhood—to these black youth.

Winkler's ethnography additionally provides clear evidence, first, that racial bipolarism remains strongly intact in places like Detroit; second, that despite notions of postblackness discussed previously, this racial formation continues to entail sharp boundaries via notions of authenticity and other limited forms of belonging. Parents in this study convey a strong frustration over the ways notions of "authentic blackness" limit their children's choices about how to identify (148). On the first point, the strongest indication of the enduring power of racial bipolarism is that many of these parents and their children articulate or repeatedly encounter the view that there are really *only two races*: white and black. Even though many other racial groups reside in Detroit—conspicuously, one of the largest concentrations of Arabs outside the Middle East, as well as a significant Latino presence—race is typically construed as a matter of just two categories. This perception is most powerfully evident in relation to *colorism* (see Chapter 6). The children "do notice skin tone and use it as an indicator of status or authenticity" (152). Along with other facial features and physical attributes, they often "make mention of this in relation to beauty and attractiveness as well as access to education, employment, and privilege." The continuum between lighter and darker hued African Americans in Detroit, though, is readily construed instead as clearly delineated orders of polar opposite terms: "white" and "black." Winkler observes, "Among the mothers and children in this study, many explicitly identified both Latinos and, especially, Arabs as white" (152). For these Detroiters, additional racial categories are eminently collapsible into what they consider to be more relevant and consequential binary terms. Conversely, the colorism Winkler observes produces situations where light-skinned black children, at times, are identified by schoolmates as racially other; "they are called 'white' or 'Chinese' or 'Hispanic' or 'Asian.' The relative homogeneity at their schools—not just of race but of skin color—creates a space in which lighter skin serves to mark them as other" (163). The enduring power of colorism strongly indicates that racial bipolarism remains a defining feature of life in this country and may well undermine the "browning thesis" (see Chapter 6). Whiteness extends into blackness, not just as constraining forms of racism but also by influencing notions of beauty and status-based appearances, resulting in a situation where our social and phenotypic variety is rendered in stark terms of white or black. But is the prevalence of racial bipolarism in Detroit representative of how dynamics of racial identity are sorted throughout the United States?

The central point here is that places matters a great deal in shaping the meanings and encounters that are associated with race. While these ethnographies offer developed views of particular locales, they do not cover the entire range of possibilities regarding racial dynamics. Hughey's ethnography of white nationalists and antiracists on the East Coast, combined with Winkler's perspective on the Midwest, strongly indicate the enduring power of racial bipolarism. But we get a rather different view on these dynamics if we shift to consider the Southwest or the West Coast, where in states like Texas and California—as we have seen—the pending national shift to majority-minority status has already occurred. An excellent glimpse of these regions is provided in Wendy Cheng's ethnography *The Changs Next Door to the Díazes: Remapping Race in Suburban California* (2013).

Specifically, this is a study of Los Angeles' West San Gabriel Valley (SGV), but analytically it is an ethnography of "nonwhite space" in California. The cluster of suburban communities Cheng examines is about two-thirds Asian, Asian American, and Latino, and is probably best known for Monterey Park, the first majority Asian American city in the continental United States (see Chapter 4). Economically, the West San Gabriel Valley has been distinctly shaped by the interlinked processes of deindustrialization and reindustrialization, set in motion in the 1970s. "Deindustrialization left warehouse and manufacturing spaces empty and available in the SGV, which also had well-developed infrastructure in large part due to the construction of freeways in the 1950s and 1960s. Changes in immigration laws in 1965 opened the door to an influx of Asian immigrants both at the top (e.g., professionals) and at the bottom (e.g., low-wage labor) of the economic spectrum" (6). Chinese immigrants, with their capital networks, fueled the rise of local banking institutions that, in turn, facilitated "ethnic Chinese business growth and home ownership," producing a sprawling community "in which Latina/o immigrants work alongside Chinese and other Asian immigrants in the kitchens of ethnic-Chinese-owned restaurants, garment factories, and manufacturing firms" (6–7). On the whole, regarding class identity, "Asian Americans and Latinas/os living in this core region have relative parity in terms of socioeconomic status, both earning median household incomes slightly below the countywide median income" (7), which is "significantly less than area whites" earned in 2010.

Cheng's basic questions are cultural: "How do people's daily paths and whom they encounter on them—shaped by family histories, regional and global economies, and localized knowledge—inform their racial and political consciousness? How do people experience these shifting formations daily, especially in an area in which the local hierarchy does not match up easily to national racial ideologies?" (3). Her answers to these questions emphasize the importance of place in how people perceive and articulate racial identities, similarly to Winkler's findings. Instead of emphasizing national dynamics, Cheng argues that "**regional racial formation** reveals an openness of meanings and outcomes rooted in place-based, everyday knowledge and interactions, which create the possibility of unexpected social and political consequences of proximity" (11). The important development in this region, Cheng finds, is an "emergent nonwhite identity rooted in middle-class and suburban contexts" (13), one that might be interestingly contrasted to blackness in Detroit.

Cheng describes "nonwhite spaces as 'worlds of their own,' in which white people are peripheral to the main act: people remaking their everyday lives and places within particular constraints but also emphatically on their own terms" (13) Unlike Detroit, where racial identity assumes a kind of fixity linked to its indelible inscription on the segregated landscape, "people-of-color identities" in the SGV

are "characterized by frequently shifting alliances, with uncertain political outcomes depending on the individuals involved and the situation" (14). This results
in a great deal of specificity in how social identity manifests. In SGV "positional-
ity within a generalized nonwhite identity varies by race, ethnicity, immigrant-
generational status, and class. With regard to Asian Americans and Latinas/os,
one must also pay attention to differential racializations vis-à-vis Asian American
model minority discourse and the ambiguously white status of Mexican Americans
(referring to both day-to-day experiences of 'passing' and historical and legal factors)" (15). Cheng is attentive here to the varying politics around citizenship and
whiteness that operate regionally and nationally in various periods: initially, being
relatively inclusive of Mexicans—in legal terms, related to the U.S. conquest of portions of northern Mexico—while excluding Asian through specific immigration
restriction acts; then, more recently, allowing Asian Americans "honorary status"
in whiteness, based on their high-profile forms of academic and economic success,
while disparaging Mexican Americans for failing to assimilate to Anglo "mainstream"
ideals and values. In the background here is the current and historical complex social
dynamics of whiteness within the category Latino.

These nuances generate a distinctive regional version of nonwhite Cheng explains, "West San Gabriel Valley, as a majority-Asian American and Latina/o lower-
middle-income to middle-income, semisuburban space, is distinct from mainstream
conceptions of nonwhite spaces (as poor, central urban ghettoes, barrios, or enclaves) as well as mainstream conceptions of suburbs (as normatively white and
economically homogeneous)" (19). Assuming these "mainstream conceptions" reference a place like Detroit, it is well worth noting an additional, important contrast
between these two locations: there are very few black people in the West San Gabriel
Valley. Cheng attributes this both to the spatial boundaries whites initially drew in
keeping blackness out and to the relative degrees of ease with which Asian Americans
and Mexican Americans were able to cross those lines. Historically, Cheng points to
"the differentiated racial hierarchy that allowed Asian Americans and Mexican
Americans, but few African Americans, to purchase homes in the West SGV marks
the area as undeniably shaped by anti-Black racism" (33). In terms of racial bipolarism, this process raises important questions of how permeable whiteness may be
to certain groups of nonwhites and how enduring is this opposition to blackness.
Cheng sees these dynamics as deeply interrelated: "the increasing ability of Asian
Americans and Latinas/os to buy houses was characterized by grudging acceptance posted in contradistinction to and often facilitated by racism against African
Americans" (31). While this process can be viewed in terms of the broad ethnic
identities at play here, Cheng allows that "strategic uses of whiteness might function
simply to facilitate individual gain and looked a lot like complicity" (39). How this
dynamic plays out today, with the continuing absence of blacks in the "multiracial"
neighborhoods of SGV, is not directly addressed by Cheng.

In considering the relative power and influence of nonwhite spaces to cultivate
distinctive orientations toward race, over and against national discourses and representations, schools are a central proving ground. As institutions, they are certainly

local in orientation but, as well, they are increasingly sites of standardization according to nationally determined politics and economics. Cheng aims to understand this interplay by exploring students' and teachers' ideas about and perceptions of success and failure as they materialize along racial lines. She focuses particularly on high school as a key site for understanding social relations. In this critical institutional setting she found that "students' ways of making sense of the social order were tied intimately with the particular regional context in which they were growing up—in a majority-Asian American and Latina/o, immigrant, metropolitan suburb in which the alignments of race and privilege were neither fixed nor clear cut" (65). In these contexts, students' active efforts to make sense of race are informed by the local versions of cultural "common sense," but they also directly encounter national discourses on academic success and failure. Schools are often volatile institutions sites where "societal orders and mores are being taught but have not yet been internalized as common sense, taken-for-granted truths." In West San Gabriel Valley, students entering local schools have already developed "regionally based forms of common sense, based on what they see and experience in their own lives, in local and familial contexts" (65). But the local high school also featured "the racialization of Asian American academic excellence, along with a concomitant racialization of Latina/o deficiency" (66), which certainly reflects national discourses and assumptions. In the context of the schools, identities that "were neither fixed nor clear cut" begin to assume a great deal of fixity, as ascribed, categorical identities.

In the schools, Cheng found that "Asian American students within this social order often experienced and enacted a distinct form of racialized privilege—in which the particulars are predicated by one's racialization, or ascribed group identity, by dominant society" (66). The concept of *racialized* privilege entails a subtle but important contrast to *racial* privilege, with the latter being the capacity to function as racially unmarked in everyday life and institutional settings. Contrastingly, "racialized privilege foregrounds the centrality of racialized meanings and outcomes—the circulation of model minority discourse is not merely incidental or external but itself participates in the production and reproduction of privilege." Being racially marked as "Asian," thus, "constitutes not a privilege to be considered normal but a privilege to be considered *exceptional*." Where whites may typically have their success and advantages attributed to their qualities as an individual, this form of advantage involves "an internalization of privilege accorded to one's ascribed racial identity"—"One's *race is not irrelevant but integral*" (75). Another aspect of this form of racialization is that important social differences within *Asian* are either ignored or dismissed; Cheng observes that "under the common umbrella of 'Asianness,' ethnic, class, and other differences are obscured" (76).

Two features fundamental to any racial dynamic—naturalization of categories and their relationally established meanings and contents (see Chapter 3)—are readily evident in the differential ways Asian and Latino students move through the school. These two categorical identities are consistently construed in polarized terms, one associated with academic achievement and the other with failure. Cheng illustrates this by noting "the degree to which the discrepancy in 'achievement' and a concomitant 'segregated' social order were seen as 'natural' by both Asian and Latina/o students indicated their acceptance as common sense. For Asian Americans, this amounted to a form of privilege predicated on racial terms" (74). Cheng further observes, "like all processes of racial formation, these racial discourses around achievement were fundamentally relational. This became apparent in the categorical use of the term *non-Asian*, which often functioned as a euphemism for Latina/o" (77). In school settings, anything "construed as Mexican or Latina/o culture (often used interchangeably) was stigmatized" (77), and "nearly all the teachers and administrators had stories of Latina/o students who were openly discouraged from reaching more ambitious goals" (78). Everyone involved faced a pronounced "difficulty of breaking polarized expectations of Latina/o versus Asian students," largely because "the 'rule' for Latina/o students—to not excel and progress academically—formed a warped, reverse mirror image of prevalent characterizations of Asian American achievement" (77–79). The sobering point here is that, even in distinctive, well-established nonwhite spaces, very powerful racial dynamics, naturalizing categorical identities as polar oppositions, can come to dominate locals' place-based, interpretive orientations and sensibilities.

Not surprisingly, categorical perceptions of individual and group played a key role here, though with a twist in this nonwhite space—"interlinked narratives of individual merit and immigrant success" in the schools result in a fundamental confusion or conflation of these key categories. Cheng makes the important point that "immigrant success narratives, such as the model minority myth, are somewhat contradictory. Although they often rest on essentialist precepts about race and culture, they are also anchored by core 'American' principles of individualism and the Protestant work ethic—that anyone can succeed in democratic, capitalist America, if they only work hard enough" (84). The result is exactly a marked version of individual, as seen with "racialized privilege." That is, for Asians, the individual slot is closely linked to an essentialized racial identity that attributed their success to race; for Latinos, similarly, their failure is also associated with race. But for Latinos, the categorical group identity is underscored, construing them as at risk students.

CONCLUSION

Postracial, as a concept, provokes the question, why is race still with us? Why does it still endure when, by every reasonable expectation, we should be long finished with race? Postracial directs our attention to cultural, rather than exclusively racial, dynamics, highlighting the categories and perceptions that reproduce race when we appear to not be doing it or being racial at all. "Post" is a reminder that we need more than racial analytics to explain the enduring significance of race; that it is, after all, epiphenomenal to culture. As cultural beings in the United States we do race in multiple ways via our most basic cultural concepts, often without referencing race directly; often while potentially referring to multiple other critical registers at once, including gender, class, and nation. Are we to explain all these cultural dynamics as racism, or should we recognize the great power cultural analysis has to reveal to people the profound depths of their socialization into a "common sense" notion that views the world in categorical terms? The advantages of the latter are twofold: first, we don't have to be reductive and assert that "everything" is about race; second, we can show how this cultural condition operates in so many other forms of identity at once, particularly gender and class and nation. Crucially, categories like "individual" and "group" can accomplish a great deal of racial work without referencing race at all. What makes this racial dynamic more intractable is that these are not racial categories; these two key terms play copious roles in sorting out belonging and difference in American culture. Postracial serves as a reminder that, to effectively depict and challenge racialization, we have to continuously return to focus on fundamental cultural dynamics that make racial thinking both possible and coherent.

∽

Taking It to the Field: Analyzing Race in a Cultural Framework

This appendix treats a host of practical aspects of using ethnographic approaches to analyze the enduring and changing significance of race. It is arranged in two parts. The first part presents general pointers about studying race in cultural terms, and the second offers a series of research prompts based on material discussed in each of the eight chapters. These discussions about race all come down to a series of empirical questions that ethnography is well designed to pose and answer. The basic question is: How do people think about and respond to race in everyday contexts? More expansively, though, the question is about what role race plays in people's lives, shaping their forms of social interactions as well as their perceptions and understandings of the larger social world. Yet another key question is: When and how do people lose sight of race? How does it slip in and out of their forms of attention, gaining or losing relevance in relation to the various ways they articulate their identities and think about the kinds of groups that constitute society? Each of these questions can be addressed via a cultural perspective on how race matters.

The general pointers on cultural analysis are arranged in the following categories:

- Four fundamental aspects to cultural analysis
- Seeing culture in order to analyze it
- The basic elements of racial identification
- Not entirely conflating the "cultural" with the "racial"
- Formulating an ethnographic topic of study
- Formulating and answering a cultural question
- Reviewing basic findings of the ethnographies covered in this book

Keep in mind *four fundamental aspects of cultural analysis*. First is the recognition that *culture shapes an interaction prior to an individual forming a distinct sensibility about a situation*. In this sense, culture precedes and forms the basis for individual beliefs and behaviors. This touches on the basic fact that culture entails generally shared patterns of thought and action. The second point is that *culture requires and features interpretive work to sort out meanings*; this is the process by which we establish, recognize, and follow sets of associations or linkages in the words and gestures that we and others use. Third, *culture both guides interactions and is reproduced interactively*; it is not something that resides simply in people's heads but, rather, *takes place* in social interactions. Finally, *culture has the power to shape what we recognize and what we do not notice*, making aspects of the world around us alternately highly visible or practically invisible. Culture involves the process by which we formulate perceptions of the world, particularly in terms of our sense of belonging to or being different from particular groups of people. As well, culture involves meanings, and meaning is a function of systems of signification that are variously bound to or embedded in or reference the material world around us. We learn to see these meanings in everyday gestures, images, and actions.

How do you see culture in order to analyze it? Look for ways that meanings become manifest and accessible in the words and actions of the people around you. Start by thinking analytically about the ways people talk about themselves. There are some basic things that people generally do in this regard. First, they will identify themselves as a certain *kind or type* of person. Sometimes this identification works oppositionally, as in "I'm not the kind of person who . . ." or "I'm the kind of person who . . ." These gestures at identification present a crucial inroad into cultural processes because they depict *categories of people*. A second gesture that people typically make is to orient themselves toward a set of "natural" facts or orders. As we saw in Chapter 3, one of the basic operations of culture is to ground its conventions and structures of meaning in "nature." Listen for this in the ways people use statements such as "I'm naturally like that" or "It just feels natural to me." Third, when we describe ourselves, we typically do so in relation to broader public discourses, conversations, or narratives. This involves the ways we draw on elements of popular culture—from movies to music to news stories—to make clear what things matter to us or that we feel are important. These sometimes take the form of "arguments" or "debates" that are unfolding in public discourse, often in relation to charged moral or political issues. Finally, as we speak. we generally feel some sense of constraint over what we can say or express. Sometimes this manifests in the form of topics about which people do not feel comfortable talking; other times it is evident in the feeling that certain aspects of our identity are improper to describe openly. This aspect is perhaps the most tangible manifestation of culture, because it reveals the operation of social conventions and forms of decorum that constrain and channel our self-presentations.

These four aspects of how people identify provide central guideposts for recognizing and then following cultural patterns of thinking and action. They represent the basic focal points of a cultural analysis. The next step, then, is to ask how these aspects form a basis for processes of racial identification and disidentification. Taking this step requires considering, also in fairly schematic terms, *the basic elements of racial identification*. Thinking back to Chapter 2 will help in this regard.

In quite cursory terms, racial identities are also composed of four basic elements. First, they are categorical, as when we characterize people as "white" or "black" based on our perceptions of a vast continuum of actual skin tones that often only tenuously match given color categories. Second, it follows that these categories are keyed to phenotype—they latch onto or reference some aspect of a person's physical appearance. Third, they are generally assumed to reflect indelible or inherent characteristics. As with most social stereotypes, racial identities are typically assumed to entail fixed or given qualities and features. Finally, racial identities matter to how people negotiate the social world, either facilitating or complicating their ease of passage through a variety of places and in an array of social interactions.

The crucial point to realize here is that there is a great deal of overlap between cultural and racial dynamics. That makes sense because the "reality" of race is predicated on our thorough socialization into a world where race matters. But it is important to recognize that the two are not simply equivalent. The key point of contrast is that the dynamics for culture listed earlier can operate or manifest in a variety of other critical registers. For instance, these dynamics are also the basis by which we articulate gender and class identities. The way to determine if the dynamic you are witnessing is generally cultural, rather than specifically racial, is exactly if it has the ability to register simultaneously in these other forms of social difference, such as gender and class. That is, if the comments or points of reference are multivalent or equivocal, with multiple possible inflections, you are likely onto a cultural dynamic.

It is important *not to entirely conflate the "cultural" with the "racial"* because there are important differences between them. Consider the matter of naturalizing some aspect of identity or difference. Just because someone is "naturalizing" does not necessarily mean they are "racializing," though we do know that racial thinking frequently manifests in or draws on assertions about "natural differences." There are countless ways we naturalize without necessarily "doing" race. For instance, as we also saw in Chapter 3, a basic set of interrelated social concerns are inheritance, relatedness, and reproduction. These are fundamental to how we establish belonging, in terms of family and kinship, but also for the ways we think about society and social relations generally. Think for just a moment how often the category of "family" is used to describe workplace relations or social networks—"We're all family here." For that matter, the keen concern today with generational identity—as in GenNext or the Millenials—fundamentally involve an anxiety or uncertainty about social inheritance and reproduction: How different is one generation from the next? What, if anything, is being passed on? These concerns are often broached in naturalistic frameworks, but this does not then imply that these are inherently racial discourses. The challenge in all this, though, is first to become attuned to both cultural and racial dynamics and then to try to discern their interplay.

The best way to proceed in this is by *formulating an ethnographic topic of study*. This will allow you to delineate the particular contours of racial thinking and acting as they arise from more general cultural orientations and positions. More than a particular set of methods, ethnography involves posing cultural questions— questions that are attentive, first, to the role of place in shaping peoples expressions and sentiments and, second, to the performative dynamics of social interactions. Ethnographic accounts fundamentally feature an attention to patterns of cultural thought and action as well as to the contexts where they unfold or emerge. Ethnographic method is directed toward identifying and tracing interrelated elements within these interweaving patterns and contexts. This approach, in addition to revealing the role of place and interpretation in how race matters, allows us to grasp two important aspects of race. The first involves the ways race, as a set of interests, perceptions, or anxieties, slides in and out of view in particular moments of social interaction; the second is simply the point that specificity matters when talking about race. The value of both of these insights can be grasped in relation to one of the most perplexing aspects of race: the difficulty of emphatically fixing or demonstrating "its" presence in someone's thoughts or actions.

A contribution the ethnographic approach makes to this problem is to show how "race" slips in and out of focus, in particular places and interactions, as people respond to shifting concerns and interests, sometimes keyed to race but then, alternately, to class or generation or religion or politics, etc. The second, related aspect stems from the central feature of ethnographic analysis. As anthropologist Harry Walcott explains, "Ethnography *is* a matter of detail. Ethnographic questions beg for relevant and complex detail" (2008, 85). Race is not the abstraction we often construe it to be; rather, it is a composite of countless specific gestures, comments, and features that are varyingly read and reacted to by people in everyday settings. Ethnography makes this aspect of race apparent and provides a valuable reminder of the importance of being specific when talking about race. This runs counter to the most common ways we talk about or study race, which is in terms of generalities—abstractions such as whiteness or blackness, for instance.

As already noted, ethnography is not simply a method. It is a means of *formulating and answering a cultural question*—in this case, about race. Cultural question are about meanings and interpretations, so make that your focus rather than trying to objectify people in racial terms. That is, these types of projects work best if you set out not to characterize a particular racial group but, rather, to record and analyze *how people think about and position themselves in relation to ideas about racial groups.* How do people project or respond to images of racial groups? What images do they hold in mind as they look at or address people around them? If you maintain this type of focus, you will become attuned to the points of commonalities, as well as the contrasting experiences, across racial fault lines.

In formulating an ethnographic project, *keep in mind some of the basic findings of the ethnographies covered in this book.* The first is the simplest and most direct: *Racial identity is not homogeneous.* This might seem at first to be an obvious point, but it actually runs counter to the ways we talk about race, which is typically in terms of generic referents to "whites" and "blacks," for instance. To whatever extent we can trace out tangible racial formations—in terms of forms of inequality, especially—people within these formations both are distinctly positioned in particular locales and regularly rearticulate their sense of identity in relation to these formations. The second point is that, within these formations, people still are faced with the cultural task of establishing and maintaining a *self*. The self is not a given property of bodies; rather, it is a cultural construct that reflects and conforms to social conventions, particularly with regard to the critical registers of class, race, and gender. The self is not simply a fundamental manifestation of persons; it represents beliefs about what constitutes a *person* and, for that matter, what it means to be human. The extent to which any self is constituted in racial terms is a reflection of social location and interactions within the material structures of advantage and disadvantage. But, as we have seen in these ethnographies, such a self is typically more than a function of race—it involves a host of other cultural elements as well, as in the *multiracial self* identified by Pamela Perry (2002).

Based on both of these points—the recognition that racial identities are heterogeneous and that the construction of self involves an array of elements in addition to race—ethnographic projects centrally feature the ability to ask about and examine the role of race in people's lives. From an ethnographic perspective, it is easy to see that "race" is not all-encompassing, explaining "everything" about the social. This view allows us to ask and examine how people delineate when, where, how, and why race matters. In pursuing such questions, you have a considerable stockpile of social science knowledge about race that has been reviewed in this book. Let that knowledge sharpen your listening skills, observations, and questions. Avoid simply characterizing their views as "wrong" or "right" about race by using that knowledge base. The more important goal is to trace their understandings of race as it emerges through the linkages and associations they make in relation to encounters, stories, and situations. Then you have to ask how these understandings contribute to a central characteristic of race today: that it remains quite significant, even as people insist that it matters less and less. Why? How?

Prompts for Ethnographic Research

CHAPTER 1: GETTING STARTED
WITH CULTURAL ANALYSIS

Over the past twenty years in anthropology, *self-reflexivity* has become a basic component of ethnographic research. This involves the ethnographer's endeavor to account, first, for how his or her social interests bring him or her to certain topics and, second, how his or her social position and identity may influence his or her findings (Behar 1996). Self-reflexivity is a crucial component of research on race, because our cultural conditioning can potentially lead us to reproduce the very thing we aim to study when we develop a racial topic of investigation. But self-reflexivity brings with it an added benefit: Since we are "natives"—and hence experts—of the culture we aim to study, self-reflexive accounting allows us to articulate what we already "know," typically at a subconscious level, about how race works.

In order to develop a self-reflexive perspective on racial matters, begin by itemizing the ways race affects your life circumstances. How does skin color influence your relative ease of movement through social settings? When do you notice race, and when do you ignore it? Then consider the concept of "unmarked" identities. Listen for how you and others either do or do not make explicit reference to (i.e., "mark") racial identity in certain circumstance or in reference to certain people. Listen, in particular, for how infrequently "white" gets explicitly mentioned. As you do these tasks, think about how you might study some of these dynamics further; as you do, try itemizing the interests you would bring to a possible project and how your racial identity may affect your research and your findings.

Another set of preliminary tasks involves learning to recognize basic cultural dynamics, such as *boundary work*, or cultural components, such as *interpretive repertoires*. With boundary work, begin systematically to pay attention to the material and immaterial ways people draw "lines" in everyday life, perhaps starting with "personal space" and then considering how an informal gathering of people unfolds.

Notice how people can be inclusive or exclusionary with gestures and expressions; then think about more concrete forms of social boundaries. For instance, notice the ways classrooms and college spaces are variously bounded or open, encouraging and discouraging a range of behaviors. Strive to feel or recognize the ways cultural boundaries constrain or influence certain kinds of actions and thoughts.

With interpretive repertoires, try to recognize these in the ways people you know talk about the world. Listen for particular stories and try to identify their sources: personal experience or news accounts or movie dramas, and so forth. Then think about how certain stories or images become shared among people or at least familiar enough to be recognized as commonsensically linked to a particular line of conversation. What type of experiences or social locations do these stories reflect? What type of "template" do they form for making sense of the social world? In this line of reflection, you want to be able to sketch the types of associations people make in linking one story to another as ways of talking about the world around us.

Another task involves becoming familiar with the ways people explain racial matters. Begin with the issue of racial inequality, which we examined in some detail at the opening of Chapter 1. Find ways of informally raising this issue with others, and see if you can get them to talk about why these forms of inequality exist. That is, ask them to speculate on the origins or bases of racial inequality today. This task should not be approached as a sort of scavenger hunt to find racism, where you are only interested in detecting stereotypes or explicitly racist sentiments. Rather, use this exercise to attend to the types of linkages people make with the facts of inequality and the ways the social world operates. Cultural analysis involves attention to the associations and linkages people make between certain topics or in regard to "types" and "kinds" of people—this is how we begin identifying the *patterned* aspects of thoughts and actions. Some of these patterns will likely involve race explicitly, but others may not seem to be about race at all. The interesting question, in cultural terms, is how we move in and out of direct references to race in relation to the ways race goes unmarked the rest of the time.

CHAPTER 2: IDENTIFYING THE SOURCES
OF RACIAL THINKING AND PERCEPTIONS

This chapter featured two primary ways of examining and engaging racial thinking—ethnography and antiracist practices. Though the chapter dealt with each approach in some detail, both of these modes of engagement will likely require a good deal more discussion for you to understand them comfortably. The purpose of the following prompts, then, is to get you thinking about how to apply both of these two methods as a means of examining racial matters.

With ethnography, begin by thinking about what kinds of sites and situations might be intriguing, productive locations for an ethnographic project. What places interest you, and how would you go about examining them ethnographically? What would you be watching for or trying to understand? Also consider what types of conversations or exchanges you might want to record and analyze. What prompts might you offer people as a way to jump-start certain discussions? How would you go about producing a transcript? How would you think analytically about what people said?

Then consider some of the key anthropological concepts from this chapter, such as *body work* and *spatializing practices*. Are these things that you can easily recognize? Think about ways of objectifying and discussing the forms of *etiquette* that guide how we comport our bodies and occupy particular spaces. How can you identify cultural ideals or patterns as manifest in the ways people discipline their bodies? As well, can you recognize material and social boundaries at work in distinct spaces? How do these function to make place more inclusive or exclusive? Each of these questions involve the matter of actually seeing or recognizing the operation of culture. Can you distinguish patterns of behavior and their associated meanings? That is, can you trace linkages between the things people say and do and the types of cultural meanings they express? Think about the particular terms, "nice," "friendly," and "work." Can you recognize these terms in your everyday conversations, and, if so, can you specify some of the meanings or values they are used to impart? Then think about the variety of expressive media that we use every day (clothes, language, music, etc.). How would you go about discussing these in cultural terms? Do these offer ways for making sense of American culture?

Then think about antiracism and the challenge of dealing with racial matters today. Antiracism, as this chapter conveys, is a means of both identifying and critically engaging racial thinking and practices. You may already be somewhat familiar with this approach if you have gone through any kind of workshop, seminar, or open forum on multiculturalism. Can you identify, and identify with, the methods and goals of antiracism? How do you think it is best to educate people about race, particularly peers, friends, and family members? If you have participated in antiracist activities, what reflections do you have about how they worked and, perhaps, how they might work better?

One of the guiding principles of antiracist work is the goal of changing, not just studying, racial thinking and practices. This stands somewhat in contrast to ethnographic approaches, which primarily are concerned with learning from the field. What are some ways that you can see these two approaches resulting in opposite modes of studying race? Can you both study something and try to change it at the same time? What conflicts would likely arise and where would your priorities lie? What about the idea of participant-observation? How do you think this works in studying or engaging issues related to race?

Then take a topic like "white talk," as identified by Alice McIntyre. She defines this as a way of talking or monitoring conversation developed by whites as a means of forestalling direct discussions of racism. Can you recognize and identify "white talk" in everyday conversations or discussions in the classroom? Think of ways this concept can be useful in getting at routine racial dynamics. Can you think of other potential concepts for designating racial dynamics in social situations? Is it helpful or distorting to try to distinguish "racist" statements and beliefs from words or thoughts about race that do not assert ideas about the superiority or inferiority of particular groups? Can you think of comments or expressions involving race that might be *equivocal*, having a variety of meanings that may not be reducible entirely to "racism"?

Now think about stereotypes and controlling images. What are the best ways to study these? How would you go about demonstrating and defining their presence in American culture? How might you analyze their relevance or impact in everyday contexts? Where are stereotypes located—in peoples' heads or in the culture all around us? Does studying stereotypes offer us a different way to think about the issues of observation and critique raised by contrary approaches to racial problems by antiracism and ethnography? How do stereotypes fit into a larger context, as with something huge, like American culture? Do they implicitly embody cultural ideals or do they warp fundamental values in a culture?

CHAPTER 3: EXAMINING THE TRAFFIC IN NATURE AND CULTURE RELATED TO RACE

Despite all the debates over the status of scientific claims linking race and biology, it is not clear whether or to what degree such findings influence the daily, social ways that people think about race. Social scientists assume these claims have a great impact, which is why their arguments over "social construction" are so developed and animated. But given the low rates of scientific literacy in this country, the impact that genetics research on race has on the larger public is uncertain. For that matter, it is not entirely clear how people actually link "race" and "nature" in commonplace, everyday manners. We do not know to what extent such an association merely *confirms* what they already believe or, in contrast, perhaps *forms the basis* of their thinking about race, from which everything else follows. Anthropologist Peter Wade (2002) characterizes the state of our social science knowledge on these matters as minimal: "There are not many studies about how laypeople in their everyday lives perceive and experience racial identity in relation to concepts of 'blood,' 'genes,' or 'the environment'; about how they think they came to be as they are, what they owe to their parents in terms of 'inheritance' (however that is construed) and how they are connected to others perceived as 'like' and 'different'" (71). Wade's point is that, rather than assume people are deterministic in thinking about race in relation to biology and genes (as scientists sometimes are), we need to investigate this question directly.

There are several lines of possible inquiry on these matters. One involves colloquial use of the "nature/nurture" distinctions. Anthropologist Bruno Latour (1999) argues that people generally "operate the distinction" rather than invest in one or the other category as being determinate. That is, we typically strive to prove we can make the distinction—often in a provisional manner—rather than stridently insist on one set of facts as belonging to either category. Does this happen with people's notions about race? Can you use the contrast between ideas of fixity and mutability (highlighted in the opening of Chapter 3) to track the ways people may see "nature" as composed of alternately essential and variable characteristics? What ideas do people hold about racial essences, human nature, and racialized bodies? Specifically, how do people think about the role of blood, genes, and biology in relation to racial identity? Do they hold one set of beliefs in referring to the realm of sports, another for matters of expressive culture, and still another for the domains of politics and education? These questions are ways of following and analyzing the traffic in nature and culture in relation to race. With each of these sets of questions, it is crucial to keep cultural dynamics in view by concentrating on how people think about and deploy categories as they interpret or perform them.

In Chapters 4 and 5 we examined issues of inheritance in a social sense, linked to wealth and cultural capital. Once you have covered that material, it might be useful to return to some of these research prompts in order to pursue a more developed inquiry related to people's ideas about inheritance and race. In this regard, Wade (2002) suggests that, rather than asking people about experiences of racism, researchers should "inquire more specifically into how they, and their parents, think about their 'natures,' how they as embodied persons come to be as they are, *what mechanisms of 'inheritance' they feel to be operating on them* [cultural or biological, for instance]; to ask how they view their 'origins' and their connectedness with, and difference from, other people" (121). In this line of inquiry, Wade suggests paying close attention to people's use of metaphors for genealogy (trees, bridges, blood) as a means of imagining forms of relatedness with racial collectives. These are all topics that anthropologists and sociologists have yet to explore in much depth in everyday circumstances.

CHAPTER 4: INQUIRING ABOUT WHITENESS

This chapter presented two basic points: (1) that whiteness is at the heart of racial matters but that (2) there is a difference between whiteness as a racial formation and the particular situations of whites in specific locales. The research prompts for this chapter each orbit around these two aspects of white racial identity.

In the first regard, a range of inquiries opens up from an initial attention to the larger system of white privilege and the advantages of being white. You could begin simply by testing where and how this advantaged condition shapes the lives of particular whites. An important question here is whether or how whites recognize "white skin privilege." A related issue is the general inability of most whites to see the facts of racial inequality. What is the basis for this inability? Is it a denial of "race," generally, as in stressing ideas linked to individualism, or is it an avoidance of acknowledging the forms of advantage that whiteness often ensures? A fairly concrete way of exploring these questions involves following the discourse of "merit." To what extent do whites see "social conditions" as countervailing against this ideal? For that matter, when or how do whites recognize group circumstances, over and against registers of individual achievement or failure, as highlighted by merit discourse?

This question opens up from an attention to the categories of "individual" and "group" to a more general matter of whether or how whites recognize cultural conditioning, particularly as an element of social success. Are they conscious of a shared set of social relations with other whites, and to what extent do they objectify people of color in cultural frames? In both questions, you want to get at the racial aspects of white people's lives via their articulation of forms of sameness and difference. With the issue of sameness, see whether you can sound out the way whites talk about their social ties with other people: What is it that they find in common? And how do they explain those ties and forms of attraction? With difference, listen for the ways that whites talk about racial issues. Importantly, how do whites explain the facts of inequality? But also, how do they approach generalizations about race? Listen for the "work/lazy" contrast but also for manifestations of "racial resentment."

With racial matters generally, *be attuned to the discourse of "comfort."* When and how do whites use the linked concepts of "comfort"/"uncomfortable" to characterize their feelings around race? Do they use this seemingly to avoid or recharacterize racial matters? Also, what forms of *taboos* around race do they recognize? Try to sketch out the conventions governing race for whites, asking whether or how these might produce anxiety around public words and actions. Finally, ask how it is that whites *perform* racial identities. In doing this, return time and again to the issues raised by many ethnographers about the specificities of white racial identity, especially as it manifests in relation to their experiences of and attachments to particular places. To what extent do these places become "invested" by whiteness? Or when or how might they disrupt a seamless equation of whiteness with particular locations, such as neighborhoods, schools, or recreation areas? Finally, think about central concerns such as inheritance, relatedness, and the reproduction of the social groups. How do whites frame such concerns, and what types of idioms (e.g., biological, economic, etc.) do they use for talking about such matters? When and how would you identify a racial component in such concerns and interests?

CHAPTER 5: INQUIRING ABOUT BLACKNESS

As you move from asking questions about whiteness to thinking about other racial identities, it is important to keep in mind that we must aim not to reproduce racial thinking in the very process of studying it. Nowhere is this more important than with blackness, since representations of it have so profoundly obscured the social heterogeneity and complexity of black life. Keep in mind the history of distorted representations by social scientists who were driven to objectify the "real" or "authentic" core of a singular, homogeneous black culture. By all means, avoid reproducing the "pathologizing perspective" on blackness. Instead, carry over the kind of specificity that we learned to adopt in talk about whites in relation to whiteness. This attention to specific circumstances—and the attendant awareness of the heterogeneous aspects of racial identity—is all the more important with blackness.

One way of doing this is by keeping basic questions close at hand. For instance, who counts as black, and what counts as blackness? What *meanings, practices,* and *places* are associated with blackness? Are these associations changing in how they are valued in the larger society? How can you tell? These kinds of questions open up a range of inquiries that move away from objectifications of blackness toward *an attention to the ways people talk about, contest, and imagine blackness.* That is, these questions move you toward a cultural attention to this racial identity. This is probably most useful in thinking about the kind of *boundary work* that goes on around blackness, as evidenced in the phrase *acting white*. What lines of inclusion and exclusion can you see being performed around blackness? In pursuing such inquiry, think back to the Pew Research poll question "Are blacks still a single race?"

But "acting white" is not just about boundaries; as John L. Jackson (2001) found in Harlem, it is about the slippage between identity and action as well as the jostling for certainty over what kinds of behaviors, stances, and expressions will be regarded as "authentically" black. Jackson's work opens up a broad attention not only to how people perform race but also how we theorize it as well, as in the *folk theories* about race that manifest in relations to notions of authenticity in relation to blackness. Then think about how such forms of theorizing relate to what Kary Lacy (2007) identified as the *black middle-class toolkit*.

This *toolkit* refers to a set of improvisational tactics that middle-class blacks maintain as a means of preempting certain racial projections and assumptions by whites. What type of theorizing of race is implied or evident in such improvisational tactics? This activity of "script switching" in relation to the "white social world" and encounters with racism is also linked to another kind of *racial anxiety*— that over the possible "inauthenticity" of being at a remove from "black social worlds." How do these dynamics reflect different notions about public and private forms of racial identity? Is race imagined similarly or differently in these various different spheres and, importantly, in the process of transit between them? With these questions, keep an ear tuned to what both Stephen Gregory (1999) and Jackson referred to as the conflicting interpretations of black experience.

The questions regarding blackness get larger and deeper the closer we attend to the specificity and nuance of black lives. There are, of course, a range of somewhat polemical questions relating to the "end of blackness" or the end of the "Black American narrative" that are sparked by the rise of Barack Obama. But these lead to more interesting questions, for instance, around the coding of ethnicity in the United States. Where do notions of the "black community" stand today? Is blackness increasingly being figured in terms of ethnicity as well as, or in contrast with, racial representations? Does the answer hinge on class position and regional location for African Americans? As well, what of diasporic forms of identity? What forms of diasporic representations are being forged in terms of blackness? How do such images or ideas relate to basic cultural concerns with *inheritance*, *relatedness*, and the *reproduction* of social relations, particularly with regard to parenting? When are such cultural concerns framed in biological or genetic registers, and when, instead, are they articulated in social terms? These questions are directed toward understanding some of the emergent meanings related to blackness.

CHAPTER 6: EXPLORING THE "RACIAL MIDDLE"

The dynamism of demographics and politics in the United States is slowly displacing the centrality of the black/white paradigm for understanding race in this country. But do whiteness and blackness still maintain the principle polarity that contours and organizes racial meanings? When we move into the "racial middle," away from a focus on whites and blacks, the questions grow only more complex and intriguing. That is because, from the vantage point of the middle ground between these mammoth formations, we glimpse processes that potentially will transform the basic dynamics that have shaped the meanings of race for hundreds of years. Consider just the concepts of *Latinization* and *Asianization*—these terms point to transformations of the cultural textures and contents of American life. But, as we have seen, such processes are not easily comprehended or summarized. That is where the work of ethnographic inquiry begins.

Question about the racial middle can be posed from a variety of angles—in terms of politics, demographics, and economics. Ethnographic approaches carve out a particular form of attention to these matters by addressing how people in particular social contexts strive to make sense of these large-scale processes. Consider how much of the debate over these transformations has been framed in terms of whiteness and blackness as rather absolute formations. We saw this in Chapter 6 in terms of the contrasting theses regarding "whitening" and "blackening." We also saw in that chapter, though, that there is sufficient cause to believe these theses too reductively formulate and answer questions about how the significance of race is changing. Ethnographic work proceeds in a different fashion simply by taking its starting point and primary focus to be the continuum of racial meanings. This continuum is predicated on a fundamentally relational dynamic by which various practices, interactions, and cultural material are differentially considered in marked and unmarked terms. Starting with this recognition, the question becomes much simpler: *How are people in the racial middle making sense of the significance of race*, both in their immediate circumstances and in their views of the nation at large?

Beyond this general question, a host of specificities emerge. As we have seen, the historical and political circumstances for Latinos and Asian Americans are quite distinct. Certainly, there are points of overlap, such as in the perception of "foreignness," but the contestations over belonging and difference within these larger panethnic constructs also reflect distinct trajectories of national and international politics. For that matter, there are copious other national, transnational, and fourth-world dynamics playing out in the racial middle, quite removed from these principal panethnic formations. Addressing such particular circumstances that inform the lives of people you may be interviewing will be important. Think of how issues such as *colorism* and *skin-color stratification* involve distinct colonial and postcolonial dynamics, as we saw in Chapter 6. These are histories and stories that may or may not be clear to people whom you interview. That might be the best starting point: asking them, while inquiring for yourself, about the particular pasts that contour life in the racial middle.

These pasts and their uncertain presents have long been processed in the United States via the competing discourses of ethnicity and race. As we saw in Chapter 6, the ability to control one's labor and to amass capital in a community have been the basis by which peoples *achieve escape velocity* from conditions of racial markedness. How do these relational discourses play out in the lives of people today in the racial middle?

In the past, this question has been fairly easily addressed in terms of advantage and disadvantage. Is that still the case today? If not, how and it what ways is it changing? Do transformations of racial meanings in the public sphere shape people's assessments of this question? Think in terms of various forms of marketing, as examined by Arlene Dávila (2001). How do people alternately associate with and distance themselves from representations of panethnic identities? Do consumerist practices provide a ground for making these abstract issues fairly tangible in people's daily lives?

The other key issue is "internal" contestations of belonging and difference from within panethnic identities. Sometimes these play out in clashes over who best represents, or how to best represent, the larger group identity in public space. How much do particular historical, political, and demographic processes influence these contests? Do the ways these contestations unfold confirm, complicate, or repudiate the whitening and blackening theses? We have seen examples of racialization of certain groups within panethnic identities. Are these reproductions of whiteness and blackness? Or are other cultural dynamics at work here? You will have to be attentive to the multiplicity of meanings related to ethnicity and race as you listen to people's stories about their childhood experiences or narrate their constructions of particular lifestyles. Listen for how boundaries are developed between public and private contexts. How does the tension between "individual" and "group" play out here? In all this, be very attentive to the role of humor and joking, as highlighted by José Limón (1994) and Nicholas De Genova (2005). Joking—which demarcates statements, values, and objectifications between "serious" and "just joking"—remains one of the most crucial means by which people both perform and make sense of race.

CHAPTER 8: POSTRACIAL AMERICA?

The question of whether America is postracial can be framed and examined ethnographically in a variety of contexts. First, attune yourself to the ways the claim is asserted and contested currently. In what arenas and with what evidence do people promote or challenge this idea? Sketch out what counts as race in these settings, and then undertake the task of directly asking people for their thoughts on this matter. What kind of observations—in locales or social interactions—would help you contextualize what people tell you?

One of the best locations to pursue this question is on college campuses, because these are sites where race-specific programs (admissions policies, themed dorms, community events) brush up against ideals of meritocracy and colorblindness. These are also locations where young people are thinking actively about their identities in relation to larger social institutions; these are sites of privilege, too, though not everyone is similarly advantaged. How do students think about the relational aspects of these matters? Importantly, how is their thinking shaped by particular organizations that they may belong to or participate in?

Consider some of the topics examined in Chapter 8—the fracturing of whiteness, postblackness, the rise of multiracial identities and "nonwhite" spaces. Can you make these the focus of an ethnographic inquiry? With whiteness, think especially about the ways whites are becoming increasingly conscious about race: How do they name or specify "white" in relation to their identity or social milieu? What factors may influence this self-marking? In terms of the always "selective" aspect of cultural perception, what does this attention to race perhaps ignore? Importantly, too, look for instances where whites may be purposefully marking their racial identity, as in the case of "race shifters" described by Circe Sturm. Is there a perceived advantage in being racially marked in certain, "ethnic" ways? If so, what might this notion of advantage be overlooking? For that matter, how are peoples' understandings of success colored? What are the racial subtexts to the idea of "getting ahead" in life?

With postblackness, the main idea is that a limited notion of a homogenous, authentic black identity or community is dissolving. In its place new forms or ways of being black are emerging. Some of these may heighten the differences between black people, as in the typologies suggested by Eugene Robinson. But perhaps there are some forms that try to reimagine blackness as a collective condition or identity. Importantly, how might individuals move in and out of identifying with blackness or postblackness in the course of a day or over a life history? How are notions of blackness complicated by "multiracial" identities? Do people find it easy to articulate multiple forms and meanings of racial identity? When do categories breakdown, and what new ones are being invented? You can ask the same questions about other identities like Latino or Asian: How do these categories alternately splinter or solidify in relation to national and regional differences as well as direct or indirect experiences of racism? Think, too, about what "nonwhite spaces" look like, or how regional variations might influence notions and perceptions of race. What about the concept of "risk"; can you find ways of asking people about how this notion is differently colored in relation to white and nonwhite.

In each of these cases, the underlying questions are similar. What are the dynamics of belonging and difference, and what categories do people rely upon or develop to negotiate the boundaries between them? In thinking about and deploying categories, are people still relying upon a notion of hypodescent, even when talking about multiracial identities or relations? Or are they imaging race through different substances than blood and genes, perhaps more in cultural terms of achieved statuses? What notions of "mixing" are involved; what does it mean to be "part" or "half" white or black, Latino or Asian? As you ask people these questions, think about major hypotheses discussed in this book, such as the whitening or browning thesis, or the "Latinization" or "Asianization" of American culture. Rely upon the basics of cultural analysis: you don't have to decide whether people are right or wrong in their accounts, whether the country is or isn't becoming postracial. Your task is to identify the criteria and discourses by which these questions are debated and provisionally answered in everyday life. Your goals are to understand and analyze how people interpret and perform racial identities and how do they do so by drawing upon or in response to fundamental categories in American culture.

Glossary

acting white: A rhetorical form of boundary maintenance that projects or polices a more or less bounded sense of black identity over and against the larger white society.

African diaspora: The dispersion of peoples of African descent, initially via slavery throughout the Americas but then later through migration to Europe and across the globe. This concept seeks to identify forms of commonality—historically and contemporarily—in the experiences of African-descended peoples.

anthropology of science: A perspective on scientific practice that focuses on the cultural dynamics that shape research through both the production of data and its interpretation. This perspective locates scientific practice—the problems it confronts, the solutions it generates, and the technologies it produces—in specific cultural milieus.

antiracism: A movement that covers a broad range of efforts to counter directly the reproduction of racism in its manifest institutional and personal forms. Antiracism, as a political practice, also encompasses efforts to generate critical knowledge about race while also challenging, destabilizing, and short-circuiting the social routines by which racial dominance is reproduced.

Asian diaspora: The dispersion of peoples from Asian countries throughout the Pacific and around the globe. This concept is used to sound out the potential depth and strength of an overarching "Asian" identity, over and against many differences of class and national identity.

Asianization: The transformation of cultural practices in the United States reflecting Asian influence. This term also references the degree to which the social content of representations of American identity are shifting from a primary equation with Euro-Americans.

belonging: A central concern of culture involving perceptions of sameness regarding other humans in relation to possible group identity. Belonging is typically negotiated via a series of boundary markers.

biocultural: The dynamic interaction between human biology, social structure, and cultural practices. This concept highlights the ways culture impacts biology and how biological features gain cultural significance.

black middle-class toolkit: An interpretive repertoire that anticipates and provides a basis for responding to white stereotypes in public encounters. This toolkit also features different forms of "black cultural capital" that can be variously invoked for drawing inclusionary and exclusionary boundaries around black identity in relation to class.

black public spaces: Locales where blackness may be a central focus of discussion or a criterion for belonging. The defining feature of such arenas is that they provide forums for black people to talk back to dominant narratives and beliefs in the culture at large.

body work: Involves the various ways social orders, identities, and behaviors are embodied—literally incorporated into our bodies—in terms of meanings and comportment, and also the disciplinary practices to which bodies are subject.

browning thesis: A view that posits the emergence of a collective identity of "people of color" that reflects both a rejection of whiteness and an insistence by whites on maintaining a delimited form of racial dominance.

categorical identities: A homogenized form of personhood established through putative assertions or ascriptions of collective identity via political and social categories of people. Such identities are often topics of public discourse and presuppose notions of in-group sameness.

clines: Human physical traits, such as the features we use for classifying races, that manifest along a continuous gradient. These traits reflect the varying impacts of natural selection in particular environments rather than emblemizing the permanence of racial characteristics.

code words: Adjectives or phrases that carry subtle racial connotations but that ostensibly make no direct reference to race.

color-blind racism: A form of racial thinking that rejects open assertions of racial superiority or inferiority but that continues to reproduce a more subtle series of practices that racially differentiate while professing an adherence to the ideal of being color-blind. These practices seek to elude the charged conflicts over race linked to the open expression of racist beliefs and ideals in the public sphere.

colorism: An enduring belief that skin color reflects inherent qualities or characteristics. This concept particularly references contests over gradations of identity and belonging typically read within largely subordinated racial groups, where skin-tone hierarchy influences people's social standing and life chances.

comprehensive racial learning: In contrast to the widespread view that children passively adopt their understandings of race from their family or the media, this concept highlights their active interpretive work in making sense of racial matters in their everyday lives.

cultural conventions: The largely implicit or unstated strictures that limit or inform what people feel they can express or do. These conventions are embedded in social contexts and interactions, and they influence how people anticipate they will be perceived and regarded by others.

culture: The interpretive, performative process by which humans make sense of the world largely in relation to group identities. Culture shapes social interactions before individuals form distinct sensibilities concerning a situation. Culture primarily involves meaning—systems of signification that are variously bound to or embedded in or revise the material world around us.

diasporic identities: Forms of identification keyed to the experiences of people who have left an original homeland and who experience racialization in other societies. The strength of such identities is often manifest in the maintenance of symbolic or material ties to that homeland.

difference: The delineation of a limit to shared identity or group belonging. Differences can alternately be highlighted or deemphasized in relation to competing perceptions of sameness.

discourse: Patterned linguistic operations that constitute cultural objects and subjects. Discourse analysis involves the study of how people recognize and reference such objects and subjects; broadly, it entails analyzing what can be said by whom and to whom.

discourse of choice: A powerful cultural rhetoric that selectively highlights the importance and value of individual actions or decisions, while obscuring or downplaying the social resources that person may be drawing upon or lacking.

environmental racism: Locating hazardous waste or noxious industrial operations in minority communities. This may occur directly due to racist intent or it may reflect the lack of political representation or social capital in such neighborhoods to prevent such concentrations of dangerous materials and practices.

equivocal: The variety of meanings one phrase or statement may have, alternately keyed, for instance, to race, generation, class, or nation.

ethnicity: As with the concept of race, ethnicity is used to categorize groups of people based on notions of similarity and difference as well as on common history, culture, and social ties. Ethnicity plays an additional role in mediating marked and unmarked identities in relation to race in the United States.

ethnography: A means of producing social knowledge about the patterns of belief and behavior that shape daily life as a meaningful condition. Ethnography generally features a systematic attention to the ways specific contexts shape—and, in turn, are shaped by—social interactions.

etiquette: A means for establishing select ways of being, acting, and perceiving as "natural." This involves expectations for how people should comport their bodies as well as what qualities—offensive or not—we judge bodies to posses.

expressive forms: The various modes of meaning—in language, music, and various forms of material culture—that we use to relate to other people. Culture combines material and symbolic media into patterned ways of interacting with people in everyday contexts.

foreignness: A racial perception derived from an equation of American identity with whiteness or blackness that obscures or ignores the generational depth of Latino and Asian belonging in the United States. Foreignness is a form of markedness, particularly in relation to whiteness, that has powerful social, economic, and political effects.

genetic diseases: Diseases that are rare and that generally affect only 6% to 8% of a population and that are still made the focus of attention when people try to build a case for a genetic basis for race.

genotypes: These can be construed at a variety of levels—a cell, an organism, an individual—but all involve genetic content, generally as it is differentiated from an underlying genome.

groups: Units by which humans sort out matters of belonging and difference. Belonging to a group is a cultural matter established by interpretation and negotiation of forms of sameness and differentiation.

hypodescent: A belief that one's racial identity is fixed by any trace of physical inheritance—generally in terms of "blood"—from dominated racial groups. This idea is epitomized in the notion that "one drop of black blood" fixed a person's racial identity as black.

ideology: A worldview that both grounds and reproduces particular social orders. This concept keys on rationalizations (or contestations) of the use of power to maintain operations of social advantage and disadvantage.

individualism: In American culture, a central belief that highlights individual accomplishments or failings while obscuring the role of social advantage and disadvantage in shaping a person's life chances, experiences, and understandings of the world.

interpretation: The process of establishing or discerning meaning in relation to images, words, gestures, and actions. Interpretation is the central activity of culture.

interpretive repertoires: Collections of stories, gossip, narratives, and images on which we rely to make sense of any particular situation. Such repertoires are linked to the places we inhabit and traverse, in that they resonate with how these setting are arranged, maintained, and reproduced.

Latinidad: Notions of an overarching Latino identity that can be represented or encapsulated by various forms of expressive culture or political mobilization that reflect or are drawn from sometimes competing national identities or class positions.

Latinization: Refers to the transformation of cultural practices in the United States linked to the increased demographic presence of Latinos. This term references the degree to which the social content of representations of American identity are shifting from a white Anglo image.

linkages: The string of cultural associations people make between various mundane references and big-meaning concepts, such as *individualism* and *merit*.

meaning: The forms of significance that imbue social relations and actions with relevance. Meaning is established relationally via mutually reinforcing structures of signification; it derives from and is reproduced in social interactions and in particular social contexts.

merit: A discourse on who should be elevated to top positions in U.S. society. This discourse features a keen attention to measures of individual achievement while largely ignoring the powerful role of social class and race.

otherness: A symbolic form of identity construed in opposition to a generally privileged condition or position. With otherness, specific forms of difference are abstracted into an essentialist notion of absolute difference.

participant observation: A method of generating social data in which an ethnographer seeks to both participate in various everyday cultural practices while also maintaining a detached stance that allows them to think analytically about these activities.

performance: The means by which we manifest and revise cultural beliefs and identities via social interactions. Performances both draw on and reproduce interpretive repertoires. When we perform our identities, we do so with a host of cultural ideas about how such performance should go.

performative model of race: An approach that focuses on the active interpretive and performative work of establishing, reproducing, and contesting racial identities. This model views racial identity as subject to ongoing revision and debate in the context of everyday life.

phenotypes: The level of manifest biology—our physical features, anatomy, and physiology—or the outward appearance of an organism.

populations: Units of frequency that geneticists use to talk about and analyze human biological variation. Boundaries of populations are fixed in the process of establishing and pursuing particular questions about evolutionary forces: mutation, selection, drift, and migration. These units can be defined in local, regional, or global terms, depending on the type of questions geneticists are trying to answer.

race: A system of classifying people into groups, either explicitly or implicitly promoting the notion that these groups are ranked in terms of superiority or inferiority. Race is meaningful in a variety of ways that reflect both the historical import of the concept and its rapidly shifting current significance.

racial bipolarism: An aspect of the classificatory system for race in the United States that differentiates among immigrants who are assigned different positions along an imagined path toward whiteness. In a bipolar racial order, immigrant groups are located along a continuum from black to white based on relative degrees of social capital, as well as phenotype.

racial formalism: The perspective that there are unchanging racial types, characterized by immutable physical, mental, and spiritual qualities.

racial formation: The particular state and significance of racial identities and categories as informed by large-scale demographic, political, and economic developments. The relevance and meaning of racial matters continually register and reflect the influence of an array of social forces active across the national landscape.

racial middle: A complex social landscape dominated by the fastest-growing panethnic groups, Latinos and Asian Americans, whose numbers are expected to double by 2050. A defining feature of life in the "racial middle" is the experience of marginalization in U.S. society.

racial optic: Social scientists' myopic focus—primarily on blacks but on "people of color" generally—in research on race. The racial optic delineates the "problem" of race in a way that too often leaves whites out of the picture.

racial paranoia: A condition of heightened anxiety over the potential significance of race in social interactions or in the public culture at large. This condition is induced by an awareness of the enormous potential significance of race coupled with an uncertainty over the subjective sentiments and perceptions of others.

racial profiling: The targeting of people of color by law enforcement official based on race or ethnicity. Though this practice is specifically prohibited in many jurisdictions, the U.S. Supreme Court upheld the practice in 1996, as long as there is no countervailing data indicating disparate treatment by law.

racial resentment: A strong sentiment formulated in response to efforts at addressing racial inequality in this country. This sentiment is linked to a firm conviction that racial equality has already been achieved in the United States.

racialization: The extension of racial meanings to peoples and practices that were not previously characterized racially. This concept highlights the developing novel aspects of racial meanings, which change and shift in conjunction with broad, national developments.

racism: The belief that racial identity is an inherent and inherited human characteristic, linked to innate capacities assumed to be permanent and common across a particular race. Racism also involves the belief that these races are hierarchically ranked or differentially valued in terms of capacities (e.g., intelligence) judged inferior and superior.

Regional racial formation: modifies the general concept of racial formation by highlighting the place-specific aspects of race, recognizing, too, that racial meanings and dynamics can vary substationally by region within the larger national context.

relational identity: A process of identification where the signifying elements are drawn oppositionally in symbolic terms. The cluster of meanings that comprise a particular identity are established in relation to other identities, frequently as a set of contrasts.

social boundaries: Boundaries that are established, contested, and transgressed in various media of popular culture. Social science perspectives on boundaries primarily emphasize their symbolic role in the process of group formation, specifically in terms of the relational dynamics that influence how collectives cohere and establish their forms of integration.

social heterogeneity: The manifest forms of difference or variation within a group that are obscured by the projection of a collective identity.

spatializing practices: Ways of organizing space and localities as meaningful sites, typically involving various forms of boundary work to mark some people as belonging and others as outsiders. Places influence our interpretations of others' words and actions and are crucial to how we articulate our identities via feelings of rootedness in a particular locale called home.

totemism: The process by which social groups become established and are reproduced largely in relation to being identified with natural phenomena. Totemic identities involve the relational interplay of notions of sameness and difference linked to the realm of "nature," as with skin color.

traffic in nature and culture: The process by which idioms of nature are employed to establish, revise, and extend cultural identities and discourses. With race, this "traffic" easily moves between everyday realms, where people make sense of bodily attributes and substances, and the domains of specialized knowledge practices involving genetics and biological research.

transnational identity: Forms of cultural identity that cross national boundaries, reflecting the movement of peoples and cultural practices. This concept recognizes that for many people today questions of identity are not reducible to forms of national belonging.

unmarked: A concept that delineates between conditions when a certain attribute is considered to be absent or present. "Race" is generally construed as present in "people of color"—a category defined racially—but absent in whites, who are unmarked and presumed to represent the "normal" condition from which race is set apart.

wealth factor: The forms of advantages bestowed on those who come from relatively privileged backgrounds and that are crucial to success in school and in the job market. These forms of advantage are generally obscured by an attention to *merit*.

white privilege: The array of advantages that accrue to whites regardless of whether, as individuals, they maintain racist beliefs. White privilege is most manifest in the ways whites are generally able to maintain an unmarked racial identity.

white spatial imaginary: Identifies, generally, the role racial thinking plays in shaping our cultural landscape; more specifically, it refers to the interests whites develop in maintaining residential segregation even without holding expressly racist ideals.

whitening thesis: A view that success and acceptance into the mainstream of American social life by Latinos and Asian Americans is predicated on an implicit identification with whiteness and a disidentification with blackness.

References

Anderson, Elijah. 1990. *Streetwise: Race, class, and change in an urban community*. Chicago: University of Chicago Press.

AP-Yahoo. 2008. http://news.yahoo.com/page/election-2008-political-pulse-obama-race. Page no longer available.

Alexander, Michelle. 2010. *The New Jim Crow: Mass incarceration in the age of colorblindness*. New York: New Press.

Aptheker, Herbert. 1995. Anti-racism in the United States: 1865–1900. In *Racism and anti-racism in world perspective*. Thousand Oaks, CA: Sage.

Austin, Algernon. 2006. *Achieving blackness: Race, black nationalism, and Afrocentrism in the twentieth century*. New York: New York University Press.

Barkan, Elazar. 1992. *Retreat of scientific racism: Changing concepts of race in Britain and the United States between the world wars*. Cambridge: Cambridge University Press.

Barr, Donald. 2008. *Health disparities in the United States*. Baltimore: Johns Hopkins University Press.

Baum, Bruce David. 2006. *The rise and fall of the Caucasian race: A political history of racial identity*. New York: New York University Press.

Bauman, Richard. 1977. *Verbal art as performance*. Prospect Heights: Waveland Press.

Behar, Ruth. 1996. *The vulnerable observer: Anthropology that breaks your heart*. Boston: Beacon Press.

Bertrand, Marianne, and Mullainathan, Sendhill. 2003. Are Emily and Greg more employable than Lakisha and Jamal? NBER Working Paper 9873, National Bureau of Economic Research.

Blanton, Hart, and Jaccard, James. 2008. Unconscious racism: A concept in pursuit of a measure. *Annual Review of Sociology* 34:277–97.

Boas, Franz. 1912. Changes in bodily form of descendents of immigrants. *American Anthropologist* 14:530–562.

Bolnick, Deborah. 2007. The science and business of genetic ancestry testing. *Science* 318:399–400.

Bonilla-Silva, Eduardo. 2006. *Racism without racists: Color-blind racism and the persistence of racial inequality in the United States*. 2nd ed. Lanham, MD: Rowman & Littlefield.

Bowser, Benjamin. 1995. *Racism and anti-racism in world perspective*. Thousand Oaks, CA: Sage.

Braun, Bruce, 2003. "On the raggedy edge of risk": Articulations of race and nation after biology. In *Race, nature, and the politics of difference*, edited by Moore, Kosek, and Pandian, Durham: Duke University Press.

Burchard, E. G. et al., 2003. The importance of race and ethnic background in biomedical research and clinical practice. *New England Journal of Medicine* 348(12): 1170–1175.

Bush, Melanie. 2004. *Breaking the code of good intentions: Everyday forms of whiteness*. Lanham, MD: Rowman & Littlefield.

Carlson, Marvin. 1996. *Performance: A critical introduction*. New York: Routledge.

Centers for Disease Control and Prevention. 2003. Youth risk behavior surveillance system: Youth 2003, Online Comprehensive Results, 2004.

Cheng, Wendy. 2013. *The Changs next door to the Diazes: Remapping race in suburban California*. Minneapolis: University of Minnesota Press.

Chin, Elizabeth. 2001. *Purchasing power: Black kids and American consumer culture*. Minneapolis: University of Minnesota Press.

Collins, Patricia Hill. 2000. *Black feminist thought: Knowledge, consciousness, and the politics of empowerment*. New York: Routledge.

Cooper, R., Jay Kaufman, and Ryk Ward. 2003. Race and genomics. *New England Journal of Medicine* 348(12): 1166–1170.

Daniel, H. 2003. Genetic epidemiology of hypertension: An update on the African diaspora. *Ethnicity & Disease* 13(2) sppl 2: S53–66.

Dávila, Arlene. 2001. *Latinos inc.: The marketing and making of a people*. Berkeley: University of California Press.

Dávila, Arlene M. 2004. *Barrio dreams: Puerto Ricans, Latinos, and the neoliberal city*. Berkeley: University of California Press.

Dávila, Arlene M. 2008. *Latino spin: Public image and the whitewashing of race*. New York: New York University Press.

De Genova, Nicholas. 2005. *Working the boundaries: Race, space, and "illegality" in Mexican Chicago*. Durham, NC: Duke University Press.

Dei, George Sefa. 1996. *Anti-Racism Education: Theory and Practice*. Halifax, N.S.: Fernwood Pub.

Dickerson, Debra. 2004. *The end of blackness: Returning the souls of black folk to their rightful owners*. New York: Pantheon Books.

Dickerson, Debra. 2007. Colorblind. Salon.com http://www.salon.com/opinion/feature/2007/01/22/obama/.

DiTomaso, Nancy. 2013. *The American non-dilemma: Racial inequality without racism*. New York: Russell Sage Foundation.

Downey, Liam. 2007. Metropolitan-area variation in environmental inequality outcomes. *Urban Studies* 44: 953–977.

Drake, St. Clair. 1987. *Black folks here and there: An essay in history and anthropology*. Berkeley: University of California Press.

Drake, St. Clair, and Horace Cayton. 1945 (1993). *Black metropolis: A study of Negro life in a northern city*. Chicago: Chicago University Press.

Drummond, Lee. 1980. The cultural continuum: A theory of intersystems. *Man* 15(2): 352–374.

Du Bois, W. E. B. 1915. The Negro. New York: Holt.

Du Bois, W. E. B. 1980 (1940). *Dusk of dawn: An essay towards an autobiography of a race concept*. Franklin Center, PA: Franklin Library.

Du Bois, W. E. B. 1996 (1899). *The Philadelphia negro: A social study*. Philadelphia: University of Pennsylvania Press.

Du Bois, W. E. B. 2000 (1903). *The souls of black folks*. Bensenville, IL: Lushena Books.

Du Bois, W. E. B., and David L. Lewis. 1992. *Black reconstruction in America: 1860–1880*. New York: Atheneum.

Duster, Troy. 2003: Buried alive: The concept of race in science. In *Genetic nature/culture: Anthropology and science beyond the two-culture divide*. Berkeley: University of California Press.

Editorial. 2001. Genes, drugs, and race. *Nature Genetics* 29(3): 239–240.

Epstein, Steven. 2007. *Inclusion: The politics of difference in medical research, Chicago studies in practices of meaning*. Chicago: University of Chicago Press.

Fordham, Signithia. 1996. *Blacked out: Dilemmas of race, identity, and success at capital high*. Chicago: University of Chicago Press.

Frankenberg, Ruth. 1993. *White women, race matters: The social construction of whiteness*. Minneapolis: University of Minnesota Press.

Franklin, Sarah, Celia Lury, and Jackie Stacey. 2000. *Global nature, global culture, gender, theory and culture*. London: Sage.

Fredrickson, George. 2002. *Racism: A short history*. Princeton, NJ: Princeton University Press.

Gannet, L. 2003. Making populations: Bounding genes in space and in time. *Philosophy of Science* 70:989–1001.

Gans, Herbert. 1967. *Levittown: Ways of life and politics in a new suburban community*. New York: Pantheon Books.

Gilroy, Paul. 2000. *Against race: Imagining political culture beyond the color line*. Cambridge, MA: Harvard University Press.

Goffman, Erving. 1959. *The presentation of self in everyday life*. New York: Anchor Books.

Goode, Judith. 2002. How urban ethnography counters myths about the poor. In *Urban Life: Readings in the anthropology of the city*, edited by George Gmlech. Prospect Heights: Waveland Press.

Gould, Stephen Jay. 1996. *The mismeasure of man*. New York: Norton.

Graves, Joseph. 2005. *The race myth: Why we pretend race exists in America*. New York: Plume.

Gravlee, Clarence. 2005. Skin color, social classification, and blood pressure in southeastern Puerto Rico. *American Journal of Public Health* 95(12): 1–7.

Gregory, Steven. 1999. *Black corona: Race and the politics of place in an urban community*. Princeton, NJ: Princeton University Press.

Greenberg, Stan. 2013. Inside the GOP: Report on focus groups with evangelical, Tea Party, and moderate Republicans. Greenberg Qunilan Rosner Research.

Gwaltney, John Langston. 1980. *Drylongso: A self-portrait of black America*. New York: Vintage.

Hammond, Evelynn. 2006. Straw men and their followers: The return of biological race. Is "race" real? Posted on A webforum organized by the Social Science Research Council. http://raceandgenomics.ssrc.org/Hammonds/.

Haney-Lopez, Ian. 1994. The social construction of race: Some observations on illusions, fabrication, and choice. *Harvard Civil Rights—Civil Liberties Law Review* 29: 1–62.

Haney-Lopez, Ian. 2006. *White by law: The legal construction of race*. New York: New York University Press.

Harris-Lacewell, Melissa Victoria. 2004. *Barbershops, bibles, and BET: Everyday talk and black political thought*. Princeton, NJ: Princeton University Press.

Harrison, Faye. 1991. *Decolonizing anthropology: Moving further toward an anthropology for liberation*. Washington: Association of Black Anthropologists.

Harrison, Faye. 1992. The Du Boisian legacy in anthropology. *Critique of Anthropology* 12(3): 239–260.

Harrison, Faye. 1998. Expanding the discourse on "race." *American Anthropologist* 100(3): 609–631.

Hartigan, John Jr. 1999. *Racial situations: Class predicaments of whiteness in Detroit*. Princeton, NJ: Princeton University Press.

Hartigan, John Jr. 2005. *Odd Tribes: Toward a cultural analysis of white people*. Durham: Duke University Press.

Hartigan, John Jr. 2008. Is race still socially constructed? The controversy over race and genetics. *Science as Culture* 17(2): 163–193.

Hess, David. 1995. *Science & technology in a multicultural world: The cultural politics of facts and artifacts*. New York: Columbia University Press.

Hill, Jane. 2008. *The everyday language of white racism*. Malden: Wiley-Blackwell.

Hochschild, Jennifer L., Vesla Weaver, and Traci Burch. 2012. *Creating a new racial order: How immigration, multiracialism, genomics, and the young can remake race in America*. Princeton, NJ: Princeton University Press.

Hughey, Matthew W. 2012. *White bound: Nationalists, antiracists, and the shared meanings of race*. Stanford: Stanford University Press.

Hunter, Margaret L. 2005. *Race, gender, and the politics of skin tone*. New York: Routledge.

Ignatiev, Noel. 1995. *How the Irish became white*. New York: Routledge.

Jackson, John L. 2001. *Harlemworld: Doing race and class in contemporary black America*. Chicago: University of Chicago Press.

Jackson, John L. 2005. *Real black: Adventures in racial sincerity*. Chicago: University of Chicago Press.

Jackson, John L. 2008. *Racial paranoia: The unintended consequences of political correctness*. New York: Basic Books.

Jacobson, Matthew. 1998. *Whiteness of a different color: European immigrants and the alchemy of race*. Cambridge, MA: Harvard University Press.

Jiménez, Thomás, and Adam Horowitz. 2013. When white is just alright: How immigrants redefine achievement and reconfigure the ethnoracial hierarchy. *American Sociological Review* 78(5):849–871.

Johnson, Charles. 2008. The end of the black American narrative. *American Scholar* 77(3): 32–42.

Joint Center for Political and Economic Studies. 2011. "Fact Sheet: National Roster of Black Elected Officials."

Katznelson, Ira. 2006. *When affirmative action was white: An untold history of racial inequality in twentieth-century America*. New York: Norton.

Kefalas, Maria. 2003. *Working-class heroes: Protecting home, community, and nation in a Chicago neighborhood*. Berkeley: University of California Press.

Kelley, Robin. 1997. *Yo' mama's disfunktional!: Fighting the culture wars in urban America*. Boston: Beacon Press.

Kenney, Lorraine. 2000. *Daughters of suburbia: Growing up white, middle-class and female*. New Brunswick, NJ: Rutgers University Press.

Kim, Nadia Y. 2008. *Imperial citizens: Koreans and race from Seoul to LA*. Stanford, CA: Stanford University Press.

King-O'Riain, Rebecca Chiyoko. 2006. *Pure beauty: Judging race in Japanese American beauty pageants*. Minneapolis: University of Minnesota Press.

Klein, Debra. 2007. *Yoruba Bata goes global: Artists, culture brokers, and fans*. Chicago: University of Chicago Press.

Krieger, Nancy, ed. 2004. *Embodying inequality: Epidemiologic perspectives*. Amityville, NY: Baywood.

Krieger, Nancy. 2006. If "race" is the answer, what is the question?—on "race," racism, and health: A social epidemiologist's perspective. Posted on A webforum organized by the Social Science Research Council. http://raceandgenomics.ssrc.org/Krieger/.

Lacy, Karyn R. 2007. *Blue-chip black: Race, class, and status in the new black middle class*. Berkeley: University of California Press.

Lamont, Michele. 2000. *The dignity of working men: Morality and the boundaries of race, class, and immigration*. Cambridge, MA: Harvard University Press.

Lander, Christian. 2008. *Stuff white people like: The definitive guide to the unique taste of millions*. New York: Random House.

Lasch-Quinn, Elisabeth. 2001. *Race experts: How racial etiquette, sensitivity training, and New Age therapy hijacked the civil rights revolution*. New York: W. W. Norton.

Latour, Bruno. 1999. *Pandora's hope: Essays on the reality of science studies*. Cambridge, MA: Harvard University Press.

Lemann, Nicholas. 2000. *The big test: The secret history of the American meritocracy*. 1st rev. ed. New York: Farrar, Straus and Giroux.

Lévi-Strauss, Claude. 1966. *The savage mind (La pensée sauvage)*. London: Weidenfeld & Nicolson.

Lewontin, R. 1972. The apportionment of human genes. *Evolutionary Biology* 6: 381–398.

Limón, José Eduardo. 1994. *Dancing with the devil: Society and cultural poetics in Mexican-American south Texas*. Madison: University of Wisconsin Press.

Limón, José. 1998. *American encounters: Greater Mexico, the United States, and the erotics of culture*. Boston: Beacon Press.

Lipsitz, George. 1998. *The Possessive investment in whiteness: How white people profit from identity politics*. Philadelphia: Temple University Press.

Lipsitz, George. 2011. *How Racism Takes Place*. Philadelphia: Temple University Press.

Livingstone, F. *1962*. On the non-existence of human races. *Current Anthropology* 3(3): 279.

Low, Setha M. 2003. *Behind the gates: Life, security, and the pursuit of happiness in fortress America*. New York: Routledge.

Lynd, Robert. 1929. *Middletown: A study in American culture*. New York: Harcourt, Brace.

MacLeod, Jay. 2009. *Ain't no makin' it: Aspirations and attainment in a low-income neighborhood*. Boulder: Westview Press.

Manalansan IV, Martin. 2000. *Cultural Compass: Ethnographic explorations of Asian America*. Philadelphia: Temple University Press.

McClaurin, Irma, ed. 2001. *Black feminist anthropology: Theory, politics, praxis, and poetics*. New Brunswick, NJ: Rutgers University Press.

McDermott, Monica. 2006. *Working-class white: The making and unmaking of race relations*. Berkeley: University of California Press.

McIntosh, Peggy. 1989. White privilege: Unpacking the invisible knapsack. *Peace/Freedom*, July, 1–4.

McIntyre, Alice. 1997. *Making meaning of whiteness: Exploring racial identity with white teachers*. Albany: State University of New York Press.

McWhorter, John. 2005. *Winning the race: Beyond the crisis in black America*. New York: Gotham Books.

McWhorter, John. 2006. The color of his skin. *The New York Sun*, September 21, 12.

Mead, Margaret. 1928 (2001). *Coming of age in Samoa: A psychological study of primitive youth for Western society*. New York: Perennial Classics.

Mendelberg, Tali. 2001. *The race card: Campaign strategy, implicit messages, and the norm of equality*. Princeton: Princeton University Press.

Modan, Gabriella Gahila. 2007. *Turf wars: Discourse, diversity, and the politics of place*. Maden: Blackwell.

Moffatt, Michael. 1986. The discourse of the dorm. In *Symbolizing America*, edited by H. Varenne. Lincoln: University of Nebraska Press.

Moffatt, Michael. 1989. *Coming of age in New Jersey: College and American culture*. New Brunswick, NJ: Rutgers University Press.

Montague, A. 1942. *Man's most dangerous myth: The fallacy of race*. New York: Columbia University Press.

Morris, Edward W. 2006. *An unexpected minority: White kids in an urban school*. New Brunswick, NJ: Rutgers University Press.

Morrison, Toni. 1992. *Playing in the dark: Whiteness and the literary imagination*. Cambridge, MA: Harvard University Press.

Moss, Kirby. 2003. *The color of class: Poor whites and the paradox of privilege*. Philadelphia: University of Pennsylvania Press.

Mukhopadhyay, Carol, Rosemary Henze, and Yolanda Moses. 2007. *How real is race? A sourcebook on race, culture, and biology*. Landham, MD: Rowman & Littlefield.

Mullings, Leith. 1997. *On our own terms: Race, class, and gender in the lives of African American Women*. London: Routledge.

Mullings, Leith. 2005. Interrogating racism: Toward an antiracist anthropology. *Annual Review of Anthropology* 34:667–93.

Myrdal, Gunnar. 1996 (1944). *An American Dilemma: The Negro Problem and Modern Democracy*. New Brunswick, NJ: Transaction.

Nader, Laura. 1996. *Naked science: Anthropological inquiry into boundaries, power, and knowledge*. New York: Routledge.

Nagourney, Adam. 2008. "Near-Flawless run is credited with victory," *New York Times*, November 5.

Nobles, Melissa. 2000. *Shades of citizenship: Race and the census in modern politics*. Stanford, CA: Stanford University Press.

Norton, Michael, and Samuel Sommers. 2011. Whites see racism as a zero-sum game they are now losing. *Perspectives on Psychological Science* 6(3): 215–218.

Obama, Barack. 2004. *Dreams from my father: A story of race and inheritance*. New York: Broadway.

Oboler, Suzanne. 1995. *Ethnic labels, Latino lives: Identity and the politics of (re)presentation in the United States*. Minneapolis: University of Minnesota Press.

O'Brien, Eileen. 2008. *The racial middle: Latinos and Asian Americans living beyond the racial divide*. New York: New York University Press.

Olshansky, S. Jay, Toni Antonucci, Lisa Berkman, Robert H. Binstock, Axel Boersch-Supan, John T. Cacioppo, Bruce A. Carnes, et al. 2012. "Differences In Life Expectancy Due To Race And Educational Differences Are Widening, And Many May Not Catch Up." *Health Affairs* 31 (8): 1803–13.

Omi, Michael, and Howard Winant. 1986. *Racial formations in the United States: From the 1960s to the 1980s*. New York: Routledge.

Ong, Aihwa. 2003. *Buddha is hiding: Refugees, citizenship, the new America*. Berkeley: University of California Press.

Ong, Aihwa. 2006. *Neoliberalism as exception: Mutations in citizenship and sovereignty*. Durham, NC: Duke University Press.

Owens, K., and Mary-Claire King. 1999. Genomic views of human history. *Science* 286:451–453.

Pattillo-McCoy, Mary E. 1999. *Black picket fences: Privilege and peril among the black middle class*. Chicago: University of Chicago Press.

Pattillo-McCoy, Mary E. 2007. *Black on the block: The politics of race and class in the city*. Chicago: University of Chicago Press.

Pew Research Center. 2012. February 16, 2012, The Rise of Intermarriage: Rates, Characteristics, Vary by Race and Gender.

Perin, Constance. 1988. *Belonging in America: Reading between the lines*. Madison: University of Wisconsin Press.

Perry, Pamela. 2002. *Shades of white: White kids and racial identities in high school*. Durham, NC: Duke University Press.

Pew Research Center. 2007. *Blacks see growing values gap between poor and middle class*. Washington.

Pluviose, David. 2006. "Acting white" accusation has damaging legacy for black students. *Diverse: Issues in Higher Education* 23(4): 6.

Pollock, Mica, ed. 2008. *Everyday antiracism: Getting real about race in school*. New York: W.W. Norton.

Powdermaker, Hortense. 1966. *Stranger and friend: The way of an anthropologist*. New York: W.W. Norton.

Powdermaker, Hortense, Brackette F. Williams, and Drexel G. Woodson. 1993 (1939). *After freedom: A cultural study in the Deep South*. Madison: University of Wisconsin Press.

Prager, Devah. 2003. The mark of a criminal record. *American Journal of Sociology* 108(5): 937–975.

Reed, Adolph Jr. 2000. *Class notes: Posing as politics and other thoughts on the American scene*. New York: New Press.

Ripley, William. 1910. *The races of Europe: A sociological study*. New York: D. Appleton.

Risch, N., Esteban Burchard, Elad Ziv, and Hua Tang. 2002. Categorization of humans in biomedical research: genes, race and disease. *Genomebiology.com* 3(7): 1–12.

Robinson, Eugene. 2011. *Disintegration: The Splintering of Black America*. New York: Anchor Books.

Rodriguez, Clara. 2000. *Changing race: Latinos, the census, and the history of ethnicity in the United States*. New York: New York University Press.

Roberts, Sam. 2008. A nation of the none and all of the above. *New York Times*, August 17.

Roediger, David. 1992. *The wages of whiteness: Race and the making of the American working class*. New York: Verso.

Roediger, David. 2005. *Working toward whiteness: How America's immigrants became white*. New York: Basic Books.

Rondilla, Joanne L., and Paul R. Spickard. 2007. *Is lighter better?: Skin-tone discrimination among Asian Americans*. Lanham, MD: Rowman & Littlefield.

Rosenberg, Noah et al. 2002. Genetic structure of human populations. *Science* 298:2381–2385.

Rugh, J. S., & Massey, G. S. 2010. Residential segregation and the American foreclosure crisis. *American Sociological Review*, 75, 629-651.

Saito, Leland. 1998. *Race and politics: Asian Americans, Latinos, and whites in a Los Angeles suburb*. Urbana: University of Illinois Press.

Saluny, Susan. 2011. "Counting Mixed-Race America Grows Ever More Complex," *New York Times*, February 9.

Sanjek, Roger. 1998. *The future of us all: Race and neighborhood politics in neighborhood New York*. Ithaca, NY: Cornell University Press.

Schmidt, Peter. 2007. *Color and Money: How Rich White Kids Are Winning the War over College Affirmative Action*. New York: Palgrave Macmillan.

Schwartz, R. 2001. Racial profiling in medical research. *New England Journal of Medicine* 344(18): 1392–1393.

Shankar, Shalini. 2008. *Desi land: Teen culture, class, and success in Silicon Valley*. Durham, NC: Duke University Press.

Shapiro, Thomas M. 2004. *The hidden cost of being African American: How wealth perpetuates inequality*. New York: Oxford University Press.

Smedly, Audrey. 1993. *Race in North America: Origin and evolution of a worldview*. Boulder: Westview Press.

Skerry, Peter. 2000. *Counting on the census?: Race, group identity, and the evasion of politics*. Washington: Brookings Institution Press.

Srivastava, S. 1996. Song and dance? The performance antiracist workshops. *The Canadian Review of Sociology and Anthropology* 33: 291–315.

Stack, Carol B. 1974. *All our kin: Strategies for survival in a black community*. New York: Harper & Row.

Steinberg, Stephen. 2007. *Race relations: A critique*. Stanford: Stanford University Press.

Stephen, Lynn. 2007. *Transborder lives: Indigenous Oaxacans in Mexico, California, and Oregon*. Durham, NC: Duke University Press.

Sturm, Circe. 2011. *Becoming Indian: The struggle over Cherokee identity in the twenty-first century*. Santa Fe: School for Advanced Research Press.

Tapper, Melbourne. 1999. *In the blood: Sickle cell anemia and the politics of race*. Philadelphia: University of Pennsylvania Press.

Thomas, Darryl. 2005. The black radical tradition—Theory and practice. *Race & Class* 47(2): 239–260.

Touré. 2011. *Who's afraid of post-blackness?: What it means to be black now*. New York: Free Press.

Tuan, Mia. 2001. *Forever foreigners or honorary whites?: The Asian ethnic experience today*. New Brunswick, NJ: Rutgers University Press.

Tyson, Karolyn. 2005. It's not a "black thing": Understanding the burden of acting white and other dilemmas of high achievement. *American Sociological Review* 70(4): 582–605.

Urban Institute. 2013. "Less Than Equal: Racial Disparities in Wealth Accumulation". April 26. http://www.urban.org/publications/412802.html.

Uriciuoli, Bonnie. 1996. *Exposing prejudice: Puerto Rican experiences of language, race, and class*. Boulder, CO: Westview Press.

Varenne, Herve. 1986. *Symbolizing America*. Lincoln: University of Nebraska Press.

Vargas, João Helion Costa. 2006. *Catching hell in the city of angels: Life and meanings of blackness in south central Los Angeles*. Minneapolis: University of Minnesota Press.

Venter, C. 2000. Reading the book of life: White House remarks on decoding of genome. *New York Times*, 8.

Wade, Peter. 2002. *Race, nature, and culture: An anthropological perspective*. London: Pluto Press.

Wailoo, Keith. 1997. *Drawing blood: Technology and disease identity in twentieth-century America, The Henry E. Sigerist series in the history of medicine*. Baltimore: Johns Hopkins University Press.

Wailoo, Keith. 2003. Inventing the heterozygote: Molecular biology, racial identity, and the narrative of sickle-cell disease, Tay-Sachs, and cystic fibrosis. In *Race, nature, and the politics of difference*, edited by Donald Moore, et al. Durham: Duke University Press.

Wailoo, Keith, and Stephen Gregory Pemberton. 2006. *The troubled dream of genetic medicine: Ethnicity and innovation in Tay-Sachs, cystic fibrosis, and sickle cell disease.* Baltimore: Johns Hopkins University Press.

Warner, Lloyd. 1941. *Yankee City: The social life of a modern community.* New Haven: Yale University Press.

Weismantel, Mary. 2001. *Cholas and Pishtacos: Stories of race and sex in the Andes.* Chicago: University of Chicago Press.

Williams, Brackette. 1989. A class act: Anthropology and the race to nation across ethnic terrain. *Annual Review of Anthropology* 18:401–444.

Williams, David et al. 2003. Racial/ethnic discrimination and health: Findings from community studies. *American Journal of Public Health* 93(2): 200–208.

Wilson, J., Michael Weale, Alice Smith, Fiona Gratrix, Benjamin Fletcher, Thomas, Mark Thomas, Neil Bradman, and David Goldstein. 2001. Population genetic structure of variable drug response. *Nature Genetics* 29:265–269.

Winant, Howard. 1994. *Racial conditions: Politics, theory, comparisons.* Minneapolis: University of Minnesota Press.

Winkler, Erin N. 2012. *Learning Race, learning place: Shaping racial identities and ideas in African American childhoods.* New Brunswick, NJ: Rutgers University Press.

Wise, Tim. 2001. A new round of white denial: Drugs and race in the 'burbs. *Alternet*, 14.

Wolcott, Harry. 2008. *Ethnography: A way of seeing:* Lanham, MD: AltaMira Press.

Womack, Ytasha. 2010. *Post black: How a new generation is redefining African American identity.* Chicago: Lawrence Hill Books.

Wray, Matt. 2006. *Not quite white: White trash and the boundaries of whiteness.* Durham: Duke University Press.

Wright, Michelle. 2004. *Becoming black: Creating identity in the African diaspora.* Durham, NC: Duke University Press.

Yancey, George A. 2003. *Who is white?: Latinos, Asians, and the new black/nonblack divide.* Boulder, CO: Lynn Rienner.

Index